CLEOPATRA

Major Literary Characters

**THE ANCIENT WORLD THROUGH
THE SEVENTEENTH CENTURY**

ACHILLES
Homer, *Iliad*

CALIBAN
William Shakespeare, *The Tempest*
Robert Browning, *Caliban upon Setebos*

CLEOPATRA
William Shakespeare, *Antony and
 Cleopatra*
John Dryden, *All for Love*
George Bernard Shaw, *Caesar and
 Cleopatra*

DON QUIXOTE
Miguel de Cervantes, *Don Quixote*
Franz Kafka, *Parables*

FALSTAFF
William Shakespeare, *Henry IV, Part I,
 Henry IV, Part II, The Merry Wives
 of Windsor*

FAUST
Christopher Marlowe, *Doctor Faustus*
Johann Wolfgang von Goethe, *Faust*
Thomas Mann, *Doctor Faustus*

HAMLET
William Shakespeare, *Hamlet*

IAGO
William Shakespeare, *Othello*

JULIUS CAESAR
William Shakespeare, *Julius Caesar*
George Bernard Shaw, *Caesar and
 Cleopatra*

KING LEAR
William Shakespeare, *King Lear*

MACBETH
William Shakespeare, *Macbeth*

ODYSSEUS/ULYSSES
Homer, *Odyssey*
James Joyce, *Ulysses*

OEDIPUS
Sophocles, *Oedipus Rex, Oedipus
 at Colonus*

OTHELLO
William Shakespeare, *Othello*

ROSALIND
William Shakespeare, *As You Like It*

SANCHO PANZA
Miguel de Cervantes, *Don Quixote*
Franz Kafka, *Parables*

SATAN
The Book of Job
John Milton, *Paradise Lost*

SHYLOCK
William Shakespeare, *The Merchant
 of Venice*

THE WIFE OF BATH
Geoffrey Chaucer, *The Canterbury
 Tales*

**THE EIGHTEENTH AND
NINETEENTH CENTURIES**

AHAB
Herman Melville, *Moby-Dick*

ISABEL ARCHER
Henry James, *Portrait of a Lady*

EMMA BOVARY
Gustave Flaubert, *Madame Bovary*

DOROTHEA BROOKE
George Eliot, *Middlemarch*

CHELSEA HOUSE PUBLISHERS

Major Literary Characters

DAVID COPPERFIELD
Charles Dickens, *David Copperfield*

ROBINSON CRUSOE
Daniel Defoe, *Robinson Crusoe*

DON JUAN
Molière, *Don Juan*
Lord Byron, *Don Juan*

HUCK FINN
Mark Twain, *The Adventures of Tom Sawyer, Adventures of Huckleberry Finn*

CLARISSA HARLOWE
Samuel Richardson, *Clarissa*

HEATHCLIFF
Emily Brontë, *Wuthering Heights*

ANNA KARENINA
Leo Tolstoy, *Anna Karenina*

MR. PICKWICK
Charles Dickens, *The Pickwick Papers*

HESTER PRYNNE
Nathaniel Hawthorne, *The Scarlet Letter*

BECKY SHARP
William Makepeace Thackeray, *Vanity Fair*

LAMBERT STRETHER
Henry James, *The Ambassadors*

EUSTACIA VYE
Thomas Hardy, *The Return of the Native*

TWENTIETH CENTURY

ÁNTONIA
Willa Cather, *My Ántonia*

BRETT ASHLEY
Ernest Hemingway, *The Sun Also Rises*

HANS CASTORP
Thomas Mann, *The Magic Mountain*

HOLDEN CAULFIELD
J. D. Salinger, *The Catcher in the Rye*

CADDY COMPSON
William Faulkner, *The Sound and the Fury*

JANIE CRAWFORD
Zora Neale Hurston, *Their Eyes Were Watching God*

CLARISSA DALLOWAY
Virginia Woolf, *Mrs. Dalloway*

DILSEY
William Faulkner, *The Sound and the Fury*

GATSBY
F. Scott Fitzgerald, *The Great Gatsby*

HERZOG
Saul Bellow, *Herzog*

JOAN OF ARC
William Shakespeare, *Henry VI*
George Bernard Shaw, *Saint Joan*

LOLITA
Vladimir Nabokov, *Lolita*

WILLY LOMAN
Arthur Miller, *Death of a Salesman*

MARLOW
Joseph Conrad, *Lord Jim, Heart of Darkness, Youth, Chance*

PORTNOY
Philip Roth, *Portnoy's Complaint*

BIGGER THOMAS
Richard Wright, *Native Son*

CHELSEA HOUSE PUBLISHERS

Major Literary Characters

CLEOPATRA

Edited and with an introduction by
HAROLD BLOOM

CHELSEA HOUSE PUBLISHERS
New York ◇ Philadelphia

Jacket illustration: Cleopatra (1875) by Lawrence Alma-Tadema.
Courtesy of the Art Gallery of New South Wales,
Sydney, Australia.

Chelsea House Publishers

Editor-in-Chief Nancy Toff
Executive Editor Remmel T. Nunn
Managing Editor Karyn Gullen Browne
Picture Editor Adrian G. Allen
Art Director Maria Epes
Manufacturing Manager Gerald Levine

Major Literary Characters

Managing Editor S. T. Joshi
Copy Chief Richard Fumosa
Designer Maria Epes

Staff for CLEOPATRA

Editorial Assistant Katherine Theodore
Picture Researcher Nisa Rauschenberg
Assistant Art Director Loraine Machlin
Production Manager Joseph Romano
Production Assistant Leslie D'Acri

Library of Congress Cataloging-in-Publication Data

Cleopatra / edited and with an introduction by Harold Bloom.
p.   cm.—(Major literary characters)
Includes bibliographical references.
ISBN 0-7910-0915-7.—ISBN 0-7910-0970-X (pbk.)
1. English drama—History and criticism.   2. Cleopatra, Queen of Egypt,
d. 30 B.C., in fiction, drama, poetry, etc.   3. Shakespeare,
William, 1564–1616. Antony and Cleopatra.   4. Shaw, Bernard,
1856–1950. Caesar and Cleopatra.   5. Dryden, John, 1631–1700. All for love.
I. Bloom, Harold.   II. Series.
PR635.C65C5   1990
822.009'351—dc20
89-29607
CIP

CONTENTS

CONTENTS

THE ANALYSIS OF CHARACTER
Harold Bloom

"Character," according to our dictionaries, still has as a primary meaning a graphic symbol, such as a letter of the alphabet. This meaning reflects the word's apparent origin in the ancient Greek *charactēr*, a sharp stylus. *Charactēr* also meant the mark of the stylus' incisions. Recent fashions in literary criticism have reduced "character" in literature to a matter of marks upon a page. But our word "character" also has a very different meaning, matching that of the ancient Greek *ēthos*, "habitual way of life." Shall we say then that literary character is an imitation of human character, or is it just a grouping of marks? The issue is between a critic like Dr. Samuel Johnson, for whom words were as much like people as like things, and a critic like the late Roland Barthes, who told us that "the fact can only exist linguistically, as a term of discourse." Who is closer to our experience of reading literature, Johnson or Barthes? What difference does it make, if we side with one critic rather than the other?

Barthes is famous, like Foucault and other recent French theorists, for having added to Nietzsche's proclamation of the death of God a subsidiary demise, that of the literary author. If there are no authors, then there are no fictional personages, presumably because literature does not refer to a world outside language. Words indeed necessarily refer to other words in the first place, but the impact of words ultimately is drawn from a universe of fact. Stories, poems, and plays are recognizable as such because they are human utterances within traditions of utterances, and traditions, by achieving authority, become a kind of fact, or at least the sense of a fact. Our sense that literary characters, within the context of a fictive cosmos, indeed are fictional personages is also a kind of fact. The meaning and value of every character in a successful work of literary representation depend upon our ideas of persons in the factual reality of our lives.

Literary character is always an invention, and inventions generally are indebted to prior inventions. Shakespeare is the inventor of literary character as we know it; he reformed the universal human expectations for the verbal imitation of personality, and the reformation appears now to be permanent and uncannily inevitable. Remarkable as the Bible and Homer are at representing personages, their characters are relatively unchanging. They age within their stories, but their habitual modes of being do not develop. Jacob and Achilles unfold before us, but without metamorphoses. Lear and Macbeth, Hamlet and Othello severely modify themselves not only by their actions, but by their utterances, and most of all through *overhearing themselves,* whether they speak to themselves or to others. Pondering what they themselves have said, they will to change, and actually do change, sometimes extravagantly yet always persuasively. Or else they suffer change, without willing it, but in reaction not so much to their language as to their relation to that language.

I do not think it useful to say that Shakespeare successfully imitated elements in our characters. Rather, it could be argued that he compelled aspects of character to appear that previously were concealed, or not available to representation. This is not to say that Shakespeare is God, but to remind us that language is not God either. The mimesis of character in Shakespeare's dramas now seems to us normative, and indeed became the accepted mode almost immediately, as Ben Jonson shrewdly and somewhat grudgingly implied. And yet, Shakespearean representation has surprisingly little in common with the imitation of reality in Jonson or in Christopher Marlowe. The origins of Shakespeare's originality in the portrayal of men and women are to be found in the *Canterbury Tales* of Geoffrey Chaucer, insofar as they can be located anywhere before Shakespeare himself. Chaucer's savage and superb Pardoner overhears his own tale-telling, as well as his mocking rehearsal of his own spiel, and through this overhearing he is emboldened to forget himself, and enthusiastically urges all his fellow-pilgrims to come forward to be fleeced by him. His self-awareness, and apocalyptically rancid sense of spiritual fall, are preludes to the even grander abysses of the perverted will in Iago and in Edmund. What might be called the character trait of a negative charisma may be Chaucer's invention, but came to its perfection in Shakespearean mimesis.

The analysis of character is as much Shakespeare's invention as the representation of character is, since Iago and Edmund are adepts at analyzing both themselves and their victims. Hamlet, whose overwhelming charisma has many negative components, is certainly the most comprehensive of all literary characters, and so necessarily prophesies the labyrinthine complexities of the will in Iago and Edmund. Charisma, according to Max Weber, its first codifier, is primarily a natural endowment, and implies a primordial and idiosyncratic power over nature, and so finally over death. Hamlet's uncanniness is at its most suggestive in the scene of his long dying, where the audience, through the mediation of Horatio, itself is compelled to meditate upon suicide, if only because outliving the prince of Denmark scarcely seems an option.

Shakespearean representation has usurped not only our sense of literary character, but our sense of ourselves as characters, with Hamlet playing the part of the largest of these usurpations. Insofar as we have an idea of human disinterestedness, we tend to derive it from the Hamlet of Act V, whose quietism has about it a ghostly authority. Oscar Wilde, in his profound and profoundly witty dialogue, "The Decay of Lying," expressed a permanent insight when he insisted that art shaped every era, far more than any age formed art. Life imitates art, we imitate Shakespeare, because without Shakespeare we would perish for lack of images. Wilde's grandest audacity demystifies Shakespearean mimesis with a Shakespearean vivaciousness: "This unfortunate aphorism about art holding the mirror up to Nature is deliberately said by Hamlet in order to convince the bystanders of his absolute insanity in all art-matters." Of *Hamlet*'s influence upon the ages Wilde remarked that: "The world has grown sad because a puppet was once melancholy." "Puppet" is Wilde's own deconstruction, a brilliant reminder that Shakespeare's artistry of illusion has so mastered reality as to have changed reality, evidently forever.

The analysis of character, as a critical pursuit, seems to me as much a Shakespearean invention as literary character was, since much of what we know about how to analyze character necessarily follows Shakespearean procedures. His hero-villains, from Richard III through Iago, Edmund, and Macbeth, are shrewd and endless questers into their own self-motivations. If we could bear to see Hamlet, in his unwearied negations, as another hero-villain, then we would judge him the supreme analyst of the darker recalcitrances in the selfhood. Freud followed the pre-Socratic Empedocles, in arguing that character is fate, a frightening doctrine that maintains the fear that there are no accidents, that overdetermination rules us all of our lives. Hamlet assumes the same, yet adds to this argument the terrible passivity he manifests in Act V. Throughout Shakespeare's tragedies, the most interesting personages seem doom-eager, reminding us again that a Shakespearean reading of Freud would be more illuminating than a Freudian exegesis of Shakespeare. We learn more when we discover Hamlet in the Freudian Death Drive, than when we read *Beyond the Pleasure Principle* into *Hamlet*.

In Shakespearean comedy, character achieves its true literary apotheosis, which is the representation of the inner freedom that can be created by great wit alone. Rosalind and Falstaff, perhaps alone among Shakespeare's personages, match Hamlet in wit, though hardly in the metaphysics of consciousness. Whether in the comic or the modern mode, Shakespeare has set the standard of measurement in the balance between character and passion.

In Shakespeare the self is more dramatized than theatricalized, which is why a Shakespearean reading of Freud works out so well. Character-formation after the passing of the Oedipal stage takes the place of fetishistic fragmentings of the self. Critics who now call literary character into question, and who proclaim also the death of the author, invariably also regard all notions, literary and human, of a stable character as being mere reductions of deeper pre-Oedipal desires. It becomes

clear that the fortunes of literary character rise and fall with the prestige of normative conceptions of the ego. Shakespeare's Iago, who wars against being, may be
the first deconstructionist of the self, with his proclamation of "I am not what I am."
This constitutes the necessary prologue to any view that would regard a fixed ego
as a virtual abnormality. But deconstructions of the self are no more modern than
Modernism is. Like literary modernism, the decentered ego came out of the
Hellenistic culture of ancient Alexandria. The Gnostic heretics believed that the
psyche, like the body, was a fallen entity, mechanically fashioned by the Demiurge
or false creator. They held however that each of us possessed also a spark or
pneuma, which was a fragment of the original Abyss or true, alien God. The soul
or psyche within every one of us was thus at war with the self or pneuma, and only
that sparklike self could be saved.

Shakespeare, following after Chaucer in this respect, was the first and remains
still the greatest master of representing character both as a stable soul and a
wavering self. There is a substance that endures in Shakespeare's figures, and there
is also a quicksilver rendition of the unsettling sparks. Racine and Tolstoy, Balzac and
Dickens, follow in Shakespeare's wake by giving us some sense of pre-Oedipal
sparks or drives, and considerably more sense of post-Oedipal character and
personality, stabilizations or sublimations of the fetish-seeking drives. Critics like Leo
Bersani and René Girard argue eloquently against our taking this mimesis as the only
proper work of literature. I would suggest that strong fictions of the self, from the
Bible through Samuel Beckett, necessarily participate in both modes, the sublima-
tion of desire, and the persistence of a primordial desire. The mystery of Hamlet
or of Lear is intimately invested in the tangled mixture of the two modes of
representation.

Psychic mobility is proposed by Bersani as the ideal to which deconstructions
of the literary self may yet guide us. The ideal has its pathos, but the realities of
literary representation seem to me very different, perhaps destructively so. When
a novelist like D. H. Lawrence sought to reduce his characters to Eros and the
Death Drive, he still had to persuade us of his authority at mimesis by lavishing upon
the figures of *The Rainbow* and *Women in Love* all of the vivid stigmata of
normative personality. Birkin and Ursula may represent antithetical and uncanny
drives, but they develop and change as characters pondering their own pronounce-
ments and reactions to self and others. The cost of a non-Shakespearean representation is enormous. Pynchon, in *The Crying of Lot 49* and *Gravity's Rainbow,*
evades the burden of the normative by resorting to something like Christopher
Marlowe's art of caricature in *The Jew of Malta.* Marlowe's Barabas is a marvelous
rhetorician, yet he is a cartoon alongside the troublingly equivocal Shylock. Pynchon's personages are deliberate cartoons also, as flat as comic strips. Marlowe's
achievement, and Pynchon's, are beyond dispute, yet they are like the prelude and
the postlude to Shakespearean reality. They do not wish to engage with our hunger
for the empirical world and so they enter the problematic cosmos of literary
fantasy.

No writer, not even Shakespeare or Proust, alters the available stock that we agree to call reality, but Shakespeare, more than any other, does show us how much of reality we could encounter if only we retained adequate desire. The strong literary representation of character is already an analysis of character, and is part of the healing work of a literary culture, which implicitly seeks to cure violence through a normative mimesis of ego, *as if it were stable,* whether in actuality it is or is not. I do not believe that this is a social quest taken on by literary culture, but rather that we confront here the aesthetic essence of what makes a culture *literary,* rather than metaphysical or ethical or religious. A culture becomes literary when its conceptual modes have failed it, which means when religion, philosophy, and science have begun to lose their authority. If they cannot heal violence, then literature attempts to do so, which may be only a turning inside out of the critical arguments of Girard and Bersani.

I conclude by offering a particular instance or special case as a paradigm for the healing enterprise that is at once the representation and the analysis of literary character. Let us call it the aesthetics of being outraged, or rather of successfully representing the state of being outraged. W. C. Fields was one modern master of such representation, and Nathanael West was another, as was Faulkner before him. Here also the greatest master remains Shakespeare, whose Macbeth, himself a bloody outrage, yet retains our imaginative sympathy precisely because he grows increasingly outraged as he experiences the equivocation of the fiend that lies like truth. The double-natured promises and the prophecies of the weird sisters finally induce in Macbeth an apocalyptic version of the stage actor's anxiety at missing cues, the horror of a phantasmagoric stage fright of missing one's time, of always reacting too late. Macbeth, a veritable monster of solipsistic inwardness but no intellectual, counters his dilemma by fresh murders, that prolong him in time yet provoke him only to a perpetually freshened sense of being outraged, as all his expectations become still worse confounded. We are moved by Macbeth, however estrangedly, because his terrible inwardness is a paradigm for our own solipsism, but also because none of us can resist a strong and successful representation of the human in a state of being outraged.

The ultimate outrage is the necessity of dying, an outrage concealed in a multitude of masks, including the tyrannical ambitions of Macbeth. I suspect that our outrage at being outraged is the most difficult of all our affects for us to represent to ourselves, which is why we are so inclined to imaginative sympathy for a character who strongly conveys that affect to us. The Shrike of West's *Miss Lonelyhearts* or Faulkner's Joe Christmas of *Light in August* are crucial modern instances, but such figures can be located in many other works, since the ability to represent this extreme emotion is one of the tests that strong writers are driven to set for themselves.

However a reader seeks to reduce literary character to a question of marks on a page, she will come at last to the impasse constituted by the thought of death, her death, and before that to all the stations of being outraged that memorialize her own drive towards death. In reading, she quests for evidences that are strong representations, whether of her desire or her despair. Such questings constitute the necessary basis for the analysis of literary character, an enterprise that always will survive every vagary of critical fashion.

EDITOR'S NOTE

This volume brings together a representative selection of the best criticism, old and new, that has been devoted to Cleopatra as a major literary character. The critical extracts and essays are reprinted here in the chronological order of their original publication. I am deeply grateful to S. T. Joshi for his erudition as a researcher, and for his acute judgment as an editor. Though this book necessarily centers upon William Shakespeare's *Antony and Cleopatra*, with particular emphasis also upon John Dryden's *All for Love* and G. B. Shaw's *Caesar and Cleopatra*, it also covers the entire range of literary representations of Cleopatra, from Horace to Thornton Wilder.

My introduction seeks to apply the criteria of my essay, "The Analysis of Character," to some of the ways in which Shakespeare's Cleopatra achieves an apotheosis that evades all our modern modes of reduction, including Freud's.

The critical extracts begin with Dryden's preface to *All for Love,* and with the celebrated remarks upon *Antony and Cleopatra* by Hazlitt and by Coleridge. Among the excerpts following are such delights as Bernard Shaw affirming the superiority of his Cleopatra over Shakespeare's, and the now classic observations upon Shakespeare's (greatly superior) Cleopatra by A. C. Bradley, G. Wilson Knight, and Rosalie L. Colie. There are also illuminating comments upon Dryden's more formal Queen of Egypt by Ruth Wallerstein, Eugene M. Waith, and Norman Suckling, and numerous brief overviews of other instances of Cleopatra as a literary character.

The critical essays begin with Harold C. Goddard's remarkable analysis of Cleopatra's transformation after Antony's death, and continue with Franklin M. Dickey's survey of how unflattering to Cleopatra nearly all of the pre-Shakespearean treatments tended to be, Chaucer being the grand and amiable exception. Steele Commager's masterly interpretation of Horace's Cleopatra Ode is followed by six essays on Shakespeare, and one each on Dryden and on Shaw. Between them, these eight interpretations give us a conspectus of the characteristic critical modes of the last three decades. Here, they serve to open up many of the hidden complexities of Cleopatra as a major literary character.

INTRODUCTION

The representation of women by male authors, when those authors are of authentic imaginative strength, hardly seems to me less persuasive than comparable portrayals by women writers. One wonders at some of the presuppositions of contemporary feminist criticism when one remembers how difficult it is to surmise an author's gender on the basis of his or her art of representing women. Clarissa Harlowe and Isabel Archer seem of one family with Emma Woodhouse and Dorothea Brooke, all heroines (however secularized) of the Protestant Will. And yet, did I not know otherwise, I might guess that Clarissa and Isabel were the work of women writers, while Emma and Dorothea were visions seen by male novelists. Cleopatra—whether in Shakespeare, Dryden, or Shaw—does seem the creation of a man's imagination, if only because the image of desire that activates and torments most men seems better represented by Cleopatra, as a literary character, than by anyone else. Certainly she is Shakespeare's most memorable image of desire, surpassing the notorious Dark Lady of the Sonnets. Only Rosalind, among Shakespeare's heroines, is as individual a figure as Cleopatra. Rosalind is beyond Cleopatra in wit and intellect, formidable as Cleopatra is, but Rosalind has no Antony, only an Oliver, and the Forest of Arden cannot vie with the vast theater of the world in *The Tragedy of Antony and Cleopatra*.

I do not know of any woman writer's attempt at a Cleopatra, in that long procession that goes from Horace through Plutarch to Shakespeare, Corneille, and Dryden, and then on to Pushkin, G. B. Shaw, and Thornton Wilder. Is it that Cleopatra truly is just a male projection of desire, or are we only now entering an era in which changed and raised female consciousness will find Cleopatra a figure fit for new representations of the possible relations between gender and power? As I read Shakespeare's play, it has very little concern with morality, and is centered wholly upon heroic love, and upon the limits of such grand and destructive passion. But those limits are neither moral nor social; they are psychological, and finally imaginative. Through them, Shakespeare shows us again that he more than antici-

I

pates Freud, and rather *contains* Freud, dwarfing the inventor of psychoanalysis in the mapping of the dialectics of passions and society.

I take it that Freud's deepest insight into love was his realization that desire for another begins always in desire for the self, and then is capable of being diverted back to the self again. Such insight is Shakespearean, and is manifested more vividly in *Antony and Cleopatra* than elsewhere, if only because both Cleopatra and Antony possess prodigiously healthy self-regard. Their authentic mutual passion founds itself firmly upon their fiercely accurate and again wholly mutual self-esteem. Such overwhelming egotism ought to have its unattractive aspects, both for every-one else within the drama and for spectators and readers, but Shakespeare has given us the love relationship of two titanic charismatics, and charisma disarms audiences. Antony and Cleopatra believe in their own greatness, and so does everyone else. What matters most about them is that greatness, more available to the sensibility of a Renaissance audience than it can easily be to us. Cleopatra doubtless is the premier Western instance of the image that men desire, yet her eminence has more to do with her greatness than with her seductiveness.

Charismatics induce enormous ambivalences in most of us, this late in our catastrophic century, and it is another tribute to Shakespeare's art that Cleopatra so little moves us to ambivalence. Like Antony, she is a world in herself, and with him she very nearly is *the* world, or would have been except for the political genius of Octavius. The East goes down with Cleopatra, not to give us a triumph of Roman order, but to bring on a world closer to the one that Shakespeare himself knew. Why Shakespeare modified Plutarch in having Antony abandoned by the god Hercules, rather than by Bacchus, while a puzzling matter, is not beyond all con-jecture. A Herculean hero is more properly to be consigned to the past than is a Dionysiac or Bacchic figure. Antony's death, while gloriously noble, is not, as is Cleopatra's, the most life-enhancing of suicides. The god abandons him, and Antony dies a human death. But Cleopatra dies upward, as it were, becoming fire and air, an Isis who forever has lost her redemptive Osiris.

Shakespeare, strongest of all Western writers, necessarily is our chief source for representations of charismatic men and women, with the simple exception of the Bible. Even Hamlet falls short of the charismatic King David, if only because David has the Blessing of Yahweh, without reservations and in perpetuity. If we consider the Jesus of the Gospels as a literary character, then he too is the un-matched charismatic, like his ancestor David, not to mention the charismatic-of-charismatics, the Yahweh of the J writer, the original Biblical author. The Geneva Bible, rarely Shakespeare's overt source, nevertheless was the dominant influence upon the dramatist's sense of human personality and character. Cleopatra is as little Biblical as a figure can be, and yet her charismatic intensities have a strange debt to Scripture. Her "strong toil of grace" is a snare, rather than a gift of God, and yet her final ecstasy brings her to the gods of Egypt, where she belongs. Charisma is not a gift of nature, or of society. Octavius, beyond Shakespeare's play, will become Augustus, and will be deified into a Roman godling, but no gods will receive him.

Antony, the Bacchic Hercules, ends as a charismatic mortal, yet Cleopatra dies as Egypt, and so she does not die.

Freud did not comment directly upon Shakespeare's Cleopatra, but his subtly outrageous puzzlement at the problematic image of the seductress is informed by Cleopatra's threat to Roman canons of male authority. It is not the Decadent Cleopatra of Gautier or Klimt that hovers in Freud's awe of the seducing goddess of Death in whose arms the hero dies, but rather the robust gypsy of Shakespeare's erotic vision. A purely Freudian reading of Shakespeare's Cleopatra would reduce her to the role of the castrating temptress that Antony invokes only in his worst moment:

> The witch shall die.
> To the young Roman boy she hath sold me, and I fall
> Under this Plot. She dies for't.   (IV, xii, 47–49)

Antony does break apart, just after this, but hardly because Cleopatra has castrated him. The limbs of this Osiris have been scattering long before he came to Egypt and fell in love with its queen. It is the nature of Antony's Dionysiac greatness that he must come apart. He belongs to the order of Shakespearean tragic heroes that includes Othello and Lear, and the hero-villain Macbeth, while Cleopatra's final affinities are with Hamlet. Cleopatra and Hamlet each dominate a fifth act marked by transcendental apotheosis at the close, and by a growing detachment or quietism that enables the apotheosis. Shakespeare, still the most original of authors (unless the J writer or Yahwist owns that distinction), achieved in Hamlet and Cleopatra a new mode of the charismatic, one that calls Max Weber's formulations into considerable question. For Weber, the holder of charisma depends completely upon success; recognition by followers is everything. Cleopatra is defeated by the world, by Octavius, even as Hamlet finally is content to be passive in the face of Claudius's plot with Laertes. Nothing could be further from the accents of defeat than the deaths of Cleopatra and of Hamlet. The Shakespearean transcendence of these grand dyings has little with Christian coloring in it. Hamlet stands upon the threshold of life and death and speaks from there with the charismatic authority that is beyond will and almost beyond affect. Cleopatra, upon her threshold, fuses temptress and mother as Freud learned from Shakespeare to see them fused:

> CHARMIAN: O eastern star!
> CLEOPATRA: Peace, peace!
> Dost thou not see my baby at my breast,
> That sucks the nurse asleep?
> CHARMIAN: O, break! O, break!
> CLEOPATRA: As sweet as balm, as soft as air, as gentle—
> O Antony! Nay, I will take thee too: (V, ii, 308–13)

The asps are at once Antony and her sons by Antony, but she is more than a seducing mother, more even than Isis. Like Hamlet, she knows finally what it is that she herself represents, and through that knowledge she has learned something that we need to know, about the nature of representation itself. Rather than tell us, Hamlet decides to let it be. Cleopatra, more than Hamlet, has become fire and air, has gone beyond the world and beyond theater. Metaphors of the stage cannot encompass Cleopatra any longer, because she has ceased performing. No Freudian reduction is possible, or appropriate, for this greatest of male representations of the female as it attains apotheosis. Shakespearean paradox, so ample as to contain Freud without being contained by him, has given us a literary character at once totally sensual and totally transcendental.

—H. B.

CRITICAL EXTRACTS

JOHN DRYDEN

The death of *Antony* and *Cleopatra,* is a Subject which has been treated by the greatest Wits of our Nation, after *Shakespeare;* and by all so variously, that their example has given me the confidence to try my self in this Bowe of *Ulysses* amongst the Crowd of Sutors; and, withal, to take my own measures, in aiming at the Mark. I doubt not but the same Motive has prevailed with all of us in this attempt; I mean the excellency of the Moral: for the chief persons represented, were famous patterns of unlawful love; and their end accordingly was unfortunate. All reasonable men have long since concluded, That the Heroe of the Poem, ought not to be a character of perfect Virtue, for, then, he could not, without injustice, be made unhappy; nor yet altogether wicked, because he could not then be pitied: I have therefore steer'd the middle course; and have drawn the character of *Antony* as favourably as *Plutarch, Appian,* and *Dion Cassius* wou'd give me leave: the like I have observ'd in *Cleopatra.* That which is wanting to work up the pity to a greater heighth, was not afforded me by the story: for the crimes of love which they both committed, were not occasion'd by any necessity, or fatal ignorance, but were wholly voluntary; since our passions are, or ought to be, within our power. The Fabrick of the Play is regular enough, as to the inferior parts of it; and the Unities of Time, Place, and Action, more exactly observ'd, than, perhaps, the *English* Theater requires. Particularly, the Action is so much one, that it is the only of the kind without Episode, or Underplot; every Scene in the Tragedy conducing to the main design, and every Act concluding with a turn of it. The greatest errour in the contrivance seems to be in the person of *Octavia:* For, though I might use the priviledge of a Poet, to introduce her into *Alexandria,* yet I had not enough consider'd, that the compassion she mov'd to her self and children, was destructive to that which I reserv'd for *Antony* and *Cleopatra;* whose mutual love being founded upon vice, must lessen the favour of the Audience to them, when Virtue and Innocence were oppress'd by it. And, though I justified *Antony* in some measure, by making *Octavia*'s departure, to proceed wholly from her self; yet the force of the first Machine still remain'd; and the dividing of pity, like the cutting of a River into many Channels, abated the strength of the natural stream. But this is an Objection which none of my Critiques have urg'd against me; and therefore I might have let it pass, if I could have resolv'd to have been partial to my self. The faults my Enemies have found, are rather cavils concerning little, and not essential Decencies; which a Master of the Ceremonies may decide betwixt us. The *French* Poets, I confess, are strict Observers of these Punctilio's: They would not, for example, have suffer'd *Cleopatra* and *Octavia* to have met; or if they had met, there must only have pass'd betwixt them some cold civilities, but no eagerness of repartée, for fear of offending against the greatness of their Characters, and the modesty of their Sex. This Objection I foresaw, and at the same time condemn'd: for I judg'd it both natural and probable, that *Octavia*, proud of her new-gain'd Conquest, would search out *Cleopatra* to triumph over her; and that *Cleopatra*, thus attacqu'd, was not of a spirit to shun the encounter: and 'tis not unlikely, that two exasperated Rivals should use such Satyre as I have put into their mouths; for after all, though the one were a *Roman*, and the other a Queen, they were both Women. 'Tis true, some actions, though natural, are not fit to be represented; and broad obscenities in words, ought in good manners to be avoided: expressions therefore are a modest cloathing of our thoughts, as Breeches and Petticoats are of our bodies. If I have kept my self within the bounds of modesty, all beyond it is but nicety and affectation; which is no more but modesty deprav'd into a vice: they betray themselves who are too quick of apprehension in such cases, and leave all reasonable men to imagine worse of them, than of the Poet.

—JOHN DRYDEN, "Preface" to *All for Love*, 1678

WILLIAM HAZLITT

The character of Cleopatra ⟨in *Antony and Cleopatra*⟩ is a master-piece. What an extreme contrast it affords to Imogen! One would think it almost impossible for the same person to have drawn both. She is voluptuous, ostentatious, conscious, boastful of her charms, haughty, tyrannical, fickle. The luxurious pomp and gorgeous extravagance of the Egyptian queen are displayed in all their force and lustre, as well as the irregular grandeur of the soul of Mark Antony. Take only the first four lines that they speak as an example of the regal style of love-making.

> CLEOPATRA: If it be love indeed, tell me how much?
> ANTONY: There's beggary in the love that can be reckon'd.
> CLEOPATRA: I'll set a bourn how far to be belov'd.
> ANTONY: Then must thou needs find out new heav'n, new earth.

The rich and poetical description of her person beginning—

> The barge she sat in, like a burnish'd throne,
> Burnt on the water; the poop was beaten gold,
> Purple the sails, and so perfumed, that
> The winds were love-sick—

seems to prepare the way for, and almost to justify the subsequent infatuation of Antony when in the sea fight at Actium, he leaves the battle, and 'like a doating mallard' follows her flying sails.

Few things in Shakespear (and we know of nothing in any other author like them) have more of that local truth of imagination and character than the passage in which Cleopatra is represented conjecturing what were the employments of Antony in his absence—'He's speaking now, or murmuring—*Where's my serpent of old Nile?*' Or again, when she says to Antony, after the defeat at Actium, and his summoning up resolution to risk another fight—'It is my birthday; I had thought to have held it poor; but since my lord is Antony again, I will be Cleopatra.' Perhaps the finest burst of all is Antony's rage after his final defeat when he comes in, and surprises the messenger of Cæsar kissing her hand—

> To let a fellow that will take rewards,
> And say God quit you, be familiar with,
> My play-fellow, your hand; this kingly seal,
> And plighter of high hearts.

It is no wonder that he orders him to be whipped; but his low condition is not the true reason: there is another feeling which lies deeper, though Antony's pride would not let him shew it, except by his rage; he suspects the fellow to be Cæsar's proxy.

Cleopatra's whole character is the triumph of the voluptuous, of the love of pleasure and the power of giving it, over every other consideration. Octavia is a dull foil to her, and Fulvia a shrew and shrill-tongued. What a picture do those lines give of her—

> Age cannot wither her, nor custom steal
> Her infinite variety. Other women cloy
> The appetites they feed, but she makes hungry
> Where most she satisfies.

What a spirit and fire in her conversation with Antony's messenger who brings her the unwelcome news of his marriage with Octavia! How all the pride of beauty and of high rank breaks out in her promised reward to him—

> —There's gold, and here
> My bluest veins to kiss!—

She had great and unpardonable faults, but the grandeur of her death almost redeems them. She learns from the depth of despair the strength of her affections.

She keeps her queen-like state in the last disgrace, and her sense of the pleasurable in the last moments of her life. She tastes a luxury in death. After applying the asp, she says with fondness—

> Dost thou not see my baby at my breast,
> That sucks the nurse asleep?
> As sweet as balm, as soft as air, as gentle.
> Oh Antony!

—WILLIAM HAZLITT, *Characters of Shakespear's Plays,* 1817

SAMUEL TAYLOR COLERIDGE

This play ⟨*Antony and Cleopatra*⟩ should be perused in mental contrast with *Romeo and Juliet;*—as the love of passion and appetite opposed to the love of affection and instinct. But the art displayed in the character of Cleopatra is profound; in this, especially, that the sense of criminality in her passion is lessened by our insight into its depth and energy, at the very moment that we cannot but perceive that the passion itself springs out of the habitual craving of a licentious nature, and that it is supported and reinforced by voluntary stimulus and sought-for associations, instead of blossoming out of spontaneous emotion.

—SAMUEL TAYLOR COLERIDGE, *"Antony and Cleopatra"* [1819], *Literary Remains,* ed. Henry Nelson Coleridge (London: Pickering, 1836), Vol. 2, p. 143

PAUL STAPFER

"Had Cleopatra's nose been shorter," says Pascal, "the whole face of the world would have been changed." We have no precise information as to the shape and size of Cleopatra's nose; medals and statues here are wanting, and history, which tells us that Antony had an aquiline nose, forgets to say anything with regard to the Queen of Egypt about this interesting feature, which is doubly remarkable, from its function as the organ of smell, and also, as Hegel justly remarks, from its intermediary position between the forehead and the chin. But we know that Cleopatra's beauty was not of a regular character: hers was not the absolute perfection of line, as was that of Venus, or of Helen, or even of Octavia, who, Plutarch distinctly states, yielded neither in youth nor in good looks to Cleopatra. Neither the noble severity of ancient Greece, nor the majesty of Rome, belonged to Cleopatra: after reading Plutarch's account of her successful method of introducing herself unseen into Cæsar's presence, wrapped up in a mattress, and so carried by Apollodorus on his shoulder, she remains for ever associated in our imagination with an idea of graceful littleness, of a sort of feline suppleness and sinuosity. Other women may be of the antique type of beauty and grandeur, but this little creature is fascinatingly pretty. That wonderful chivalric romance, written by a Greek historian in the first century and called *The Life of Antony,* is irradiated by the presence of Cleopatra as by a premature apparition of modern beauty,—animated and subtle, more mental than physical, dazzling, less by purity of form than by ever-varying expression. To speak of her as charming, as enchanting, is to say little or nothing—she was an *enchantress,* a charmer not of snakes but of men, and what was felt in her presence was something more than attraction; she was simply bewitching, and her spell was all the stronger and the more irresistible because it wound itself round its victim closer and closer by slow degrees.

—PAUL STAPFER, *Shakespeare and Classical Antiquity,* tr. Emily J. Carey (London: C. Kegan Paul, 1880), pp. 393–94

GEORGE BERNARD SHAW

The very name of Cleopatra suggests at once a tragedy of Circe, with the horrible difference that whereas the ancient myth rightly represents Circe as turning heroes into hogs, the modern romantic convention would represent her as turning hogs into heroes. Shakespear's *Antony and Cleopatra* must needs be as intolerable to the true Puritan as it is vaguely distressing to the ordinary healthy citizen, because, after giving a faithful picture of the soldier broken down by debauchery, and the typical wanton in whose arms such men perish, Shakespear finally strains all his huge command of rhetoric and stage pathos to give a theatrical sublimity to the wretched end of the business, and to persuade foolish spectators that the world was well lost by the twain. Such falsehood is not to be borne except by the real Cleopatras and Antonys (they are to be found in every public house) who would no doubt be glad enough to be transfigured by some poet as immortal lovers. Woe to the poet who stoops to such folly! The lot of the man who sees life truly and thinks about it romantically is Despair. How well we know the cries of that despair! Vanity of vanities, all is vanity! moans the Preacher, when life has at last taught him that Nature will not dance to his moralist-made tunes. Thackeray, scores of centuries later, was still baying the moon in the same terms. Out, out, brief candle! cries Shakespear, in his tragedy of the modern literary man as murderer and witch consulter. Surely the time is past for patience with writers who, having to choose between giving up life in despair and discarding the trumpery moral kitchen scales in which they try to weigh the universe, superstitiously stick to the scales, and spend the rest of the lives they pretend to despise in breaking men's spirits. But even in pessimism there is a choice between intellectual honesty and dishonesty. Hogarth drew the rake and the harlot without glorifying their end. Swift, accepting our system of morals and religion, delivered the inevitable verdict of that system on us through the mouth of the king of Brobdingnag, and described Man as the Yahoo, shocking his superior the horse by his every action. Strindberg, the only genuinely

Shakespearean modern dramatist, shews that the female Yahoo, measured by romantic standards, is viler than her male dupe and slave. I respect these resolute tragi-comedians: they are logical and faithful: they force you to face the fact that you must either accept their conclusions as valid (in which case it is cowardly to continue living) or admit that their way of judging conduct is absurd. But when your Shakespears and Thackerays huddle up the matter at the end by killing somebody and covering your eyes with the undertaker's handkerchief, duly onioned with some pathetic phrase, as The flight of angels sing thee to thy rest, or Adsum, or the like, I have no respect for them at all: such maudlin tricks may impose on tea-drunkards, not on me.

Besides, I have a technical objection to making sexual infatuation a tragic theme. Experience proves that it is only effective in the comic spirit. We can bear to see Mrs Quickly pawning her plate for love of Falstaff, but not Antony running away from the battle of Actium for love of Cleopatra. Let realism have its demonstration, comedy its criticism, or even bawdry its horselaugh at the expense of sexual infatuation, if it must; but to ask us to subject our souls to its ruinous glamor, to worship it, deify it, and imply that it alone makes our life worth living, is nothing but folly gone mad erotically—a thing compared to which Falstaff's unbeglamored drinking and drabbing is respectable and rightminded. Whoever, then, expects to find Cleopatra a Circe and Cæsar a hog in these pages, had better lay down my book and be spared a disappointment.

—GEORGE BERNARD SHAW, "Better Than Shakespear?" [1900], *Three Plays for Puritans* (1901; rpt. London: Constable, 1930), pp. xxx–xxxii

A. C. BRADLEY

Shakespeare has paid Cleopatra a unique compliment. The hero dies in the fourth Act, and the whole of the fifth is devoted to the heroine. In that Act she becomes unquestionably a tragic character, but, it appears to me, not till then. This, no doubt, is a heresy; but as I cannot help holding it, and as it is connected with the remarks already made on the first half of the play, I will state it more fully. Cleopatra stands in a group with Hamlet and Falstaff. We might join with them Iago if he were not decidedly their inferior in one particular quality. They are inexhaustible. You feel that, if they were alive and you spent your whole life with them, their infinite variety could never be staled by custom; they would continue every day to surprise, perplex, and delight you. Shakespeare has bestowed on each of them, though they differ so much, his own originality, his genius. He has given it most fully to Hamlet, to whom none of the chambers of experience is shut, and perhaps more of it to Cleopatra than to Falstaff. Nevertheless, if we ask whether Cleopatra, in the first four Acts, is a tragic figure like Hamlet, we surely cannot answer 'yes.' Naturally it does not follow that she is a comic figure like Falstaff. This would be absurd; for, even if she were ridiculous like Falstaff, she is not ridiculous to herself; she is no humorist. And yet there is a certain likeness. She shares a weakness with Falstaff—vanity; and when she displays it, as she does quite naïvely (for instance, in the second interview with the Messenger), she does become comic. Again, though like Falstaff she is irresistible and carries us away no less than the people around her, we are secretly aware, in the midst of our delight, that her empire is built on sand. And finally, as his love for the Prince gives dignity and pathos to Falstaff in his overthrow, so what raises Cleopatra at last into pure tragedy is, in part, that which some critics have denied her, her love for Antony.

Many unpleasant things can be said of Cleopatra; and the more that are said the more wonderful she appears. The exercise of sexual attraction is the element of her life; and she has developed nature into a consummate art. When she cannot exert it on the present lover she imagines its effects on him in absence. Longing for the living, she remembers with pride and joy the dead; and the past which the furious Antony holds up to her as a picture of shame is, for her, glory. She cannot see an ambassador, scarcely even a messenger, without desiring to bewitch him. Her mind is saturated with this element. If she is dark, it is because the sun himself has been amorous of her. Even when death is close at hand she imagines his touch as a lover's. She embraces him that she may overtake Iras and gain Antony's first kiss in the other world.

She lives for feeling. Her feelings are, so to speak, sacred, and pain must not come near her. She has tried numberless experiments to discover the easiest way to die. Her body is exquisitely sensitive, and her emotions marvellously swift. They are really so; but she exaggerates them so much, and exhibits them so continually for effect, that some readers fancy them merely feigned. They are all-important, and everybody must attend to them. She announces to her women that she is pale, or sick and sullen; they must lead her to her chamber but must not speak to her. She is as strong and supple as a leopard, can drink down a master of revelry, can raise her lover's helpless heavy body from the ground into her tower with the aid only of two women; yet, when he is sitting apart sunk in shame, she must be supported into his presence, she cannot stand, her head droops, she will die (it is the opinion of Eros) unless he comforts her. When she hears of his marriage and has discharged her rage, she bids her women bear her away; she faints; at least she would faint, but that she remembers various questions she wants put to the Messenger about Octavia. Enobarbus has seen her die twenty times upon far poorer moment than the news that Antony is going to Rome.

Some of her feelings are violent, and, unless for a purpose, she does not dream of restraining them; her sighs and tears are winds and waters, storms and tempests. At times, as when she threatens to give Charmian bloody teeth, or hales the luckless Messenger up and down by the hair, strikes him and draws her knife on him, she resembles (if I dare say it) Doll Tearsheet sublimated. She is a mother; but the threat of Octavius to destroy her children if she takes her own life passes by her like the wind (a point where Shakespeare contradicts Plutarch). She ruins a great man, but shows no sense of the tragedy of his ruin. The anguish of spirit that appears in his language to his servants is beyond her; she has to ask Enobarbus what he means. Can we feel sure that she would not have sacrificed him if she could have saved herself by doing so? It is not even certain that she did not attempt it. Antony himself believes that she did—that the fleet went over to Octavius by her orders. That she and her people deny the charge proves nothing. The best we can say is that, if it were true, Shakespeare would have made that clear. She is willing also to survive her lover. Her first thought, to follow him after the high Roman fashion, is too great for her. She would live on if she could, and would cheat her victor too of the best part of her fortune. The thing that drives her to die is the certainty that she will be carried to Rome to grace his triumph. That alone decides her.

The marvellous thing is that the knowledge of all this makes hardly more difference to us than it did to Antony. It seems to us perfectly natural, nay, in a sense perfectly right, that her lover should be her slave; that her women should adore her and die with her; that Enobarbus, who foresaw what must happen, and who opposes her wishes and braves her anger, should talk of her with rapture and feel no bitterness against her; that Dolabella, after a minute's conversation, should betray to her his master's intention and enable her to frustrate it. And when Octavius shows himself proof against her fascination, instead of admiring him we turn from him with disgust and think him a disgrace to his species. Why? It is not that we consider him bound to fall in love with her. Enobarbus did not; Dolabella did not; we ourselves do not. The feeling she inspires was felt then, and is felt now, by women no less than men, and would have been shared by Octavia herself. Doubtless she wrought magic on the senses, but she had not extraordinary beauty, like Helen's, such beauty as seems divine. Plutarch says so. The man who wrote the sonnets to the dark lady would have known it for himself. He goes out of his way to add to her age, and tells us of her wrinkles and the waning of her lip. But Enobarbus, in his very mockery, calls her a wonderful piece of work. Dolabella interrupts her with the cry, 'Most sovereign creature,' and we echo it. And yet Octavius, face to face with her and listening to her voice, can think only how best to trap her and drag her to public dishonour in the streets of Rome. We forgive him only for his words when he sees her dead:

> She looks like sleep,
> As she would catch another Antony
> In her strong toil of grace.

And the words, I confess, sound to me more like Shakespeare's than his.

That which makes her wonderful and sovereign laughs at definition, but she herself came nearest naming it when, in the final speech (a passage surpassed in poetry, if at all, only by the final speech of Othello), she cries,

> I am fire and air; my other elements
> I give to baser life.

The fire and air which at death break from union with those other elements, transfigured them during her life, and still convert into engines of enchantment the very things for which she is condemned. I can refer only to one. She loves Antony. We should marvel at her less and love her more if she loved him more—loved him well enough to follow him at once to death; but it is to blunder strangely to doubt that she loved him, or that her glorious description of him (though it was also meant to work on Dolabella) came from her heart. Only the spirit of fire and air within her refuses to be trammelled or extinguished; burns its way through the obstacles of fortune and even through the resistance of her love and grief; and would lead her undaunted to fresh life and the conquest of new worlds. It is this which makes her 'strong toil of grace' unbreakable; speaks in her brows' bent and every tone and movement; glorifies the arts and the rages which in another would merely disgust or amuse us; and, in the final scenes of her life, flames into such brilliance that we watch her entranced as she struggles for freedom, and thrilled with triumph as, conquered, she puts her conqueror to scorn and goes to meet her lover in the splendour that crowned and robed her long ago, when her barge burnt on the water like a burnished throne, and she floated to Cydnus on the enamoured stream to take him captive for ever.

—A. C. BRADLEY, "Antony and Cleopatra" [1905], Oxford Lectures on Poetry (London: Macmillan, 1909), pp. 299–303

G. WILSON KNIGHT

On casting retrospect over Cleopatra's tale we are struck by her variety. It surpasses that of any other Shakespearian person. In this way she is all womankind, rather than a single woman: or again, we may say she is universal in the sense that any one person, or, indeed, any one object of any sort, becomes a symbol of universal meaning and content if properly understood. And Cleopatra's 'variety' is so vividly depicted that it is easy to understand. Thus her two main qualities are: (i) the essential femininity we have continually observed, and (ii) her profuse variety of psychic modes: which two are clearly one, since a profound and comprehensive delineation of essential woman is necessarily very varied, and built of contradictions. Thus in analysis we have not inaptly made reference, not only to Shakespeare's previous heroines, but to Eve, Jezebel, Helen of Troy, Amazons, St. Joan, Dido, Delilah, Andromache, Dante's Beatrice, Medusa, the Madonna. All women of legend or literature combine to make our Cleopatra. She is a silk shot with dazzling, shifting, colours. The same is true of the play as an artistic whole. She, more than any other, is the play. Hence, the femininity in the vowel-sounds and the style generally, which I have noted already, and its shifting, dazzling opalescent interplay of imagery. Now it will be clear that Cleopatra is the divinity of the play in the sense that Desdemona is the divinity of *Othello*. Her transcendent divinity and beauty is stressed in Enobarbus' description of her in her barge. The sombre plays ever revolved on such ideals: Hamlet's father, Isabella, Helen of Troy (in *Troilus*), Desdemona, Duncan and the English King in *Macbeth*, Cordelia, Timon himself: all are at some time vividly idealized, all but equated with divinity. Such divinity was ever divine by nature of a certain limited perfection, a certain limited beauty. Cleopatra is divine by nature of her divine variety and profusion. Queen of romance, she is yet, like Antony, old: 'wrinkled deep in time'. The contrast is the same as that between the two theological conceptions of a God containing all qualities good and evil, and a God partial and exclusive: God the Father, and God the Son. The same contrast is reflected in the ethic of the Duke in *Measure for Measure,* who knows both good and evil within himself, and that of Angelo who prides himself on a false, because exclusive, sanctity. Here Cleopatra has beside her Octavia to point the same contrast: and Octavia is a thing of cardboard in this comparison. Now since Cleopatra is so comprehensively conceived, it will be clear that the streak of serpentine evil in her is part of her complex fascination: and, though real and as truly part of her as any other quality, it will be found to melt into her whole personality, enriching rather than limiting her more positive attractions. A limited perfection is sand on which to build: thus Isabella was exposed to shame, her very virtue turned against her when it claimed all-importance. Troilus could not accept Cressid's faithlessness as hers; Desdemona's purity could not save her in a world where an Iago exists. In Cleopatra we find a personification blent of 'good' and 'evil', a Cordelia with a streak of Lady Macbeth. The perfection is one of totality, not exclusion. Thus, from a limited view, her treachery is nauseating; but, from the view of eternity, the whole and all its parts observed, the 'evil' is seen otherwise, as part of a wider pattern. This is why Antony, when his anger is thrown suddenly into relation with death's eternity, so completely alters: his rage abates, its 'reason' now meaningless. Indeed, Enobarbus speaks truth of Cleopatra:

> Age cannot wither her, nor custom stale
> Her infinite variety: other women cloy
> The appetites they feed; but she makes hungry
> Where most she satisfies: for vilest things
> Become themselves in her; that the holy priests
> Bless her when she is riggish.   (II. ii. 240)

Her power to assimilate all qualities and gild them with the alchemy of her rich personality was observed, too, by Antony. She is one

> Whom every thing becomes, to chide, to laugh,
> To weep; whose every passion fully strives
> To make itself, in thee, fair and admired!   (I. i. 49)

She is, indeed, 'a most triumphant lady' (II. ii. 193): and she triumphs where others failed. I conclude, therefore, that the Cleopatra-vision, without shirking the problems of the sombre plays, yet answers them imaginatively.

—G. WILSON KNIGHT, "The Diadem of Love: An Essay on *Antony and Cleopatra," The Imperial Theme* (1931; rpt. London: Methuen, 1951), pp. 308–11

RUTH WALLERSTEIN

If we start with Shakespeare's Cleopatra, it is, of course, impossible that we should make anything of Dryden's. For Shakespeare's Cleopatra offers us not only the variety and fascination of her nature at play with all the forces of empire. She offers us the transformation in a character of supreme spontaneity and energy, of sensationalism, lust, greed and selfishness, into profound emotion, through the instrumentality of suffering and the confrontation with death. Of this transformation Dryden's Cleopatra offers us nothing, nor does she offer that Racinian struggle between passion and reason by which Racine abstracted his dramas out of the formalistic prison of dramatic justice in which the critics were trying to bind the French theatre and into the realm of pure psychological ethics. Dryden conceived her without internal conflict and as a wholly 'good' woman. The tragic issue he reduced to the purely formal moral one of her illicit relation to Antony; and even this issue remained actually outside his play, since the play was a study of emotions and not of history. Granting these severe limitations, however, let us look at her as she is.

Dryden did not conceive of her as a passional character, in the sort in which a man was so. All that interested him in her was her capacity for loving in such a way as to make her, in happy circumstances, the final complement of the active and intellectual sides of man's nature. We must remember Dryden's famous comment on the love lyrics of Donne and Cowley. The view was not original with Dryden; he repeated it because it represented the reflection in literary comment of the social attitude of the age. This attitude in general is conveniently defined by Saint-Evremond, speaking of Corneille, though of the range and refinement of Saint-Evremond's conceptions, neither Dryden nor most of his Restoration audience had any grasp.

> Rejeter l'amour de nos tragédies comme indigne des héros, c'est ôter ce qui nous fait tenire encore à eux par un secret rapport, par je ne sais quelle liaison qui demeure encore entre leurs âmes et les nôtres; ... D'ailleurs, comme les femmes sont aussi nécessaires pour la représentation que les hommes, il est à propos de les faire parler, autant qu'on peut, de ce qui leur est le plus naturel et dont elles parlent mieux que d'aucune chose. Otez aux unes l'expression des sentiments amoureux at aux autres l'entretien secret où les fait entrer la confidence, vous les réduisez ordinairement à des conversations fort ennuyeuses. Presque tous leurs mouvements, comme leurs discours, doivent être les effets de leur passion; leurs joies, leur tristesses, leurs craintes, leurs désirs doivent sentir un peu d'amour pour nous plaire. ...
>
> ... La douleur des maîtresses, tendre et précieuse, nous touche bien plus que l'affliction d'une veuve artificieuse ou intéressée, & qui, toute sincère qu'elle est quelquefois, nous donne toujours une idée noire des enterrements et de leurs cérémonies lugubres.

It is this *maîtresse, tendre et précieuse,* who forms Dryden's central conception of Cleopatra, and her sufferings are his theme in this aspect of his play. To her he has sought to unite as much of the passion of Shakespeare's Cleopatra as he felt could be absorbed into his idea. It is notable that in the closing scene he has stripped from his imitations of Shakespeare all imperial thoughts either in relation to herself or to Antony and has focused only on the final satisfaction and justification of her tenderness. Sedley, in his *Antony and Cleopatra,* just before Dryden's play, had handled the relation between Antony and Cleopatra on précieuse or platonician theses. And Antony's jealousy of Photinus—which very conceivably suggested to Dryden the use of the Dolabella incident—is in Sedley met by Cleopatra with a charge of the unworthiness of jealousy. The contrast of this with Dryden's treatment of her suffering tenderness brings out clearly the realism and sincerity in his handling of Cleopatra. Nowhere is his conception more vividly realized than in the close of the fourth act, which is quite independent of Shakespeare.

For this conception of Cleopatra, Dryden's own distinctive style was the proper instrument. Certain motifs of her view of her own life, such as the claim to meet Antony as his wife, derive from Shakespeare though they originate in Plutarch (of their transmogrification into the theme of free love I say nothing); in the earlier part of the play the concrete expression of her sensuousness perhaps owes much to Shakespeare, and in the last act the grave directness of her speech may owe something to the effect on Dryden of Shakespeare's last act. But her moving definition of her own sorrow and fate springs from Dryden's mastery of the analytical drama, and of the poetry of reflection and logical statement.

—RUTH WALLERSTEIN, "Dryden and the Analysis of Shakespeare's Techniques," *Review of English Studies* 19, No. 2 (April 1943): 179–81

G. S. GRIFFITHS

In *Antony and Cleopatra* there is relatively much more of the ecstasy of passion while there is less of the life of the practical will than in the four great tragedies, and the tragedy needs therefore a different approach from that of Bradley's study. The play exists much more than any other of Shakespeare's in its ecstatic moments, its pure sensations, its gusts of sheer passion: pride, jealousy, remorse, anger, above all love, absolute sole lord of Life and Death, presented with rapturous lyrical energy. In no other play does Shakespeare so stress this by inventing a choric commentator, robuster than the Henry James personal chorus in the later novels but an even rarer and subtler instrument, in the person of Enobarbus, a mere name in Plutarch, whose sole function is to interpret this emotion, a conductor who is himself electrocuted by it before the full force of the play's emotional energy has been released. But all these moments of ecstasy which really compose the passional life of the play 'integrate and become one continuous point'—the expression is Shaw's and he is using it in the interpretation of a Shakespeare play.

It is Cleopatra as Shakespeare creates her who contributes most to this effect. Enobarbus, the best guide to Shakespeare's attitude to his creature, does not think of her as a 'person' or a 'character' at all, she is a phenomenon, 'a wonderful piece of work'. Her agitations he refuses to conceive in the framework of Elizabethan psychology and physiology of animal and vital spirits, humours—in the terms, say, of Orsino's cogitations on the passions: appetite, the motion of the liver or the palate, suffering surfeit, cloyment and revolt, though there are traces in *Twelfth Night* that show Shakespeare even then groping for an image that may equal the undulation and variableness of passion—changeable taffeta, a very opal, the sea—to fit the fancies giddy and infirm, more longing, wavering, soon lost and worn, that will put constancy to sea, that will 'yield an echo to the seat where Love is throned'.

When Enobarbus corrects Antony's commonplace reflection on Cleopatra, 'She's cunning past man's thought', he describes her passions as 'made of nothing but the finest parts of pure love'. The significance of this to the Elizabethan is made clear in many a passage in Donne's poems. 'Love's Growth' begins:

> I Scarce beleeve my love to be so pure
> As I had thought it was,
> Because it doth endure
> Vicissitude, and season, as the grasse;
> Methinkes I lyed all winter, when I swore
> My love was infinite, if spring make it more.
>
> But if this medicine, love, which cures all sorrow
> With more, not onely bee no quintessence,
> But mixt of all stuffes, paining soule, or sense,
> And of the Sunne his working vigour borrow,
> Love's not so pure and abstract, as they use
> To say, which have no Mistresse but their Muse.

'The finest parts of pure love' are the quintessence of love, complete possession. It is significant, too, that Shakespeare makes Cleopatra's beauty a spirit and a motion. She is represented by Shakespeare as at the extreme limit of the thirty-eight years Plutarch gives her at death, her lip is waned, she is wrinkled deep in time, has a tawny front, is sunburnt, but she is love's medium and can 'make defect perfection, and, breathless, power breathe forth'.

At each successive crisis in the play's action Enobarbus directs Antony's attention and ours to this demonic force which has to be reckoned with. The first situation in the play is a challenge to Antony, whose wife, Fulvia, had died, leaving Antony's partisans virtually at war with Octavius in Italy. He proposes to go to Italy with the purpose of a general appeasement. Enobarbus warns him that Cleopatra will be opposed with all her force to his going, that Antony is involved with her and she cannot be ignored, that now Antony has a fair opportunity to choose a woman for himself. Enobarbus is snubbed and Antony goes, but not before Cleopatra has pursed up his heart even more securely by letting him go. This is Antony's first tragic blindness and Enobarbus warns us. Then in Rome Antony makes his second marriage 'for his peace' with Octavia. It is like the marriage of Cathy Earnshaw and Edgar Linton in *Wuthering Heights,* a fatal mistake, and like that it is done out of policy from merely prudential (political) motives. It is the act of a man afraid of his own warm, sensuous, passionate temperament, who senses his error even as he blunders and is completely distracted and passionally detached at his own proposal and marriage. Enobarbus and the Soothsayer both stress the tragic error and Antony in a way knows it himself: 'I' the East my pleasure lies.' Enobarbus even anticipates the further concatenation of circumstances, that this new tie with Octavius will but exacerbate their differences—that Antony can never leave Cleopatra.

Then again before Actium Enobarbus notes emphatically the tragic and moral infatuation of Antony's choice to fight by sea and by Cleopatra's side, and he blames Antony alone for what happens. It is true that Enobarbus is a 'character', a humorist, a *raisonneur,* and he is engulfed in Antony's tragedy by following the dictate of his reason, but this does not invalidate, rather vindicates it. Shakespeare clearly intends him as an example of the truth-seer who perishes, the blinded prophet. Shakespeare no doubt regards Enobarbus's reason as a revealer of truth divorced from charity and the affective will, the lightning-flash into the nature of things—the human heart only excepted—the wisdom of Silenus. His vision has the aloofness of the Lucretian gods, its pure appreciation of life and the human spectacle as an aesthetic phenomenon, an object of wonder and contemplation. But Enobarbus is also a human being, and by passing judgement on Antony in his own person and acting against him by going over to Octavius he attempts to live, to be, to incarnate the vision of reason, and thereby delivers himself into the tragic process. He dies as he sees it fit for Cleopatra to die by taking thought. Shakespeare has in fact touched here the mood described in the passage from Valéry. 'To take thought—metaphysical thought—is fatal: the real in its pure state instantly stops the heart.'

Cleopatra, too, knows the truth of this, the horror of the void—the eternal silences of contemplation. She fills the great gap of time her Antony is away with his living and moving image and the quest of the absent-present Antony in drugged reverie, but she wonders significantly how the unseminar'd exist, these unencumbered thinkers with no affective passional magnet for their thought. Herself she is perpetual motion and emotion, most busy least when she renews herself in dream reverie, and she is always the artist, the great actress-artist, in every extreme and excess of emotion, even in the tempest and whirlwind of passion. She is the greatest of all Shakespeare's coquettes. Cressida goes limp in the morning, shuns the accusing daylight, loses face and fence, but there is no situation of which Cleopatra is not the conscious form-imposing mistress. Here again Enobarbus understands and interprets when he denies design, 'cunning' to these great displays of passion. The only other character in fiction who reminds me of Cleopatra's clairvoyant anticipation of overpowering emotion is Emily Brontë's Cathy Earnshaw who is misunderstood by Nelly and the other characters, as Cleopatra is by Antony and all but Enobarbus. Nothing is done 'deliberately' by either. When the storm comes it is more like possession than hysteria or nervous vapours. Both show an infallible psychological insight into others and themselves at such moments, and each is in command of her wits throughout. Both have the same expectation of adjustment and indulgence from others, of acceptance of the inspiration or afflatus, and expect submission to the spell. Each has the capacity of Love's full intuition of the beloved's nature, and craves absorption by it though struggling incessantly against it. Cleopatra is completely aware of the 'Enemy' in Antony, the Roman element of Will, and she also realizes the limitations of the Roman and those further depths of Antony that can be stirred against the Roman strain. Cathy and Cleopatra both centre outside themselves. 'I am Heathcliffe' balances 'O my oblivion is a very Antony and I am all forgotten', and Cleopatra's vision of Antony after his death, 'Nature's piece 'gainst fancy'.

Only at the very end, at the point when Cleopatra has lost Antony and turned to Death, do the various manifestations of her complicated nature arrange themselves in a sort of perspective; but even then what emerges is a state of trance, a vision of the divine lover, Antony, filling Heaven and Earth, the kiss of the bridegroom, Love lifted to a higher plane among the Homeric gods, all an aspiration and a wild desire, the eagle and the dove. 'O Eastern Star.' How much cosmic vision and imagery is given Cleopatra throughout this last phase:—

> O sun!
> Burn the great sphere thou movest in; darkling stand
> The varying shore o' the world. O Antony!
> Antony, Antony!...

> Shall I abide
> In this dull world, which in thy absence is
> No better than a sty?...

> The odds is gone,
> And there is nothing left remarkable
> Beneath the visiting moon....

> His face was as the heavens, ...
> A sun and moon, which kept their course, and lighted
> The little O, the earth.

Is not Yeats right, with this play in his mind, in speaking of this vision of woman (Cleopatra at the end) 'as though the individual woman is lost in the labyrinth of its lines, as though life were trembling into stillness and silence or at last folding itself away'?

This is not to deny that striking reality, the minute realization of the temperament and the ultimately subordinated personality of Cleopatra which makes Mr. Aldous Huxley, a good judge of this quality, speak of her as the only 'real' woman in all Shakespeare. This aspect of Cleopatra—and it is not more than that—is so magnificent, façade or mask as it proves ultimately to be, that it deserves substantiation here. Thus throughout the whole of Act I, where Cleopatra is on the defensive, she is consistently the female sphinx, enigmatic in action, perverse, contradictory, provocative, she is the thorn, the scourge of love; when she opens her lips mocking, shrill, resisting flow, mood, temperament, irritating, countering, contending, wrangling, stemming the current of passion like a cold stone, or making herself the medium or mocking instrument of the hostile impinging forces from without, obstinately echoing the knocking at the door, harping on the Roman thought, the other Antony, the Self that is eternal and can never be fused. Even her lapses to tenderness and longing are controlled. All the time she keeps her secret, she provokes passion but withdraws herself. It is the very virtuosity, the art of Love. Yet, still in the first act, after Antony has been released and has gone, this Cleopatra is revealed plunged in reverie of a quality that reminds one of Shakespeare's intuition for the movement of the subconscious mind that he shows in all his scenes of madness and mental disturbance or derangement—and they offer a considerable variety: Edgar as poor Tom, and as decayed courtier, the Fool and Lear, Hamlet, Ophelia, Lady Macbeth, Leontes, the secret thoughts of the witches. Cleopatra's passionate reverie has few parallels. Like Marion Bloom's in *Ulysses,* the train of imagery is associative, and like hers it is a reverie of love, all the past enriching the present. Like Marion's too and Chaucer's Wyf of Bath's the evocations make the heart's core glow with gratitude for the demon in her that has given life to passion after passion in others and in her. Here, too, one sees that continuum, that echo of past and anticipation of the future and fusion of all three, that marks the dream reverie and makes it the richest of all mediums of the inner, the quintessential life. Moreover, this pride of life and love, this familiarity with the demon within, is quite free from the vulgarity of vanity which Cleopatra only condescends to. She alludes to the narcotic of vanity as poison only to invoke—invite— her absent lover's thought on her, like the blazing eyes of dead lovers, with all her physical disadvantages when fixed in the still life of memory, the infinite variety at a stay. She is quite as obviously and completely in love with Antony as he with her. It is a perfect reciprocity. She too feels that all his acts are kings and she knows him and is subdued to his element, is incorporated in him, values his every moment's existence as the divine presence in the world—real living. He can make no ungraceful move. From reverie she springs to life and action, like an untamed beast.

—G. S. GRIFFITHS, *"Antony and Cleopatra," Essays and Studies* 31 (1945):
38–44

WILLARD FARNHAM

Samuel Daniel gives the Countess of Pembroke all due credit for stimulating him to rise above the level of his Delia and achieve his Cleopatra. His *Tragedie of Cleo-*

patra, which first appeared in 1594 in a collection of his works entitled *Delia and Rosamund Augmented. Cleopatra,* is dedicated to the countess. Daniel says of her in the dedication that she called up his spirits from low repose to sing of state, to frame tragic notes, to give her *Antonius* company in a *Cleopatra,* and to take part with whatever poor strength he had in the war begun by her valiant brother against "Grosse Barbarisme," that foul foe grown strong enough to become the "tyrant of the North." With Senecan weapons, then, Daniel was to fight Gothic barbarism, particularly, one may suppose, its domination of drama written for the English public stage. With his *Cleopatra* he was to fight a power which would soon produce Shakespeare's *Antony and Cleopatra.*

Daniel did so little to change the prevailing character of popular tragedy that *Antony and Cleopatra* is outstanding as a flagrant but successful violation of Renaissance classical rules; and yet Daniel apparently had his effect upon *Antony and Cleopatra,* chiefly because he had spontaneous poetry in him, despite his allegiance to cut-and-dried Senecanism, and because Shakespeare was therefore not averse to reading him and not unappreciative of some of his best images and turns of phrase. Daniel had the imaginative power to take a long step beyond Garnier and the Countess of Pembroke in what he did with the character of Cleopatra. He gave his Cleopatra a certain complexity and thus made her more subtly tragic than the heroine of *Antonius.* ⟨. . .⟩

In the *Cleopatra* of 1594 the heroine offers much self-analysis in long passages of soliloquy that follow the right Senecan pattern. At the opening of the play, Antony is dead, and Cleopatra, soliloquizing, wonders that she remains alive, since it is not because she still loves life that she still lives. As she looks back upon her life she finds that it has been "foule." Her lusts have brought Antony and herself to ruin and have destroyed her kingdom. She has been cast down from a lofty place of glory, honor, and delight, to be

> Leuell'd with low disgrac'd calamitie.

Thus her "loathsome soule" finds her body only a "hatefull prison." This is a repentant Cleopatra but not an abject one, for she vows never to forget that she was born a queen and never to let anything that comes to her take away her royal spirit.

Hence, as she considers what she is to do, her first thought is of Octavius and his desire to take her to Rome as an adornment of his triumph. That Octavius has this desire she does not doubt. She assumes that because he plans to lead her captive in the streets of Rome, he "seekes to entertaine" her life "with wiles," with promises, flatteries, and threats, but she is confident that he cannot keep her alive to enslave her. The royal courage with which she was born will not desert her, and as a queen she will kill herself. She declares:

> I must not be, vnlesse I be mine owne.
> Tis sweet to die when we are forst to liue.

Cleopatra's second thought is of her children. She says that she would not have remained alive thus long had she not feared that Octavius would offer injury to them after her death. She decides that she still lives, still feigns content, and still soothes Octavius because calamity has made her crafty, and that she temporizes with Octavius out of a desire to procure her children's safety. But she promises that it will not be for long. Honor calls.

> My soule yeelds honour vp the victory,
> And I must be a Queene, forget a mother:
> Yet mother would I be, were I not I.

Perhaps the heavens have decreed, and her sins have deserved, that the line of the Ptolemies should fail. If so:

> Yet let a glorious end conclude my dayes,
> Though life were bad, my death may yet be prais'd.

Cleopatra's third and last thought is of Antony. According to her interpretation of their tragedy, she and Antony have been equally faulty, though faulty in different ways, and they have grappled in an ocean of pride.

> To sinke each others greatnes both together.

Her basic fault has been ambition, and his has been folly. She was enamoured of his greatness, and he was bewitched by her vanity. He came to her "lasciuious Courte" inured to wars but unlearned in woman's wiles, and he fell "to love in earnest," even became her "doting Louer," while she feigned love for him because her ambition sought to use his greatness. At that time she was incapable of love. Her greatness and her beauty made her think that all men must love her duty-bound and that she must love none in particular. She had "vagabond desires" and, moreover, "to thinke one loue had neuer leysure." But now that Antony is dead she has come to love him. She makes this avowal:

> Our like distresse I feele doth sympathize
> And euen affliction makes me truly loue thee.
> Which *Antony,* (I must confesse my fault,)
> I neuer did sincerely vntill now;
> Now I protest I doe, now am I taught,
> In death to loue, in life that knew not how.

She is determined not to survive their "common faulte," since, for one thing, the world would hate her if she did (she has already shown regard for the world's opinion in wanting to make a "glorious end"), and, for another thing, she owes a debt to the sincere lover Antony, who deserves much more than she has given him. In dying she will pay that debt to him faithfully at the same time that she proves herself a courageous queen able to deceive and elude Caesar:

My death, my loue and courage shall reueale,
The which is all the world hath left t'vnstaine me.

Octavius knows that he has captured but not yet conquered a woman of royal spirit. He wants to vanquish her utterly and lead her in triumph, but fears he may not be able to do so. For, as he says to Proculeius, who to capture Cleopatra has entered her monument by trickery and who has had to keep her from stabbing herself at the moment of capture:

Princes (like Lyons) neuer will be tam'd.
A priuate man may yeeld, and care not how,
But greater harts will breake before they bow.
And sure I thinke sh'will neuer condiscend
To lyue to grace our spoyles with her disgrace.

Octavius goes to talk with Cleopatra, hoping against hope to get her to live and allow herself to be made "the greatest Trophey" of his travels. He reproaches her for wrongs she has done to Rome and to himself, and she excuses herself by saying that she did all she did because she was dominated by the greatness of Antony. When her treasurer exposes her concealment of a large amount of treasure, and when she beats the informer, Octavius forgives her, as in Plutarch, and promises that she will have generous treatment. He is deceived into thinking that she is now content to live.

Dolabella, who accompanies Octavius when this interview takes place, admires Cleopatra and is smitten with love for her. Octavius tells him that he plans to send her and her children to Rome immediately, and Dolabella informs Cleopatra in a letter that Octavius means to do this and that he intends to place both her and her children in his triumph. In the letter Dolabella makes known his love. Cleopatra gets satisfaction from the knowledge that her face can still win a lover, and she is grateful to Dolabella for his message, but she does not have any thought of making capital once more of her power to charm. She replies to Dolabella by messenger:

As for my loue, say *Anthony* hath all,
Say that my hart is gone into the graue
With him, in whom it rests and euer shall.

Dolabella's message makes Cleopatra determine to die without more delay. She will shun disgrace, fly to her love, escape her foe, free her soul, and act the last of life with glory by dying like a queen. A *nuntius* tells the Chorus of her death. He was sent by her to procure two aspics and he brought them to her in a basket of figs. She bared an arm to receive the poisoned sting, saying:

And heere I sacrifize these armes to Death,
That Lust late dedicated to Delights.

For a moment she hesitated while Life and Honor struggled within her for victory. Honor won. She received the sting and died. Her face retained a grace that graced death,

> And in that cheere, th'impression of a smile
> Did seeme to shew shee scorned Death and *Cæsar,*
> As glorying that she could them both beguile.

Messengers from Caesar found Charmion dying, while she rearranged Cleopatra's crown with her last strength, and Eras dead at Cleopatra's feet. Cleopatra they found stretched on a bed of gold in her richest royal attire. One of them asked Charmion whether this was well done, and received the memorable reply that it was well done indeed and that it was a proper act for one descended from a race of great kings.

What Daniel does, then, is to make Cleopatra into a heroine with mixed motives, instead of letting her remain one with a single motive, as he has found her in the Countess of Pembroke's *Antonius.* Furthermore, though in *Antonius* Cleopatra has a love for Antony important enough to be her single motive, Daniel gives her a love for Antony that is not even her dominant motive. Before all else his Cleopatra is a queen. Since Antony's death she has come to have true love for him, and the proof lies in her ability to forego a pleasure that would once have been irresistible, that of making a conquest of the doting Dolabella. But she has always had royal pride, even when vagabond desires made her most vain as a light-o'-love. The roots of her royal pride have grown through all the years of her life, and those of her sincere love for Antony through only a few days at the end of her life. In making this plain, Daniel shows himself to be a very respectable artist, as he does also in complicating and to some extent mingling the two motives of royal pride and love for Antony. In dealing with a third motive, Cleopatra's love for her children, he is not so successful, but is not without skill and understanding.

To show Cleopatra's royal pride as her dominant motive, Daniel seizes upon the theme of Caesar's coming triumphal progress through the streets of Rome—a theme only slightly developed by Garnier from Plutarch—and makes much of it. At the opening of the play, as we have seen, he has Cleopatra think of the triumph first of all as she considers suicide and has her decide that she, a queen, will never be exhibited as Caesar's slave. Then he has Caesar express doubt that her royal spirit can be so tamed that she will grace a triumph with her disgrace. Then he has Dolabella, with his news of Caesar's decision to send her to Rome, give her the effective impulse toward suicide. In a sense Daniel builds his drama on the theme of Caesar's triumph.

But aside from Daniel's employment of this theme there is much to let the reader know that his tragedy is primarily that of a royal Cleopatra. His heroine is guided by a truly aristocratic conception of honor, even when she takes account of her new-born love for Antony. By dying she will "fly to her love," but she will also pay an honorable debt owed by a queen to an emperor, will show courage and scorn of death, without which aristocracy has no honor, and will keep herself from being hated by the world as dishonorable—indeed, will gain glory. Her last inner struggle is between life and honor, not between life and love, though it is true that after honor has gained the victory she feels that her soul "parts free to *Antony.*" As for what she feels for her children, that is so much less than her regard for honor that, in order to be a queen, she is entirely willing to forget that she is a mother.

The choruses of *Cleopatra* are not filled with conventional complaints against Fortune, but consistently interpret the tragedy as showing a train of suffering caused by the faults of Antony and Cleopatra. The last chorus puts the question whether man's pride is not limited by a tendency in greatness to destroy itself:

> Is greatnes of this sort,
> That greatnes greatnes marres,
> And wracks it selfe, selfe driuen
> On Rocks of her owne might?
> Doth Order order so
> Disorders ouer-thro?

Though the choruses bring moral fervor to the condemnation of Cleopatra's sins, they are not at odds with the body of the play. They hold up for the reader's sympathy and admiration a true queen, who, whatever her faults, can win glory by dying honorably.

—WILLARD FARNHAM, *Shakespeare's Tragic Frontier: The World of His
Final Tragedies* (Berkeley: University of California Press, 1950),
pp. 156–65

EUGENE M. WAITH

Of all the plays in which Fletcher had a hand, *The False One,* based on the history of Caesar and Cleopatra, comes closest to the tragic norm of his day. The plot has a logical development, not distorted by purely sensational scenes. Though the happy ending makes the tragedy the sort often cited as a precedent for tragicomedy, the evil of the play is convincingly solid, and the emphasis falls upon the temptations to which the protagonists are subjected. The illustrious hero and heroine are (unlike the hero of *Cupid's Revenge*) consistently and rather fully presented and their tragic situation is firmly related to the world in which they live. Septimius, "the false one" who betrays and murders Pompey, serves to focus attention on the theme of honor which unites the play. This is much more than a series of theatrically effective scenes.

And yet, considered as tragedy in relation to other tragedies of the period, *The False One* seems to pretend to more than it in fact possesses. Its great moments are hollow in spite of every merit. The treatment of the two protagonists explains much about this failure. Caesar is first presented at the moment of his meeting with Ptolemy, when Photinus, the evil counselor, offers the conqueror the head of Pompey. Caesar's reaction of horror, dramatically effective in being the exact opposite of the gratitude expected by the Egyptians, establishes the moral superiority of the hero. In his first long speech praise of his Roman enemy is matched by contempt of Egyptian perfidy:

> What poor fate follow'd thee, and pluckt thee on
> To trust thy sacred life to an *Egyptian;*
> The life and light of *Rome,* to a blind stranger,
> That honorable war ne'r taught a nobleness,   (II, i)

Somewhat later he says to Ptolemy:

> And study not with smooth shews to invade
> My noble Mind as you have done my Conquest.   (II, i)

"Noble" and "honorable" are the key words. Caesar is as honorable as the traitor Septimius, corrupted by Photinus, is dishonorable, and the contrast is pointed up by the speeches of Septimius in the scene immediately following the first appearance of Caesar. For Septimius gold is "the Lord I serve, the Power I worship," which makes him honorable no matter what heinous crimes he commits. The irony is unmistakable.

The first suggestion of ambiguity in Caesar's character is given in the soliloquy (II, iii) where he regrets his civil wars. He blames himself for his ambition, thinks sadly of Cato and other Romans whom he has made his enemies, and ends by characterizing himself an "honorable rebel." Here is a human failing—the hint of a tragic flaw—but the impression it makes is counterbalanced by the patent nobility of the hero's self-reproach. He remains honorable after all.

Caesar's reflections are interrupted by the arrival of Cleopatra in a "packet," carried in by the bluff captain Scaeva. The presentation of the heroine is an antiphon of coarse, soldierly observations from Scaeva and enraptured comments from Caesar:

> CAES.: What heavenly Vision! do I wake or slumber?
> ....
> SCE.: A tempting Devil, o' my life;
> ....
> A Spunge, a Spunge to wipe away your Victories:
> And she would be cool'd, Sir, let the Souldiers trim her!
> ....
> CAES.: But that I see her here, and hope her mortal,
> I should imagine some celestial sweetness,
> The treasure of soft love.   (II, iii)

The contrast recalls *Antony and Cleopatra,* but instead of developing gradually as in Shakespeare's tragedy, it is compressed into one scene and, in the process, greatly sharpened and simplified. Here there is no Enobarbus to weigh seductiveness and greatness or to suggest infinite complexities; the loss is incalculable. Fletcher's contrast (for the scene is probably his), brilliant and finite, presents us with a goddess and a whore. And it soon becomes clear that Scaeva's opinion is merely a foil for Caesar's intuitive perception of the nobility of Cleopatra, for, despite her scheming, the heroine of *The False One* has nothing of the hoyden in her. She has much more in common with the dignified enchantress of *All for Love,* but even Dryden's Cleopatra is more wicked.

The characters of both Caesar and Cleopatra are developed by the spectacular incident of Ptolemy's attempt to impress Caesar with the wealth of Egypt. It is another scene of contrast, but now the contrast is most insistently made between Cleopatra and Egyptian materialism. Ptolemy has planned the show to distract Caesar from his sister, and as the treasure is brought in, Cleopatra tries in vain to retain Caesar's attention. After a masque of Isis and Nilus celebrating the fertility of Egypt, Caesar leaves with the words: "The wonder of this wealth so troubles me, / I am not well: good night." (III, iv) In this way another doubt is thrown upon the character of the hero, but the heroine is put on the side of the angels. She is disappointed in Caesar not only because he has neglected her but because:

> He is no man:
> The shadow of a Greatness hangs upon him,
> And not the vertue: he is no Conquerour,
> H'as suffer'd under the base dross of Nature:
> Poorly delivered up his power to wealth,
> (The god of bed-rid men) taught his eyes treason
> Against the truth of love: (IV, ii)

When Cleopatra confronts Caesar directly her nobility is made unmistakable, and also her ideal for Caesar:

> You flung me off, before the Court disgrac'd me,
> . . . .
> Gave all your thoughts to gold, that men of glory,
> And minds adorn'd with noble love, would kick at:
> Souldiers of royal mark, scorn such base purchase:
> Beauty and honour are the marks they shoot at;   (IV, ii)

But Caesar's defection is only temporary. The last act shows him once more his noble self, defending Cleopatra against all calumny and finally setting the crown of Egypt on her head. He is, in her words, "all honour."

Honor and nobility. Precisely what virtues are implied by these terms, reiterated from the beginning to the end of the play? We seem to be closest to a definition in the first act and again in the fifth (both of which were probably written by Massinger). When Achoreus has advised Ptolemy to keep his faith with Pompey, Photinus makes a Machiavellian distinction between honor and policy:

> *Achoreus* (great *Ptolomy*) hath counsell'd
> Like a Religious, and honest man,
> Worthy the honour that he justly holds
> In being Priest to *Isis:* But alas,
> What in a man, sequester'd from the world,
> Or in a private person, is prefer'd,
> No policy allows of in a King,
> To be or just, or thankfull, makes Kings guilty,
> And faith (though prais'd) is punish'd that supports
> Such as good Fate forsakes: (I, i)

A similar distinction is implied in Caesar's paradoxical term for himself, an "honorable rebel," and in his choice of Cleopatra rather than gold, but honor remains, nevertheless, a most inclusive virtue. Cleopatra gives the essence of her conception of honor and nobility when she defies fortune, asserting that she is still herself and that whatever happens her mind will always be free. (V, iv) She touches here upon the Stoical ideal of personal integrity valued by the Duchess of Malfi or Shakespeare's Troilus and expressed in Polonius' famous words: "This above all: to thine own self be true." But the honor of Caesar and Cleopatra is so much more than personal integrity—it is so stuffed with every virtue—that it becomes an equivalent for goodness and loses any distinctive character. The hero and heroine are like the ideal characters of romance, where honor is also a most inclusive term. It is, so to speak, the moral qualification of a hero. To say that Caesar and Cleopatra are honorable is to say little more than that they are heroic.

Thus the meaning of honor in the play is extremely vague and yet suggestive of all that is highest and best. It is closely associated with nobility, that other indefinable quality constantly referred to. Once the breadth and haziness of these key concepts are recognized, it is not difficult to see why the tragedy as a whole is disappointing. Caesar and Cleopatra, paragons of honor and nobility, conform to a general notion of what is heroic rather than being truly particularized. Because their virtue is so comprehensive, the efforts of their enemies seem not only despicable but puny. The defense of personal integrity is a theme which may well evoke pity and terror, especially when the individual is obliged, like Troilus or the Duchess, to defend his ideal against the superior force of a materialistic and faithless world. But Caesar and Cleopatra are much more than a match for Septimius, Photinus, and Ptolemy. Easy victors over all forms of evil, the hero and heroine are almost superhuman. From the Fletcherian conception of the hero it is a short step to the "heightened" figure of the Restoration heroic drama.

—EUGENE M. WAITH, *The Pattern of Tragicomedy in Beaumont and Fletcher*
(New Haven: Yale University Press, 1952), pp. 124–27

NORMAN SUCKLING

⟨. . .⟩ Shakespeare's Cleopatra does not love Antony at all, until the last act. A real love could be attributed to her only by those who are so unaware of the truth of the matter as to suppose that love is compatible with coquetry. Shakespeare's Cleopatra is a coquette—Professor Bonamy Dobrée has called her "a flashy vulgarian." She is more concerned with her power over Antony than with his happiness or his honour; always until the last act, when a realization of the irrevocable end rouses her to unsurpassed lyric heights and to a genuine love too late, as it comes to so many of us. I should not like to state categorically that this is the more frequent type of woman, but it is the type that attracted more of Shakespeare's attention, to the extent of encouraging in some of his critics the suggestion that in his portrayal of this type he was drawing on his own experience. That was the point of Miss Clemence Dane's play of *Will Shakespeare*—to present the poet in the toils of a woman who was capable of love only on exceptional occasions, and to show him as so affected by this experience that it coloured most of the feminine portraits he drew. But Dryden's Cleopatra is a very different character, and may be said genuinely to love Antony, not merely to exploit him. She had deserted at Actium, but there is no reason to doubt her own statement that her flight was due to simple fear. She has genuinely refused Octavius' offer, where the Cleopatra of Shakespeare would have used it as a stake in her game (and in fact begins to do something of the kind in her scene with Octavius' messenger Thidias). We need not, doubtless, take at its face value her statement that

> Nature meant me
> A wife, a silly, harmless, household dove,
> But Fortune, that has made a mistress of me,
> Has thrust me out to the wide world, unfurnished
> Of falsehood to be happy

and if there were no other option than to explain her in terms of the two types noted by Valéry, the *matrone essentielle* and the *danseuse-née*—with regard to whom it is important not to fall into the error of trying to seduce the former or marrying the latter—one would hesitate to qualify her exclusively as the *matrone!* But neither is she at all recognizably the *danseuse;* certainly she is not compounded all of feminine wile and power-hunger like her Shakespearean counterpart. The only time she stoops to the coquette's trick of arousing jealousy it is by Alexas' suggestion, and what is more she does not do it at all cleverly. The scene is vitiated a little by Dryden's making her accept the sentimental convention that "jealousy's a proof of love"—whereas in reality they exclude each other—but it is clear that in embarking on this line of policy she is acting against her own nature. Shakespeare's Cleopatra on the other hand would have found no difficulty in it, and would not moreover have needed the promptings of her counsellor to suggest it—those promptings whereby, as I have indicated, Alexas in Dryden absorbs the odium of the action. Later in the play it is again Alexas who (to save his own "bacon" as much as Cleopatra's) feigns her death, *unknown to her;* but in Shakespeare the same development is presented as of Cleopatra's own invention—or, at any rate, with no more than a word from Charmian—and it is she who deliberately instructs Mardian to "word it piteously."

Dryden's Cleopatra has in fact shed most of the features of her traditional "serpentine" character and acquired many of those of the lover who is a fulfilment rather than a fatality to him whom she loves; without, one must admit, being in any way quotable as a partner in Christian marriage. There is indeed a certain ambiguity evident throughout Dryden's play in his simultaneous exploitation of "official" sympathy for Octavia as a lawful wife and of Cleopatra's scorn for "that thing, that dull insipid lump." The one can clearly count on as ready a predisposition in the audience as the other, and can do so in our own day as well as in Dryden's own. We should in fact find it difficult nowadays to attach even as much weight as Dryden did to the fact that the love of Antony and Cleopatra was "illicit"—which may point, according to one's predilections, to the triumph in modern times of M. de Rougemont's "myth" of love outside morality, or to a recognition of the nature of genuine love as unrelated (like all other ultimately precious states of mind) to any finalities of social ethics or survival-values. But at least Dryden has pointed the way to a consciousness of the love which, working outside the framework of social morality and therefore as likely to be manifested in the absence as under the sanction of the marriage-bond, offers those who are capable of it the prospect of recognizing and realizing their highest nature—as against the obscure satisfaction of uneasy stirrings for their own sake which, as M. de Rougemont noted, the devotees of "dark passion" wilfully stimulate to their own undoing.

—NORMAN SUCKLING, "Dryden in Egypt: Reflexions on *All for Love*,"
Durham University Journal 45, No. 1 (December 1952): 5–6

DONALD PEARCE

Horace's achievement in this poem ⟨*Odes* 1.37⟩ was to present Cleopatra on a plane transcending the world of temporal contradictions without at the same time withdrawing her from history. It was a remarkable feat considering the image of Cleopatra that prevailed among Romans, but more especially in view of the deep paradox of her nature. She was licentious, insolent, cruel: when her fourteen-year-old brother, who by Egyptian custom was also her husband, requested his rightful share in the government of his country, her response was to poison him and become sole ruler. At the same time, she was cultivated and intellectually resourceful. She had made herself fluent in the languages of the tribes over which she ruled. She was a brilliant conversationalist. She had strong scholarly learnings, even exchanging rare books on a familiar basis with no less a connoisseur than Cicero.

According to Plutarch, Antony found it perfectly appropriate, in view of her intellectual interests, to present her with the celebrated library of Pergamum.

She was a genuine enigma; and it is doubtful that any Roman saw her objectively, unless it was Horace. His solution to the "problem" of her character was to come out not on the side of politics, that *vox dei* of the Roman world, but on the side of romance. This is the real meaning of Cleopatra's death-scene as he presents it. For though it is one of the most familiar pictures in history or in literature, it is not really a "documentary" scene at all, but one deliberately constructed by Horace out of several competing versions of her death which were circulating at the time: that she had died from the use of a poisoned comb, that she had swallowed poison, that she had pricked her arm with a poisoned pin, that she had been bitten by an asp. According to some sources the postmortem revealed a small puncture halfway up her arm, and no other mark; though accounts vary here, too, for others (Plutarch's, for example), record that her body bore the marks of the beatings which she had inflicted on herself in grief over Antony's death. She was given a splendid funeral by Octavian and laid in state beside her lover Antony, as she had requested. The glorification of her death was thus the work of the one Roman who while she lived had been the most insusceptible to her charms. But now that her death had been, so to speak, officially romanticized by Octavian, Horace was free—in another sense, bound—to choose the version of her death that combined what probably happened with the greatness of what ought to have happened.

As one thinks about this complex and mysterious death, so personal and self-fulfilling in its inwardness, yet so self- and world-transcending, the final image of Cleopatra shines back through the poem, rinsing and defining those "anniversary sentiments" with which the poem opens. For the effect is not merely rhetorical. Primarily it is moral and transvaluative. The final picture of the queen, drawn in these very verses as history was forever after to remember her, must have been brimful of social and political implications in 23 B.C. The Cleopatra of this ode was not just a clever literary portrait, but a subversive transformation of the *regina demens* of official and popular imagination into a superb and touching figure of heroic romance.

 —DONALD PEARCE, "Horace and Cleopatra: Thoughts on the Entanglements
  of Art and History," *Yale Review* 51, No. 2 (Winter 1962): 244–45

EUGENE M. WAITH

Cleopatra (in *All for Love*) is first seen as the cause of Antony's unmanning. The theatrical strategy of this first unfavourable impression, established only to be radically altered later on, is almost the only similarity between Dryden's treatment of his heroine and Shakespeare's. After exposure to the charms of Shakespeare's Cleopatra, who manages to remain marvellously attractive even at her most hoydenish and deceitful ("holy priests bless her when she is riggish"), one is apt to find the Cleopatra of Dryden shockingly tame and stiff. While it is easy to picture Shakespeare's Cleopatra in anything from Egyptian dress to the bodice and far-thingale she probably wore on the Elizabethan stage, Dryden's Cleopatra belongs in late seventeenth-century court dress, complete with train. Passion never quite robs her of dignity. There is no haling of messengers by the hair, no riggishness. To understand this Cleopatra is an essential preliminary to understanding the play.

She dominates the second act as Ventidius does the first. In her initial appear-ance with Iras and her eunuch, Alexas, she proclaims her love a "noble madness" and a "transcendent passion" which has carried her "quite out of reason's view" till she is "lost above it" (II, 17–22). Force and excessiveness combine here with nobility as they do in Ventidius' first description of Antony. The heroine is no mere temptress to lure the hero from the path of virtue. She is herself carried away by a passion of heroic proportions like his. Serapion's description of the flood, already suggested as an analogue for Antony's love, may be associated even more properly with Cleopatra's:

> Our fruitful Nile
> Flow'd ere the wonted season, with a torrent
> So unexpected, and so wondrous fierce,
> That the wild deluge overtook the haste
> Ev'n of the hinds that watch'd it . . .   (I, 2–6)

Dryden has taken over Shakespeare's insistence on the resemblances between the lovers and added another in giving Cleopatra a heroic stature like Antony's. Gran-deur and largeness of mind are hers as much as they are his. In fact it is her high-mindedness rather than her sensual attraction which persuades Antony not to leave her. The telling blow is her announcement that she refused a kingdom from Caesar because of her loyalty to Antony (in her noble contempt for wealth she resembles the Cleopatra of Fletcher and Massinger's *The False One*). By the end of the act these similar lovers have been brought together to the dismay of Ventidius, but it is to be noticed that Antony's conviction that Cleopatra is worth more than all the world does not alter his heroic determination to fight with Caesar. There is now the additional motive of revenge for Caesar's attempt to corrupt Cleopatra. Love for her is not entirely the effeminizing passion Ventidius thinks it to be, and despite her dignified bearing she is far from tame.

One sentence of self-description has exposed Cleopatra to a great deal of unfriendly laughter:

> Nature meant me
> A wife; a silly, harmless, household dove,
> Fond without art, and kind without deceit.   (IV, 91–3)

The comparison is not apt, and it is particularly unfortunate that the incongruity blocks the understanding of a crucial point—Cleopatra's attitude towards being a wife. In Shakespeare's play "Husband I come" owes its brilliance as much to its unexpectedness as to its rightness. It signals a transformation in Cleopatra matching

the re-emergence of the heroic Antony. In Dryden's play the change is a much
smaller one, and so thoroughly prepared that it is no shock to hear:

> I have not lov'd a Roman, not to know
> What should become his wife; his wife, my Charmion!
> For 'tis to that high title I aspire . . .   (V, 412–14)

Her first reference to marriage is contemptuous, as one might expect. Charmion
has brought a message that, though Antony is leaving, he will always respect
Cleopatra, and she picks up the word with obvious irritation:

>   Is that a word
> For Antony to use to Cleopatra?
> O that faint word, *respect!* how I disdain it!
> Disdain myself, for loving after it!
> He should have kept that word for cold Octavia.
> Respect is for a wife: am I that thing,
> That dull, insipid lump, without desires,
> And without pow'r to give 'em?   (II, 77–84)

The speech not only expresses Cleopatra's pique but establishes an attitude towards the cold and the dull exactly like that of Antony (the speech precedes
Antony's comments on Caesar by only thirty lines). Though Cleopatra in other
moods and other circumstances speaks more favourably of being a wife, she retains
to the end her scorn of a "dull, insipid lump". Immediately after vowing to follow
the dead Antony as a dutiful wife, she adds:

>   Let dull Octavia
> Survive, to mourn him dead: my nobler fate
> Shall knit our spousals with a tie too strong
> For Roman laws to break.   (V, 415–18)

The opposition between "spousals" and "Roman laws" provides the necessary clue
here. Cleopatra considers her love above and beyond law as it is above and
beyond reason, yet she borrows from marriage law the terms which distinguish this
love from an infatuation of the senses. Her unfortunate self-comparison to a
household dove (the context of which will have to be examined later) is part of this
process of distinguishing her feelings both from the dullness of the routine and
every-day and from the purely sensual and transient.

   A glance back at *The Conquest of Granada* will make the distinction clear.
Cleopatra's love (and Antony's too) is the sort that Queen Isabella defines:

> Love's a heroic passion which can find
> No room in any base degenerate mind:
> It kindles all the soul with honor's fire,
> To make the lover worthy his desire.   (2 *Conquest*, I, 1, 145–8)

The fire and honour of such a love distinguish it from the "lethargy" to which Abdalla succumbs under Lyndaraxa's spell and also from the mere legality of Almahide's relationship to Boabdelin, "When all I knew of love, was to obey!" Almanzor at first takes love for a "lethargy", but by the time of his debate with Lyndaraxa he has learned that though it is not controlled by reason it is both constant and strong:

> 'Tis an enchantment where the reason's bound;
> But Paradise is in th'enchanted ground . . .
> My love's my soul; and that from fate is free;
> 'Tis that unchang'd and deathless part of me.
>
> (2 *Conquest*, III, 3, 146–7, 179–80)

Similarly, Antony is lethargic at the opening of the play, seemingly unmanned by love. He is "fired" first by Ventidius, though still half unwilling to leave Cleopatra. When she has persuaded him of the nobility of her love, he identifies his passion with his heroism, much as Almanzor does, and prepares with a whole heart for his battle with Caesar. The spectacle of triumph with which the third act opens presents the momentarily successful fusion of warrior and lover.

When Cleopatra compares herself to a household dove she is explaining to Alexas why she does not want to adopt his plan of flirting with Dolabella to arouse Antony's jealousy: she is opposed to all deceit. Repeatedly during the play her plainness is brought out. Though she finally takes the advice of Alexas, she is unable to maintain the counterfeit. Later, when the false news of her death is carried to Antony, she, unlike Shakespeare's heroine, is unaware of the ruse. Antony, too, has a transparent nature, and both of them in this respect resemble Almanzor, who compares his heart to a crystal brook. Antony complains of his "plain, honest heart", and compares himself to "a shallow-forded stream" (IV, 432–40). Plainness is another heroic trait which Dryden has given to Cleopatra; his desire to emphasize it in the scene with Dolabella leads him to force the comparison of his heroine to a wife, who is further compared to a fond and artless dove. If Cleopatra lacks the dullness of a wife, she hopes to prove that she lacks the meretriciousness of a mistress.

The comparison of two kinds of love is best seen in Cleopatra's interview with Antony's legal wife, who is hardly more like a household dove than Cleopatra. Dryden was well aware that the unhistorical introduction of Octavia in Act III was his most daring innovation. I doubt whether it has the effect which Dryden most feared, of dividing the audience's sympathies (and he notes that no critic made this objection), but it has other consequences, very likely unintentional, though by no means damaging to the total effect of the play. Briefly stated, they are the shift from the contrast between Cleopatra and Caesar to the contrast between Cleopatra and Octavia and the resulting transfer of heroic values to the realm of love.

In Shakespeare's play Caesar remains throughout the chief embodiment of the Roman point of view as Cleopatra of the Egyptian. Caesar's ideal of heroic man is a Stoic concept of the warrior, whereas Cleopatra's includes both warrior and lover. The same might be said of the ideals of these two characters in *All for Love,* but from the moment that Octavia appears, she usurps her brother's antipodal position. The confrontation with Cleopatra establishes her firmly as Antony's alternative choice. Even Ventidius, who represents Roman values though qualified by his admiration for Antony, relies on Octavia to make the Roman ideal compelling. Thus, though the issue remains Antony's choice of love or his responsibilities in the world, the stage presents as the dramatic symbols of these alternatives two women, Cleopatra and Octavia, and the choice at the centre of the play becomes one between love and marriage. The turn of the third act which determines Antony for the second time to leave Cleopatra is not, as it was in the first act, the responsibility to fight Caesar in order to show the world who is master, but duty to a wife, through whom he may reach a peaceful understanding with Caesar. Octavia's weapons are her unrequited love and her children. Cleopatra, who was portrayed in the first act as a deterrent to heroic action, now appears as an alternative to domestic love. When the two women meet, they naturally quarrel over which one of them loves Antony more, and Cleopatra stakes her claim on the very extravagance of her love, which has made her give up her good name in order to become Antony's mistress. The fourth act in effect tests the truth of this love in the episode of Dolabella, showing that it is too great to be concealed. Octavia's love, in this same act, is overwhelmed by outrage. When she leaves in the midst of angry (though justifiable) accusations, it is reduced to duty, its basic component all along.

In the fifth act Antony is separated from both women. Octavia has left and he has quarrelled with Cleopatra over her supposed liking for Dolabella. The problems of empire are raised again but only to be reabsorbed in the problems of love. Though the Egyptian fleet has deserted and Caesar is at the gates, Antony is primarily concerned with Cleopatra's feelings towards him. When he thinks that she has fled, his first thought is that she has "fled to her Dolabella"; the accusation that she has turned to Caesar comes second. The idea of a heroic last stand is banished in an instant by the false news of Cleopatra's death, which seems to prove her innocence. The only possible heroic action now is suicide, since

> I was but great for her; my pow'r, my empire,
> Were but my merchandise to buy her love . . .   (V, 270–1)

The structure of the play has been called episodic. Noyes says that "like that of *The Conquest of Granada,* it deals with successive adventures in the life of one man, not with one central crisis." Jean Hagstrum says the play "is not a closely concatenated action that unfolds moral justice. It is a gallery of related heroic poses intended to arouse our sympathy . . . and our admiration . . ." The second judgment is much the more acceptable, and surely the relatedness which Hagstrum recognizes is provided by the crisis in the love-relationship of Antony and Cleopatra, the concern of each act in the play. It is strange to complain of looseness of structure in a play whose strength resides in concentration upon one problem. In this respect the structure is a refinement upon that of *The Conquest of Granada* and *Aureng-Zebe*. The three plays constitute a series in progressive tightness and simplification.

—EUGENE M. WAITH, "Dryden," *The Herculean Hero in Marlowe, Chapman, Shakespeare and Dryden* (New York: Columbia University Press; London: Chatto & Windus, 1962), pp. 193–98

DENZELL S. SMITH

⟨. . .⟩ the two acknowledged classical sources for ⟨Thomas⟩ May's play which treat the Cleopatra story at length offer different interpretations of her character. Plutarch shows a queen concerned about worldly affairs of course, but a captivating, intelligent, witty, charming, and beautiful consort for an aging yet great man. Dio Cassius shows a queen mainly concerned about advancing her own fortunes, unscrupulously using the love of an infatuated and easily led general to do it. Sometimes to the confusion of his play, especially in the character of Antony, May draws heavily on both sources.

Thus May's play is clearly dependent on Dio Cassius and Plutarch for its main outlines and partly dependent on Dio Cassius for its skeptical interpretation of Cleopatra's character. However, it also shows the skeptical spirit of May's age. His skepticism concerning the character of a person long famous in narrative and dramatic literature chiefly indicates his doubts about the abilities of men to remain steadfastly loyal when changes in fortune wrought by the accidents of history or men's actions and temperaments create situations in which loyalty and self-interest clash. May shows that but a minute fraction of men are capable of unselfish devotion, while most men choose the easier course. He does not condemn those who do waver or change their loyalty; the dilemma in which he places them and the choices he has them make demonstrate his underlying assumption that life requires men to commit themselves to absolute loyalties in a world made up of seemingly irreconcilable viewpoints. One is either for or against a man, a government, or a way of life, and that man, government, or way of life has somewhere its opposite, which also commands absolute loyalties. Some viewpoints are claimed to be more worthy than others, but the real reason for characters choosing one position over another is not the moral superiority of the new position, but rather the satisfaction of personal aims such as love, gain, or physical well-being.

While some characters utter traditional moral judgements of the conduct of others pursuing their selfish interest, the judgements do not convince the reader that May believed traditional moral patterns governed men's real conduct, partly because at times the characters making the evaluations are themselves suspect. When he required characters to choose between Antony or Caesar, or between license or morality, he shows us characters adopting one loyalty or another without regard for traditional modes of judging men's actions. Those who change loyalties for selfish reasons are not condemned by those whom they forsake, those whom they join, or the higher powers, since retributive justice seems not to operate in the play. Those who remain loyal to Antony are but a handful; and although Antony praises their fidelity, the priase is hollow when loyalty brings them either death or a post in the enemies' camp no better or worse than the post they had before. To be faithful is to die, as Eros and Cleopatra's servants show; to be disloyal is merely to change the color of one's coat.

The shifting loyalties of May's play even make Cleopatra's suicide not an act of fidelity—which is what she claims for it—but a selfish escape from her wretched future as a Roman captive. The dramatist makes clear by explicit statement that she chooses death as the alternative to captivity, and once death is all that is left for her, she as wholeheartedly devotes herself to Antony's memory as she, moments before, was devoted to furthering her earthly estate. Loyalty corresponds to self-interest for her at the end of the play, making her last act peculiarly ambiguous.

A detailed description of May's play will show that he places not only Cleopatra but also other characters in situations which require the choice of one loyalty or the other. Except for a handful, his characters are loyal for motives which either are unstated or ignoble. By making his characters choose between different loyalties, he reveals the demand of the late Jacobean age for decisions in real life requiring a choice between disparate loyalties, and by showing Cleopatra's selfish motives he shows his spirit is attuned to his age's skeptical view of the nature of women.

Cleopatra first appears to be an intelligent, charming, and courtly mistress who commands and receives Antony's every attention, but who soon more truthfully shows herself as scheming and treacherous. Before her first appearance she is described by three of Antony's lieutenants as "a state beauty . . . ordain'd by fate / to bee possest by them that rule the world." Further, "her Soule is full of greatnesse, and her witt / Has charms as many as her beauty has," but she is said to have "ambitious aimes," aims beyond Antony's gift of three kingdoms. Antony, however, dotes on her: he compliments her beauty and her taste, he foregoes examining letters from Rome in order not to "disturbe the pleasures of [the] night," he debases a king to honor her, and he makes a gift to her of a famous library.

In return for his trust she selfishly hires Antony's lieutenant Canidius to persuade Antony that she ought to accompany him to the war because she fears that she will lose her "state . . . hopes and fortunes" if Octavia should successfully intercede between husband and brother a second time. Cleopatra hides her real reason for going by pleading that her love for Antony urges her to be "a partner in his higher cares," a partner "whose soule hee [thinks] . . . fitt to share / In all his dangers." Antony believes her. When she gets her way, she says aside, "My wishes are effected," sounding like the scheming villain of a melodrama. She repays Antony's confidence in her courageous heart by fleeing from the battle, feigning victory when she lands in Egypt, offering "herselfe, and all her fortunes to [Caesar's] service" soon after landing in Egypt, and offering to Caesar, in return for her liberty and the crown of Egypt for herself and her children, a "great masse of gold" which she has hidden "unknowne t' Antonius."

Thus she is correctly described by Agrippa as a queen with an "ambition greater than her fortunes" who has ruled "halfe the Roman world, / Trodd on the necks of humbled kings," and is possessed of a "haughty spirit" that "will never stoope [to] captivity." Her "haughty spirit" leads her to seek a poison that first will enable her to "controll the spite of Fortune" and second to save herself from servitude and loss of honor; but only as a last resort will she die, because her aim is to achieve such eminence that "her glorious name" will be "fix[ed] . . . above the starrs." No longer does Antony serve her purpose; the agent who will now achieve this greatness for her is Caesar, and control of Caesar is to be gained by her beauty. In short, she will sell herself to the highest bidder.

Her double dealing reaches a climax in Act IV. After seeking to "devise some meanes . . . to deserve great Caesar's love," she, seconds later, addresses Antony, just returned from Pharos, as "my dearest lord"; assuring him that his welcome feast, "the feast of fellow-dyers," shows the "firme" bond of those who "live in love, that meane to dy togither." Antony's acceptance of her statement exemplifies Miss Ellis-Fermor's claim that "the sense of defeat . . . was so marked a characteristic of the Jacobeans." Believing her, Antony has no reason to suspect that she commands Pelusium to be "rendred upp to Caesar" except that his lieutenants expose the treachery of Caesar's messenger Thyreus. But when Antony accuses her of treachery, she claims "a faithfull heart," threatening to use the asp, which she is keeping as a "preservation / 'Gainst Caesar's cruelty," "against Antonius' baseness, a worse foe / Then Caesar is." Antony callowly relents, fawning on her before leaving for a final attack on Caesar.

When the false report of her death causes Antony to slay himself, she does not mourn Antony, but is torn by doubts about her future. She says that "knowne mischiefes have their cure; but doubts none"; she prefers "despair" to "fruitless hope Mixt with a killing feare." She would willingly choose either an honorable life or death, but she cannot live in an undetermined position. Her "doubting soule" is "afflict[ed]" to know whether Caesar's "love will proove / Feigned or true." The reader knows which alternative was long before decided on; the dramatist constructs a situation which holds the reader's attention not by doubt about the outcome, but because men's actions, temperaments, and the accidents of history demand that a character choose between alternate absolute positions—between life or death. Once she sees that the situation will not allow her to pursue her selfish interests, and that she has no honorable way out, she chooses immediately.

The situation is striking in Act V because Cleopatra clearly prefers death to doubt, a known position to a non-determined position. Her long temptation scene with Caesar shows her begging for death rather than the indeterminate, doubtful future of a captive in Rome, and after she sees no sign of love in Caesar, she cryptically replies to the question "How fares youre Majesty?" by saying "never so well— / As now I am." That is, she now knows that she will not be empress of the world but must choose either captivity or death. With two choices open to her, she has no fears about preferring death to a life of dishonor. Once she is resolved, she wholeheartedly commits herself to her new role which in fact results from a selfish choice but which appears to be loyalty to Antony; she now claims to be Antony's loving and loyal mistress. She truthfully says that she was "never till now [his] true and faithfull love"; and once she decides, all other alternatives are forgotten. With the greatest pomp she dies so that she can "begge [his] pardon in the other world."

Cleopatra's motives are not difficult to determine; throughout the play she has but one end in view: to be empress of the world, to be "the Queene of fortune." She cannot know which general to cast her lot with until the final battle shows the victor, because presumably Caesar, who appears ascendant, could by chance die in the final skirmishes. Thus she barters with Caesar while feigning loyalty to Antony. Cleopatra articulates her dilemma; should Antony win, he would find out she has been treacherous; should Caesar win, she is unsure of his love because she has only dealt with his messenger. Her solution is "to make all sure" by going to the tomb; when she does so she is *not* the queen of fortune because she says:

> If fates contrive
> A future state of happinesse for mee,
> It is my castle; if my death they doome,
> I am possest already of a tombe.

The alternatives are clear: either happiness or death.

Clearly, Cleopatra is not loyal to Antony. The dramatist places her in situations which show her scheming to gain her own selfish goals; he shows her claiming loyalty to Antony while bartering with Caesar. If she loves Antony she ought to be against Caesar, but she is not; if she is against Antony, she ought to be for Caesar, but she is not. In her attempt to bestride the twin colossi of Antony and Caesar lies the focal point of the play. She wants to be the manipulator of both men, the queen of fortune who operates through the agencies of Rome's ostensible rulers. She can be said to be continually loyal only to herself; she uses the doting Antony for her own gain, and she would use Caesar, if she could but ensnare him, for the same end. Her "ambitious aimes" seek to control the world through the figurehead who has her momentary loyalty. Three great Romans have so far been her lovers; she had just as soon add a fourth.

—DENZELL S. SMITH, "Literary Introduction" to *The Tragoedy of Cleopatra Queene of Aegypt* [1965] (New York: Garland, 1979), pp. lxxxv–xcii

ROBERT E. FITCH

As for Cleopatra (in *Antony and Cleopatra*), is it a fair proposal that we should look upon her as a sort of female Falstaff? Both the one and the other seek to transcend the contingencies of circumstance and the soilures of sin by a secret inward power. For Falstaff it is an inexhaustible humor; for Cleopatra, an inexhaustible personal charm. But when either of them is made to confront love, the limitations become apparent. Love for Falstaff, in *The Merry Wives of Windsor,* must be subordinated to avarice. Love for Cleopatra is strangely mingled with pride and power, with cruelty, caprice, jealousy, and deceit. Nor is this Cleopatra some other than the true Cleopatra, any more than the Falstaff of *The Merry Wives* is some other than the Falstaff of *Henry IV* and *Henry V.* Surely "Q" (Sir Arthur Quiller-Couch) has it upside down when he tells us that Shakespeare had to kill off Falstaff in order not to bring further disgrace on the hero king. Shakespeare had to kill off Falstaff as he had to kill off Cleopatra, because if they were to stay around longer they would, in effect, kill off themselves. Shakespeare, knowing that in reality age *can* wither and custom *can* stale even the most gay and the most graceful, led Falstaff to death in beauty and in pathos and led Cleopatra to death in beauty and in triumph, so that the immortal part of them—reputation—should not be dimmed by envious and calumniating time nor yield to its razure of oblivion.

However, it is quite another thing to talk of this sort of love as mature, or as being the expression of Shakespeare's mature experience in love. Doubtless Cleopatra sees her affair with Antony as belonging to the maturity of her career, since she is no longer green in judgment as in her "salad days", and now has a more discriminating palate than when she feasted with Julius Caesar. But what is the mark of maturity in love? If maturity means growth in sensual awareness, and in a temper that alternates between reckless self-abandon and shrewd manipulation of the lover, then no doubt Cleopatra has arrived at it. But if maturity means love that has parted with false pride, that gives itself to sincerity, humility, and truthfulness, that is strengthened in loyalty by the toughest ordeal, that has discovered the full meaning of tenderness, that is unafraid at last to stand alone, and goes to meet death like a bridegroom, then Juliet has more maturity at fourteen than Cleopatra could dream of at twenty-eight. In any case it is altogether incredible that the Shakespeare who could give us Brutus' Portia and Bassanio's, who could delineate a Desdemona and even a Lady Macbeth, whose vision could move from Juliet to Cordelia to Imogen, and who early and late in his career rejoiced in innocence, loyalty, and love, before lust with all its cruel splendors, could have presented Cleopatra as a model of the mature woman in mature emotion.

—ROBERT E. FITCH, "No Greater Crack?," *Shakespeare Quarterly*
19, No. 1 (Winter 1968): 11–12

LOUIS CROMPTON

In his interpretation of *The Ring of the Nibelungs* Shaw divides the actors in Wagner's allegory into four categories: the predatory, lustful, greedy people; the dull, patient plodders; the "gods" or lawgivers who invent the religious, moral, and legal codes society is bound by; and finally, the heroes who free men from the rule of the "gods" when their codes become obsolescent. Clearly, Cleopatra belongs to the first of these categories as Caesar belongs to the last. Of Caesar's two servants in the play, Rufio is loyal and affectionate as a dog is loyal and affectionate, but Britannus stands on a level of development beyond Cleopatra's naïve passionateness or Rufio's simple devotion. He is a man of the third class, a moralist, a legalist, and a rhetorician, shocked when Caesar challenges the "gods" by sanctioning the incestuous royal marriage, careful to restate Caesar's blunt demand for money in legal terms, and appalled at his not bothering to punish those who are plotting against him. What makes his character comical, of course, is his trick of translating all his enthusiasms and antipathies into resounding moral imperatives. Britannus cannot conceive of a world without punishment or "justice," as he calls retaliation. To him, Caesar's anarchist vision of a society without punitive laws or deterrents is unthinkable and frightening. But to Shaw as to Wagner, it is exactly the highest developments of civilization that stand directly in the way of further advance through their moral prestige; and law and order as presently incorporated in Church and State are merely swaddling bands humanity has wrapped itself in until it is ready to burst them and proceed a stage onward.

The result is that Caesar must, like Dick Dudgeon, appear to the morally hidebound as another sort of "devil's disciple"; the embryonic superman will usually impress others as shockingly immoral. The difference is that where Dick is always attended by a faint smell of sulphur, Caesar commits his impieties with Olympian serenity. This debonair quality of its hero is one of the sources of the play's remarkable charm. Another is what we may call its "musicality." From the delicate rhythms of Caesar's prose-poem soliloquy onward, *Caesar and Cleopatra* has about it a happy air of improvisation, so that its mood reminds us of one of the freer musical forms, say a fantasia or a divertimento. In this it contrasts strongly with the more closely knit, but rather mechanical, structure of the other two *Plays for Puritans.*

Yet these musical and poetic qualities should not blind us to the fact that *Caesar and Cleopatra* is also a melodrama. It is, for Shaw, a remarkably violent play. Two murders actually take place in the course of the action, and we are implicitly asked to judge three others. This is an almost Shakespearean quota of deaths, but, unlike Shakespeare, Shaw is not interested in the dramatic poetry of murder either on the sensational, theatrical side or from the point of view of what Samuel Johnson would call poetic justice. Rather, Shaw wants us to think critically about the moral and social significance of killing. Hence each of the five violent deaths has a distinctly different context and meaning. First we have the cold-blooded murder of Pompey by Septimius at the behest of the Egyptians, who have ordered the death of the defenseless refugee in the hope of winning political favor with Caesar. Shaw's Caesar reacts to this cold-blooded butchery of his enemy and rival with all the horror that Plutarch and Appian ascribe to him. Then follows the discussion of the judicial murder of Vercingetorix, which Caesar now repudiates as mere terrorism parading as statecraft. In the play itself we are all but spectators at the murders of Pothinus and Ftatateeta. And finally, we learn of the impending assassination of Caesar on his return to Rome, an act which Shaw regarded as a particularly outrageous blunder on the part of well-intentioned political idealists.

As we have already seen, melodrama has its roots in certain moral religious feelings of which Shaw strongly disapproved. Though a critic as civilized as A. C. Bradley found it consoling that *Hamlet* and *King Lear* vindicated retributive justice in their gory endings, Shaw would have pointed out that this is a feature they share with any movie or television western in which the audience feels gratification when the villain gets his thrashing. Once again, as in *The Devil's Disciple,* Shaw is trying to draw our attention to the contradiction in popular Christianity, which illogically mixes Yahweh-worship with the Sermon on the Mount without any sense of their incongruity. It is exactly this endorsement of Christianity on its Tolstoyan, and repudiation of it on its Pauline side that underlies the banquet scene which is the climax of *Caesar and Cleopatra.* Here Ftatateeta, goaded on by Cleopatra, vows vengeance on Pothinus for betrayal of the queen, and shortly after, kills him.

At this point it is interesting to compare Shaw with the one other major dramatist who has dramatized Caesar's relation to Cleopatra. Corneille, in *La Mort de Pompée,* wrote a typical revenge melodrama, the theme of the play being the struggle of Pompey's widow, Cornelia, to avenge her husband's death, and its denouement the overwhelming of Pothinus, Ptolemy, and the others who had connived at it. Shaw turns Corneille's ethic upside down. Cleopatra, still smarting from Pothinus' accusation, thinks her honor has been vindicated by his death and appeals haughtily to Lucius Septimius, Britannus, and Apollodorus to justify her. Each man gives an answer in keeping with his life-philosophy: Septimius discreetly equivocates, calling the murder just but unwise (since it will not please Caesar); Britannus applauds it as a moral deterrent to others; and Apollodorus regrets that he was not allowed to kill the man in a chivalrous duel. Only Caesar disagrees:

> If one man in all the world can be found, now or forever, to know that you did wrong, that man will either have to conquer the world as I have, or be crucified by it. [*The uproar in the streets again reaches them.*] Do you hear? These knockers at your gate are also believers in vengeance and in stabbing. You have slain their leader: it is right that they shall slay you. If you doubt it, ask your four counsellors here. And in the name of that right [*he emphasizes the word with great scorn*] shall I not slay them for murdering their Queen, and be slain in my turn by their countrymen as the invader of their fatherland? Can Rome do less then than slay these slayers, too, to shew the world *how Rome avenges her sons and her honor.* [Italics added.] And so, to the end of history, murder shall breed murder, always in the name of right and honor and peace, until the gods are tired of blood and create a race that can understand.

This "trial" of Cleopatra corresponds, by analogy, to the other trial scenes in Shaw's melodramas, and ends like them, not with justice triumphant, but with justice repudiated. But Caesar's speech was, of course, much more than a rebuke to Cleopatra. It was, among other things, a criticism of the English, who, having waged war in the Anglo-Egyptian Sudan to revenge their national honor and the death of Gordon, had at its conclusion dug up and mutilated the body of the dead Mahdi, an act of public policy which Shaw thought revealed how little English mentality was removed from the outlook of the barbarous tribesmen they were fighting.

At the end of the scene Cleopatra sees Ftatateeta's red blood streaming over the white altar of the god she worshiped. In response to a murder done out of spite, Rufio has added another death. What, Shaw now asks, are we to make of this new killing? It is a measure of the hardheadedness that goes with his humanitarianism that he has Caesar justify the slaughter of Ftatateeta. In his essay on prisons Shaw denounces the idea of punishment relentlessly, but argues for the social necessity of killing irremediably dangerous people as one might kill dangerous animals, without malice or any pretense of moral superiority. In reply to Desmond MacCarthy's charge that he had made Caesar overly squeamish, Shaw wrote:

> To confess the truth, if there is a point in the play on which I pride myself more than another, it is the way in which I have shewn how this readiness to kill tigers, and blackguards, and obstructive idealogues (Napoleon's word) is part of the same character that abhors waste and murder, and is, in the most accurate sense of the word, a kind character.

Like Christ's "I came not to send peace but a sword," this is a hard saying, but one that will bear pondering by those who, while objecting to the death penalty, think that half a century of incarceration is a humane alternative.

It is now possible to see further into the significance of the animal symbolism in *Caesar and Cleopatra*. Morally, Shaw's refusal to draw a line between men and animals, which has its roots in eighteenth-century humanitarianism and nineteenth-century biological science, is fraught with all sorts of radical consequences. If we look at the animal-human world from Shaw's perspective, we arrive at a drastic transvaluation of values. No one pretends to be morally superior to an animal he has decided to destroy, or hopes that its death will encourage other animals to refrain from manslaughter or depredations. Nor does one speak of its crimes against society, or ask it to pay for its deeds, or cage it as a punishment for its sins or under the pretense that this will reform its character. Instead we accept animal nature for what it is, and act accordingly. In so doing, Shaw would argue, we treat animals far more sensibly and kindly than we do human beings. But on the other hand, we do not speak of the sacredness of animal life or hesitate to kill dangerous animals or suffering and neglected ones. Caesar, who looks at men and women from the Shavian vantage point, regards human beings in the same way that the keeper of the Humane Society pound looks at its inmates. As the new animal toward which nature is evolving, Caesar is as free of malice toward, or passionate regard for, Cleopatra and the other people in the play as the ordinary man is toward monkeys in a zoo. It is in a mood of profound irony that Shaw has the devil in *Man and Superman* warn us: "Beware the pursuit of the Superhuman: it leads to an indiscriminate contempt for the Human. To a man, horses and dogs and cats are mere species, outside the moral world. Well, to the Superman, men and women are a mere species too." But if Shaw disagreed with his cynical-sentimental devil, neither did he share the philosophy of Carlyle, who regarded the finding of the ablest poundkeeper as the solution to the political problem. Rather, Shaw counts on the race as a whole leaving Yahoodom behind; as he puts it in the preface to his next play, he wants his mob to be "all Caesars." Thus *Caesar and Cleopatra* is not a glorification of Caesar as a hero we should worship, but as a goal we should strive toward.

These are the currents that run through the depths of Shaw's play. But the surface is covered with gay ripples, and the mood of Caesar's final leave-taking is that of a festival. So little is Caesar enamored of Cleopatra that he forgets all about her in the press of business. When she does appear, she demonstrates that she has learned nothing since they met but poise and histrionic effectiveness. Acting the grand tragedienne, she demands vengeance for the death of Ftatateeta. But Caesar simply refuses to play the scene in this key. Napoleon once remarked that the difference between tragedy and comedy was the difference between standing up and sitting down, and told how, when the Queen of Prussia appeared before him "à la Chimène," he simply offered her a chair. Caesar similarly reduces a tragic pose to farce by stuttering over the dead nurse's name, and then coaxes Cleopatra out of her sulks by promising to send Mark Antony. The Siegfried motif swells buoyantly in the background: Caesar has subdued the Egyptians and will conquer three or four more armies on the way home. He goes lightheartedly to Rome and his death, as Cleopatra, childishly enraptured, awaits the coming of her demigod—and Shakespeare's.

—LOUIS CROMPTON, *"Caesar and Cleopatra," Shaw the Dramatist*
(Lincoln: University of Nebraska Press, 1969), pp. 68–73

ROSALIE L. COLIE

Unquestionably, the preoccupation with sex and with the shared sexuality of Antony and Cleopatra runs as an undercurrent through the play ⟨*Antony and Cleopatra*⟩. The difference between Egyptian and Roman talk of sex is instructive: Charmian and the Soothsayer, Cleopatra and the Eunuch, speak playfully and naturally; Enobarbus speaks cynically to and about Antony, on "death," on horses and mares; and the other Romans show their prurience and crudity when they speak, as they compulsively do, about the subject. The imagery too carries its sexual meanings: Cleopatra's "sweating labour" joins with the imagery of bearing and of weight to remind us of the woman's part in the act of love. This language in turn conjoins with the marvelous and varied horse-imagery which reaches its peak as she imagines the absent Antony on horseback: "O happy horse, to bear the weight of Antony!" Such language assumes sexuality to be a normal part of life; the Nile-imagery, with its "quickenings" and "foison" references, suggests procreation and creation as part of a natural cycle. Nature provides reproductive images for sexuality, and war another sort. The constant reference to swords, in fact as in image, keeps manliness ever at the forefront of our awareness, as it is at the forefront of the dramatic characters' awareness, too.

There is more than the suggestion, then, that love is no more than appetite or a drive; if that were all there was to love, the Roman view of this affair would be correct, Cleopatra simply a whore and Antony besotted, "ne'er lust-wearied." But can a man remain "ne'er lust-wearied" by the same woman, however infinite her variety, if she is merely a whore, however aristocratic her birth? Enobarbus, in so many ways faithful to Antony and Cleopatra in spite of his disapproval of their behavior, sees something more in her and tries to say what that "more" is. Once again, significantly, he speaks in terms of food—"Other women cloy / The appetites they feed, but she makes hungry, / Where most she satisfies." Mere sexuality, strong sexual love, idealized love: however it is described, the emotions shared by Antony and Cleopatra challenge the heroic world of Roman military organization.

This miracle of love (or whatever it is) we do not see acted out onstage. Instead, we never see Antony and Cleopatra alone, as we do Romeo and Juliet, Desdemona and Othello. What we see is something quite different: a man and a woman playing, quarreling, making up; a woman sulking, pretending to anger, flying into real rages, running away from danger, flirting even in deep disgrace and danger. Except on Roman tongues, there is little that can be called shameless or lascivious in Cleopatra's or Antony's utterances about love: her language on this preoccupying subject is remarkably clean—which is not the case with Roman commentators on these spectacular lovers.

To make so commonplace, so vulgar a mixture into a woman worth losing the world for is a considerable task for any playwright. Our playwright accomplishes it by fairly simple, even domestic, means. His Cleopatra has, among other things, a girlish, hoydenish companionability. She is obviously amusing company; she will try anything once. She has a lovely imagination and considerable command of language. She tries to rise to occasions, and sometimes she does. We hear much of Cleopatra's whoredom, and we see Antony blundering after her, twice fatally; we hear him speak of the less pleasant side of his love, of the "Egyptian fetters" which tie him in Alexandria, of his "dotage," and later, when he misses her in Rome, of his "pleasure" with Cleopatra. There is every reason to think very little of Cleopatra—although, to balance her crudities (as when she had a salt-fish attached to Antony's line), we are made to see that even in her breaches of decorum, her riggishness, her foolish middle age, she is delightful. She is earthy, and down-to-earth; her sudden accessions of realism puncture both the romanticizing of the lovers and Antony's simplistic view of love and Cleopatra as satisfaction to his appetite. This woman is something more:

Sir, you and I must part ...
Sir, you and I have lov'd. . . .   (I.iii.87–88)

In praising Antony, I have disprais'd Caesar. . .
I am paid for't now.   (II.v.107–109)

Think you there was, or might be such a man
As this I dreamt of?   (V.ii.93–94)

       Antony
Shall be brought drunken forth, and I shall see
Some squeaking Cleopatra boy my greatness
I' the posture of a whore.   (V.ii.218–20)

When her ironical common sense pierces her own theatricals, her charm is irresistible: though she rarely acts on that knowledge, we see that at moments she knows herself and the precarious, politicking world she lives in. It is this side of her, the practical, real woman, that is picked up in Charmian's farewell epithet: to "a *lass unparallel'd.*" Age, apparently, could not wither her, nor a rakish life, nor childbearing.

But in her first parting from Antony, as in her exchange with Dolabella after Antony's death and just before her own, Cleopatra's common sense rises to something greater:

Sir, you and I must part, but that's not it:
Sir, you and I have lov'd, but there's not it. . . .

The facts are clear enough—but they do not provide Cleopatra with an explanation for the pressure of her feelings, that this love for Antony is unduly significant, that parting from him must radically diminish her. Her sentence loses its direction as she seeks to express the "more" of her feeling for him:

That you know well, something it is I would,—
O, my oblivion is a very Antony,
And I am all forgotten!   (I.iii.89–91)

As she later says, she wants to sleep out "the great gap of time" that Antony is away from her; in his absence, even by herself, she is, imaginatively, "forgotten" and therefore does not exist. Both Antony and Cleopatra speak feelingly and movingly about their sense of identity lost. Part of their tragedy lies in Antony's feeling himself dissolve when he is with her, and Cleopatra's feeling her "nothingness" when he is not with her.

Cleopatra makes clear that her love for Antony is fully sexual; but, as has been noted, this emphasis comes in reverie, not in lascivious action or exchange. What is significant, surely, is that in a life given to sexual conquest and enjoyment, her relation to Antony means more to her than anything else. It is not that Cleopatra does not want to be reminded of her old connection with Caesar; it is that she knows its qualitative difference from the connection with Antony. Certainly Cleo-patra does not shirk the facts of her sexual past; however giddy and irresponsible her behavior with Antony, though, she knows that for him, she has quit being a rake. For her, sexuality is never just the "pleasure" that Antony implies early in the play it is for him. It has (at last, one has the impression) risen above itself to become love of a sort that defies definition in psychological ways, not just in "literary" ways. Indeed, in literary ways, the lovers' extreme preoccupation with one another is almost *too* resonant to the conventional language of love: as in *Othello,* but in an entirely different context, the petrarchan mixture of love and war has here been actualized in the necessary conditions, unmetaphored into actuality, of everyday life for this general and this queen. But the love-poet's transcendent aim is the same as theirs: how to express the indefinable love they share, a love that to unsympathetic onlookers seems ordinary enough, vulgar enough, but to the lover experiencing it inexpressibly glorious and valuable. Their language is pitched at the familiar literary goal, to make the "new heaven, new earth" of lovers' cliché into a universe for their exclusive dwelling. Their *folie à deux* is in part a matter of language, manipulated to record heightened experience and to displace both conventional and particular renditions of their experience by others.

Cleopatra's imagination particularly works at this task: if sex is the reality and imagination the fantasy of love, then the two fuse in Cleopatra's speech in Antony's absence from her, when she imagines him as he at that very moment actually *is:*

> Stands he, or sits he?
> Or does he walk? or is he on his horse?   (I.v.19–20)

Her sexual memories crowd into the single line, "O happy horse, to bear the weight of Antony!" Her images of weight, realistic enough in any woman's expe-rience of love, come to their culmination in the terrible scene of Antony's death, as she draws him into her monument:

> How heavy weighs my lord!
> Our strength is all gone into heaviness,
> That makes the weight.   (IV.xv.32–34)

The reality is there, although not displayed to us, of the children she has borne him; "the lap of Egypt's widow," as Pompey so rudely said, has actually held Antony and known what it was to do so. Finally, to her "demi-Atlas" she attributes more weight than any man can carry; she turns her love into an even more colossal personage than the world will recognize or can, in the person of Dolabella, accept.

—ROSALIE L. COLIE, *Shakespeare's Living Art* (Princeton: Princeton University Press, 1974), pp. 186–91

RICHARD B. GRANT

Théophile Gautier wrote two important stories whose action is set in ancient Egypt. "Une Nuit de Cléopâtre" ("One of Cleopatra's Nights"; 1838) was the first of these.

It tells a story considerably less complex than "Le Roi Candaule." A young com-
moner named Méiamoün has fallen hopelessly in love from afar with beautiful
Queen Cleopatra. He has always been a man who dared to face extreme danger.
He would often go out hunting in the desert lightly armed and be gone for months.
He had no fear of death. Indeed, "the abyss beckoned to him." Eventually, eager to
end the misery of loving in vain, he shoots an arrow with a note attached through
a window of the queen's chambers. It reads: "I love you." As luck would have it,
Cleopatra is bored and is intrigued by the mysterious note. Méiamoün next swims
through an aqueduct into the queen's outdoor gardens and bathing pools where he
is caught spying on her in her bath. As in "Le Roi Candaule" the penalty for this
outrage must be death, but Cleopatra's vanity is flattered at finding a man who
would so gladly throw away his life for her, so she proposes to entertain him
lavishly for one night. At daybreak he will die. They feast sumptuously together, she
dances erotically before him, and then as dawn breaks, Cleopatra is so touched by
Méiamoün's courage that she is about to spare him so he may have the joy of loving
her a little longer. But Marc Antony appears at that crucial moment, and Méiamoün
says: "You see that the moment has come; it's the hour when beautiful dreams fly
away." He drinks a deadly poison and dies. Cleopatra "sheds one burning tear, the
only one she ever shed" and then lightheartedly turns toward Marc Antony. The
story ends with her ironic explanation that the corpse on the floor is merely a slave
on whom she was trying out a new poison.
        The theme of impossible love is by now entirely familiar to our readers and
need not detain us further. But the mythic substructure of the tale is worth closer
scrutiny. Gautier first establishes the closed quality of his Egyptian universe. He
points out that the blue of the Nile is doubled by the blue of the sky and that it is
"difficult to decide whether the Nile reflected the sky or the sky reflected the Nile."
One would expect that Gautier would then show the unity of this closed Egyptian
universe as a fusion of the timeless male and female principles. The sun and flooding
Nile waters would combine to produce Egypt's agricultural fertility, and the divine
family of Osiris, Isis, and their child Horus would reflect this climactic reality. But
Gautier proceded a bit differently, and it is this difference that gives the tale
distinctiveness.
        The Egyptian landscape is presented as totally desolate and sterile. "Nothing
offset this aridity; no leafy oasis refreshed one's view; green seemed a color
unknown to this nature; once in a while a palm tree spread its fronds against the
horizon like a vegetal crab; a thorny cactus brandished its leaves as sharp as bronze
swords." The sun is described in the same language of sterility that Gautier was to
use in 1840 when describing the desolate regions south of Madrid for his *Voyage
en Espagne:* "A harsh light, so intense that it was dazzling and dusty, poured out in
torrents of flame, the blue of the sky turned white with the heat like metal in a
smelting furnace; a blazing reddish haze smoked on the burned-out horizon. Not
a cloud broke the uniformity of this sky, as unchanging and desolate as eternity."
What is normally a life-giving male principle, the sun, becomes something "sinister,"
a principle of death.

Egyptian culture, too, is desolate. Instead of trees there are granite obelisks, instead of the good earth, granite paving and steps. The living (of whom we see none, incidentally) seem to have "no other function than to bury the dead." This ancient world communicates a sense of total discouragement and seems to crush everything beneath its weight.

We find a strong contrast to the depressing landscape and burning sky, however, in the images of moon and water associated with the feminine principle of fertility. As the story opens, we see the queen in a magnificent boat shaped like a golden crescent moon gliding swiftly down the Nile. Her robe, so light that it seems woven out of air, undulates like a white vapor over her beautiful body. Feminine imagery is particularly evident in the description of Cleopatra's palace garden. Its luxurious coolness, its many pools and fountains, even its statuary all suggest feminine fecundity. Here is a good example: "At the end of the walk, one could find a large pool with four sets of porphyry stairs; through the transparency of the water which sparkled like diamonds, one could see the steps go down to the bottom which was sanded over with gold dust; from the breasts of women whose lower halves were encased in sheaths, spurted a perfumed water which fell back down into the pool in a silver spray." It is in this inviting area that the bored and dissatisfied Cleopatra waits for some fulfillment: "If I only had some passion, some interest in life," she complains, "if I loved someone or was loved ... this arid and frowning Egypt would seem to me more charming than Greece, with its ivory, its temples of white marble, its copses of rose laurels, and its springs of living water."

Obviously, Méiamoün seems destined to fulfill Cleopatra's longing for a great passion. But one notes that their orgy stops short of sexual unity as if to suggest that Méiamoün cannot accomplish this desired goal. In fact, he is like the sterile climate he represents. He brings not creative love but a death wish. It is he who chooses to die as Marc Antony appears, for he is in love not with Cleopatra, or even with love, but with death. He is a precursor of all those sterile heroes of decadent fiction that populate so many works of literature, especially in the latter half of the nineteenth century. They all wish to die in a spasm of voluptuousness at the feet of some dominating, inaccessible woman. One may enjoy or be repelled by such a vision, but there is no doubt that in technical terms, Gautier's story is a success, for he harmonized his characters and his landscape perfectly. The ending, too, is well conceived. Its irony and detachment provide just the right tone for a story that celebrates the failure of human union.

"Une Nuit de Cléopâtre," like "Le Roi Candaule," emerges as an important story in the development of nineteenth-century fiction. It is well known, of course, that after 1835 prose fiction in France was moving away from Romantic medievalism in the direction of social Realism, but Gautier's stories point to another important direction that fiction was taking. Profiting from new discoveries in ancient cultures and religions, Gautier was wrestling with the problem of how to reconcile modern style and vision with the truths communicated by ancient mythic literature in a century dedicated to science and the doctrine of progress. By making his characters incarnations of opposing principles, he could have his human drama without abandoning a sense of the cosmic. Only Flaubert in *Salammbô* (1862) succeeded better than Gautier in recreating that mythic universe where the pre-Hellenic gods reigned supreme.

—RICHARD B. GRANT, *Théophile Gautier* (Boston: Twayne, 1975), pp. 113–16

MARY JO MURATORE

In comparison to Camille ⟨in *Horace*⟩, Corneille's next self-indulgent heroine is very subdued. Not only is Cléopatre, in *La Mort de Pompée,* less volatile than Camille, but her role has a minimal influence on the main action of the drama. Cléopatre has lost to her brother Photin her share of the royal power which she inherited from her father. As the play begins, Photin, still dissatisfied with his lot, attempts to persuade his sister to aid him in assassinating Pompée, whose death he believes will best serve their combined interests. She refuses to help him in his criminal plan, but Photin forges ahead, killing Pompée in the hope of thereby obtaining César's gratitude. César, however, not pleased but angered by Photin's ignoble act, promises to avenge Pompée by killing those responsible for his death.

Many critics view Cléopatre as an ambitious queen anxious to recapture her stolen crown; and such an assessment she herself would not contradict. She clearly states that ambition is the only passion worthy of a princess:

> J'ai de l'ambition, et soit vice ou vertu,
> Mon coeur sous son fardeau veut bien être abattu;
> J'en aime la chaleur et la nomme sans cesse
> La seule passion digne d'une princesse.   (431–434)

The love she professes to have for César appears little more than a device to help her realize her royal aspirations. Although she claims to love him (357–360), she shows little concern that he may divorce her, since she will still have had the opportunity to be mistress of the world, if only for a moment (427–430).

Yet Cléopatre is not motivated by ambition alone. Though she does not deny the ambitious nature of her personality, she insists that her desire to obtain the royal scepter has its limits:

> J'ai de l'ambition, mais je la sais régler:
> Elle peut m'éblouir, et non pas m'aveugler.   (623–624)

She maintains that she wants power only if it can be honorably attained (435–438), and although Albert Gérard questions the sincerity of such a statement, there is evidence to support her contention. Cléopatre prides herself on her integrity (370–374), and she is not alone in believing herself a model of virtue. Antoine, for example, has nothing but praise for her moral character (947–948). Cléopatre is fiercely protective of this reputation, and when she feels it is jeopardized, she consistently acts in a way to endanger rather than further the acquisition of the throne. When Photin speaks of assassinating the man whose efforts have helped restore his crown, Cléopatre is shocked by her brother's ingratitude and adamantly opposes his plan. Photin, believing she wants only to obtain a document from Pompée that will guarantee her the right to reign, accuses her of acting solely for her own interests. Cléopatre disagrees, pointing out that if this were the case, she too would act to please César by acting against Pompée (283–286). When César unexpectedly expresses anger at Pompée's assassination, Cléopatre dares ask that her brother and his aides be forgiven (1339–1344). When César learns that these same men are now plotting his own death, Cléopatre still endeavors to win clemency for her brother (1433–1436). Finally, when Cornélie predicts César's demise and blames it on his love for Cléopatre, Cléopatre is ready to offer her own life in order to save César from this foretold disaster:

> Plutôt qu'à ces périls je vous puisse exposer,
> Seigneur, perdez en moi ce qui les peut causer:
> Sacrifiez ma vie au bonheur de la vôtre;
> Le mien sera trop grand, et je n'en veux point d'autre.   (1755–1758)

Cléopatre's ambition represents a new quality for the heroines of this category. The Infante, Sabine, and Camille are separated from their society by emotional attachments which differentiate them from their peers. Cléopatre does not condemn emotional sensitivity, but she considers it less important than political power. Opportunistic yet magnanimous, ambitious but not ruthless, Cléopatre is a transitional heroine in Cornelian tragedy. As Pierre Corneille continues his development of the self-assertive, individualistic heroine, virtue and honesty in his plays assume progressively smaller importance than this newly-emphasized attribute of ambition. This change of focus might be considered a reflection of contemporary changes occurring in the author's society. Between 1643 and 1650, the social order, threatened by a new emphasis placed on self-interest, showed signs of decay. At this very time, the author's conception of the heroine also changed. He no longer presents his individualistic heroines as virtuous, but as deceitful and her ambition is no longer limited, but all-consuming. In short, the heroine becomes a social menace ready to create chaos when her designs are thwarted.

—MARY JO MURATORE, *The Evolution of the Cornelian Heroine* (Madrid: José Porrua Turanzas, 1982), pp. 77–80

LESLIE O'BELL

In 1824 Pushkin composed "Cleopatra," the original version of the poem which figues in "Egyptian Nights." In 1828 he revised it and also wrote the first in a series of prose fragments which frame the poetic material, "The Guests Gathered at the

Dacha." In 1830 he returned briefly to that fragment. This is the pre-history of the later developments of 1835. In 1833, however, a Cleopatra anecdote appeared in a different setting, the "Tale from Roman Life," also known as "Caesar was Traveling." Work on this fragment was renewed in January of 1835 but soon broken off. The Cleopatra anecdote was then recast into a story related to "Guests," "Evening at the Dacha"; at the same time the poem "Cleopatra" again underwent revision, this time rather extensively. Finally, the idea of "Cleopatra" was absorbed by a new one, "Egyptian Nights"—these are alternative titles for the last story of this cycle. Another productive line was now grafted onto the old material, namely an artist story concerning a pair of poets, Charsky and the Italian improvisor, a line which has its own genealogy.

⟨. . .⟩ Pushkin wrote the Cleopatra story for three successive heroes: first, the youth, then, the man of the world, and finally, the poet. His Cleopatra accompanied them but changed in less essential ways, even as society heroine. In 1824 the divided character of Cleopatra was set off by the youth, her third lover; in 1828, by the provincial girl of the plan for "Guests." In 1833 and 1835, the period whose spirit Cleopatra embodied was explicitly defined as the Decadence, a historical concept which implies a boundary with a new age; and, finally, in "Egyptian Nights" itself, Cleopatra was paired with the poets. At none of these stages was the artistic aim to present only the incarnation of lust, cruelty and satiety.

From the psychological tension of the original historical elegy, its paradox of compassion, sprang the lifeline of the entire cycle, characterized by the pathos of a desire for renewal balanced against the expectation of a fatal reckoning. The animation which Cleopatra had imparted to her feast, and which Volskaya had restored to jaded high society, found its ultimate expression in the dynamic action of the improvisation, where it is the poet as mover who attempts to leaven the inert social mass. The largely decorative historical side of the 1824 poem "Cleopatra" was discarded in 1828 for a contemporary tale with an emphasis on the biographical past of its characters. Then it re-emerged in 1833 and 1835 as continuous historical stylization, only to be absorbed into the parodistic plan of "Evening at the Dacha," in the possibility of historical repetition. In "Egyptian Nights," the past of antiquity meets the present of Petersburg society through the mediation of the Italian improvisor, but historical repetition is possible there only because a true consciousness of history is absent, because the time of the story is the *bezvremen'e*, the "dead time" of the Russian/Egyptian nights.

Certain outside influences, really literary stimuli, helped to move the cycle forward. Aurelius Victor's anecdote and Parny's Persephone from the "Déguisements de Vénus" contributed to its formation; then came Baratynsky's *Ball*, Janin's *Barnave*, Petronius' *Satyricon* and Tacitus' *Annals*, the Cleopatra of Shakespeare and of Plutarch, the wit of Madame de Staël, and the fantasy of E. T. A. Hoffmann. French, German, Italian and classical style-images overlap in "Egyptian Nights." The general conversation which the poets come to conduct there in place of the public shared its critical terms with Chaadaev's pessimistic *Philosophical Letters*. The night which witnessed their exchange entered the annals of other such "nights" and "evenings": Batyushkov's "An Evening with Kantemir," Maistre's *Saint Petersburg Evenings,* Odoevsky's *Russian Nights.*

The development of the cycle can also be seen in terms of genre: the mixed "historical elegy" of 1824 containing the possibilities of the erotic ballad, of drama and of satire found new incarnations first in the analytic society tale, then in a historically stylized Satyricon, really a form of philosophical prose, and, finally, in the artist story. All three narratives strongly involved lyrical and dramatic modes of presentation: in "Guests," the balcony scene and figurative social stage; in "A Tale from Roman Life," the public declamation of the odes which formed part of the Satyricon; in "Egyptian Nights," the device of the improvisations. In the end the approach of parody offered the closest equivalent to the ambiguity of the original psychological situation, but expressed as plot.

This is the new analytic prose of a poet, in which thought has been reabsorbed into style and form and in which the most disturbing personal complexes have been made objective. Akhmatova felt that fragments like "A Tale from Roman Life" or "Evening at the Dacha" rivalled the *Little Tragedies* in their laconic, concentrated power. At Pushkin's death, his friends were amazed to discover that this man of letters had continued to develop as a poet. Annenkov later commented: "In the unpublished verse you can see how the phenomena of life begin to present themselves to his mind under an aspect which somehow lies in proximity to a historical or religious idea." Yet "Cleopatra" had always been a philosophical poem about the value of life, echoing the cry, "did it not all come down to one or two nights?" The final story of 1835 is simply one last statement about those few nights, made with a fuller consciousness of the things that make them count.

It is now possible to see how this succession of literary realizations of the Cleopatra theme emerged from the dynamic of Pushkin's unfolding work. In 1824 the original conception was born of the disintegration of the "southern poems," side by side with the "Imitations of the Koran." It also shared important motifs and something of the moral atmosphere of a central ballad complex about "the bridegroom." In the middle stage of the development, "Guests," the Cleopatra material was drawn into the evolution of *Onegin.* Stanzas from Onegin's "Journey" and from his "Album" led to the point of departure for "Guests," whose arrangement of characters anticipated, in turn, the final grouping of Chapter VIII in *Onegin,* where the "brilliant Nina Voronskaya, that Cleopatra of the Neva" was seated beside Tatyana in the society salon. "Guests" also clearly recapitulated Chapter I of the novel in verse, set in the world of Petersburg society. The pair of heroes whose presence would be the mark of all the further Cleopatra stories appeared for the first time in "Guests," out of the sphere of *Onegin,* where in Chapter I the hero was doubled by his friend, the narrator, and where the pair Onegin and Lensky represented the clash of prose and poetry. In addition, the Cleopatra intrigue of "Guests" was intertwined in its genesis with the writing of Maria's love story in *Poltava,* another use of the bridegroom ballad. "Guests" was thus situated in the manuscripts between the historical and the contemporary, between *Poltava* and *Onegin*. The next stage in the development of the Cleopatra material was influenced by reflections arising out of the *The Journey to Arzrum*. It was at this point in the history of the cycle that an artistic image connected with Egypt first appeared, the "Egyptian tombs." The return from Arzrum left its mark on "Guests" (1830), "A Tale from Roman Life," and the so-called "Fragment" which was later revised for the characterization of Charsky. The end of *Onegin* and the return from Arzrum were the creative events that shaped the middle of the Cleopatra cycle, acting to highlight the arrival of a moment of fate, which might bring either retribution or renewal.

Like "Scenes from the Days of Chivalry" or indeed *The Captain's Daughter*, the Cleopatra fragments of 1835 are works of the renegade poet who threatens the aristocratic establishment from the inside. However, the end of the cycle was governed less by any new connections with other works of Pushkin than by what might be termed the aesthetic event of indirection. Pushkin developed and varied the figure of the "conversationalist" who had been mentioned in an 1828 draft of "Guests"—first in Petronius, then in Aleksey Ivanych and finally in the Italian improvisor. In the place of conversations are put various kinds of performances, and, meanwhile, the poem "Cleopatra" which was buried or perhaps dissolved in "Guests" is restored to independent life. The overall sequence was poetry into prose, then prose again into poetry. Under its final aspect, the poetry is meant to be sensed precisely as such, as something poetic with a power to move and magically to animate. The poetic improvisations return in their function to the very first line of the original Cleopatra poem, in which the queen "with voice and glance animated her luxurious feast."

Tynyanov once wrote, "The concept of breadth of genre range turns out to be less fundamental with respect to Pushkin than is the rapid and even catastrophic evolution of his work." He wished to direct attention away from the undoubted scope and universality of Pushkin to the impetuous unfolding of the writer's creation. However, in the case of the history of the Cleopatra material, as with any cycle, the development was also in a sense circular. Akhmatova remarked upon the fact that the plots and imaginative patterns of Pushkin's works in the 1830's often were derived from strata of experience laid down ten years earlier or more. The patterns "settled" or clarified but were not replaced by new ones. The later stages of the Cleopatra cycle are likewise notable for the way in which aspects of earlier Pushkin persist and are reinterpreted, a process for which parody is an inadequate term unless parody is understood partly as a creative rather than a destructive relationship. "A Tale from Roman Life" witnessed a revival of Pushkin's interest in the Roman historians, in anacreontic verse and in the occasion of the poetic feast. "Evening at the Dacha" presented its Cleopatra poem as a fragment from an unfinished romantic narrative poem. The opening lines of the poem echoed "Reminiscence," and a harem scene re-emerged from the buried layer of the "southern poems." In "Egyptian Nights," the Cleopatra improvisation was based on a theme suggested by the Petersburg poet, whose dandified existence calls to mind Onegin's; it also represented an auto-reminiscence of the author's own poetry.

The retrospective elements in late Pushkin are best perceived as romantic stylization—as part of the author's own artistic repertoire and not as purely polemical in application. In "Evening at the Dacha" the Cleopatra poem still represented something genuine, something literally true, something quite opposed to the fashionable rantings of the "new novels." The "ornamental" quality of the 1835 "Cleopatra" served to persuade its doubting audience of the reality of the scenes and events depicted in the poem. In its turn, the first improvisation in "Egyptian Nights" defended a form of "romantic realism," based only on a radical freedom from all convention. Of course, the Cleopatra anecdote itself possessed a life-or-death seriousness. Thus, as Bocharov has written in another context, in the development of Pushkin's work "poetic tradition" (*poèticheskoe predanie*) does not become outworn; rather it acquires the force of literal truth. When Pushkin turned again to the Cleopatra anecdote in 1835, he touched one of the "nerve-centers of long-accumulated poetic energy."

The self-contained literary quality of "Egyptian Nights," along with its problems of modernity and decadence, of periods of transition, give the work a contemporary relevance. The split time perspective and, above all, the multi-layered narrative structure of the story (or really story within a story) lend it a strong appeal for the twentieth-century reader and writer. The story fuses personal reminiscence, historical reminiscence, and literary reminiscence into a single whole; the poem conceived in 1824 retains a personal meaning for the story's poet, but one overlaid by the perspective of historical repetition and the poetic spell cast by the ancient anecdote. But the almost crystalline symmetry of the form in which the story is cast, and the relentless logic of the artistic syllogism upon which it is built, these qualities belong to Pushkin alone. "Egyptian Nights" shows the writer enmeshed in a situation of potentially tragic compromise, the writer who is beleaguered by the "social command" to which he responds whether he wills or no. It displays a writer who is isolated and faced with a silent audience, one who communicates within the privileged but restricted community of the poets. The fragment, belying its fragmentary nature, contains the complete expression of a continuing and perhaps haunted predicament.

—LESLIE O'BELL, *Pushkin's "Egyptian Nights": The Biography of a Work*
(Ann Arbor, MI: Ardis Publishers, 1984), pp. 4, 121–25

DAVID CASTRONOVO

The Ides of March is a curiosity of twentieth-century literature: it is an epistolary novel, a historical evocation, a fantasia, and a series of discourses. Divided into four books that cover and re-cover the last year of Julius Caesar's life, the narrative form is complicated by an odd use of repetition. Wilder, the writer who plays with time and history in *The Skin of Our Teeth* and the short one-act plays, has devised a new way of forcing us to attend to man's relationship to the temporal order by moving across the same period in sections that take in longer and longer stretches of Caesar's life. The structure could be represented visually by lines (corresponding to Books I, II, III, and IV) that are longer to denote the extended time frame. Book I covers September 45 B.C.; Book II begins earlier and ends in October. Book III begins earlier still and extends to December; the final book goes farther back and extends forward in time to end with Caesar's assassination in March 44 B.C. The effect of this extension and retroversing of one period is to make the reader feel all the currents that swirled around Caesar and all the different lives that touched his. No single story, Caesar's life becomes a series of retellings presented in letters exchanged by historians, the poet Catullus, his friends, and political opponents ⟨. . .⟩

While Book I focuses on choice and freedom, Book II explores the idea of love and the reality of a number of erotic relationships. Cleopatra—before her entrance in October and thereafter—is the most gossiped-about character in Roman correspondences. To many women she is vulgar, dangerously ambitious, and likely to destabilize Roman politics. Her son Caesarion is Caesar's child, and the Queen has come to Rome to establish his claims. Many patrician women see her as a barbarian, a pretentious Easterner who brings corruption to the city. This surface characterizing is counterpointed by Caesar's correspondence. Book II comes alive as an emotional experience when we listen to Caesar's passionate but ambivalent responses: he is drawn to her beauty and intelligence, her conversation and exoticism; and yet he is fearful that she is another of the enemies of order. Caesar's love becomes powerful and complex as it alternates between feeling for a woman and devotion to Roman order and progress. This section ends as Cleopatra begins her Roman escapades with Marc Antony: she is caught in a romantic situation with Caesar's nephew, and this betrayal of Caesar becomes a foreshadowing of his eventual betrayal by others.

—DAVID CASTRONOVO, *Thornton Wilder* (New York: Ungar, 1986), pp. 126–28

Harold C. Goddard

ANTONY AND CLEOPATRA

VI

It is not by chance that Shakespeare puts the description of the meeting of Antony and Cleopatra at Cydnus right after the account of the selling of his sister by Octavius to Antony. Caesar issues his orders and Octavia obeys. Cleopatra does not have to issue orders. The winds fall in love with the very sails of the barge she sits in. The water is amorous of its oars and follows faster. Boys and maids, like Cupids and Nereides, fan and tend her. The city pours out its multitudes to behold her. But for the gap it would have left in nature, the air itself would have gone to gaze on her.

I saw her once,

says Enobarbus,

Hop forty paces through the public street;
And having lost her breath, she spoke, and panted,
That she did make defect perfection
And, breathless, power breathe forth.

Here is power of another species than power military or political. Cleopatra's beauty may have been more the Dionysian beauty of vitality than the Apollonian beauty of form, but whatever it was it justifies Keats's dictum:

'tis the eternal law
That first in beauty should be first in might.

And yet the magnetism that emanates from her at her first meeting with Antony at Cydnus is mere witchcraft and magic compared with the authentic "fire and air" that descends on her before her second immortal meeting with him at the end.

From *The Meaning of Shakespeare* (Chicago: University of Chicago Press, 1951), pp. 581–93.

It is this magic and witchcraft that captivate Antony in the first place.

I must from this enchanting queen break off.

The adjective shows that it is with the semi-mythological Cleopatra, the ancestral image of Woman she evokes within him, the gypsy, Egypt, the Serpent of old Nile, that he is in love. The fascination is mutual, and she in turn endows him with superhuman attributes. He is anything to her from the demi-Atlas of the Earth to Mars. The tradition that Antony was descended from Hercules, son of Zeus, abets this cosmic overvaluation of the human being, as does, for him, her assumption of the role of the goddess Isis. In so far as these things amount to a conscious affectation or attribution of divinity—and, even more, a willingness to make political use of them—they degrade the pair deeply in our estimations, proving them victims not only of infatuation with each other but of a self-infatuation far less excusable. But infatuation, analyzed, generally turns out to be more a failure to locate the origin of compelling forces from underneath or from overhead than mere vanity, folly, or egotism in the usual sense. "No man," says Robert Henri, "ever over-appreciated a human being." And so when Cleopatra, about to part from Antony, exclaims,

> Eternity was in our lips and eyes,
> Bliss in our brows bent; none our parts so poor
> But was a race of heaven,

it strikes us less as affectation of divinity than as genuine perception of the divine element in love—insight into the heart of something which their wildest words about each other are abortive or rapturous attempts to express. In such poetry as Cleopatra attains in those three lines the illusion becomes almost indistinguishable from the truth.

Far more subtly than in the case of Cleopatra and earth, Shakespeare suggests correspondingly that Antony is like the sun. Not until near the end does this analogy shine forth so clearly that we know the author must have intended it. But looking back we can see that he has insinuated it from the beginning. Granted that if Antony is the sun he is an intermittent and often obscured luminary, uncertain of his course across the heavens and subject to frequent total eclipse or worse, as when he orders Caesar's emissary whipped and sends word that, if Caesar does not like it, he may "whip, or hang, or torture" an enfranchised bondman of Antony's in requital. But these things strike us as mere aberrations of that real Antony in whose presence alone Cleopatra germinates and blossoms and matures into her full self as does the earth under the sun. Antony's power to attract and hold men in his sphere is sun-like also, as is the bounty he dispenses as freely and widely in his degree as the sun does his warmth. It was Eros who referred to his face as

> that noble countenance
> Wherein the worship of the whole world lies.

Yet this is a sun that, reversing all known laws of heavenly bodies, when the planet he should illuminate and hold in her course flies off at a tangent at the Battle of Actium, follows ignominiously after her. What wonder that he cries, when he realizes what he has done:

> ANT.: Hark! the land bids me tread no more upon't!
> It is asham'd to bear me. . . .
> CLEO.:   O, my lord, my lord,
> Forgive my fearful sails! I little thought
> You would have follow'd.
> ANT.:   Egypt, thou knew'st too well
> My heart was to thy rudder tied by the strings,
> And thou shouldst tow me after. O'er my spirit
> Thy full supremacy thou knew'st, and that
> Thy beck might from the bidding of the gods
> Command me.

But the shame is not the whole story. Even here Shakespeare seems less interested in the outcome of the Battle of Actium than in the nature of that force that at the height of the action can obliterate utterly in the mind of this greatest soldier of the world all thought of military conquest and glory, all concern for what the world will think of his disgrace. Here is a mystery indeed. In the Battle of Actium, war and love—or at least war and something akin to love—grapple, and war wins. Yet does it win? To deepen the enigma the poet proceeds to show that it is precisely out of the dishonor and defeat that the spiritual triumph emerges which is always found at the heart of the highest tragedy. More and more as it nears its end, *Antony and Cleopatra* seems to recede from mere history into myth, or, if you will, to open out and mount above history into a cosmic sunset of imagination.

Sunset is the inevitable figure, and Antony himself gives us the cue for it in the superlative passage in which he compares himself with black vesper's pageants.

But even before this, Shakespeare has given our imaginations a hint of the element into which the action is to pass when it rises above earth. In a little scene that reminds one of nothing so much as the opening of *Hamlet,* a group of soldiers discuss rumors of strange happenings about the streets. Suddenly mysterious music is heard. Where is it? "Under the earth," says one.

> 'Tis the god Hercules, whom Antony lov'd,
> Now leaves him,

says another. But still another one (of rarer sensibility than the others, we cannot but believe) locates the sound in the air. It is a premonition of the transubstantiation that is to overtake Antony in defeat. In defeat he puts off the strength and renown that are like those of his mythical ancestor, and with them, by implication, his spurious claim to divinity through descent from the gods, putting on, in exchange, the true divinity of his own guardian angel who, as the Soothsayer foresaw, is the enemy and the opposite of the demon of power. Antony's metaphor of the sunset is but a confirmation of this scene, adding, however, the element of fire to the element of air.

The marks of a sunset are beauty and insubstantiality—a splendor that makes whatever it touches more real than earth, a transiency that makes it seem less than a dream. It is all in the evanescence and dissolution of the shapes and colors in the sky that Antony sees the likeness to himself:

> Here I am Antony;
> Yet cannot hold this visible shape.

But we see more than that. Only when the sun nears or goes under the horizon do men catch a glimpse reflected on the clouds of what they dared not gaze on directly when it was overhead. The sun, when it goes down, has an alchemic power to transmute the material world into its own substance. (Compare the 33d sonnet for alchemy at sunrise.) It is the same with a great man when he dies. The world in which he had lived is lit up with his afterglow; the common scene where he once walked seems changed into a vision. This is the miracle that Antony, dead, performs on Cleopatra. His devotion to her, even unto death, is what does it, bringing to the surface at last a Cleopatra that his love has long been shaping underneath. In this revolution of everything, Cleopatra the enchantress disappears forever—except in so far as she survives as the willing servant of the new Cleopatra that takes her place. So fully does this new Cleopatra realize the splendor of Antony at death that her memory of him transforms what little of life is left for her on earth into heaven. She enters heaven, as it were, in advance. And we enter it with her.

VII

Incredibly, many readers and critics find in the conclusion of *Antony and Cleopatra* only the old Cleopatra, thinking at bottom just of herself, bent above all things on saving herself from being shown in Caesar's triumph. That the old Cleopatra, bent on precisely this end and with every histrionic device still at her command, is still present cannot indeed be questioned. But that she is now the only or the predominant Cleopatra everything in the text converges to deny. What has happened is that a new Cleopatra is now using the old Cleopatra as her instrument. It is the new one who issues the orders. It is the old one who obeys.

When Cleopatra, frightened by Antony's reaction to his belief that she has betrayed him and caused the surrender of his fleet, sends word to him that she is dead, it is the culmination of Cleopatra the actress and deceiver, of the woman who will go to any extreme to attain her end. Little does she realize at the moment—though soon afterward she has a premonition of what she has done—that by her lie she has thrust a sword into the man she loves and who loves her even unto death, as certainly as if she had done it with her own hand. But from the moment when the dying Antony is lifted into her monument and she finds no word of reproach on his lips for what she has done, scales seem to drop from her eyes, and never from then on does she waver in her undeviating resolution to join him in death. What looks like hesitation and toying with the thought of life is but deception utilized with the highest art to make certain that her determination to die is not thwarted. The fact is that the new Cleopatra, with all the histrionic devices of the old Cleopatra at her command, acts so consummately in these last hours of her life that she deceives not only Octavius Caesar but full half the readers of the play. She stages a mousetrap beside which Hamlet's seems melodramatic and crude, enacts its main role herself, and, unlike the Prince of Denmark, keeps her artistic integrity by never for a second revealing in advance what its purpose is or interrupting its action for superfluous comment. Blinded by victory and the thought of his triumph in which she is to figure, Octavius is clay in her hands, infatuated in a sense and to a degree that she and her lover never were. She twists him, as it were, around her little finger. If this still be acting, it is acting of another order. It is no longer "art" vaingloriously exhibited as personal triumph or the pride of personal power. It is art, rather, tragically impressed in the service of death. Those who think that Cleopatra is driven to suicide only when she is certain that if she does not kill herself she will be shown in Caesar's triumph are taken in by her as badly as is Caesar himself.

The text corroborates this interpretation to the point of supererogation.

Antony in almost his last words begs Cleopatra to seek of Caesar her honor and her safety. "They do not go together," she replies with a ringing finality. Trust none about Caesar but Proculeius, Antony adds.

My resolution and my hands I'll trust;
None about Caesar.

Who cannot hear the tone in which that "none" is uttered, and who can fail to understand from that reference to her hands that her determination to do away with herself is already taken? Antony dies, and no one will ever debate, as in the case of Lady Macbeth, whether the swoon into which Cleopatra falls is genuine or not. It is as if in those few moments of unconsciousness she visits some other world and comes back divested forever of all mere earthly royalty. Now for the first time she is a woman—and not Woman.

No more but e'en a woman,

are her first words as consciousness returns,

and commanded
By such poor passion as the maid that milks
And does the meanest chares.

It is as if she must compensate for having been queen by being not merely a woman, but the humblest of women, a menial, a servant. And as the fourth act

ends, she confirms to Iras and Charmian the promise she made to Antony before
he expired:

> We'll bury him; and then, what's brave, what's noble,
> Let's do it after the high Roman fashion,
> And make death proud to take us. . . .
> Ah women, women! come; we have no friend
> But resolution, and the briefest end.

Resolution: it is the same word she had used to Antony. This Egyptian has become
a Roman, not an imperial Roman like Caesar, but a noble Roman like the angel of
her own Emperor—

> Noble, courageous, high, unmatchable.

The change in Cleopatra is again confirmed in the first words we hear from
her in the last act:

> My desolation does begin to make
> A better life.

Better!—a word, in that sense, not in the lexicon of the original Cleopatra. The
rapidity of the change going on within her is registered in another word in the
message she sends by Proculeius to Caesar:

> I *hourly* learn
> A doctrine of obedience.

Caesar, poor fool, thinks, as she intends he shall, that it is obedience to his will that
she is hourly learning. But it is obedience to her own new self and to her own
Emperor, Antony, to which she of course refers. The very words with which she
hoodwinks Octavius most completely are made to express, on another level, the
highest fidelity to her own soul. When Caesar first enters her presence, she kneels
to him:

> CAES.: Arise, you shall not kneel.
> I pray you, rise; rise, Egypt.

He wishes to dupe her into thinking she can still remain a queen. But to be a queen
in that sense is the last thing that she wishes.

> CLEO.: Sir, the gods
> Will have it thus; my master and my lord
> I must obey.

"You, Caesar, are now my lord and master; I have no choice but to kneel and
obey," Caesar thinks she means. It sounds like obeisance to the point of prostration.
But what Cleopatra is really saying is that she now listens only to divine commands.

She must obey her master and her lord, her Emperor Antony, not the mere emperor of this world to whom she is kneeling in mockery.

The interlude with her treasurer Seleucus is to the undiscerning overwhelming proof that Cleopatra is still angling for life, if she can only get it on her own terms. But surely this is the old histrionic Cleopatra placing all her art at the disposal of the new Cleopatra who is bent only on death and immortal life. Whether this little play within the play was planned in advance in consultation with Seleucus and he too is acting, or whether it is a piece of inspired improvisation on her part alone, struck off at the instant of her treasurer's betrayal of her, makes little difference. The reason Cleopatra kept back some of her treasures is the same in either case: to throw the gullible Caesar off the track of her intention. How completely he is deluded by her hint that she is planning to sue with gifts for the mediation of Livia and Octavia! It is the old wily Cleopatra of course who knows how to devise this trap, and her undertone of exultation at her success in springing it is heard almost to the end. But the wily Cleopatra is now the mere servant of another Cleopatra who is intent only on her own freedom, to whom traps for others are nothing except as they help her to escape from the trap that has been set for her.

Caesar is so beguiled that he makes a fulsomely magnanimous speech in which he thinks he is finally ensnaring his victim but in which he is really only entangling himself. His comparisons and metaphors, as usual, fairly blurt out the very truth he is trying to conceal. "Caesar's no merchant," he protests, revealing that a merchant is precisely what he is at heart. "Feed, and sleep," he advises—as if Cleopatra were a beast being fattened for the slaughter and he were already licking his lips at the prospect. "My master, and my lord!" once more, is all she says. To him the words confirm her abject submission. To her—however aware she may be of the irony— they are no less than a prayer to Antony for strength. "Not so," says the over-confident Caesar, seeming to reject her obeisance, as he goes out. The two words, as he means them, are the mark that his self-stultification is complete. But, in a sense he could never divine, they are the very truth echoed from Cleopatra's heart.

> He words me, girls, he words me, that I should not
> Be noble to myself,

she cries the moment she is alone with her women. His pretended mercy has not fooled her.

> But hark thee, Charmian,

and she whispers in her maid's ear. What she tells her of course is that she has already ordered the instrument of death, the asp.

> I have spoke already, and it is provided,

and bids her "Go, put it to the haste." This tiny incident is calmly left out of the account by those who think that Cleopatra has been seriously debating between life and death in the previous scene and that the interlude with her treasurer is just what it seems to be—a provision for avoiding death if a way of escape with safety to her person should present itself at the last moment. Caesar, as I said, is not the only one these scenes deceive.

Shakespeare sees to it that it is only *after* this sending for the asp, with its clear implication that the die is cast, that Dolabella—with one exception the last of many men to come under Cleopatra's spell—confides to her the fact that Caesar does indeed intend the worst. The effect of the information is merely to fortify further what needs no fortifying.

Left alone with Iras, Cleopatra draws a final picture of the fate she has escaped. Charmian returns from her errand.

Now, Charmian,

she cries without a second's hesitation,

> Show me, my women, like a queen; go fetch
> My best attires; I am again for Cydnus
> To meet Mark Antony.... Bring our crown and all.

Here, it will be said, Cleopatra gives the lie to everything I have just been saying. Here, once for all, she proclaims herself actress, first, last, and forever. As if she were about to appear upon the stage, she calls for her costume, her robe and crown. Once more she will assume the role of queen—in her "best attires." She will play-act the very act of death. The woman is an incorrigible exhibitionist.

On the contrary, it is the extreme opposite of all this, I believe, that Shakespeare intends. We become new not so much by rejecting the old as by imparting to the old a new meaning. So here. What we have is not the old Cleopatra reverting to the theatrical and all its meretriciousness, but a new Cleopatra, rather, aspiring to make the symbol indistinguishable from the thing, to rise into that region where art is lifted into life and life into art, the goal, alike, of art and life.

As the clown brings the asp, she cries:

> I have nothing
> Of woman in me; now from head to foot
> I am marble-constant, now the fleeting moon
> No planet is of mine.

What follows confirms this inversion and reversal. (And we can be the more confident of this interpretation because, strangely, however much more swift, the change in Cleopatra parallels a change of like character in her creator, who, as in the cases of Falstaff and Hamlet, has endowed her with not a little of his own dramatic genius. Shakespeare, by his own confession, was at one time almost "subdued" by the theater, and his evolution traces his successful effort to elude its grasp. From *The Comedy of Errors* to *Antony and Cleopatra,* the story is one of the gradual subjection of the theatrical to the poetical. Cleopatra's development is a sort of parable of Shakespeare's. "Shakespeare led a life of allegory: his works are the comments on it.")

Four times, in her haste to be rid of him, Cleopatra says "farewell" to the loquacious clown who has brought the asp. When he is gone and Iras has returned, she begins her own farewell:

> Give me my robe, put on my crown; I have
> Immortal longings in me. Now no more
> The juice of Egypt's grape shall moist this lip. . . .

As she renounces the intoxicants of earth a celestial intoxication comes over her—she feels herself being transmuted from earth into fire and air. Whoever, as he listens to her, does not feel, in however diminished degree, a like effect within himself, misses, I believe, one of the supreme things in Shakespeare. The atmosphere of sunset—which Charmian's single phrase, "O eastern star!" turns into sunrise—the universal character of every image and symbol, and above all perhaps the sublimity of the verse, conspire with the action itself to produce this alchemic effect. Here, if ever, is the harmony that mitigates tragedy, the harmony, better say, that creates it.

VIII

Whoever questions or is insensible to all this should consider the contrast between the two meetings of Antony and Cleopatra at "Cydnus," the earthly meeting as described by Enobarbus, and the spiritual meeting to which the death scene is the vestibule. Around these two passages, as we can see fully only when we have finished the play and hold it off in perspective, the drama is described as an ellipse is about its two foci. The antithesis between them is complete: the "poetry" of the senses versus the poetry of the imagination. In the first we have Cleopatra as the earthly Venus, enveloped in incense, waited on by everything from the winds to the populace, conscious to the last degree, we cannot but feel, of the universal adulation. Antony is absent, and is brought in at the end almost as an afterthought. In the second he is in a sense more present than she is, and she unconscious of everything save him, her Emperor, whom she is about to meet—of him, and of the courage with which his love has endowed her. The only memories that cross her mind of a world that "is not worth leave-taking" are those of *its* emperor that by contrast serve to make her Emperor great. "Ass unpolicied"! It is her Last Judgment on all Caesars—hers and Shakespeare's—the revenge of poetry, which is the politics of heaven, on empire. For the rest, what unprecedented words on the lips of Cleopatra: "husband," "baby," "nurse"! Even that "kiss" which it is to be her heaven to have is of another order from the many thousand kisses that Antony once placed upon her lips, of which his dying one, he thought, was the "poor last." The first meeting at Cydnus, as Enobarbus gives it to us, is like an immense tapestry or historical picture, a word painting, just the overdecorated sort of thing that the world mistakes for supreme art. The second is more than the greatest art. It is an apocalypse.

IX

Yet, even after this, Shakespeare, incredibly, has something in reserve, the most miraculous single touch in the whole play, a touch that, like a flash of lightning at night, illuminates everything.

Caesar enters. He is first told the truth and then looks down upon it. The sight seems to lift him outside of himself. Quite as if he had overheard those earlier words of Cleopatra,

> I dream'd there was an Emperor Antony.
> O, such another sleep, that I might see
> But such another man,

and had come to declare that prayer answered, he exclaims:

> she looks like sleep,
> As she would catch another Antony
> In her strong toil of grace.

Another Antony indeed, her Emperor! Whatever has happened elsewhere, here on earth, in those perfect words, the lovers are reunited. And Octavius, of all men, spoke them!

Many, including Bradley (who says that to him they sound more like Shakespeare than Octavius), have declared the lines out of character, entirely too imaginative for this boy politician whom Cleopatra herself derided so unmercifully. They are. And yet they are not. And when we see why they are not we have seen into the heart of the play.

Caesar, practically alone, has shown himself immune to the fascination of this woman, and only now is he in a position to realize how utterly, even at his own game, she has outplotted and outwitted him, led him, as it were, by the nose. Conqueror as he is, she has dragged him behind the chariot of her superior insight and power. But all that now is nothing to him, less than nothing, not even remembered, and, gazing down as if entranced, this man, who had been cold to her and to her beauty while she lived, utters the most beautiful words ever spoken of her. Dead, she proves more powerful than the most powerful of men alive. She makes him realize that there is something mightier than might, something stronger than death. She kindles the poet within him. She catches him in her strong toil of grace. She leads him in her triumph!

X

  Nothing in his works perhaps illustrates better than the conclusion of *Antony and Cleopatra* what I have called the integrity of Shakespeare, by which I mean the psychic interdependence of those works and their consequent power to illuminate one another.

  The imaginative germ of *Antony and Cleopatra* is found in Romeo's opening speech in the fifth act of *Romeo and Juliet:*

> I dreamt my lady came and found me dead—
> Strange dream, that gives a dead man leave to think!—
> And breath'd such life with kisses in my lips
> That I reviv'd and was an emperor.

So specific is this, down even to the conception of a spiritual emperor, that it not merely presages the situation at the end of *Antony and Cleopatra* but is a perfect comment on and interpretation of its transcendental meaning.

  Cleopatra and Othello seem incongruous figures to connect. Yet Cleopatra in the end is in the same position as Othello: she has killed the one she loves, not with her own hand, to be sure, as he did, but not less actually. And in one respect her situation is far worse. He did his deed under a complete delusion, but in good faith. She did hers by a lie that was wantonly selfish. But if Cleopatra and Othello make strange companions, Antony and Desdemona make even stranger ones—the greatest soldier in the world and the simplest and most modest girl. Yet here the link is even closer—and we remember Othello's greeting, "O my fair warrior!" Desdemona dies with no reproach for the wrong he has done her, and when he discovers the truth he is shaken to the foundation by a profound spiritual change. Similarly, not one word, not one thought, of the part Cleopatra has played in his death crosses Antony's lips, or his mind, in his last moments. Instead he merely says:

> I am dying, Egypt, dying; only
> I here importune death awhile, until
> Of many thousand kisses the poor last
> I lay upon thy lips.

Here is the counterpart of Desdemona's last words:

> Commend me to my kind lord. O, farewell!

and here the only conceivable cause commensurable with the change effected in Cleopatra. If it seems a more incredible change than that which occurs in Othello, it is because Othello had from the first a nobility to which the earlier Cleopatra could make no claim. The motif of the transcendental reunion of the lovers, which is only faintly hinted at and kept wholly in the overtones in *Othello,* becomes the main theme, openly announced and developed like music, at the end of *Antony and Cleopatra.* It is as if what the violins vaguely suggested there were played here by the full orchestra. At last we know that we were not deceived in what we hardly dared believe we heard in the earlier play.

But it is *King Lear* that comes closest of all. King Lear, summing up a dozen figures that preceded him, shows that it is greater to be a man than to be a king, greater to be a king in the imaginative than in the worldly sense. Antony's story says the same. He refuses to sacrifice to the Roman Empire his heritage as a man. He shows that it is greater to be an Emperor in Romeo's and Cleopatra's sense than to be emperor of the earth. "A man needs but six feet of ground," an old proverb has it, and though he has owned the whole earth six feet is enough when he has become a corpse. Even having been a universal landlord will not help him. "The earth I have seen cannot bury me," said Thoreau in one of the most astonishing sentences that even his genius ever struck off. The conclusion of *Antony and Cleopatra* makes clear what he meant.

The analogy between King Lear and Cleopatra is even more striking than that between King Lear and Antony, if for no other reason than that a contrast between the sexes is here involved. Just as Lear had to lose his title and recognize that he was only

> a very foolish fond old man
> Fourscore and upward, not an hour more or less,

before he could regain his kingdom as spiritual King, so Cleopatra had to realize that she was

> No more but e'en a woman, and commanded
> By such poor passion as the maid that milks
> And does the meanest chares,

before she could become a spiritual Queen worthy to meet her Emperor. Through humility both Lear and Cleopatra discover their humanity. Anger and violence in him are tamed to patience. Pride and passion in her are lifted to love. So faithful even in detail is Shakespeare to his earlier pattern that Lear's crown and robe of weeds and common flowers is the very counterpart of Cleopatra's symbolic robe and crown which she puts on before her death. And yet—what could be more splendidly different from the piercingly swift and simple ending of *King Lear* than the prolonged sunset glory of *Antony and Cleopatra?* The difference corresponds precisely to the two characters. But the likeness goes deeper than the difference. The end of the earlier play gives us a single lightning-like glimpse into heaven; that of the other ushers us to its very threshold.

Further plays, *Troilus and Cressida* especially, afford more comparisons and contrasts. But we must restrict ourselves to a last one, a link with *Hamlet* which is of another sort. When the Prince of Denmark discovers the truth about the poisoned rapier and realizes that he is trapped, he turns it on the King with the cry,

> The point envenom'd too!
> Then, venom, to thy work.

Cleopatra, as she applies the asp to her breast, exclaims:

> Poor venomous fool,
> Be angry, and dispatch.

It is as if Shakespeare had chosen the dying Cleopatra to make his ultimate comment on the dedication to the most futile of human passions, revenge, of the most gifted character he ever created.

Franklin M. Dickey

THE TRAGEDY
OF *ANTONY AND*
CLEOPATRA

First of the stories of saints who died for love in Chaucer's *Legend of Good Women* is the pitiful martyrdom of Cleopatra who marches naked into a pit of serpents. This conception of the Egyptian queen, which makes her an example of love true unto death, accords with Chaucer's purpose. He wrote the poem, the Prologue tells us, to make amends for having written *Troilus and Criseyde* and for having translated *Romaunt of the Rose,* both of which disparage love and feminine constancy. But one suspects that he wrote the conclusion of the tale with his tongue in his cheek:

> Now, or I fynde a man thus trewe and stable,
> And wol for love his deth so frely take,
> I preye God let oure hedes nevere ake.
> Amen.

Without Chaucer's ironic reservation, modern critics of Shakespeare's *Antony and Cleopatra* praise the play as an Elizabethan "Seintes Legende of Cupyde." True, many concede that among the themes in Shakespeare's love tragedy are the torments of passion and the incompatibility of politics and private desire.[1] Few, however, would agree that Shakespeare takes any moral stand on the meaning of passion in the tragedy, and many of the most eloquent contend that the play hymns a love so great as to transcend ordinary morality. If the lovers have lost a kingdom, they have gained a more "ethereal diadem of love." For life on earth they have traded an eternal passion.[2]

Actually this widespread exaltation of the love of Antony and Cleopatra is new. Chaucer speaks only for a very small minority of those who from classical times to the end of the seventeenth century wrote of the fatal love which cost Antony and Cleopatra their thrones and their lives. In fact Chaucer's is the only charitable version of any note before Shakespeare. Even Lydgate, who liked to

From *Not Wisely but Too Well: Shakespeare's Love Tragedies* (San Marino, CA: Huntington Library, 1957), pp. 144–60.

think of himself as carrying the torch which Chaucer lit, follows the tradition of abuse toward the lovers that began with Cicero and continued until Dryden's day.

When Dryden got around to revising Shakespeare's play in 1678 to make it square with neo-classical literary theory, the story had long been an exemplum, as Dryden makes clear in his Preface. "I doubt not," he explains in defense of his choice of tragic matter,

> but the same Motive has prevailed with all of us in this attempt; I mean the excellency of the Moral: for the chief persons represented, were famous patterns of unlawful love; and their end accordingly was unfortunate.

Nevertheless most critics since Dryden have preferred to dismiss the "excellency of the Moral" which he saw in the story. Almost without exception they agree that the final meaning of Shakespeare's tragedy is expressed by the subtitle which Dryden chose for his recension of it—"The World Well Lost."[3] Because the traditions which made Antony and Cleopatra patterns of unlawful love and modern criticism are so much at odds, it will be worth our time to look again at the literary portraits of the lovers to see what Shakespeare's audience might have expected when they attended the first performance of the play.

Needless to say Shakespeare was under no compulsion to give them what they expected. Romantic critics argue that he did not; that in fact Shakespeare's tragedy is unique because, unlike Plutarch and unlike the Renaissance imitators of Seneca, he "dares to defend the illicit passion that set the halves of the world at war and destroyed its possessors."[4]

We will begin our survey with the more familiar accounts of Antony and Cleopatra in classical antiquity from Cicero (d. 43 B.C.) to Sidonius (fifth century A.D.). Next we will pursue the story through its medieval modifications. Then, since we are trying to determine the *idées reçues* of Shakespeare's audience, we shall see how Elizabethan moral philosophers and poets used the lives of the lovers as exempla. ⟨. . .⟩

I. The Classical View of the Lovers

The first charges against Antony's private character were made by his political opponent Cicero, who in the second Philippic accuses him of profligacy, lechery, drunkenness, pederasty, and the indecorum of keeping company with mimes and players.[5] Most of these accusations are dutifully recorded in Plutarch, along with Cicero's charges that as a public man Antony was cruel and traitorous, building his own estate at the expense of the people. The other thirteen Philippics repeat and embroider these accusations, but this oration is the most opprobrious. Cleopatra has not yet entered his life.

Horace, writing shortly after the Battle of Actium for his patron, Cleopatra's conqueror, calls her "fatale monstrum," the mad leader of an effeminate crew. As Thomas Hawkins translates Ode 37 of Book I:

the mad Queen
Prepar'd the ruine, and disastrous fall,
Both of the Empire and the Capitoll,
With her scabb'd Troop of men effeminate,
Proud with vast hopes, & *drunk* with prosp'rous state . . .[6]

Horace concludes the ode with grudging tribute to this *non humilis mulier* because she had the courage to die rather than be led in a Roman triumph. In Epode 9 he deplores the subjection of Antony and his army to the oriental queen:

The *Roman* Souldier by a woman ty'd
In slavish bands (ah this will be deny'd
By after times) lugs armes, earth, stakes, and tent,
Striving her with'red Eunuches to content;
And *Phoebus* 'mongst their *ensignes* doth espy,
Her net-like and lascivious canopie.[7]

Virgil, extolling the same great patron, makes the standard comparison between noble Rome and degenerate Egypt. In Book VIII of the *Aeneid* Venus gives Aeneas a shield which pictures the future of Rome. Here he sees the Battle of Actium in which "all manner of monstrous gods and dog-headed Anubis" lose to the Roman deities; here too he sees Antony sail into the engagement, "to his shame, with his Egyptian mistress."[8]

Velleius Paterculus, an officer in the Roman army under Augustus, denigrates Antony's character as enthusiastically as Cicero does. In Sir Robert Le Grys' translation (1632) we read that both fiery love for Cleopatra and "the greatnesse of his vice (which are ever fomented by wealth, libertie, and flatteries)" caused him to have himself crowned as the god Bacchus. Like Horace Paterculus attributes Antony's decline in spirit to Cleopatra's love. The phrase *post enervatum amore eius Antonii animum* epitomizes his attitude toward the lovers, "after the mind of Antonius was by her love enfeebled."[9]

Lucan too excoriates Cleopatra, but more for her relations with Caesar than for those with Antony. She is another Helen, not for her beauty but for the wars she occasioned. Arthur Gorges's free and vigorous translation apostrophizes her

O *Egypts* impudence and shame!
Erynnis fierce to *Latium* name!
A strumpet to the *Roman* state,
Unchast, our fuell of debate!
Looke how much woe and wretched toyle
Fell out upon the *Grecian* soyle,
And with what wracks and ruine wrought
That *Spartan* face, the *Trojans* bought;
In no lesse fury, and mishap
Did *Cleopatra Latium* wrap![10]

Eager to drive home the moral, Gorges amplifies Lucan, who is censorious enough. Where Lucan excuses Antony because even stern Caesar's heart was ignited, Gorges embroiders the passage thus:

> O *Anthonie* who will disprove
> Thee, for thy lawlesse filthy love.
> Since Caesars haughtie heart so fries,
> With this bewitcing harlots eyes...[11]

Shortly after, where Lucan lists a series of treacherous peoples, none of whom are so infamous in crime as the Egyptians, Gorges's Renaissance bias carries him from his text completely. Gorges tells us that none of these fierce peoples were so dangerous to Caesar as his "banqueting and wantonnesse" with Cleopatra. In his marginal gloss Gorges adds the typical precept,

> Luxury and pleasure dangerous to great men.   (sig. Qq 3 verso)

Josephus's indignant estimate of Cleopatra's worth drags her one step lower. The insinuation that Cleopatra used witchcraft to hold Antony suggests the direction which her reputation is to take in the Middle Ages. Cleopatra, Josephus says, was "by nature very covetous, and stuck at no wickedness." She poisoned her brother and persuaded Antony to murder her sister, "for if there were but any hopes of getting money, she would violate both temples and sepulchres." She was "a slave to her lusts," and was never content. Against Antony Josephus again repeats the charge of pederasty and hints darkly that

> he was so entirely overcome by this woman, that one would not think her conversation only could do it, but that he was some way or other bewitched to do whatsoever she would have him...[12]

Suetonius has nothing new to offer. Sourly anti-imperial, he adduces the Egyptian affair as one of the very human faults of the "deified Julius," whose lechery and intemperance he seeks to establish. By inference and indirection, he too blackens Cleopatra's reputation.

The fullest account of the lovers, however, is Shakespeare's source, the *Parallel Lives* of Plutarch, which appeared in Sir Thomas North's translation of Amyot's French in 1579. Amyot's Preface makes it clear that he interpreted Plutarch as a series of exempla which, by exhibiting the precepts of moral philosophy in the lives of famous men, would both profit and delight.[13]

Plutarch leaves no doubt about the nature of the lessons to be learned from the love of Antony and Cleopatra. Plutarch's Antony is a dissolute man given to the same unmanly behavior of which Cicero accuses him. Although unlike Cicero Plutarch praises his generosity as a commander and his great skill and endurance as a soldier, he condemns him as cruel and wanton. Moreover Plutarch emphasizes the fact that Antony is a man ruined by women. The first step in his decline and fall is his marriage to Fulvia, a lady, writes Plutarch, not so basely minded to spend her time in spinning and housewivery, and was not contented to master her husband at home, but would also rule him in his office abroad . . . so that Cleopatra was to give Fulvia thankes for that she had taught Antonius this obedience to women, that learned so well to be at their commaundement. (XII, ii)

The next step in his downfall is his encounter with Cleopatra, a meeting for which a luxurious life had predisposed and softened him. "Antonius being thus inclined," says Plutarch in North's English,

the last and extreamest mischiefe of all other (to wit, the love of Cleopatra) lighted on him, who did waken and stirre up many vices yet hidden in him, and were never seene to any: and if any sparke of goodnesse or hope of rising were left him, Cleopatra quenched it straight, and made it worse then before. (24)

In the end the "sweete poyson" of Cleopatra's love and the "unreyned lust of concupiscence" combine to end "Antonius abominable life."

Pliny the Elder uses Antony and Cleopatra frequently to illustrate his discourses in the *Naturall Historie*. In Pliny's eyes the lovers are famous patterns of extravagance and intemperance. He describes with horror the destruction of a gem valued at sixty million sesterces which Cleopatra, as befitting "a noble curtezan, and a queene withall," drank in a cup of vinegar while Antony, in Philemon Holland's phrase, "looked wistly upon her."[14]

Elsewhere in the *Historie* Pliny presents Cleopatra as past master in giving sumptuous banquets and as an expert in subtle poisons (XXI, iii). In the chapter he devotes to the subject of drunkenness Pliny cites Antony as the great example of this vice, maintaining that he wrote a book

with this title, *Of his owne drunkennesse:* wherein he was not ashamed to avow and justifie his excesse and enormities that way: and thereby approved (as I take it) under pretence and colour of his drunkennesse, all those outrages of his, all those miseries and calamities that hee brought upon the whole world. (sig. Oo 4 verso)

Aside from North's great Plutarch, however, the most interesting version of the story Englished in the sixteenth century is the anonymous translation of Appian's *Auncient Historie* which appeared in 1578. The translation is accompanied by an equally interesting *Continuation* based upon Plutarch which carries the history to the death of Antony and Cleopatra. Both parts embody the classical and Elizabethan attitude toward the lovers and toward the political significance of their lives. MacCallum has shown that Shakespeare knew Appian and used details from the history for *Julius Caesar* and *Antony and Cleopatra*. As I shall demonstrate elsewhere, there is some reason for thinking that he used the *Continuation* rather than North's Plutarch for at least one important speech in the play.

But that Shakespeare may have used Appian is not to our immediate purpose. Very much to the point though is Appian's censure of the love which ruined Antony, a love which did not sort well with his years. Antony, Appian writes, loved Cleopatra "like a yong man, though he were fourty yeeres of age, his nature (as it seemeth) ever being pliant to that thing . . ."[15] As in Plutarch and the other classical authors, Cleopatra is responsible for Antony's final degradation, for after he met her, "hee did all things as *Cleopatra* woulde have him, without respecte of God or mannes lawe"; and his love for her "was the beginning of his troubles, and ende of his life."[16]

By the time we reach Florus in the second century, the pattern is thoroughly set. In familiar phrases Florus inveighs against the "wanton lust, and riot" of Antony's life and love. Of Cleopatra's influence he says, "This *Egyptian* woman did value her companie at no lesse a rate to *Antonie* drunken with love, then the *whole Roman* empire, and he promised it . . ." Under Cleopatra's spell Antony "absolutely degenerated into no lesse a monster in his understanding, then hee did in his affection, and fashion."[17]

The other late classical authorities carry on the tradition that Antony and Cleopatra were shameless voluptuaries, although generally Antony appears nobler than his mistress. Dion Cassius's portrait of the lovers is drawn from those of his predecessors. His fickle and treacherous Cleopatra achieves "a genuine desire to die" only when it develops that Octavius is not seduced by her charms. Dion's Antony is characterized "equally by greatness of soul and servility of mind."[18] The third-century "art of dining," Athenaeus' *Deipnosophistae,* chooses Cleopatra to typify the prodigal hostess.[19] In the fifth century Sidonius compares the enemies of his patron to the cowardly and luxurious Egyptians under Cleopatra and predicts a like defeat for them because of their decline from Roman virtue.[20]

From the classics then the Elizabethan audience might have learned how to judge Antony and Cleopatra: whatever virtues the lovers had, they were notorious for their lust and extravagance. It would have taken "small Latine and lesse Greeke" to find out these facts, for the most important classical accounts of the lovers had appeared in English before Shakespeare wrote his play.

II. The Medieval Tradition

The medieval world embroidered the legend of Antony and Cleopatra freely. A tradition which continued into the Renaissance makes Cleopatra the author of a book on cosmetics and another on gynecology.[21] But in all the major accounts of her before Chaucer, she is made a moral exemplum to warn others by her unhappy life of the end of those who live for pleasure. Dante sees her like this. Accompanied by her peers Semiramis, Helen, and Dido, she sweeps about the second circle of his hell with carnal sinners, those in whose lives

Reason by lust is swayed.[22]

So far as I can discover, the most popular and extensive accounts of the "lustfull queen" and her fatal love in the late Middle Ages are Boccaccio's. Boccaccio devotes sections of both *De Casibus Virorum Illustrium* and *De Claris Mulieribus* to the fatal love of Antony and Cleopatra. The former opens with the story of Antony who rose to power through cruelty and greed until, spurred by Cleopatra, he fell through overwhelming ambition. Rather than credit Antony with any virtue, Boccaccio tells us that it was the good fortune of Octavius rather than Antony's might that defeated Brutus at Philippi. But Antony in Cleopatra's toils was worse than Antony alone. Under her influence he "flung himself," Boccaccio writes, "into voluptuousness and idleness," and "ever ready for carousing, let himself by unbridled lust be dragged into so great infamy."[23] Once caught, he is Cleopatra's creature and at her command discards Octavia.

Boccaccio's Cleopatra is a cruel and designing woman who murders, robs, and seduces her way to empire. At Actium she flees in a gilded ship with purple sails, followed by her doting Antony. After Antony has killed himself she tries in vain to seduce Caesar, applies the asps to her breasts, and dies. Boccaccio's summation of the meaning of this familiar tale is precisely what one would expect. Antony and the *meretrix* Cleopatra got exactly the fate they deserved for their wicked lives. Her soft limbs used for the pleasure of so many men, writes Boccaccio with ferocious relish, in the end were the pleasure of serpents.[24]

The *De Claris Mulieribus* repeats much of Boccaccio's earlier invective but adds the incidents, related by Pliny, of the dissolved pearl which this *lasciva mulier* drank in Antony's honor and of the poisoned chaplet by which she proves that Antony's tasters are no proof against her skill. Boccaccio's second treatment of Cleopatra goes even beyond the first in its scorn for her promiscuity and prodigality, the vices for which she paid with her life.[25]

Out of Boccaccio, surprisingly, comes Chaucer's martyr of love, the only praiseworthy Cleopatra we have seen. Chaucer was hard put to alter his source, for he begins like Boccaccio by censuring Antony for rebelling against Rome and deserting Octavia to take another wife. But then he tosses his source aside to praise Antony as a knight worthy of Cleopatra, adds a vigorous medieval version of the Battle of Actium, and describes Cleopatra's self-immolation for love. His almost flippant conclusion suggests that his heart was not in his work, and that had he not perhaps been writing for Queen Anne, he might have painted a more orthodox queen of Egypt.

Lydgate rights the balance again, although with considerable deference to his master Chaucer. He translates Premierfait's French recension of Boccaccio's *De Casibus* with infuriating prolixity until he comes to the tale of Antony and Cleopatra. Their story, he writes, it would be "presumpcioun" to "make ageyn," for Chaucer has already told it faultlessly. But for all his apologies to the "cheef poete of Breteyne," he offers a condensed version of the story as Boccaccio saw it. Retaining the moral judgment, if not the words of his source, Lydgate rhymes:

> Cleopatras
> Caused Antonye that he destroied was.
>
> Hir avarice was so importable,
> He supprised with hir gret fairnesse,
> Folwyng ther lustis foul & abhominable,
> She desirying to have be emperesse;
> And he, alas, of froward wilfulnesse,
> To plesen hire, unhappily began
> To werreye the grete Octouyan.[26]

For all his deference to Chaucer, Lydgate really had no sympathy for the guilty lovers, and in one of his minor poems he unleashes his strongly antifeminist emotions. The lesson taught by the amusing "Beware of Doublenesse" is that neither eels nor shifting winds are as slippery or inconstant as the mind of woman:

> Sampson hadde experience
>   That women weren ful trewe founde
> Whan Dalida of innocence
>   With sheres gan his hede to rounde;
>   To speke also of Rosamounde,
> And Cleopatris feythfulnesse,
>   The storyes pleynly wil confounde
> Men that apeche her doublenesse.[27]

The medieval tradition which the Elizabethans inherited therefore follows the classical tradition but adds its own Christian moralization. The concept of God's justice which makes the punishment fit the crime appears in Dante's treatment of carnal sinners, for those who were carried away by passion are punished by a whirlwind which carries them about forever. Boccaccio, as we have seen, finds it appropriate that Cleopatra whose limbs were embraced by lovers should in the end be embraced by serpents. Save for Chaucer's, most of the medieval Cleopatras are very wicked indeed.

III. Received Opinion: The Story as Exemplum

Thus the Elizabethan reader of English, French, or Latin texts would have found an almost unanimous chorus of authority from classical times through the fourteenth century condemning the lovers for their "lustis foul & abhominable." As with most famous stories, the lovers became a byword for certain qualities. Even the good middle-class reader who was too busy or too pious or too unliterary to care for the extended treatments of the story might have run across casual references to the unfortunate lives of Antony and Cleopatra, for the popular books of moral philosophy and the equally popular commonplace books cite them regularly as examples of how not to behave. The desultory reader of poetry, if he had not discovered Cleopatra in Thomas Howell's moralized *Fable of Ovid Treting of Narcissus* (1560), might have been instructed by the much more famous poetical moralist, Edmund Spenser.[28]

Howell's *Fable of Ovid* is an awkward poem with a moral—"very pleasante to rede," according to the title page—considerably longer than the text itself. The meaning of the fable, culled from various sources including Boccaccio and Ficino, is that reason should conquer passion and that beauty, wealth, and strength all pass away. "The office of the minde," our poet writes, "is to have power / Uppon the bodye"; just as Narcissus faded away because he was enamored of appearances, so the body wastes away when the mind is "drowned with desyre" (sigs. D 3 verso– D 4). In this poem against indulgence in "raginge lustes" Cleopatra and Helen, whose names had become byword for strumpet, demonstrate that a life of pleasure brings no real joy:

> The sorowes greate, of Menelawes wyfe
> Whose bewtie fayre, so farre to se was sought
> The wretched ende, of Cleopatres lyfe
> Whose ryche araye, was all to derely bought
> Dothe plainly shewe, that all was vaine and nought
> Thus riches strength and power, confesse we muste
> Wyth bewtie eke, to slypper be to truste.   (sig. B 4 verso)

However, the Elizabethan reader at the end of the century would have been more likely to run across the story in a much more fashionable poem than this obscure version of Ovid. In Book I of the *Faerie Queene,* where even the desultory reader of that poem might easily find them, Spenser condemns both Antony and Cleopatra to the dungeon of Lucifera's House of Pride. Here with others they exemplify sinners who "Through wastfull Pride, and wanton Riotise" must "live in woe, & die in wretchednesse" (I, v, 46). Spenser's "fierce Antonius" suffers in the company of other warriors, but Cleopatra stands with Semiramis, the licentious Queen of Babylon, and Sthenoboea, the Amazon, all

> Proud wemen, vaine, forgetfull of their yoke . . .   (I, v, 50)

Spenser finds the tale of Antony and Cleopatra too valuable an exemplum to discard before more of its possibilities are exhausted. In Book I the lovers exemplify the sins of lust and pride; in Book V, which Spenser devotes to the allegory of justice, their love demonstrates the feminizing effect of passion.

Canto v of Book V describes the perversion of justice through feminine wiles. Artegal, the representative of justice, has conquered the Amazon Radigund in fair fight, but when he removes her helmet, he is smitten by her beauty and throws aside his sword, a weakness for which he must pay dearly. Jumping to her feet, Radigund defeats her conqueror who has been "Left to her will by his owne wilfull blame." When he has surrendered, she dresses him "In womans weedes, that is to manhood shame," makes him don an apron, and sets him to spin until Britomart rescues him.

Spenser does not, however, explain the allegorical significance of Artegal's unnatural bondage until Canto viii, where he makes it clear that Artegal is one with Samson, Hercules, and Antony, those other famous champions made effeminate by love. All three heroes, who could not be conquered by strong men, were defeated and made weak by women:

> Nought under heaven so strongly doth allure
> The sence of man, and all his minde possesse,
> As beauties lovely baite, that doth procure
> Great warriours oft their rigour to represse,
> And mighty hands forget their manlinesse;
> Drawne with the powre of an heart-robbing eye,
> And wrapt in fetters of a golden tresse,
> That can with melting pleasaunce mollifye
> Their hardned hearts, enur'd to bloud and cruelty.

> So whylome learnd that mighty Jewish swaine,
> Each of whose lockes did match a man in might,
> To lay his spoiles before his lemans traine:
> So also did that great Oetean Knight
> For his loves sake his Lions skin undight:
> And so did warlike *Antony* neglect
> The worlds whole rule for *Cleopatras* sight.
> Such wondrous powre hath wemens fair aspect,
> To captive men, and make them all the world reject.   (V, viii, 1–2)

If the Elizabethan reader's taste was for books of self-help and morality rather than poetry—and this sort of reading often made more money for its publishers than Elizabethan works which our taste judges far nobler—he would have taken it for granted that Antony and Cleopatra were patterns of lust, extravagance, pomp, and pride.[29] The company they keep is most interesting, for often as not Cleopatra is listed beside the same willful queens with whom Spenser companions her, and Antony joins the same great conquerors weakened and made effeminate by love.

For instance the aspiring reader who turned to Thomas Hoby's translation of Castiglione's *Courtier* (1560) would have found Cleopatra among those queens who, as the marginal gloss emphasizes, "gave themselves to all their appetites"; if he knew his Castiglione, then the reader would have recognized Cleopatra as a byword for lasciviousness (p. 248). Or if he knew his Montaigne (1603) or his Burton (1621) or any of a long list stretching from the middle of the sixteenth to well into the seventeenth century, he would have recognized the lovers as examples of the destruction caused by profligacy. All bring their stones to hurl with more or less ferocity. Thus Antony appears variously as a man feminized by lust, as a drunkard, and as a man dominated by women; his story illustrates the vanity of sensual pleasures and the sin of despair. Cleopatra if anything fares worse. With Helen of Troy, Jezebel, and Delilah she teaches men to beware of wicked women; she also serves as an example of the sins of incest, lust, and prodigality.[30]

It seems clear, after looking at these instructive and pious authors, that even the reader who confined himself to popular digests of morality and whose knowledge of the classics derived from commonplace books would have developed certain ideas about the guilty love of Antony and Cleopatra. Instead of seeing Antony and Cleopatra as patterns of nobility and of a deathless love, the Elizabethan reader must have seen them as patterns of lust, of cruelty, of prodigality, of drunkenness, of vanity, and, in the end, of despair. Nowhere does an author hint that their love enriched their lives. Instead the Elizabethans pointed to their love as destructive, not only of their own happiness but of that of their followers and subjects as well.

The vicissitudes of fortune are at the heart of medieval tragedy, which generally follows the pattern of Boccaccio's *De Casibus* in picturing the fall of men and women of high estate. Although Boccaccio and those who followed him often link catastrophe with evil actions, their main aim is to show the instability of earthly prosperity and to teach contempt of the world.

Renaissance humanism modified and broadened this concept. Mature Renaissance tragedy, while often full of references to fortune, attempted to deal with the problem of evil by linking men's fortunes to their passions. Those whom the gods would destroy, they first made passionate.[31] Building upon Aristotle and Horace, Renaissance literary theory saw tragedy as an imitation of an action which might both teach and delight. The delight comes from the liveliness of the imitation; the teaching is to be seen in the plot, which shows by example rather than precept what happens to those whose passions carry them off. Since Antony and Cleopatra were great and important personages, and since they were unfortunate because their own passions destroyed them, they were ideal dramatic material.

NOTES

[1] Goethe, *Shakespeare u. Keine Ende*, quoted in *A New Variorum Edition of Shakespeare: The Tragedie of Anthonie and Cleopatra*, ed. H. H. Furness, Jr. (Philadelphia, 1907), p. 491. Gervinus, Dowden, Paul Stapfer, Granville-Barker, G. Wilson Knight, M. W. MacCallum, and Willard Farnham all concur on this point.
[2] It is not farfetched to see neo-Hegelianism in this attitude. A. C. Bradley, the noblest Hegelian of them all, admires Antony for the violence and one-sidedness of his love. The "passion that ruins Antony," he tells us, "also exalts him, he touches the infinite in it." *Shakespearean Tragedy* (London, 1904), p. 83.
[3] Notable exceptions are the invaluable and exhaustive critique of M. W. MacCallum, *Shakespeare's Roman Plays and Their Background* (London, 1910); and of Willard Farnham, *Shakespeare's Tragic Frontier* (Berkeley, 1950).
[4] This stirring declaration comes from Donald A. Stauffer's illuminating study, *Shakespeare's World of Images* (New York, 1949), p. 234.
[5] Who, according to Edward K. Chambers (*The Mediaeval Stage* [Oxford, 1903], I, 8) were close to the bottom of the Roman scale, not being allowed even the full privileges of citizenship.

[6] *The Poems of Horace . . . Rendred in English Verse by Several Persons . . . Printed . . . for Henry Brome . . . M. DC. LXVI*, p. 48. In Loeb Classical Library (LCL), ll. 6–12:
>Capitolio
>regina dementis ruinas,
>>funus et imperio parabat
>
>contaminato cum grege turpium
>morbo virorum, quidlibet impotens
>>sperare fortunaque dulci
>>>ebria.

[7] Ibid., p. 168. LCL, ll. 11–16:
>Romanus eheu—posteri negabitis—
>>emancipatus feminae
>fert vallum et arma miles et spadonibus
>>servire rugosis potest,
>inter quesigna turpe militaria
>>sol adspicit conopium.

[8] Cf. Dryden's interesting translation of line 688, *sequiturque (nefas) Aegyptis coniunx*: "His ill fate follows him—th'Egyptian wife."

[9] *Velleius Paterculus His Romane Historie*. Rendered in English by Sr. Robert Le Grys (1632), sigs. O verso–O 5.

[10] *Pharsalia* (1614), sig. Oo 4. According to the *Short Title Catalogue* there were three issues in 1614. This is 16885a, Huntington Catalogue 17266. LCL, X, 59–62, reads:
>Dedecus Aegypti, Latii feralis Erinys,
>Romano non casta malo. Quantum impulit Argos
>Iliacasque domos facie Spartana nocenti,
>Hesperios auxit tantum Cleopatra furores.

[11] Ibid. Cf. LCL, X, 70–72:
>Quis tibi vaesani veniam non donet amoris,
>Antoni, durum cum Caesaris hauserit ignis
>Pectus?

[12] *The Works of Flavius Josephus*, trans. William Whiston (New York, 1852), p. 409. (Bk. XV. iv. 1 of the "Antiquities of the Jews.")

[13] In Tudor Translations, ed. W. E. Henley, VII (London, 1895), 8.

[14] *The Historie of the World. Commonly Called, The Naturall Historie*, trans. Philemon Holland (1601), I, sig. Z 3. The story also occurs in Macrobius *Saturnalia* II. xiii.

[15] *An Auncient Historie and Exquisite Chronicle of the Romanes Warres* (1578), sig. Rr 3 verso.

[16] Ibid. Cf. the opening of Bk. V (sig. Rr verso):
>After the deathe of *Brutus* and *Cassius*, *Octavian* went into *Italy*, and *Antonie* into *Aegipt*, where *Cleopatra* meetying with him, overcame him at the firste sight. The which love, brought them to destruction, and *Aegipt* to utter ruine.

[17] *The Roman Histories*, trans. E. M. B[olton] (1618), sigs. X 8 verso–X 9.

[18] *Dio's Roman History*, Ll. 5–15; LCL, VI, 19–45.

[19] IV. 148 c–e; V. 229 d.

[20] *Panegyric on Maiorianus*.

[21] See index of Burton's *Anatomy*, p. 1002.

[22] Canto V, 38–40. Line 62 stigmatizes her as the "lustfull queen."

[23] . . . *in luxuriam & segniciem se deiecit. et per effusam libidinem conuiuijs vacans in tantam trahi se permisit infamiam*. From *De Casibus*, the edition of Georg Husner (Strasbourg, ca. 1475), sig. [l 5 verso].

[24] Ibid., sig. [l 6]. Cf. Lydgate's *Fall of Princes*, Pt. IV, p. 262. Bergen transcribes the conclusion of the more accurate edition printed in Paris in 1507. The French version of the story published by Collard Mansion in 1476 follows Boccaccio but adds a few moralizing judgments. The French translation by Laurens de Premierfait exists in various versions. The one which I have examined in a manuscript which the Huntington Library dates at about 1450 follows Boccaccio rather loosely. It is characterized by such typically moralistic glosses added in the text as *mais escoute une chose detestable et mauldicte* (f. 173 verso).

[25] *De Claris Mulieribus*, ed. J. Czeiner (Ulm, 1473), f. lxxxvi, ff. lxxxix verso–lxxxxii. Favorable mentions of Cleopatra are very slight and very few. In the anonymous *Grete Rayson Cleopatra Is by Kyndnesse*, which the manuscript falsely attributes to Chaucer, Cleopatra is a heroine. The poem is an imitation of Chaucer, however. George Turberville's "Disprayse of Women" (1567) mentions her as an example of a woman faithful to death. Cf. Francis Lee Utley, *The Crooked Rib* (Columbus, 1944), No. 356.

[26] VI, ll. 3632–40. Lydgate's *Fall of Princes* was fairly well known, at least in the first half of the century. Four editions appeared between 1494 and 1555.

[27] *The Minor Poems of John Lydgate*, ed. H. N. MacCracken, Pt. II (1934), *EETS*, No. 192, p. 441.

[28] Douglas Bush, *Mythology and the Renaissance Tradition* (Minneapolis, 1932), pp. 48–49, finds good reasons for denying the customary attribution of Howell. But since the question of authorship is immaterial here, I have followed the *Short Title Catalogue* and the *Cambridge Bibliography*.

[29] For an analysis of the significance of "self-help" literature to the Elizabethans and its popularity, see Louis B. Wright, *Middle Class Culture in Elizabethan England* (Chapel Hill, N.C., 1935), Ch. V, "Hand-books to Improvement," and pp. 588–594, in which Wright discusses the books of moral philosophy and medicine.

[30] Although Lodowick Lloyd, *The Pilgrimage of Princes* [1573], seems to admire Cleopatra for her magnanimity, he uses her life and Antony's to illustrate the vanity of pride, lust, intemperance, and other traditional vices; cf. sig. D verso; sig. Nn 3 verso; sig. Tt verso; sig. Bbb 5; sig. Eee 2 verso; sig. Fff 2. Three editions of Lloyd appeared between 1573 and 1607. Rogers, *Anatomie*, uses Antony to exemplify licentiousness and to show the madness of despair, f. 61 verso, f. 134. La Primaudaye's *French Acade-mie*, which went through nine editions between 1586 and 1618, sees Antony as typical of princes and magistrates whose lust destroys the state, sig. Q. La Primaudaye, sig. H 3 verso, sees Augustus as the temperate ruler who "ware no other garments than such as his wife and daughters made, and those very modest"; he finds Octavia a model of virtue, sig. S 5, and Cleopatra the pattern of the woman who destroys her man, sig. G 4 verso; sig. I 2 verso. Cf. Florio's *The Essays of Montaigne* (1603), in Tudor Translations, ed. George Saintsbury (London, 1892–93), II, 474; Thomas Beard's *The Theatre of Gods Judgements* (1597), sigs. Z 3 verso–Z 4. Beard's ferocious *Theatre* was read enough to require three editions between 1597 and 1631. Cf. *Politeuphuia: Wits Commonwealth* (1597), f. 272; Sir Richard Barckley, *A Discourse of the Felicitie of Man* (1598), sig. D 6; Robert Allott, *Wits Theater of the Little World* (1599), f. 240 verso, f. 260 verso, f. 263; Bodenham's *Belvedére or The Garden of the Muses* (1600), op. cit., p. 164; Barnabe Rich, *Faultes Faultes* (1606), sig. G 3 verso. Other mentions might be cited, as for example Richard Reynoldes's *A Chronicle of All the Noble Emperours of the Romaines* (1571), ff. 17–18. This history, dedicated to Lord Burghley, emphasizes the virtues of Octavius and the discord caused in a commonwealth when the nobles envy their prince as well as the evils caused by wicked rulers. Reynoldes calls Cleopatra a harlot and speaks of her many "horrible murthers." See also Farnham, *Shakespeare's Tragic Frontier*, p. 181. I omit the similar remarks by Burton, Bacon, and Thomas Heywood because they appeared after Shakespeare's play. All agree in making Antony and Cleopatra patterns of unlawful love.

[31] Cf. Willard Farnham, *The Medieval Heritage of Elizabethan Tragedy* (Berkeley, 1936), for an analysis of these changing concepts. The best discussion of these theories of tragedy still is to be found in Lily B. Campbell, *Shakespeare's Tragic Heroes* (Cambridge, 1930), pp. 1–43.

Steele Commager

HORACE, *CARMINA* I.37

Horace's so-called "Cleopatra Ode" has excited attention more often as a historical document than as a literary one. We are frequently urged to contemplate its "Weltgeschichtliche Bedeutungsschwere," and reminded that Horace here treats the conflict not only of Cleopatra and Octavian, but of Egypt and Rome, East and West, the old and the new.[1] In the midst of these ideological reverberations Horace's individual tone seems to have been lost. Yet the Ode is as remarkable in technique as in its ultimate implications, and the figure of Cleopatra as striking as what she shadows forth. Horace's response to the Egyptian queen has a primary command upon our attention, and the Ode offers a context for the author's own feelings as well as a text for historical discourse.

The Ode has not passed without criticism. C. M. Bowra suspects that Horace exults "perhaps too noisily" at Cleopatra's downfall,[2] while another critic has levelled a more comprehensive indictment of the poet's chauvinism:

> May I add that this Ode, so much admired (allegedly) in many quarters and so rhapsodically raved over by editors and literary critics times without count, seems to me an almost perfect example of bad taste in the field of "applied patriotism". Most of us who have lived at mature years in the atmosphere of two World Wars have regretted in the second the unprofitably venemous name-calling that characterized the first, and have noted with satisfaction that it does not take very well in the second with our people. It is no special excuse, certainly no noble one, to say that the violence of the language employed in 1.37 shows how jittery the Augustan party was and Horace along with them; he had plenty of time to think it over between 30 B.C. and the publication date of the Odes. In verses 17ff. the ranting becomes rather ridiculous seeing that no *mollis columba* ever had even a sporting chance against an *accipiter*, nor a poor timid *lepus* against a *citus venator;* Horace has

From *Phoenix* 12, No. 2 (Summer 1958): 47–55.

allowed himself to become so self-propagandized by name-calling that as usually is the case in such circumstances, his logic lapses utterly.[3]

In singling out the similes of hawk and dove, hunter and rabbit, Professor Alexander has directed us to the moral, as it is the physical, centre of the poem. ⟨...⟩

More editors have endorsed Professor Alexander's instincts than his analysis, discerning the Ode to be responsible for, rather than an insult to, our magnanimity.[4] The images of pursuer and pursued are crucial, in the word's radical sense, for they mark the point where poetic intentions cross. The lines act as a kind of pivot, diverting our sympathies from Caesar to Cleopatra, and a straightforward triumph song slides into what has been justly termed a "panegyric on the vanquished queen."[5] Horace's manipulation of fact confirms such an interpretation. He deliberately magnifies the moral force of Cleopatra's final defiance. He neglects the year elapsing between Actium and her suicide: she seems to rise directly from defeat to noble death. He assigns her proud refusal to be led in Caesar's triumph as the sole motive for her suicide, one which other accounts by and large play down.[6] And finally, he omits any reference to her attempts to cajole Octavian, as she had Caesar and Antony before him. Horace's Cleopatra witnesses her defeat with stoic fortitude, *voltu sereno* (26), and then embraces a death worthy of Cato himself.[7]

In a recent article Ernst Bickel[8] seems to share Prof. Alexander's assumptions about the central images, though his sympathies are less chivalric. He too takes them as an intended glorification of Octavian, and he reminds us that the simile of hawk and dove may be an epic reference to Achilles' pursuit of Hector (*Iliad* 22.139ff.). The Greek hero's voyage to Troy becomes a paradigm for Octavian's expedition to Actium: Vergil, he thinks, had symbolically prophesied the same thing in the fourth Eclogue: *atque iterum ad Troiam magnus mittetur Achilles* (36).[9] In the mention of a hunter in Haemonian fields (19–20) Bickel also detects an occult allusion to Achilles, who came from Thessaly, or Haemonia.[10] Now even if Horace's images do imply so specific a reference, they are hardly calculated to enlist our unreserved sympathy. The Romans identified themselves with Trojans rather than Greeks, and Hector was, after all, the brother of Aeneas, from whom Octavian and all the Iulii traced their descent.[11] The Horatian lines Bickel compares (*Troiae prope victor altae Pthius Achilles, C.* 4.6.3–4) are hardly complimentary if we look at the context. Horace is hymning Apollo, Octavian's patron god.[12] The prime example of Apollo's power appears in his conquest of Achilles, whom Horace deliberately makes less sympathetic by attributing to him the vengefulness which Homer (*Iliad* 6.57ff.) recorded of Agamemnon.[13]

> sed palam captis gravis, heu nefas, heu
> nescios fari pueros Achivis
> ureret flammis, etiam latentem
>   matris in alvo ...   (*C.* 4.6.17–20)

Research only bolsters the immediate appeal of hawk and dove. Nor, if we accept Bickel's identification of the hunter in Haemonian fields, does the vision of the mighty Achilles tracking down a frightened rabbit recommend itself as a heroically compelling one.

If, then, we are correct in thinking the central images divert rather than intensify our initial sympathies, we should expect the Ode's total movement to correspond to the switch. And so it does. The difference between beginning and end is self-evident: triumphal paean has subsided into elegy, for Horace has come to praise as well as bury a *non humilis mulier*. The transition is meditated rather than impulsive, and the Ode's second half answers the first in contrapuntal detail.[14] The opening cry—*nunc est bibendum*—establishes also the poem's structural terms. It initiates the central antithesis between two types of drinking, one which has gone oddly unremarked. The Romans' finally achieved triumphal celebration (1–6) rebukes Cleopatra's previous intoxication—for before Actium she had been drunk with power, *fortunaque dulci ebria* (11–12). *Dementis* (7), *inpotens* (10), *furorem* (12), and *lymphatam Mareotico* (14) similarly suggest her heady delusions of grandeur.[15] In this case metaphor allies itself with historical fact, for the celebrations of Antony and Cleopatra approached the fabulous: in her excesses Cleopatra was said to have entertained notions of supreme rule at Rome.[16] Her notorious band of eunuchs (9–10), or *semiviri*,[17] appears as a disease (*morbo*, 10) or deformation of nature, and furthers the air of fantasy hovering over her world. For a woman to be sole ruler always presented itself as an affront to the Romans, and for Cleopatra's very men to be unreal added biological insult to military injury. With Actium, Cleopatra's unreal world and dreams of glory shatter upon the fact of Octavian's victory. Fanciful hopes (10–11) are overwhelmed by true fears (15). Caesar's sober strength has crushed the queen's intoxicated fantasies: the juxtapositions are clear, and our sympathies unequivocal.

Horace makes of Actium as much a moral as a military watershed, and the first words after the central image compel us to qualify, if not reverse, the Ode's initial distinctions. *Generosius . . . nec muliebriter expavit:* Cleopatra seems to assume the prerogatives of her conquerors. *Generosus* implies a specifically Roman sense of "well-born,"[18] and with *nec muliebriter* she sheds the effeminacy of the Egyptian court. She repudiates (*nec reparavit,* 23–24) her dreams of conquest (*funus parabat,* 8).[19] If her daring remains (*ausa,* 25) it is now founded on reality, and her serenity (26) before the fact of defeat is the more impressive for her previous agitation. As her delusions diminish (*minuit* [12] . . . *redegit* [15]) her presence expands (*invidens privata* [30–31][20] . . . *non humilis mulier* [37]), and the decline of her public fortunes is counterpointed by a rise in her personal stature.

Dr. Johnson praised Milton for his "weightily embodied" descriptions, and a comparable denseness of verbal suggestion enforces Cleopatra's acceptance of reality. We feel the snake's harsh scales (26), see its black venom (27–28), hear its hiss in the repeated sibilants (26–27), and almost taste the poison which Cleopatra "drinks in" (28) with her whole body. *Combiberet* insists upon the immediacy of her contact with actuality, and marks how far behind lie her former drunken illusions, *fortunaque dulci ebria* (11–12). *Deliberata* (29) again is pointed by her

previous fantasies, while austere negations (*nec muliebriter, nec reparavit,* culminating in *non humilis*) mark the change from past indulgence. *Superbo non humilis
mulier triumpho*—the final phrase epitomizes the double impact of the whole
poem. *Superbo* and *non humilis* are practically identical, and a consecutive reading
makes it easy to forget that *mulier* and *triumpho* are formally opposed. The
sequence of words produces a suggestion, impossible to reproduce in translation,
that the triumph belongs with Cleopatra as well. "Her life would be eternal in our
triumph," anticipates Shakespeare's Caesar, and Cleopatra's death becomes eternal
in her own. The sense of a two-fold triumph on which the poem ends has been
prepared for in *combiberet* (28). Cleopatra's final drink salutes reality, for it is she
who ultimately shatters Caesar's dream of leading her a captive. She celebrates a
triumph as surely as do the Romans, and her drink to yesterday has no less glory
than their toast to tomorrow.

A comforting rationalization might propose that Horace exalts Octavian's
enemy only to magnify Octavian.[21] Yet not until her defeat does Cleopatra become
formidable; it is the change in her character which is responsible for our altered
feelings. The Cleopatra we leave is very different from the one to whom we are
introduced. Intoxicated hopes have sobered into a meditated draught; by embrac-
ing reality she has overtopped her lofty illusions. Repudiating a dream of Roman
rule she achieves a Roman nobility; casting off her unnatural world she dies a more
than natural heroine. Public catastrophe and private renaissance are simultaneous.
Phoenix-like, Cleopatra rises from the ashes of her own defeat, and her final
wrought serenity marks an exemplary triumph over Fortune's reverses.[22]

The ninth Epode also celebrates Cleopatra's defeat, though her death had not
yet occurred. It seems to have been written either during or immediately after the
battle of Actium, and hence antedates *C.* 1.37 by about a year.[23] Whatever the
internal difficulties as to the exact *mise-en-scène,* the Epode does not complicate
its emotional demands as the Ode does. The victory is unequivocally a Roman one
(*io triumphe ... capaciores adfer huc, puer scyphos,* 21ff.), while Cleopatra is
presented with a mixture of hostility and disgust:

> Romanus eheu—posteri negabitis—
>   emancipatus feminae
> fert vallum et arma, miles et spadonibus
>   servire rugosis potest,
> interque signa turpe militaria
>   sol adspicit conopium.   (11–16)

The Ode does more than recollect the same emotions in greater tranquillity.
Cleopatra's intervening suicide compelled Horace to a refreshed consideration
which distinguishes the Ode from its predecessor. What had been a pure cry of
triumph (*io triumphe ... io triumphe,* 21–22) modulates into the ambiguity of
superbo triumpho (*C.* 1.37. 31–32); abuse of the effeminate Egyptian court becomes balanced by Cleopatra's rejection of womanly fear; festive invitation ramifies

into a dialectic of symbolic drinks. The two poems form an instructive example of the way elements of a narrative sequence in the Epodes tend to become structural principles in the Odes.

The poem's distinction emerges yet more clearly from a comparison with contemporary testimony.[24] At the centre of Aeneas' shield stands a representation of Actium, and its position is symptomatic of the national bias which informs Vergil's description (*Aeneid* 8.675ff.). The encounter lies between monstrous gods and Olympians (698ff.): Actium assumes the proportions of a Titanomachia, shadowing forth an ideological conflict between barbarism and civilization, East and West.[25] Cleopatra is almost incidental. We catch only a glimpse of her as she flees, pale at the thought of her coming death (708ff.). If Vergil largely ignores the Egyptian queen, Propertius actively depreciates her, and Professor Alexander might better have looked here for "applied patriotism." To compare Propertius' attitude with that of Horace is to raise a question as to the validity of the popular contrast between Horace's fervid patriotism and Propertius' notorious recalcitrance. His treatment of Actium is framed by a description of the recently dedicated temple of Apollo:

> Musa, Palatini referemus Apollinis aedem:
> res est, Calliope, digna favore tuo.
> Caesaris in nomen ducuntur carmina: Caesar
> dum canitur, quaeso, Iuppiter ipse vaces   (4.6.11–15)

To turn to praise of Octavian was appropriate, if not inevitable, for Romans were encouraged to believe that Apollo had at Actium stood above the ship of his most distinguished protégé, lending assistance. To further glorify the victor, *mundi servator* (37), Cleopatra's suicide is made to appear as negligible personally as it is fortunate politically:

> illa petit Nilum cumba male nixa fugaci,
> hoc unum, iusso non moritura die.
> di melius! quantus mulier foret una triumphus,
> ductus erat per quas ante Iugurtha vias!   (4.6.63–67)

The explanation seems tactful rather than authentic, for Suetonius, Dio, and Plutarch are unanimous in recording Octavian's eagerness to lead Cleopatra in Jugurtha's footsteps.[26] A victor who recorded (*Res Gestae* 4.3) with careful pride the nine kings, or children of kings who swelled his procession, could have gained small satisfaction from the image borne in place of his greatest conquest.

The Ode approaches a paradigm of the poet's alchemy of historic fact. The elements were all well known. Propertius need only refer to Cleopatra's apparently notorious fondness for drink:

> "non hoc, Roma, fui tanto tibi cive verenda:"
> dixit et assiduo lingua sepulta mero.   (3.11.55–56)

What Propertius exploits as casual abuse, Horace explores as a poetic image capable of articulating the whole Ode. Blending it with other common facts— Cleopatra's band of eunuchs, her hopes of Roman rule, her final repudiation of womanhood and royal death—he transmutes them into the very structure of the Ode. We cannot, as we can with Propertius, isolate any reference to Cleopatra's drinking. Remove it and the poem collapses. History has been concentrated into image, and image has become poetic meaning. Form and content are identical.[27]

For parallels, whether of technique or of attitude, we must look less to contemporaries than to Shakespeare's retrospective vision, *Antony and Cleopatra.* Here we find a similar crystallization of history into poetic structure, for in North's *Plutarch* Shakespeare rediscovered the same interplay between Rome's national victory and Cleopatra's individual one which had previously attracted Horace's attention. It is by maintaining the tension between these poles that *Antony and Cleopatra* generates such electricity of dramatic utterance, and Shakespeare's antitheses echo Horace's even in elaborating them. A public sense of history informs the play: we see an emerging Empire triumph over a decaying dynasty, masculine Roman over effeminate Egyptian, land force over sea power, grave sobriety over light sport, four square *virtus* over devious love, a youthful Caesar over an aging Antony and Cleopatra—the contrasts are the playwright's own. Yet private lives play against public issues, and the counterpoint recalls Horace's. Laying aside her womanhood—

> My resolution's plac'd, and I have nothing
> Of woman in me—

Cleopatra rises by "a Roman death" to an ultimate victory over Rome's very founder:

> Where souls do couch on flowers, we'll hand in hand,
> And with our springly port, make the ghosts gaze.
> Dido and her Aeneas shall want troops,
> And all the haunt be ours.

On Shakespeare's boards the conflict is played out principally in terms of Antony, in whom love vies with honour, East with West. Horace could hardly share the Englishman's distanced perspective, and even had he felt free to treat the subject in the same way, it is unlikely that he would have anticipated Shakespeare's tacit, and Dryden's explicit, verdict that the world was well lost. Horace's treatment of Cleopatra represents not so much a divided allegiance as a fondness for seeing every situation in a double aspect. The tendency is habitual, and the Cleopatra Ode, in its technique, stands as a kind of manifesto of the Horatian imagination.

NOTES

[1] See W. Wili, *Horaz* (Basel 1948) 136–137, 165; H. U. Instinsky, "Horatiana," *Hermes* 82 (1954) 126–128. Th. Birt (*Horaz' Lieder* [Leipzig 1925] 59) speaks of Horace's "politische Muse."

C. M. Bowra, *Inspiration and Poetry* (London 1955) 39.

[3] W. H. Alexander, "Nunc tempus erat," *Classical Journal* 39 (1944) 233. Cf. the same author's characterization of Horace as "superheated with Roman patriotism throughout this unpleasantly vindictive ode" (*Univ. of Cal. Publ. in Class. Philol.* 13, No. 7 [1947] 194).

[4] See the editions of C. L. Smith (Boston 1903), C. H. Moore (New York 1902), Plessis-Lejay (Paris 1911), and Kiessling-Heinze (achte Auflage, Berlin 1955). For the meaning of *fatale monstrum* (21), and for perceptive observations on the Ode as a whole, see Ed. Fraenkel, *Horace* (Oxford 1957) 160.

[5] L. P. Wilkinson, *Horace and His Lyric Poetry* (Cambridge 1946) 133.

[6] Vergil makes only a generalized reference to her death (*pallentem morte futura, Aeneid* 8.709) without even specifying that she committed suicide. Propertius grants her suicide only a scornful "this alone did she win, death at the hour of her own choice" (4.6.64). Velleius Paterculus ignores her motives (2.87). Suetonius records only that Caesar wished to keep her alive (*Augustus* 17). Plutarch gives as her motive a refusal to be part of the triumph over Antony (*Life of Antony* 84.2–4); his conception seems closest to Horace's.

[7] The similarity to Cato's suicide after his defeat at Thapsus is striking: compare Horace's admiration for him, C. 2.1.23–4, 1.12.35–6.

[8] "Politische Sibylleneklogen," *Rheinisches Museum* 97 (1954) 193–228, 210ff.

[9] Bickel also considers Vergil's Tiphys (*alter erit tum Tiphys, Eclogues* 4.34) to be a masque for Agrippa, who was to command Octavian's wing at Actium (op. cit. 228).

[10] Op. cit. 212ff.

[11] Propertius, in his description of Actium, speaks of Octavian as *Hectoreis cognite maior avis* (4.6.38).

[12] The connection between Apollo and Augustus was widely popularized, and carefully encouraged by the ruler himself. See Fr. Altheim, *A History of Roman Religion* (Engl. transl. London 1938) 365ff.; J. B. Carter, *The Religion of Numa* (London 1906) 164ff.; E. H. Haight, "An Inspired Message in Augustan Poets," *American Journal of Philology* 39 (1918) 341–366.

[13] Cf. *Ars Poetica* 120–122; if the playwright introduces Achilles, he should make him true to character, that is, *impiger, iracundus, inexorabilis, acer, / iura neget sibi nata, nihil non adroget armis.*

[14] H. L. Tracy, "Thought-Sequence in the Ode," *Studies in Honour of Gilbert Norwood* (Toronto 1952) 211, finds the Ode to be an example of "pure linear structure." Although the article is a valuable one for the study of Horace, and for the ancient Ode in general, I cannot agree with the statement that "the Cleopatra Ode runs through an uncontrived set of reflections."

[15] *Dementem strepitum* is used of a drinking bout in C. 3.19.23, as is *furere* in C. 2.7.28. Ps.-Acro explains *lymphatam* as *ebrietate insanam; cf.* Catullus 64.254; Ovid *Metamorphoses* 11.3; Pliny *Natural History* 24.17.164.

[16] Probably meant by *quidlibet inpotens sperare* (10–11). Cf. Propertius 3.11.31; Dio, 50.5.4; Florus, 2.21.2; Ovid *Metamorphoses* 15.827–828.

[17] Cf. *Epodes* 9.13–14. Kiessling-Heinze, *ad* C. 1.37.10, notes the scorn which falls upon *virorum.*

[18] Cf. *Satires* 1.6.2, 24.

[19] It seems likely that Horace intended the contrast. It is probably for this reason that he used the word *reparare*, an odd one in such a context, and one which has been frequently emended. *Penetravit, repetivit, repedavit,* have been proposed; see L. Mueller, *Q. Horatius Flaccus, Oden und Epoden* (St. Petersburg 1900) ad loc.

[20] *Privata* (31), usually translated "a private citizen," retains a strong verbal force. It suggests "stripped," or "deprived," and has connotations similar to those of *redegit* (15). Though publicly reduced, Cleopatra admits no diminution of her real self.

[21] Wickham (*Horace, The Odes, Carmen Saeculare and Epodes* [Oxford 1904] ad loc.) considers that Horace, by his admiration for Cleopatra, is merely "bringing out in stronger relief the danger from which Rome has been freed, and the glory of Octavianus, who has conquered no unworthy foe." Cf. M. Renard, "Horace et Cléopâtre," *Études Horatiennes* (Brussels 1937) 199.
    C. 1.38, with its repudiation of the exotic rose for the stern and indigenous myrtle, might be seen as a milder and less complex echo of C. 1.37. *Mitte sectari, rosa quo locorum / sera moretur* (3–4). Cleopatra herself is in a sense the last rose of summer—yet it is perhaps the rose itself, rather than the command to forget it, which we remember.

[22] We should remember Horace's enthusiasm for such equanimity: C. 2.3.1ff.; 3.29.41ff.; *Epodes* 1.6.13.

[23] For a discussion of the Epode's setting and dramatic date see L. P. Wilkinson, "Horace, *Ep.* 9," *Classical Review* 47 (1933) 2–6, who gives references to previous articles, and F. Wurzel, "Der Ausgang der Schlacht von Actium und die 9. Epode des Horaz," *Hermes* 73 (1938) 361–379.

[24] We have nothing left except the opening lines of the Alcaeus poem (frg. 39, Dl.) which Horace seems to have used as a model. It is highly improbable that Alcaeus would have shown a comparable respect for Myrsilus, or compared him to a fleeing rabbit. See Pasquali, *Orazio Lirico* (Firenze 1920) 55.

[25] Cf. Propertius 3.11.41–42, and R. Pichon, "La Bataille d'Actium," *Mélanges Boissier* (Paris 1903) 397–400. In *C.* 3.4.42ff. most editors have seen a reference to Actium in the account of Zeus' victory over the Titans and Giants. Wickham (op. cit., ad loc.) suggests the same relevance in *C.* 2.12.6–9. The political possibility of such symbolism was familiar; see Wilamowitz, *Der Glaube der Hellenen* (Basel, reprinted 1956) 2. 94, and A. Y. Campbell, *Horace* (London 1924) 109.

[26] Suetonius *Augustus* 17.4; Dio 51.11.3; 51.14.6; Plutarch *Life of Antony* 86.4; see Instinsky, op. cit. (n. I) 128. For a further attack, including some rather fanciful accusations, see Propertius 3.11.29ff. Cf. Lucan 8.693; 10.59–60; 357ff.; Pliny *Natural History* 9.119.

[27] The same use of history may be seen in *C.* 2.18. The foundations left along the shore at Baiae prove that the houses Horace describes, built upon the sea itself (17ff.), were a contemporary reality. But in the poem the rich man's blindness to the natural limit of land and sea becomes a symbol for his refusal to acknowledge nature's final limit of death: *sepulcri immemor struis* (18–19). Moreover, such a mansion is contrasted with the inescapable hall of Hades (29ff.), the only house which is ours forever. Historical fact has become absorbed into the imagistic structure of the Ode.

L. J. Mills

CLEOPATRA'S TRAGEDY

Interpretations of Shakespeare's *Antony and Cleopatra* have emphasized, with varying degrees of stress, one or another of the three principal themes in the play, which are, as summarized by John Munro:

> ... first, the East represented by Egypt and lands beyond versus the West represented by Rome; secondly, the strife in the Triumvirate who divided and governed the world, and the reduction of the three, Octavius, Lepidus and Antony, to one, Octavius; and thirdly, the love and tragedy of Antony and Cleopatra. Of all these the last is dramatically dominant.[1]

But among the commentators who regard the third theme as dominant there is much difference of opinion. Some write as if the play were entitled "The Tragedy of Antony"; for example, J. Middleton Murry:

> ... up to the death of Antony it is from him that the life of the play has been derived. She [Cleopatra] is what she is to the imagination, rather in virtue of the effects we see in Antony, than by virtue of herself. He is magnificent; therefore she must be. But when he dies, her poetic function is to maintain and prolong, to reflect and reverberate, that achieved royalty of Antony's.[2]

Others give Cleopatra more significance but yet make Antony central, as does Peter Alexander, who allots to Cleopatra a somewhat more distinct, more nearly self-contained personality than does Murry:

> Antony dies while the play has still an act to run, but without this act his story would be incomplete. For Cleopatra has to vindicate her right to his devotion.[3]

Any interpreter, however, who concentrates on the tragedy of Antony is confronted with the difficulty pointed out by Robert Speaight:

From *Shakespeare Quarterly* 11, No. 2 (Spring 1960): 147–62.

... if you are thinking in terms of Antony's tragedy alone, and if you are trying to make his tragedy conform to a classical definition, then you may find it awkward to face a fifth act, in which only his heroic and fallen shadow is left to keep Cleopatra company.[4]

Moreover, such an interpreter overlooks the title of the play as it appears in the Folio: "The Tragedie of Anthonie, and Cleopatra", with the significant comma after "Anthonie." The nature of the play *Antony and Cleopatra*, really in itself more than from the comma signal but given added emphasis by it, should be self-evident: the play presents the tragedy of Antony and then the tragedy of Cleopatra. Such recognition, however, does not obscure the fact that each tragedy gives significance to the other and increases its effect.

Judicially objective critics have granted Cleopatra more stature as a tragic figure in her own right than those who think of the play as Antony's tragedy. J. W. Mackail, for instance, though he does not point out that Cleopatra's tragedy differs from Antony's, says:

> It is the tragedy not of the Roman world, but of Antony and Cleopatra: and of both of them equally.... Here, neither single name gives the central tone to the drama; Antony does not exist for the sake of Cleopatra (as one might put it), nor does Cleopatra exist for the sake of Antony: they are two immense and in a sense equivalent forces which never coalesce, and the interaction between them is the drama.[5]

And Virgil K. Whitaker, though insisting that "the tragic action of the play is centered upon Antony, who has so yielded himself to the passion of love that it has possessed his will and dethroned his judgment", gives Cleopatra stature as a tragic figure: "Cleopatra, although she is developed almost as fully as he is, remains the seductress, and only at the end does she become a participant in a tragedy of her own."[6] "A tragedy of her own"—just what is it? "A question to be asked", and answered.[7]

It is trite to remark that an audience's first impression of a character is very important; it is not commonplace to call particular attention to Cleopatra's first word in the play: "If". It is obvious—or should be—that in saying "If it be love indeed, tell me how much", she is following up a previous declaration, on Antony's part, of great love for her by teasing and bantering him. She is playful, but within her brief demand may be discerned one of her chief devices, contradiction.[8] Immediately, by the entrance of the messenger from Rome, her tone changes; the contradictions become blunt, the taunts amazingly bold and affrontive. Antony's submitting to them proves that Philo's term "dotage" is not an exaggeration. That Cleopatra's contradictory behavior (as in I. ii. 89–91; iii. 1–5) is calculated is obvious from her rejoinder to Charmian's warning: "Thou teachest like a fool. The way to lose him!" (I. iii. 10).[9] Simultaneously Cleopatra's constant fear is revealed: that Antony will leave her.

When Antony, having determined to break off with Cleopatra and return to Rome, goes to her to announce his departure, she perceives that he is in a serious mood and, surmising his intention, gives him no chance to talk. Six times she interrupts him when he starts to speak. In her tirades she taunts him (1) by references to his wife Fulvia, charging him with falsity to her; (2) by the accusation that he has treacherously betrayed her (Cleopatra); and (3) by recounting his compliments to her when he was wooing, practically calling him a liar. And when eventually Antony commands her to listen to him and hear his reasons for leaving, ending with a reference to Fulvia's death, she then accuses him of lying, of expecting her, like a child, to believe fairy tales. When he offers proof, the letter he has received, she then charges him with insensibility for not weeping over his wife's death and predicts that he would be equally unmoved by her death. And as he protests his love for her she begins one of her fainting spells but changes her mind; she is, she says, "quickly ill, and well", as changeable as Antony is in his love. She mockingly urges him to produce some tears for Fulvia and pretend they are for her, ridicules him for not making a better show at weeping, and calls on Charmian to join her in laughing at Antony's rising anger.

Antony turns to walk away. Then Cleopatra brings him back by the one appeal that just then could do it, a quavering "Courteous lord". It is the first time in the play that she has spoken to him in anything like a complimentary fashion. Then she pretends to have something serious to say, or that she was going to say and has now forgot. Antony recognizes that she is playing for time, and she perceives his recognition.[10] She has drawn on her coquette's kit for a variety of tools, and they have failed her, even her appeal to pity (her most effective, much used tool); Antony is going despite all she can do. But perhaps, if she says something kind, for once, it may eventually bring him back:

> Your honour calls you hence;
> Therefore be deaf to my unpitied folly,
> And all the gods go with you! Upon your sword
> Sit laurel victory, and smooth success
> Be strew'd before your feet!
>
> (I. iii. 97–101)

Or something that may seem kind! Her reference to his honor is much belated; she makes another appeal to pity; and the sequence of *s* sounds and the concatenation of *b*'s and *f*'s and *e*'s and *t*'s in the last line may suggest, by the conceivable hissing and sneering, an unconscious extrusion of her essentially serpentine nature.

During Antony's absence Cleopatra's behavior is self-characterizing. She evinces no interest in the business he is engaged in; she is concerned as to what he may be thinking of her, is enveloped in thoughts physical and sensual, and reviews the list of her great lovers, "Broad-fronted Caesar", "great Pompey", "brave Mark Antony". She revels in memories of her behavior to Antony—trickery in fishing, laughing him out of and into patience, dressing him in tires and mantles while she "wore his sword Philippan", contrarieties all. She is aghast when the news comes that Antony has married Octavia and beats the messenger, but regains hope from the description he gives of her.

We do not see Antony and Cleopatra together again until just before the battle of Actium. Were it not for Enobarbus' description of her on the river Cydnus and his analysis of her charms (II. ii. 195–245), there would be little about her in the first half of the play that to an objective reader is alluring. But even Enobarbus' account hints at Cleopatra's oppositeness, for he pictures Antony, "Enthron'd i' th' market place", waiting for Cleopatra to appear before him, which she does not do, and accepting her refusal to dine with him and her counter-invitation "to come and suppe with her".[11] The description follows closely the reconciliation scene between Antony and Octavius in which Antony, then at his best, is shown as firm master of himself and thus provides the background to contrast with his sorry self when manipulated by Cleopatra. But there is no such admirable background for Cleopatra; it is apparent that her tragedy will have to be of a distinctly different sort from Antony's. It cannot be a "tragic fall", for there is nothing for her to fall from.

After Actium, where Antony at her urging has fought at sea, she offers as her reason for leaving the scene of the battle that she was afraid. But that reason does not satisfy everyone. E. E. Stoll, for instance, lists among various unanswered questions in Shakespeare's plays the query "Why does Cleopatra flee from the battle and Antony?"[12] Later he wonders whether in examining such a question as that, and about her later dealings with Thyreus and her responsibility in the second sea-fight, we may not be "then considering too curiously".[13] Certainly the question about her behavior at Actium exists and must be considered; but just as certainly it cannot be answered.[14] Cleopatra's "I little thought / You would have followed" (III. xi. 55–56), besides putting the blame on him, may reveal a more nearly true reason than her "fearful sails": Is her leaving the battle at the critical point a test of Antony, to see whether the political leader or the lover is stronger in him? Does she fear that military success and political mastery would be a dangerous rival to her charms? And when Antony reproaches her with

> You did know
> How much you were my conqueror, and that
> My sword, made weak by my affection, would
> Obey it on all cause   (III. xi. 65–68)

and she cries "Pardon, pardon!" is she really sorry? Her behavior to Thyreus soon after makes us wonder.

When Thyreus tells Cleopatra that

> He [Caesar] knows that you embrace not Antony
> As you did love, but as you fear'd him   (III. xiii. 56–57)

she exclaims "O!" What does she mean by that? There are those who seem to know; e.g., G. L. Kittredge (note on l. 57):

Cleopatra's exclamation is meant to convey to Thyreus not only eager acceptance of Caesar's theory of her union with Antony, but also gratified surprise that Caesar should have shown so sympathetic an understanding of the case. All this she expresses in plain terms in her next speech: 'He is a god,' etc.

That interpretation implies that Cleopatra, suddenly perceiving a way out of the impasse, is deserting Antony and preparing to entangle Caesar in her "toils of grace", through the pity for her that she hopes to inspire. But conceivably the "O!" may merely imply painful shock at the idea that anyone could even think she feared Antony and did not love him.[15] If so, the idea of appealing to Caesar's pity may not occur at the moment but be suggested by Thyreus'

> The scars upon your honour, therefore, he
> Does pity, as constrained blemishes,
> Not as deserv'd.   (ll. 58–60)

It is doubtful whether one is justified in saying that "All this she expresses in plain terms in her next speech", inasmuch as Thyreus' statement comes between her "O!" and "her next speech". Or, perhaps, the previous lines should be taken into consideration; Thyreus says,

>   Caesar entreats
> Not to consider in what case thou stand'st
> Further than he is Caesar,   (ll. 53–55)

which seems to promise noble treatment, with possible emphasis on the good will of Caesar the man. If the idea of attempting to entangle Caesar has already occurred to her, her enthusiastic "Go on. Right royal!" is flattery intended to be relayed to Caesar. But then Thyreus'

> He knows that you embrace not Antony
> As you did love, but as you fear'd him

is definitely cooling, and her "O!" may involuntarily escape her, indicating sudden awareness of Caesar's realization that she "embraced" Antony because of his power more than for love of the man himself and thus is on guard against any designs she might have on him now that he has conquered Antony. If that is the situation, then Thyreus' speech suggesting Caesar's pity for the scars upon her honor "as constrained blemishes / Not as deserv'd" arouses hope and prompts her flattering and pity-inviting

>   He is a god, and knows
> What is most right. Mine honour was not yielded
> But conquer'd merely,   (ll. 60–62)

a bare-faced lie, as Enobarbus recognizes.

Whatever the significance of the "O!" it is soon obvious that Cleopatra proceeds to cajole Thyreus,[16] hoping thereby to make him a friend in court. But whether she is actually deserting Antony and staking all on a hope of ensnaring Caesar or is planning a deep deception of Caesar it is impossible to tell. Nor is her behavior to Antony clear when he enters unexpectedly and in fury orders punishment to Thyreus and condemns her. She attempts to defend herself with four questions: "O, is't come to this?" "Wherefore is this?" "Have you done yet?" and, after a parenthetical "I must stay his time", "Not know me yet?" What does she mean by the fourth question? She probably intends for Antony to understand that she was just temporizing, meeting Caesar's suspected treachery with pretended submission. When Antony, still pained by what he is sure is betrayal of him, asks, "Cold-hearted toward me?" she breaks out in impassioned speech:

> Ah, dear, if I be so,
> From my cold heart let heaven engender hail,
> And poison it in the source, and the first stone
> Drop in my neck; as it determines, so
> Dissolve my life! The next Caesarion smite!
> Till by degrees the memory of my womb
> Together with my brave Egyptians all,
> By the discandying of this pelleted storm,
> Lie graveless, till the flies and gnats of Nile
> Have buried them for prey!   (III. xiii. 158–167)

Actually her plea that, if her heart is cold, from it hail, poisoned in its source (her heart), should be "engendered" only to fall in her neck, melt, and in melting dissolve her life, is basically nonsense. For if there were enough poison in the source, her heart, to kill her when, incorporated into hail, it was carried to her neck and then caused her life to dissolve, she would have been dead long ago. To say nothing of the amount of poison it would take to dispose of Caesarion and "my brave Egyptians all"! She has created a barrage of words that by the excess of emotion and the deficiency of sense seem to denote complete devotion to Antony but which by the very excesses reveal the opposite. "The lady doth protest too much, methinks." Her speech is not the bald lie that she tells Antony when later she sends him word that she has killed herself, but there is deception, masked by the barrage of words and the vehemence of her utterance.[17]

What a narrow escape that was for her! She has convinced Antony ("I am satisfied") but not Enobarbus; for him it is the last straw. He knows that Antony is now lost, for "When valour preys on reason, / It eats the sword it fights with" (ll. 199–200). Though Enobarbus speaks only of Antony, he reveals his interpretation of Cleopatra's behavior in the crisis.

Antony declares that he will fight Caesar again, gains Cleopatra's "That's my brave lord", and joins with her in anticipation of her birthday festivities. The next morning she playfully helps Antony don his armor and kisses him as he departs for battle. She comments to Charmian, "He goes forth gallantly", and expresses a wish

> That he and Caesar might
> Determine this great war in single fight!
> Then Antony—but now—
>
> (IV. iv. 36–38)

Since she apparently thinks Antony will be defeated, she is surprised at his victorious return:

> Lord of lords!
> O infinite virtue, com'st thou smiling from
> The world's great snare[18] uncaught?
>
> (IV. viii. 16–18)

Though she thus compliments Antony in exaggerated terms and rewards Scarus extravagantly ("An armour all of gold", l. 27), she hardly discloses her real thoughts. Nor is it certain that she did not betray Antony in the second sea-fight. Antony is sure: "This foul Egyptian hath betrayed me!" (IV. xii. 10) and he is exceedingly bitter about the "triple-turn'd whore" that

> Like a right gypsy hath at fast and loose
> Beguil'd me to the very heart of loss!

He calls for Eros, but Cleopatra appears, having mistakenly thought, perhaps, that Antony was summoning her by calling on the deity of love (Eros), and is met by "Ah, thou spell! Avaunt!" In innocence or seeming innocence she asks, "Why is my lord enrag'd against his love?" Then at Antony's threats she leaves. Exclaiming that he is "more mad / Than Telamon for his shield" (xiii. 1–2), she sends Mardian to Antony:

> Mardian, go tell him I have slain myself.
> Say that the last I spoke was 'Antony'
> And word it, prithee, piteously. Hence, Mardian,
> And bring me how he takes my death.
>
> (IV. xiii. 7–10)

The lie, with the appeals for pity—"I have slain myself" (for love of Antony), "piteously"—is her final deception of Antony. Knowledge about how he takes her death may be intended to provide her with a clue as to possible appeasement of his wrath, but the lie is the climax of all her tricks, and ironically causes his death. Though it be argued that she did not betray Antony, his thinking she did is understandable, in the light of her behavior throughout the play up to the time of the second sea-fight.

What would be—to return to Cleopatra's entrance and exit for a moment—the impression on an audience of Cleopatra's behavior? Antony's brief but vivid description of the fleet's surrender and his repeated charge that Cleopatra has betrayed him, plus remembrance of what happened at Actium, may well make an audience suspicious of her when she appears. And her exit, following immediately upon Antony's detailed picture of her as the captive of Caesar and the victim of Octavia's wrath, may well give the definite impression that her self-interest has been and is the force that motivates her action. She does not even think of fainting or of attempting to kill herself in disproof of Antony's accusation. And her question "Why is my lord enrag'd against his love?" is colored by her accustomed plea for pity. Altogether, whether or not she betrayed Antony to Caesar is left an unanswered question, like the motives for her behavior at Actium.

There are some obvious facts. Cleopatra, to satisfy her ego, must have as her lovers the world's greatest. The outcome of the war between Antony and Octavius, since it is for world mastery, will determine which will emerge as the greater. Suppose Antony should win: he will certainly be immersed in state affairs and neglect her. Suppose Octavius should win: then there is the question as to whether she can ensnare him. Her equivocal behavior to Antony and her flirting with Caesar through Thyreus may reflect her uncertainty.

Yet there can be no doubt that Cleopatra has love, of a sort, for Antony, and when he, dying, is brought to her in the monument it is the realization of his personality as a man, her lover, and her belated recognition of the stalwart Roman qualities he represents (emphasized by the pride in them shown in his dying speech) that for the moment overshadow everything else. Even though self-pity is not completely absent—"Noblest of men, woo't die?/Hast thou no care of me?" (IV. xv. 59–60)—she is genuine in lamenting that "The crown o' th' earth doth melt", and she is quite humbled:

> No more but e'en a woman, and commanded
> By such poor passion as the maid that milks
> And does the meanest chares.   (ll. 73–75)

Some appreciation of Antony's worth, now that he is no more, comes to her:

>   It were for me
> To throw my sceptre at the injurious gods,
> To tell them that this world did equal theirs
> Till they had stol'n our jewel.   (ll. 75–78)

But there is no admitting, apparently no perception, of the fact that she is responsible for his defeat and death. Her self-pity, her concentration on self, makes it impossible for her to see the situation objectively. If she could see it objectively, she would not be Cleopatra. It is her very Cleopatra-ness that is the basis for her ultimate tragedy. If she were a Juliet she would kill herself immediately for love of Antony, not merely talk about suicide. The fact that she does not act but talks precludes any interpretation of her tragedy as a love tragedy, even though there is pathos in her

>   what's brave, what's noble,
> Let's do it after the high Roman fashion
> And make death proud to take us.   (ll. 86–88)

She has learned something; she has gained unconsciously some insight into what virtue, Roman virtue as embodied by Antony, is. There is no sneering now at "a

Roman thought" (I. ii. 87). But though she knows no "friend / But resolution and the briefest end", she is yet a long way from declaring "Husband, I come"; her tragedy is by no means yet manifest.

When we next see her (V. ii) some time has elapsed; she still talks of suicide, but not of "the briefest end": "My desolation does begin to make / A better life." Better than what? Since she immediately speaks of Caesar and his subjection to Fortune, she will show a "life" superior to his by doing that which ends all the influence of Fortune. Is it unconscious irony that she uses the word "life" in speaking of the ending of her life? Her whole speech (ll. 1–8) is of herself in relation to Caesar, and she does not attempt suicide until the Roman guardsmen make a move to capture her. Meanwhile she has parleyed with Proculeius and through him made a bid for pity from Caesar—"a queen his beggar"—and professes "A doctrine of obedience". But she adds, significantly, "and would gladly / Look him i' th' face" (ll. 31–32).

When she is prevented from killing herself (not for love of Antony but to forestall capture) she moans,

> Where art thou, death?
> Come hither, come! Come, come, and take a queen
> Worth many babes and beggars.   (ll. 46–48)

The real reason for her attempted suicide is made plain by her outburst after Proculeius' "O, temperance, lady!":

> Sir, I will eat no meat; I'll not drink, sir;
> If idle talk will once be necessary,
> I'll not sleep neither. This mortal house I'll ruin,
> Do Caesar what he can. Know, sir, that I
> Will not wait pinion'd at your master's court
> Nor once be chastis'd with the sober eye
> Of dull Octavia. Shall they hoist me up
> And show me to the shouting varlotry
> Of censuring Rome? Rather a ditch in Egypt
> Be gentle grave unto me! Rather on Nilus' mud
> Lay me stark-nak'd and let the waterflies
> Blow me into abhorring! Rather make
> My country's high pyramides my gibbet
> And hang me up in chains!   (V. ii. 49–62)

Proculeius had been commended to her by Antony (IV. xv. 47–48), but he has proved untrustworthy. When Dolabella follows and attempts to gain her confidence by "Most noble Empress, you have heard of me?" (V. ii. 71), she tests him: "You laugh when boys or women tell their dreams; / Is't not your trick?" He does not understand what she means, and is puzzled as she pours out an elaborate eulogy of Antony (ll. 79ff.). She glorifies Antony's power and bounty and wins

Dolabella's sympathy to the degree that he answers truthfully her question as to what Caesar intends to do with her: lead her in triumph in Rome.[19] She has told Dolabella that she "dreamt there was an Emperor Antony" and asked whether "there was or might be such a man / As this I dreamt of". It appears that she was giving him an opportunity to assure her that Caesar, now Emperor, is such a man;[20] since he did not respond affirmatively, she puts her direct question. Immediately after his answer, Caesar enters.

It is through the glorified Antony of her dream that the audience is made aware of the fact that Cleopatra now has gained some conception of the worth of Antony. But that is in retrospect; she indicated no such recognition while Antony was alive. The idealization of Antony in the dream contrasts with the unideal realism of her treatment of him while he lived. (Dramatically, the idealized Antony comes between the deceitful Proculeius and the cold, unmalleable Caesar. Cleopatra's acquired recognition of Antony's excellence cannot be left to the very end of the play but must be made evident, for it is vital to the formation of her tragedy.) But she is in many ways still the former Cleopatra; she schemes, and uses a new device to arouse pity for herself. There is no admission of responsibility for what has happened, no hint of a sense of guilt. And she obviously has not given up hope of a future if one can be contrived that is not shameful to her. That future depends on what she can gain from Caesar.

Since she is still alive and has not become penitent nor admitted—even realized—any responsibility for the dire situation she is now in, it is inevitable that she should carry on. Indeed the force of momentum, not checked by a change in character, leads the audience to anticipate an attempt to captivate Caesar: Julius Caesar, Pompey, Antony; and now Octavius is Caesar, the world's greatest.[21] And it is to be expected that she will use the old tools, or rather the most effective one, the appeal to pity.[22] When Caesar enters, she kneels to him:

> Sir, the gods
> Will have it thus. My master and my lord
> I must obey;   (V. ii. 115–117)

then

> Sole sir o' th' world,
> I cannot project mine own cause so well
> To make it clear; but do confess I have
> Been laden with like frailties which before
> Have often sham'd our sex.

Caesar's response gives her little encouragement, ending as it does with a threat:

> If you apply yourself to our intents,
> Which towards you are most gentle, you shall find
> A benefit in this change; but, if you seek

To lay on me a cruelty by taking
Antony's course, you shall bereave yourself
Of my good purposes, and put your children
To that destruction which I'll guard them from
If thereon you rely.

There follows the Seleucus incident. Whether she is providing for herself if she should have a future or, as some think, tries to convince Caesar by the planned exposure of her concealing half her wealth that she has no intention of following "Antony's course", or has contrived the whole thing as a means of eliciting pity, she unquestionably utilizes it for the latter purpose:

O Caesar, what a wounding shame is this,
That thou vouchsafing here to visit me,
Doing the honour of thy lordliness
To one so meek, that mine own servant should
Parcel the sum of my disgraces by
Addition of his envy! Say, good Caesar,
That I some lady trifles have reserv'd,
Immoment toys, things of such dignity
As we greet modern friends withal; and say
Some nobler token I have kept apart
For Livia and Octavia—must I be unfolded
With one that I have bred? The gods! It smites me
Beneath the fall I have. . . .
Be it known that we, the greatest, are misthought
For things that others do; and, when we fall,
We answer others' merits in our name,
Are therefore to be pitied.   (V. ii. 159–171; 176–179)

But her flattery, her profession of complete subjection to him, and her tearful appeals for pity have no effect on the astute Caesar, who answers her by the royal "we" and to her final, more quaveringly piteous "My master and my lord," says bluntly, "Not so. Adieu." She has done her best, but her practised methods, particularly the previously much-used plea for pity, do not touch Caesar. And when he leaves she is vehement in her outburst—"He words me, girls, he words me", and adds "that I should not / Be noble to myself!"[23] There is nothing left for her but to fall back on her resolution. The confirmation by Dolabella of what he had already told her about Caesar's intentions and his specifications of a time limit,

Caesar through Syria
Intends his journey, and within three days
You with your children will he send before,   (V. ii. 200–202)

incites her to immediate action. She describes vividly to Iras the exhibition Caesar would make in Rome of Iras and herself (she would no doubt include Charmian if

she were then present) and applauds Iras' determination to pluck out her eyes
rather than see it—

> Why, that's the way
> To fool their preparation, and to conquer
> Their most absurd intents.

Caesar having proved to be untouched, she reverts to the scene of her conquest
of Antony:

> Show me, my women, like a queen. Go fetch
> My best attires. I am again for Cydnus,
> To meet Mark Antony.   (II. 227–229)

With an implied confession of dillydallying, she declares:

> My resolution's plac'd, and I have nothing
> Of woman in me. Now from head to foot
> I am marble-constant. Now the fleeting moon
> No planet is of mine.[24]   (II. 238–241)

In her final moments, as she carries out her resolution, Cleopatra has "immortal longings", hears Antony call, gloats over outwitting Caesar, addresses Antony as "husband", shows jealousy in her fear that Iras may gain the first otherworld
kiss from Antony, sneers at Caesar again, speaks lovingly to the asp at her breast,[25]
and dies with "Antony" on her lips and with a final fling of contempt for the world.
But, it should be noted, she does not "do it after the high Roman fashion", nor with
the singleness of motive that actuated Antony, whose tragedy gains ironical poignancy because he thought Cleopatra—really the lying Cleopatra—had anticipated
him in nobility (IV. xiv. 55–62).

Does she kill herself to be with Antony or to escape Caesar? It is the final
question, to be placed along with others. Would she have killed herself if she could
have added Caesar to her string of "greats"? Why did she leave the battle of
Actium? Why did she urge Antony to fight at sea? Did she betray Antony in the
second sea-fight? What was the meaning of her "O"? Why did she behave in such
a way as to lose her country instead of preserve it? Did she ever really love Antony
or did she love herself for having captivated him? Why did she tease, taunt, and
cross Antony, very rarely saying anything kind to him? These questions, and others
that could be asked, show that it was not accidental that the first word she speaks
in the play is "If". The appropriate symbol for her is a big interrogation point.

There is testimony, of course, by Antony and especially by Enobarbus, the
clear-headed, cynical logician, as to her infinite variety. Somehow she has enchanted
the world's greatest men, and she is beloved by her attendants, even to the death.
But in her behavior throughout the play, from the effrontery of her appearing on
the Cydnus to her wily proceedings with Octavius Caesar, there are repeated
evidences that she is unaccountable. It is certain that Antony never penetrates her

real character; he may call her gypsy and witch, but that is begging the question. How, in the face of and through his presentation of Cleopatra's behavior to Antony, does Shakespeare make of her a force powerful enough to bring about the downfall of the great Antony? Does he not supply the answer, paradoxically, by depicting her as the world's great question mark, alluring and magnetic because of all the unanswerable questions about her? Does he not imply that the secret of her charm lies in the fact that neither Antony nor we (including Shakespeare himself) can identify the secret of her charm? Such an interpretation was suggested by Gamaliel Bradford many years ago but apparently disregarded by most commentators on the play:

> I have said that Cleopatra was mysterious. Perhaps it is an element of the art of Shakespeare to puzzle us a little, to make us feel that we cannot interpret him always conclusively. It detracts nothing from the truth of his characters that we cannot always determine what their motives are as we can with that poor little creature of Dryden. . . . I, at least, do not feel clear as to her good faith to Antony. That she loves him there is no doubt at all, loves him as she is capable of loving. But it is more than doubtful whether she kills herself for love of him or in sheer desperation to avoid the scorn and vengeance of Caesar. I greatly fear that if she had been confident of Caesar's favor, confident of reigning in Rome as she had reigned in Alexandria, Antony's poor dust might have tossed forgotten in the burning winds of Egypt. And yet, I do not know—who can know? That is precisely what gives the character its charm.[26]

But whatever interpretation of Cleopatra's character may be given—and to survey all that has been said would demand a volume devoted to her—the final question remains: What is *her tragedy?* One can agree with Willard Farnham's statement (p. 174) that "It is part of her tragedy that with her subtlety she wins control of his [Antony's] force and by winning this control ruins him and herself", but that is hardly the whole story. Nor is it satisfactory to become rhapsodic, to glorify Cleopatra beyond warrant, as J. Middleton Murry does:

> Now [after Antony's death] in very deed, Cleopatra loves Antony: now she discerns his royalty, and loyalty surges up in her to meet it. Now we feel that her wrangling with Caesar and her Treasurer which follows is all external to her—as it were a part which she is still condemned to play 'in this vile world': a mere interruption, an alien interlude, while the travail of fusion between the order of imagination and love, and the order of existence and act is being accomplished: till the flame of perfect purpose breaks forth [V. ii. 226–229 quoted]. No, not *again* for Cydnus: but now for the first time, indeed. For that old Cydnus, where the wonder pageant was, was but a symbol and preparation of this. That was an event in time; this is an event in eternity. And those royal robes were then only lovely garments of the body,

now they are the integument of a soul. They must show her like a queen, now, because she *is* a queen, as she never was before. (Pp. 375–376)

Much nearer to the text of the play and to all the evidence is E. E. Stoll:

> ... in [an] ... audacious, sensuous key, for all her exaltation, she expresses herself on her deathbed. She is tenderer with her women, and stronger and more constant, than she has ever been; but her thoughts of Antony, though now an inviolable shade, are not celestial or Platonic. They are steeped in amorousness, and she is waiting, coiled on her couch. She loves him more than at the beginning; but neither now nor at his death is she, as Professor Schücking declares, "all tenderness, all passionate devotion and unselfish love"; nor does she quit life because it is not worth the living. On life she really never loosens her greedy grip. Her beauty she clutches to her dying bosom as the miser does his gold. Her robe and jewels are, even in death, assumed to heighten the impression of it upon Caesar—though only to show him what he has missed. She hears Antony mock him now, from over the bitter wave; and at the beginning of the scene she cried,
>
> go fetch
> My best attires; I am again for Cydnus—
>
> as one who, to please both him and herself, and vex their rival, would fain die at her best, reviving all the glories of that triumph. To an ugly death she could scarcely have brought herself; ... the death which ... she is choosing and devising [is] ... an event, a scene, well-nigh an amour ... she thinks the stroke of death is as a lover's pinch, which hurts and is desired. ... she is wrapped and folded up in sensuous imaginations to the end.[27]

Indeed, to have Cleopatra glorified and transfigured is to forgive her treatment of Antony, to imply that it was well worth the destruction of the great Roman to bring about her regeneration. If the tragedy of Antony and the tragedy of Cleopatra are to interact to intensify each other, it is necessary *not* to have a transfiguration of Cleopatra; the poignancy of Antony's tragedy is intensified by Cleopatra's unregeneracy, and it increases the pathos and tragedy of Cleopatra that she is never penitent, not even conscious of the debacle she has wrought. That she does change somewhat, that she does attain some realization of what Antony was, is to be recognized. That she did not realize it earlier, and to a much greater degree, is her tragedy: the too little and the too late. Thus the tragedy of Cleopatra is different in kind from that of Antony; the play contains the tragedy of Antony and then the tragedy of Cleopatra.

The "too little" involves a considerable pathetic element. Cleopatra, though appearing on the Cydnus as Venus, is really Isis in environment, interests, and obsessions. Of that the fertility connotations made obvious in the conversation of her companions Iras and Charmian with the Soothsayer (I. ii), the Nile imagery frequent in the play, and the trend of Cleopatra's own thoughts as revealed in her speeches give plentiful proof. Her basic interests show themselves in her imagination as she visualizes Antony in Rome (I. v. 19ff.). They permeate the glowing dream of Antony she describes to Dolabella, as she concentrates on Antony's power and his bounty (not on aspects of character and personal qualities). They suffuse her final speeches; "but even then what emerges is a state of trance, a vision of the divine lover Antony, filling Heaven and Earth, the kiss of the bridegroom, Love lifted to a higher plane among the Homeric gods, all an aspiration and a wild desire, the eagle and the dove."[28] This last characterization of her vision is over-etherealized; a more moderate statement is Willard Farnham's:

> If we are to understand that the love of Cleopatra for Antony, like her character, continues to be deeply flawed to the end of her life, we are nevertheless to understand that, like her character, it has its measure of nobility. If Cleopatra never comes to have a love for Antony to match his love for her, she at least comes to have magnificent visions of what it would be like to achieve such a love, and her climactic vision leads her to call him husband as she dies. (P. 202)

To that extent we may credit Cleopatra with some ennobling; but it is just enough to intensify and illuminate her tragedy. "She's good, being gone; / The hand could pluck her back that shov'd her on", said Antony (I. ii. 130–131), on hearing of Fulvia's death. Cleopatra only after Antony's death comes to some realization of what he was; he's good, being gone. Only after he is wounded or dead does she call him "noble"; only in a sort of funeral hymn does she recognize his power and bounty. But she never feels any sense of guilt such as Antony confesses; there is no *peccavi;* there is no repentance, no consciousness even, of the need for remorse. She is no Othello; her tragedy can be only partial, not complete. The picture she imagines of rejoining Antony in another world could never become actual; she still would have considerable explaining to do.

Cleopatra's tragedy is inherent in her equivocality, in her utter self-interest, and in her complete ignorance of the existence of an unselfish love apart from the physical. She has had no comprehension of Roman virtues, no recognition of Antony's fundamental character, no appreciation of his courtesy and devotion to her. She gloried in his greatness as a soldier and as the most powerful of the triumvirs, not for his sake but for her own—and undermined both his military prowess and his power. She evinces, throughout the play, little concern about the country of which she is queen; she is woman, not queen, in her interests and behavior. She is as innocent of morality as Falstaff of honor. But she does learn something, through frustration and suffering, of what virtue—Roman virtue— means. It is pathetic and tragic that a beginning of anything other than sensual self-interest comes when there is neither the opportunity nor the time for growth to ensue. In that irony—in the too little and the too late—lies her tragedy. That is all the tragedy there is for her, but it is none the less profound, and gains poignancy through contrast to Antony's as his gains pathos through contrast to hers.

NOTES

[1] *The London Shakespeare* (N.Y., 1957), VI, 1213.
[2] *Shakespeare* (London, 1936), p. 372.
[3] *Shakespeare's Life and Art* (London, 1939), p. 178.
[4] *Nature in Shakespearian Tragedy* (London, 1955), p. 123.
[5] *Approach to Shakespeare* (Oxford, 1931), p. 90.
[6] *Shakespeare's Use of Learning: An Inquiry into the Growth of His Mind and Art* (San Marino, 1953), p. 315.
[7] The answer is hardly to be found in the multitudinous pages that have been written about her. An excellent summary of the varying, antithetical interpretations of Cleopatra is given in Daniel Stempel's "The Transmigration of the Crocodile", *Shakespeare Quarterly*, VII (1956), 59–62.
[8] Not all critics recognize the teasing; for instance, J. Dover Wilson:
> ... when the lovers enter..., we learn from their lips that this same love is more spacious than 'the wide arch of the ranged empire', more precious than kingdoms or the whole 'dungy earth', and so boundless that it requires 'new heaven, new earth' to contain it. (*Antony and Cleopatra*, ed. Wilson, Cambridge, 1950, p. xviii);
and Robert Speaight:
> But when Antony and Cleopatra enter upon the stage, lost to everything but each other, their rapture is almost liturgical, and we remember the first meeting of Romeo and Juliet. (Pp. 127–128)
It is surely inaccurate to give the speeches of Antony and Cleopatra equal import, to fail to discriminate between the tone of her two lines and that of his two (I. i. 14–17).
[9] Citations and quotations are based on the Kittredge edition of *Antony and Cleopatra* (Boston, 1941).
[10] Some critics have interpreted the "Courteous lord" speech differently; e.g., H. N. Hillebrand:
> Until now Cleopatra has been desperately trying, with all the battery of her wit and sarcasm, to stave off the moment of parting. When at last she sees that Antony is inflexible, that he is in fact on the point of strategic flight, she suddenly breaks, abandons her attack, and becomes wholly the unhappy, loving woman. (*Antony and Cleopatra*, "The Arden Shakespeare", Boston, 1926, p. 145.)
But she does not "abandon her attack"; she merely changes tactics.
[11] North's Plutarch, "*Antonius* ... sent to command *Cleopatra* to appeare personally before him, when he came into CILICIA, to aunswere vnto such accusations as were laide against her, being this: that she had aided *Cassius* and *Brutus* in their warre against him. ... Therefore when she was sent vnto by diuers letters, both from *Antonius* himselfe, and also from his friendes, she made so light of it and mocked *Antonius* so much, that she disdained to set forward otherwise, but to take her barge in the riuer of Cydnus," etc.
[12] *Shakespeare Studies* (N.Y., 1927), p. 29.
[13] *Poets and Playwrights* (Minneapolis, 1930), p. 2.
[14] Enobarbus, in saying to Cleopatra,
> What though you fled
> From that great face of war whose several ranges
> Frighted each other?   (III. xiii. 4–6)
is not concerned with arguing about her reason for leaving; he is condemning Antony for having followed her (II. 6–12).
[15] The Folio "Oh" followed by a period may suggest only a distressful moan; Thyreus goes on speaking as if he heard nothing. Maybe modern editors imply too much by inserting an exclamation point.
[16] "And she gives Thyreus her hand to kiss. Perhaps she finds him rather good-looking; certainly she is musing on former, or on future, conquests" (Speaight, p. 142).
[17] G. B. Harrison calls that speech "the first outburst of genuine emotion that she has yet shown", and adds, "It is difficult to know at this point whether Cleopatra is loyal or false; probably she does not know herself" (*Shakespeare's Tragedies*, London, 1951, p. 218).
[18] War, "all the snares the world can set" (M. R. Ridley, rev. ed. in the "Arden Edition of the Works of William Shakespeare," p. 171), or Caesar?

[19] "Why, we may ask, should she be worried about what Caesar means to do with her if she has fully made up her mind to leave the dull world that no longer contains Antony?" (Willard Farnham, *Shakespeare's Tragic Frontier: The World of His Final Tragedies*, Berkeley, 1950, p. 198).

[20] This Dolabella incident has been interpreted in various ways. For instance, G. S. Griffiths (*"Antony and Cleopatra"*, *Essays and Studies . . . English Ass'n*, XXXI [1946], 64): "Cleopatra turns this great engine of poetry on Dolabella, but it remains primarily an apology for suicide and a declaration of faith in a love, a person that has been and is no more in time." And, more realistically, A. H. Tolman ("Act V of *Antony and Cleopatra*", *Falstaff and Other Shakespearean Topics*, N.Y., 1925, pp. 166–167):

> This high-sounding praise of her last lover is wholly genuine. . . . But Cleopatra is an infinite coquette . . . she has never been able to 'see an ambassador, scarcely even a messenger, without desiring to bewitch him'; and only death can put an end to her instinctive longing to fascinate men . . . Cleopatra is eloquent both because she is praising her beloved Antony, and because she is captivating Dolabella. Her rapturous words are about Antony, but they are also directed at her new admirer. . . . Dolabella . . . returns to declare his love, to give the queen the fullest possible information, and to take a last farewell.
>
> Most students of Shakespeare do not seem to realize the full force of this embryonic love-affair, acting itself out before us on the very brink of the grave.

[21] "Each person [in a book or play] must behave in character; that means that he must do what from their [the readers'] knowledge of him they expect him to do" (Somerset Maugham, *The Summing Up*, Chap. 72).

[22] The sequence of seeing, pitying, and loving is explicitly stated, though by a woman for a man in this instance, in *The Two Noble Kinsmen* II. iv. 7, 11, 14–15:

> Daughter: First, I saw him;
> . . . next I pitied him;
> . . . then I loved him,
> Extremely lov'd him, infinitely lov'd him.

Cleopatra's envisioning this possible sequence is suggested by her words to Proculeius, V. ii. 30–32; she wishes, of course, to be in Caesar's presence that he may see and pity her:

> I hourly learn
> A doctrine of obedience, and would gladly
> Look him i' th' face.

[23] Apparently "a desire to save herself from the ignoble fate that Caesar plans for her" (Farnham, *Shakespeare's Tragic Frontier*, p. 199). But is that really all she means?

[24] Shakespeare here reflects the contemporary popularity of Virgil's "Varium et mutabile semper/ Femina" (*Aeneid*, IV. 569–570).

[25] "The asp, wriggling its way from the basket to her breast, carries more than its mortal sting; it bears the salt and savour of all that natural life whose passionate child Cleopatra had been. The asp is very much more than a theatrical convenience; it is the symbol of nature reclaiming one part of its own" (Speaight, p. 139).

[26] "The Serpent of Old Nile", *Poet Lore*, X (1898), 529–530.

[27] *Poets and Playwrights*, pp. 14–16.

[28] Griffiths, p. 42.

Marilyn L. Williamson

PATTERNS OF DEVELOPMENT IN *ANTONY AND CLEOPATRA*

In a convincing article modestly entitled "Cleopatra's Scene with Seleucus: Plutarch, Daniel, and Shakespeare," Brents Stirling has outlined the pattern of Cleopatra's behavior from the death of Antony to her own suicide:

> I hope to show that Shakespeare's achievement is largely a structural one, an arrangement of parallel scenes in cumulative order. Each of them presents the old Cleopatra of whim and contradiction who can hold the stage as a new Cleopatra is suddenly revealed. And each time the process is more telling. Preparatory scenes thus set a pattern which is repeated with great effect in the Seleucus episode. As a result the audience, not mystified but in a proper state of wonder and expectation, is ready for Cleopatra's final role. . . . Hence in IV. xv a dialectic of resolution and back-sliding, selflessness and vanity—all of it in Cleopatra's provocative style—prepares for a decisive turn that ends the episode. The scene thus becomes a model for two subsequent scenes, including the Seleucus incident.[1]

My purpose here is to demonstrate that there are throughout the play as a whole similar patterns in Cleopatra's conduct which unify her infinite variety, that there are perceptible stages in her development, and that Shakespeare has so developed the earlier portion of the drama, where he is creating virtually out of whole cloth, that it prepares structurally for the later parts of the play where he is following Plutarch closely. This last effect gives this diverse play a unity which critics are just now beginning to notice.[2]

In I. iii, Cleopatra, sensing that Antony may be distracted by the messenger from Rome, sends Alexas to lie about her state:

> See where he is, who's with him, what he does:
> I did not send you. If you find him sad,
> Say I am dancing; if in mirth, report
> That I am sudden sick. Quick, and return.　　　　　　(I. iii. 2–5)[3]

From *Tennessee Studies in Literature* 14 (1969): 129–39.

Charmian protests that Cleopatra should not constantly cross Antony: "Tempt him not so far. I wish, forbear; / In time we hate that which we often fear." Charmian's observation is a prediction of the fatal episode later in the play, when Antony has come virtually to hate Cleopatra because of his repeated fear that she has betrayed him to Caesar and his rage frightens her into a disastrous repetition of the earlier inconsequential behavior—she sends another servant to tell another lie, the one about her death. Mardian's manner in telling Antony echoes the posturing that is the mode of conduct in the early part of the play:

> What thou wouldst do
> Is done unto thy hand: the last she spake
> Was "Antony! most noble Antony!"
> Then in the midst a tearing groan did break
> The name of Antony; it was divided
> Between her heart, and lips: she render'd life
> Thy name so buried in her.   (IV. xiv. 28–34)

Lest we conclude, however, that Cleopatra is all wiles and scheming at the beginning, Shakespeare gives her a scene (I. iii) in which she strongly anticipates her demeanor at the end of the play. As Antony prepares to leave Egypt for Rome, Cleopatra has railed against him, reproached him for loving and not loving Fulvia, accused him of falsehood and betrayal (justifiably: what is the male counterpart of a "triple-turned whore"?), revealed her wiles ("I am quickly ill, and well, / So Antony loves."), and mocked him: "Look, prithee, Charmian, / How this Herculean Roman does become / The carriage of his chafe." The instant, however, she realizes that Antony is resolved, her tone becomes dignified and deep in feeling:

> Courteous lord, one word:
> Sir, you and I must part, but that's not it:
> Sir, you and I have lov'd, but there's not it;
> That you know well, something it is I would,—
> O, my oblivion is a very Antony,
> And I am all forgotten.   (86–91)

Antony, slower to shift emotional gears than she, calls our attention to the change by not understanding it:

> But that your royalty
> Holds idleness your subject, I should take you
> For idleness itself.

In reminding the audience of her royalty Antony prepares them for the tone of her final lines to him, when she utters what Ornstein has called "the finest Roman words of the play":[4]

> Your honour calls you hence,
> Therefore be deaf to my unpitied folly,
> And all the gods go with you! Upon your sword
> Sit laurel victory, and smooth success
> Be strew'd before your feet!

The transformation she effects here becomes a kind of rehearsal for the larger one she is to undergo to end her life and the play; the process and character ingredients remain constant: the seriousness of the action changes. Here she is parting from a lover who can return to her; later she is parting from life and there is no return; but in both cases she rises to the occasion.

The next time (I. v) we see Cleopatra her wantonness is ascendant, and yet, even as the ripe sensuality of her court is developed through her bawdy talk with waiting women and eunuch, we are made constantly aware of the grandeur of her life and of her regal station. If she has played the whore, it has been with none less than the greatest in the world: broad-fronted Caesar and great Pompey preceded Antony, the man of men, in her favor. When Alexas arrives from Antony, he brings not only a pearl as love token, but news of the political implications of their love as well:

> "Good friend," quoth he,
> "Say the firm Roman to great Egypt sends
> This treasure of an oyster; at whose foot
> To mend the petty present, I will piece
> Her opulent throne with kingdoms. All the east,
> (Say thou) shall call her mistress."   (I. v. 42–47)

At the end of the scene we are simultaneously conscious of Cleopatra's enormous power and of the frivolous uses to which she puts it through her conversation with Alexas about the "twenty several messengers" she has sent to Antony and her final assertion that "he shall have every day a several greeting, / Or I'll unpeople Egypt." We leave the scene with a mingled impression of Cleopatra's lively vanity and her regal position and with a curiosity about whether her conduct will parody or dignify her role.

That impression is reinforced when the unfortunate messenger brings her news of Antony's marriage to Octavia (II. v). Cleopatra's reaction is memorable and conforms both to her earlier threat to give Charmian bloody teeth and to her later treatment of Seleucus.[5] And, in anticipation of what is to come later,[6] Cleopatra herself reminds us and herself of the standard of demeanor from which she is falling:

> These hands do lack nobility, that they strike
> A meaner than myself; since I myself
> Have given myself the cause.   (81–83)

Though the shift of tone and manner is neither so complete nor striking as in the parting scene, the shift is there, and through repetition we come to expect it. That this scene anticipates and prepares for the scene with Seleucus is supported not only by the repetition of Cleopatra's threats of violence to a servant, but also by thematic similarities. Both servants tell truths that are distasteful to Cleopatra, a fact which she points out to the audience, and both scenes contain sententious commentary about relations of greater and meaner people. Though she cannot resist threatening the messenger to make him recant the story, she knows she cannot hold him guilty of Antony's untruth to her: "O that his fault should make a knave of thee, / That art not what th'art sure of." Cleopatra's comment to Caesar about Seleucus is an interesting reversal of the same theme, for greater people answer to their servants' conduct:

> Be it known, that we, the greatest, are misthought
> For things that others do; and when we fall,
> We answer others' merits in our name,
> Are therefore to be pitied.   (V. ii. 175–178)

Shakespeare's habit of supplying a comic perspective on his major themes is not absent here either. In a later interview with the same messenger (III. iii) the queen interrogates him about Octavia, and he is careful to avoid another beating by telling her what she wants to hear ("She creeps"). Pleased by what she has heard, Cleopatra reassures herself that the messenger has high standards in his judgment of great women: "The man hath seen some majesty, and should know." Charmian's reply is a high comic touch that offers us a cue for our reaction to her queen: "Hath he seen majesty? Isis else defend! And serving you so long." Her absolute loyalty to Cleopatra is finely balanced by a keen sense of her mistress' foibles, and a good audience should strike for a similar balance.

As in the earlier court scene Shakespeare maintains a complexity of effect by continuous reminders that this is not simply a love story with political implications, but that the love story is itself a power struggle that has divided the world:

> ALEX.:   Good majesty,
> Herod of Jewry dare not look upon you,
> But when you are well pleas'd.
> CLEO.:   That Herod's head
> I'll have: but how, when Antony is gone,
> Through whom I might command it?   (III. iii. 2–6)

In the scenes we have explored Cleopatra's temptation has been to be untrue to her royalty: to let the quean rule the queen. After Actium her temptation is to be untrue to Antony and deal with Caesar to keep her throne. After Antony's death her temptation is to be untrue to herself, for she has lost both Antony and her throne: "He words me, girls, he words me, that I should / Not be noble to myself." In the final paradox of this paradoxical play, as she is noble to herself, she is true to Antony, who is more real to her dead than alive,[7] and finally true as well to her queenly role.

There is a motif in the play that punctuates these stages in Cleopatra's development and allows us to trace it: her hands. They first come to our attention in II. v before the messenger can tell her of Antony's marriage and she concludes from his facial expression that he brings bad news:

> Antonius dead!—If thou say so, villain,
> Thou kill'st thy mistress: but well and free,
> If thou so yield him, there is gold, and here
> My bluest veins to kiss; a hand that kings
> Have lipp'd, and trembled kissing.   (26–30)

Dripping with condescension, the gesture eloquently conveys the spurious royalty Charmian mocks. As Cleopatra herself admits, "These hands do lack nobility."

In the second stage of development the gesture occurs twice and demonstrates Cleopatra's ambivalent loyalties after Actium. In the scene with Thidias she again alludes to a former lover when he asks to kiss her hand:[8]

> Your Caesar's father oft,
> When he hath mus'd of taking kingdoms in,
> Bestow'd his lips on that unworthy place,
> As it rain'd kisses.   (III. xiii. 82–85)

The gesture quickly becomes for us and for Antony a symbol of her potential disloyalty to him:

> To let a fellow that will take rewards,
> And say, 'God quit you!', be familiar with
> My playfellow, your hand; this kingly seal,
> And plighter of high hearts!   (123–126)

He continues to Thidias, again calling our attention to the gesture: "Henceforth / The white hand of a lady fever thee, / Shake thou to look on't."

Like Scarus and Dercetas, Cleopatra follows Antony to the end, and this loyalty, however qualified in her case by the scene with Thidias, is figured forth in a scene that directly contrasts to that with Thidias. After the first, and for Antony successful, battle at Alexandria, he presents Scarus, who has fought with him loyally, to kiss Cleopatra's hand as a reward for his valor. In this halcyon moment the rage against feeders being familiar with his playfellow is gone, and Antony requests the gesture he earlier condemned:

> Behold this man,
> Comment unto his lips thy favouring hand:
> Kiss it, my warrior: he hath fought to-day
> As if a god in hate of mankind had
> Destroy'd in such a shape.   (IV. viii. 22–26)

And then to Cleopatra, "Give me thy hand, / Through Alexandria make a jolly march, / Bear our hack'd targets like the men that owe them." It is a fine touch that Shakespeare adds to Plutarch's narrative, and especially poignant, for we are on the brink of final disaster.

As Antony dies, Cleopatra's hands come to mean her truth to herself; she knows that once he is gone she can trust only herself:

> ANT.:   Gentle, hear me,
> None about Caesar trust but Proculeius.
> CLEO.: My resolution, and my hands, I'll trust,
> None about Caesar.
>
> (IV. xv. 47–50)

And later she demonstrates her resolution in her first suicide attempt:

> GAL.: You see how easily she may be surpris'd:
>   Guard her till Caesar come.
> IRAS: Royal queen!
> CHAR.: O Cleopatra, thou art taken, queen.
> CLEO.: Quick, quick, good hands.
>
> (V. ii. 35–39)

If Shakespeare links Cleopatra's behavior early in the play with that at the end, he also is careful to treat the middle of her development in the same way. As he dramatizes Cleopatra's scene with Thidias, Shakespeare brings to life the following sentence from Plutarch: "He was longer in talk with her than any man else was, and the Queen herself also did him great honour; insomuch as he made Antonius jealous of him."[9] In the play Cleopatra noticeably treats Thidias very much as she treats his master, Caesar, after Antony's death; she speaks of Caesar as if he had won the war rather than simply a battle. Her message to Caesar could easily be transposed to Act V without alteration:

>   Most kind messenger,
> Say to great Caesar this in deputation:
> I kiss his conquering hand: tell him, I am prompt
> To lay my crown at's feet, and there to kneel:
> Tell him, from his all-obeying breath I hear
> The doom of Egypt.
>
> (III. xiii. 73–78)

In the later scene she does in fact kneel to Caesar, saying, "Sir, the gods / Will have it thus, my master and my lord / I must obey" (V. ii. 114–116). Simple observation of the text reveals the close similarity of the two scenes, but comparison of the play with the source reinforces the interpretation. Shakespeare draws from Plutarch's description of the encounter with Caesar some of the dialogue for the scene with Thidias:

> When Caesar had made her lie down again, and sat by her bed's side, Cleopatra began to clear and excuse herself for what she had done, laying all to the fear she had of Antonius.[10]

THID.: He knows that you embrac'd not Antony
As you did love, but as you fear'd him.
CLEO.:   O!
THID.: The scars upon your honour, therefore, he
Does pity, as constrained blemishes,
Not as deserv'd.
CLEO.:   He is a god, and knows
What is most right. Mine honour was not yielded,
But conquer'd merely.   (III. xiii. 56–62)

Now, if we are inclined to be sentimental about Cleopatra's loyalty to Antony and to argue that though she assents to Thidias' insinuations, nothing she says to him indicts her, Shakespeare has included in the episode a detail that hints at her real disaffection from Antony: her allusion to Julius Caesar when Thidias kisses her hand. Caesar has been mentioned twice before in such a way that we come to see Cleopatra's feelings about him as a gauge of her emotional distance from Antony. In Act I, scene v, she begins to think of him as she imagines Antony far from her:

            Broad-fronted Caesar,
    When thou wast here above the ground, I was
    A morsel for a monarch. . . .

But after Alexas arrives with happy news of Antony, Cleopatra threatens to strike Charmian for comparing Caesar and Antony:

CLEO.:   Did I, Charmian,
Ever love Caesar so?
CHAR.:   O that brave Caesar!
CLEO.: Be chok'd with such another emphasis,
Say the brave Antony.
CHAR.:   The valiant Caesar!
CLEO.: By Isis, I will give thee bloody teeth,
If thou with Caesar paragon again
My man of men.
CHAR.:   By your most gracious pardon,
I sing but after you.   (I. v. 66–73)

The tone is light, but the seemingly inconsequential dialogue calls our attention to the comparison. Later when Cleopatra knows that Antony has betrayed her in marrying Octavia, Caesar again comes to mind with the same emotional significance:

CHAR.: Good your highness, patience.
CLEO.: In praising Antony, I have disprais'd Caesar.
CHAR.: Many times, madam.
CLEO.: I am paid for't now.   (II. v. 107–109)

Cleopatra's allusion to Caesar in the scene with Thidias may be taken, then, as a signal of the distance she feels from Antony as she deals with Octavius' deputy.

What changes, therefore, in the course of the drama is not Cleopatra's character, but her circumstances. She is many-minded throughout the play: the mixture of her motives for suicide—love of Antony and fear of Caesar's triumph—is only the culmination of others we have seen before. As her circumstances deepen and become adverse, they call out in her qualities we have known earlier, but we have paid them little heed because the stakes for which she was playing were not high. She develops in a wave-like motion through experiences of increasing intensity to the final occasion—and not without ambiguity and regression.[11] As life closes in on her, Cleopatra rises to part with it in the high Roman fashion, quite as she rose to Roman words of parting with Mark Antony in the beginning. The patterns not only unify her character, but also show us the proportions of our sorrow. In the meeting with Thidias she could hope to retain her throne by betraying Antony, but in the similar one with Caesar she has nothing left to give him for her kingdom. The repetition helps us feel that. The futility of her rage against Seleucus contrasts similarly with her earlier outburst at the messenger. We know Antony will return to her: he has told the soothsayer so. But Seleucus' betrayal sounds a death knell to a fallen ruler. The repetition gives a measure of how much she is the same and how adverse are the conditions that finally call forth the qualities we have but glimpsed before.

We may also relate Cleopatra's development to that of other characters and elements in the play as well.[12] Antony repeatedly rejects Cleopatra, each time with greater intensity until he frightens her into precipitating their final disaster. First he leaves her for Rome and Octavia, only to return as predicted. Then after the defeat at Actium, he reproaches her for flight in battle while Enobarbus blames the debacle squarely on him. This episode is followed quickly by his outburst at the meeting with Thidias, one so intense that it convinces Enobarbus to desert him. All is briefly well between them when in the next battle Antony beats Caesar to his camp, but in the following encounter he is defeated and again convinced that Cleopatra has betrayed him. His fury is this time so great that it leads her to do the very thing he fears—betray him with the lie about her death. Shakespeare found all these events in Plutarch, but he greatly increases the effect of the pattern by compressing the incidents so that the repetition is vivid, by emphasizing more than does Plutarch Antony's rage at Cleopatra in the Thidias episode, and by intensifying the magnitude of Antony's feeling each time.

Enobarbus, who is almost totally Shakespeare's creation, follows a similar line of development as he makes his crucial decision about deserting Antony.[13] This possibility first occurs to him at Actium when he talks of other defections with Canidius and Scarus, but he resolves to remain loyal. When Antony challenges Caesar to single combat, Enobarbus' doubts about his leader rise again, but once more he decides not to desert. Almost immediately thereafter he is tempted by Cleopatra's treatment of Thidias: "Sir, sir, thou art so leaky / That we must leave thee to thy sinking, for / Thy dearest quit thee." Finally, as with Cleopatra so with Enobarbus Antony's rage tips the balance:

> Now he'll outstare the lightning; to be furious
> Is to be frighted out of fear, and in that mood
> The dove will peck the estridge; and I see still,
> A diminution in our captain's brain
> Restores his heart; when valour preys on reason,
> It eats the sword it fights with: I will seek
> Some way to leave him.   (III. xiii. 195–201)

Critics have increasingly accepted the apparently tangential scene on Pompey's barge (II. vii) as a symbolic analogue to the general action of the play.[14] This interpretation is supported by the presence of the same pattern in Menas' temptation of Pompey. The situation is straight out of Plutarch, but the repetition is Shakespeare's, and Menas accents the effect. First he has to make repeated attempts to get Pompey's ear because his master is distracted by efforts to be a solicitous and jovial host. When he finally gets Pompey aside, Menas has to broach the subject three times to his tipsy and astonished leader, each time with renewed impatience and intensity:

> MEN.: I have ever held my cap off to thy fortunes.
> POM.: Thou hast serv'd me with much faith: what's else to say?
> Be jolly, lords.
> ANT.:   These quick-sands, Lepidus,
> Keep off them, for you sink.
> MEN.: Wilt thou be lord of all the world?
> POM.:   What say'st thou?
> MEN.: Wilt thou be lord of the whole world? That's twice.
> POM.: How should that be?
> MEN.:   But entertain it,
> And though thou think me poor, I am the man
> Will give thee all the world.
> POM.:   Hast thou drunk well?
> MEN.: No, Pompey, I have kept me from the cup.
> Thou art, if thou dar'st be, the earthly Jove:
> Whate'er the ocean pales, or sky inclips,
> Is thine, if thou wilt ha't.   (II. vii. 57–69)

The effect reverberates through the play, operating in major and minor characters and scenes alike, and with the same result. It unifies play and character by preparing the audience through anticipating future action; it provides insights into character, a sense of the development of character, and a measure of the emotional intensity and height of the action. But because like the play as a whole, Cleopatra has a rare complexity, it is especially significant with regard to her.

NOTES

[1] *Shakespeare Quarterly,* XV (1964), 305–307.

[2] See, for example, Thomas Stroup, "The Structure of *Antony and Cleopatra,*" *Shakespeare Quarterly,* XV (1964), 289–298.

[3] The text used throughout is the Arden Edition, ed. Case and Ridley (Cambridge, Mass., 1956), and all lineation refers to that edition.

[4] Robert Ornstein, "Love and Art in *Antony and Cleopatra,*" in *Shakespeare: Modern Essays in Criticism,* ed. L. F. Dean (New York, 1967), p. 394.

[5] Stirling, p. 310.

[6] Granville-Barker remarks, "And this is a notable touch. It forecasts the Cleopatra of the play's end, who will seek her death after the 'high Roman fashion'; it reveals, not inconsistency, but that antithesis in disposition which must be the making of every human equation." *Prefaces to Shakespeare* (Princeton, 1946), I, 440.

[7] See R. C. Harrier, "Cleopatra's End," *Shakespeare Quarterly,* XIII (1962), 63–65. It is characteristic of their love that Antony and Cleopatra are more real to each other and to the audience when they are absent from the stage. Never is Cleopatra so vivid as during Enobarbus' barge speech in Rome; the only real tribute Antony pays her comes when he thinks her dead. Similarly her most striking statements about him occur while he is in Rome or after his death.

[8] See below for the significance of Cleopatra's allusions to Julius Caesar.

[9] *Shakespeare's Plutarch,* ed. T. J. B. Spencer (Baltimore, 1964), p. 270.

[10] Ibid., p. 287.

[11] See Stirling, p. 311.

[12] Many commentators on *Antony and Cleopatra* have noted Shakespeare's use (and to some overuse) of repetitive devices in the play. Leo Kirshbaum has commented on iterative imagery in "Shakespeare's Cleopatra," *Character and Characterization in Shakespeare* (Detroit, 1962), pp. 99–110; Stroup has noted structural patterns, "The Structure of *Antony and Cleopatra,*" *passim;* Maurice Charney has also analyzed patterns of imagery in *Shakespeare's Roman Plays* (Cambridge, Mass., 1963); Sylvan Barnet has shown that Antony, Cleopatra, and Enobarbus follow Aristotelian patterns of character development in "Recognition and Reversal in *Antony and Cleopatra,*" *Shakespeare Quarterly,* VIII (1957), 331–334; and P. J. Aldus has discussed analogy in the scene on Pompey's barge in "Analogical Probability in Shakespeare's plays," *Shakespeare Quarterly,* VI (1955), 397–414.

[13] E. C. Wilson says, "Four times the audience sees that desertion is before Enobarbus as a logical course. Each time it appeals more strongly to his highly rational self—'reason' and 'judgment' are recurring words in his speeches—as the only intelligent move; for each time he beholds additional evidence of Antony's folly. A suggestion of desertion grows gradually into the definite resolve with which Enobarbus ends the act," in "Shakespeare's Enobarbus," *J. Q. Adams Memorial Studies,* ed. J. G. McManaway (Washington, D.C., 1948), p. 402.

[14] See Aldus and Stroup in notes above.

Gordon W. Couchman
"THE MOST DANGEROUS OF CAESAR'S CONQUESTS"

What kind of woman was Cleopatra? The name means 'glory of her race'[1] but according to Plutarch Cleopatra's 'glory' lay less in any remarkable beauty than in her irresistible charm of person, her bewitching ways, the sound of her voice.[2] Dio emphasizes Cleopatra's "surpassing beauty", adding that she knew "how to make herself agreeable to everyone".[3] Like Queen Elizabeth I, she was able to conduct her diplomacy in the language of many of the nations with whom she had to deal. Chroniclers and historians from Plutarch to the present, though often writing from widely differing points of view, agree in painting a picture of a woman who combined, to an unusual degree, the caprice of a hoyden with the poise of a matron, the love of life with the sobriety and shrewdness of a born ruler.

In having Enobarbus tell us that age could not wither Cleopatra, "nor custom stale / Her infinite variety", Shakespeare has, of course, fixed for all time an image of Cleopatra that has all but obliterated the historical one. It is Shakespeare's portrait, rather than whatever conjectures history had to offer, that Shaw was thinking of in his own version of the Queen. Shakespeare's Cleopatra speaks of her "salad days" and Shaw goes back to these days in his own portrayal. ⟨...⟩ he had ample justification for doing so in Plutarch, who informs us that Caesar had known her when she was "a girl, ignorant of the world", whereas when she met Antony she was "in the time of life when women's beauty is most splendid, and their intellects are in full maturity".[4] Shaw needed nothing more, and in the Prologue to his comedy which he added in 1912 to facilitate the restoration of Act III to the London revival, Plutarch's young girl reappears as "a child that is whipped by her nurse".

What Cleopatra represented to Shaw is obvious from the justly famous passage to which we have already had occasion to refer in our first chapter. "The very name of Cleopatra suggests at once a tragedy of Circe". The name is ines-

From *This Our Caesar: A Study of Bernard Shaw's* Caesar and Cleopatra (The Hague: Mouton, 1973), pp. 43–50.

capably bound up with a "romantic convention" that has turned the tradition upside down and instead of metamorphosing heroes into hogs, turns hogs into heroes. All this, as we have seen, Shaw considered "intolerable to the true Puritan" as well as "distressing to the ordinary healthy citizen" (note "healthy") because through the grandeur of his "rhetoric" Shakespeare attempts to convince the audience that the "world was well lost by the twain". And we have already seen what Shaw thought of a man, who, like Antony, would run away from a battle for love of his Queen.

Arthur Nethercot has pointed out two references, direct or indirect, to Cleopatra in other Shaw plays. Marcus Darnley's first name in *Heartbreak House* is appropriate since it comes from the name of one of those men who "think the 'world well lost' for vampire women". In the Methuselah cycle, says Nethercot, "Semiramis"–Cleopatra, along with "Ozymandias" is "unemotionally put out of the way by the Ancients, in accordance with Shaw's theory that the person dangerous to society should be destroyed without anger or revenge".[5] The tell-tale phrase "the world well lost" in Shaw's denunciation of Shakespeare's lovers clearly betrays the figure of Dryden's heroine somewhere in the background, although ⟨. . .⟩ Shaw's quarrel is basically with Shakespeare, precisely as he said it was.[6] We shall see in a later chapter how Shaw relates the subject of Puritanism and the "romantic convention" both to Cleopatra and to Caesar. To Shaw this Circe-Cleopatra symbolizes in life everything that he abhorred in the way of emotional self-indulgence and, in the arts, the notion that sexual infatuation is a tragic theme or indeed that the so-called 'love interest' is sufficient at all as a steady diet in literature of any kind, but especially in plays. Shaw might have been describing Hollywood when he wrote:

> It may seem strange, even monstrous, that a man should feel a constant attachment to the hideous witches in Macbeth, and yet yawn at the prospect of spending another evening in the contemplation of a beauteous young leading lady with voluptuous contours and longlashed eyes, painted and dressed to perfection in the latest fashions. But that is just what happened to me in the theatre.[7]

Or when he attacked the "romance in which the hero, also rigidly commercial, will do nothing except for the sake of the heroine".[8] The only answer to this was to take up Plutarch's immature girl as a kind of counterweight, as the heroine of a comedy in which Caesar and not Antony would be the hero, and this Shaw did so thoroughly that one of his most distinguished stage Caesars was to complain at the meagerness of the role he had given Cleopatra.[9] Concerning this turning of the tables one writer was unable to speak temperately: "We cannot", he fumes, "call this funny little girl by the great name", averring that it was not possible to write a farce about Cleopatra, a "holy temple aristocrat", a "prince of women". "Cleopatra", he insists, "can be only a tragic theme".[10] The vehemence of such a protest is a good measure of Shaw's success. In reality, Shaw could have summoned more witnesses than Plutarch. The same critic who objected to the "funny little girl" asserted that our picture of Cleopatra is the result of the slander of Octavius and of Catholic Rome.[11] This contention is borne out in part by Weigall in his biography, which opens with the categorical statement that the generally accepted view of the Queen stems from "those who sided against her in regard to the quarrel between Antony and Octavius", and is essentially "the simple abuse of her opponents".[12] Confirmation of this view of Cleopatra is given by W. W. Tarn in the *Cambridge Ancient History:* "The surviving accounts of her in our late sources largely represent the victor's version . . ."[13] Disputing Josephus' attack on the Queen as a slave to her lusts, Weigall asserts that "There is not a particle of trustworthy evidence to show that Cleopatra carried on a single love affair in her life other than the two recorded so dramatically by history, nor is there any evidence to show that in those two affairs she conducted herself in a licentious manner", and draws in his turn a somewhat sentimentalized picture of a kind of Alexandrian Queen Victoria.[14]

This should have been grist for Shaw's mill if unfortunately it had not appeared a quarter of a century too late. Not only was Cleopatra a mere girl when Caesar knew her; she was never the Oriental sensualist of Shakespeare's creation. Even more interesting to Shaw might have been Ferrero's insistence that the immortal lovers of legend were inescapably involved in the struggle for power between Rome and the East in the persons of the two triumvirs and that Antony himself was by no means so much Cleopatra's slave that he could not remain away from her for long periods of time. Antony's marriage to Cleopatra in 36 B.C. was made for *dynastic* reasons, and the very flight from Actium was based on a prearranged plan whereby Octavius was to be thwarted and Rome brought under the domination of Cleopatra and Antony ruling jointly from Alexandria.[15] Ferrero cites Pliny's account of Antony's fear that Cleopatra was trying to poison him at one time, a detail, says Ferrero, "in no sort of harmony with the love-story imagined by ancient writers, but . . . entirely consistent with the struggle of political interests . . .".[16] All this again is borne out by W. W. Tarn who quietly dissolves the Cleopatra legend with the simple assertion that "the keynote of her character was not sex at all, but ambition". Her love affairs were undertaken with the most deliberate intention of making use of them for political ends. "Perhaps", says this writer, in what ought surely to have made Shaw rub his hands if he had read it, "she never loved any man . . .".[17]

It is interesting to think that Shaw might have given to his girl-queen some concern with policy and greater political astuteness, not only without sacrificing his original conception but even re-enforcing its fundamental logic. Shaw was more nearly right than he knew.

As it is, he shows us a Cleopatra who grows somewhat in wisdom, insight, and the capacity to rule, but only under Caesar's tutelage; and with the best will in the world it is hard to down the suspicion that Shaw vouchsafes even this much grudgingly and that he has shamelessly played down Cleopatra (legendary or otherwise) in order to play up Caesar. The Queen in Shaw's play may be viewed in two contrasting scenes which give us the essence of what Shaw was trying to do.

The first episode is the extended passage climaxing Act I in which Caesar attempts to nerve the scared Cleopatra for the ordeal of meeting her Roman conqueror:

CAESAR [*admiring Cleopatra, and placing the crown on her head*]: Is it sweet or bitter to be a Queen, Cleopatra?
CLEOPATRA: Bitter.
CAESAR: Cast out fear; and you will conquer Caesar.   (I, 111)

It is one of the great moments in Shaw, a scene at once indulgent and wise. Its counterpart is in Act IV when Pothinus engages in some verbal sparring with a Cleopatra now, as he says, much changed. "Do you speak with Caesar", retorts Cleopatra, "every day for six months: and you will be changed."

CLEOPATRA: When I was foolish, I did what I liked, except when Ftatateeta beat me; and even then I cheated her and did it by stealth. Now that Caesar has made me wise, it is no use my liking or disliking: I do what must be done, and have no time to attend to myself. That is not happiness; but it is greatness . . . (IV, 163)

So Napoleon had spoken in *The Man of Destiny* (1895): "Happiness is the most tedious thing in the world to me. Should I be what I am if I cared for happiness?" (P. 168) So had Marchbanks spoken at the end of *Candida* (1894–5): "I no longer desire happiness: life is nobler than that." (III, 140) So also was Ann Whitefield to speak in 1903 offering in *Man and Superman* what Chesterton called "the only defense great enough" to cover her cynical pursuit of John Tanner: "It will not be all happiness for me. Perhaps death." (IV, 163) So also Undershaft to Cusins in *Major Barbara* (1905): "From the moment when you become Andrew Undershaft, you will never do as you please again." (III, 327) And so also Ellie Dunn of *Heartbreak House* (1919) commenting on Mangan's suffering: "His heart is breaking; that is all . . . When your heart is broken, your boats are burned. Nothing matters any more. It is the end of happiness and the beginning of peace." (II, 108) And when Ellie discovers that there is nothing she could not do, because she wants nothing, the Captain praises her: "Thats the only real strength. Thats genius." (II, 115)[18]

Between this scene and the preceding, the "child whipped by her nurse" has grown up in a sense, though as a character she has not gained in depth to any appreciable degree.[19] Before the end of the play she takes upon herself the responsibility for the murder of Pothinus only to cringe when Caesar calls her to account; her vindictiveness is a living demonstration of the meanness of that spirit of vengeance which Caesar has already repudiated once and now rejects with even greater intensity. At the opening of the play Cleopatra is afraid; at the end she has overcome fear sufficiently to talk up to Caesar. But all in all she is a poor second best to Caesar, who shows more interest in naming Rufio governor of Egypt than in saying goodbye to the Queen, and in fact, almost forgets to say goodbye at all.

Arthur Nethercot quotes Ftatateeta's impatient remark to Cleopatra in the play: "You want to be what these Romans call a New Woman"—one of the numerous topical allusions in the play. Professor Nethercot comments: "However much Cleopatra may want to be a New Woman, she is incapable of being anything but a womanly woman."[20] Cleopatra dreams not of Caesar's love but of the "young man with strong round arms", Antony, whom Caesar wryly promises to send to her from Rome, thereby prompting Rufio to exclaim scornfully: "You are a bad hand at a bargain, mistress, if you will swop Caesar for Antony." (V, 193) So Michelet (1798–1874) described Antony: ". . . a proud and pompous actor, who imitated Caesar without understanding the part".[21] "A spark of Caesar", says the *Cambridge Ancient History,* "glowed smokily in Antony and was extinguished: there remained Octavian."[22]

It is perhaps too much to expect of Shaw that he take into account Cleopatra's return visit to Rome and the supposition that her son Caesarion was Caesar's child. Arthur Nethercot reminds us that Shaw "artfully suppresses" the fact that Cleopatra paid a return visit to Caesar in Rome and there, according to some chroniclers, bore him a son, Caesarion.[23] Perhaps "suppresses" is too strong, since Mommsen's account stops short of Caesar's return to Rome and of course therefore says nothing about a visit to Rome or the birth of Caesarion. Moreover, Shaw refers to this episode in his article defending his play at the time of its revival, but asserts that Cleopatra, playing the role of an Alexandrian Ann Whitefield, had to chase Caesar to Rome to hold him.[24] This cavalier treatment of history may easily be corrected; according to Carcopino Caesar wanted Cleopatra in Rome as a matter of policy, but policy did not necessarily exclude amour.[25] Whether Caesarion was Caesar's child is still a matter of controversy, although Octavian evidently suspected enough truth in it to impel him to execute the boy.

Shaw's comedy, it may readily be conceded, ends at the proper point, with Caesar, as Rufio points out, under the shadow of "too many daggers" in the Rome to which he is about to return. Again, it remained for Thornton Wilder, writing in a different medium and in a more subtle vein, to recreate Cleopatra's visit to Rome. Wilder shows us Cleopatra the mother:

> A Queen, great Caesar, may be a mother. Her royal position renders her more, not less, subject to those loving anxieties which all mothers feel . . .
>
> Unfeelingly you have dealt with me, and not only with me but with a child who is no ordinary child, being the son of the greatest man in the world. He has returned to Egypt.[26]

Caesar's mother, the great lady Julia, writes of Cleopatra:

> She drew from a cabinet beside her some admirable paintings of her two children and showed them to me. 'All else', she whispered, 'is like a mirage of our deserts. I adore my children. I could wish to have a hundred. What is there in the world to equal one of those darling heads, those darling fragrant heads? But I am a Queen', she said, looking at me with tears in her eyes. 'I must go

on journeys. I must be busy with a hundred other things. Have you grandchildren?'[27]

And again, Caesar himself tells us:

> With one greatness she is in perfect harmony and on that score I did her a great injustice. I should have permitted her to bring her children here. She does not know it yet to the full; she is that figure which all countries have elevated to the highest honor and awe; she is the mother as goddess. Hence those wonderful traits that I was so long in explaining to myself—her lack of malice, and her lack of that fretful unease to which we are so wearisomely accustomed in beautiful women.[28]

This is a very different Cleopatra from Shaw's, and one that throws into sharp relief Shaw's own conception. It is noteworthy also that in revealing to us a Cleopatra who, far from being a mere child, is a part of the eternal mystery of motherhood, Wilder also gives the Queen credit for statesmanlike qualities even when Caesar knew her; for Caesar in fact her fascination lay in the rare amalgam of gypsy allure and political astuteness:

> Conversation will be a pleasure again. Oh, oh, oh, I have sat holding that catlike bundle on my lap, drumming my fingers on ten brown toes and heard a soft voice from my shoulder asking me how to prevent banking houses from discouraging the industry of the people and what are the just wages of a chief of police relative to those of the governor of a city. Everyone in our world, my Lucius, everyone is lazy in mind except you, Cleopatra, this Catullus, and myself.[29]

In equally sharp contrast to Shaw's conception is Rex Warner's, whose Cleopatra, popping out of Apollodorus' famous bundle, is for Caesar at first "impudent and roguish" but immediately thereafter assumes an aspect of "something strenuous and sublime": "I saw that she was ... indeed a queen."[30]

It is probably unnecessary to elaborate the sharp contrast that exists between this 'heroine' of Shaw's and the women of his other plays. For *Caesar and Cleopatra* is one of those plays in which Shaw allots the dominant role to the male, as opposed to the long procession of aggressive, masculine females in many of his plays, from Vivie Warren to Epifania in *The Millionairess*. To seek any resemblance between Cleopatra and Gloria Clandon in *You Never Can Tell*, though here also is a refreshing study in emotional intensity and feminine conflict, is futile. Both Grace and Julia in *The Philanderer* are take-offs on the Ibsenite "New Woman" but though Shaw makes Ftatateeta label Cleopatra thus, the resemblance stops there. What do Barbara Undershaft and Cleopatra have in common? Or Ann Whitefield? Or Candida? If, as Henderson suggests in his latest biography, Shaw created Candida out of his unconscious craving for a mother's love that he never had had, obviously no trace of such blind motivation will be found in Cleopatra. If, as seems likely, a terrifyingly competent, hideously unromantic, and surprisingly fascinating heroine like Vivie Warren, whom Shaw almost succeeds in endowing with a kind of grandeur, reflects the influence of a mother who had to keep the family going with little help from her husband, Cleopatra shows no remote traces of such a childhood environment, being thoroughly incompetent to assert her own prerogative as Queen until Caesar helps her. These examples are enough to indicate that Cleopatra is in a sense unique among Shaw's female creations; and of course the parallel with Saint Joan is not Cleopatra at all, but Caesar.

NOTES

[1] Arthur Weigall, *The Life and Times of Cleopatra Queen of Egypt*, rev. ed. (New York, 1924), 44, note.
[2] Plutarch, *Antony*, in *Lives*, trans. Bernadotte Perrin (Loeb Classical Library, 1958), IX, 195–197, par. 27.
[3] Dio XLII, 169.
[4] Plutarch, *Antony*, 193, par. 25.
[5] *Men and Supermen: The Shavian Portrait Gallery* (Cambridge, Mass., 1954), Appendix, "What's in a Name", 299, 301 respectively. The passages quoted are from Act I of *Heartbreak House* and the last part of *Back to Methuselah*.
[6] The playwright responsible for what Shaw called "Sardoodledom" made his own contribution to the "world well lost" tradition in a starring vehicle for Sarah Bernhardt. According to one writer, *Cléopâtre* by Sardou was first performed in French in New York in 1891 with Sarah Bernhardt as the Queen, after which it toured the country in an English translation with Fanny Davenport as late as 1898. This was the year in which Shaw wrote *Caesar*. The play appears as a collaboration between Sardou and Emile Moreau with music by Xavier Leroux in vol. IV of the *Théâtre Complet* (Paris, 1935). I have been unable to ascertain whether Shaw knew this play. See Jerome A. Hart, *Sardou and the Sardou Plays* (Philadelphia, 1913), 392–393.
[7] Preface, *Three Plays for Puritans* (1900; Standard Edition London: Constable, 1930), xii.
[8] Preface, *Three Plays for Puritans*, xvii.
[9] Felix Barker, *The Oliviers: A Biography* (London, 1953), 301: Olivier considered that the play left Cleopatra "in mid-air half-way through". He apparently felt that Shaw intended to write a love-story, then out of sheer perversity changed his mind.
[10] Oliver Ellis, *Cleopatra in the Tide of Time* (Timlerley, 1947), 260, 266, and "Synopsis", [1]–2.
[11] Ellis, 266.
[12] Weigall, 3.
[13] *The Cambridge Ancient History* (New York and Cambridge, 1923–39), X, 31.
[14] Weigall, 12. W. W. Tarn and Ronald Syme both point out that it was common practice to vilify enemies through sexual innuendo.
[15] Guglielmo Ferrero, *Characters and Events of Roman History from Caesar to Nero* (New York, 1909), 46, 53–54 and passim. Ferrero does not dispute Cleopatra's power over Antony. See also Sidney Hook, *The Hero in History* (Boston, 1955), 178.
[16] *The Greatness and Decline of Rome*, trans. Alfred E. Zimmern (New York, 1910), IV, "Rome and Egypt" Appendix, 274–275. For the anecdote in Pliny see Bk. XXI, par. IX of the *Natural History*, trans. W. H. S. Jones (Loeb Classical Library, 1961), VI, 169.
[17] *Cambridge Ancient History*, X, 35. Like Ferrero, Tarn fully acknowledges Antony's susceptibility to Cleopatra, "whose only devotion to him was as the instrument of her ambition . . ." Antony's memory is redeemed for us by the fact that in the end he literally lost half the world (which he might have shared with Octavius) for love (66).
[18] Quoted by Arthur Nethercot, *Men and Supermen*, 71. Ellie's words Professor Nethercot calls "a typically Shavian doctrine" (ibid.).
[19] William F. Goodykoontz applies to the early Cleopatra in Shaw's comedy the playwright's own scornful characterization of the "feverish selfish little clod of grievances" to which, in the Epistle Dedicatory of *Man and Superman*, Shaw contrasts the truly vital person, willing to be consumed by life. See

Some Aspects of John Bunyan's Influence on the Art of George Bernard Shaw, unpublished master's thesis (Chapel Hill, 1952), 103–104.

[20] *Men and Supermen,* 82.

[21] Jules Michelet, *History of the Roman Republic,* tr. William Hazlitt (London, 1847), 375. The *History* was originally published in 1839.

[22] *Cambridge Ancient History,* IX, 740.

[23] *Men and Supermen,* 82–83.

[24] *New Statesman* (3 May 1913), 112–113.

[25] Jérôme Carcopino, "César et Cléopâtre", *Annales de l'Ecole des Hautes Etudes de Gand,* Tome I (Ghent, 1937), 47, 51–52.

[26] Thornton Wilder, *The Ides of March* (New York, 1948), 106.

[27] Wilder, 139.

[28] 243–244.

[29] 93.

[30] Rex Warner, *Imperial Caesar* (Boston, 1960), 284.

John Bayley

DETERMINED THINGS: THE CASE OF THE CAESARS

'No character is very strongly discriminated,' observes Dr Johnson of the play ⟨*Antony and Cleopatra*⟩. Fate here seems to have leached out the kinds of individuality we are elsewhere accustomed to. Antony can only evade Caesar or be exasperated by him and dare him to personal combat, and again we are reminded of Cassius' way of escaping the elder Caesar's tyranny. But Cassius and Brutus, though their soldiership was not a patch on Antony's, seemed always to have an even chance of winning, a chance determined from the play's point of view by their whole mode of being and thinking. They are proper persons for conventional tragedy, working out their lot, heroically exposed to the shot of accident and dart of chance and the fatal misunderstanding which causes Cassius' suicide, in which his final words have all the recognition of appropriateness: 'Caesar, thou art revenged, / Even with the sword that killed thee.'

The lack of discrimination that Johnson noted is caused by two things—the mental processes in Antony and the lack of them in Caesar and in Cleopatra. Antony is unique in Shakespearean tragedy in being a lost man from the very beginning. The sense 'of what he has, and has not', is as emphatic in the first scene as it is in his demeanour before the final battle. The ominous precedent is that of Pompey the Great, in his dishonoured grave by the sands of Alexandria, driven to his death by the inflexible will and luck of the first Caesar. Cleopatra recalls him as she muses on her conquests when Antony is away:

> Great Pompey
> Would stand and make his eyes grow in my brow:
> There he would anchor his aspect, and die
> With looking on his life. (I. v. 31–4)

The same doomed paralysis is now to be continuously presented in Antony, but it gives us no sense of participation; no more does its opposite, the unmoved Caesar

---

From *Shakespeare and Tragedy* (London: Routledge & Kegan Paul, 1981), pp. 137–46.

and the equally unmoved Cleopatra. Antony's self in the play engages with neither of them, and for the same reason, that both have such complete confidence in themselves and where they are going. One of the tactics of the piece is the simplification of Cleopatra, by a process that is analogous to the simplification of both Caesars. In all three cases Shakespeare abandons the indications of 'wheels within wheels' in the source, and forgoes the political dimension which it indicates. There is no depth in defence here, no jockeying for position.

For in reality Antony was involved in a complicated political power-game with his rival and his mistress, and Plutarch thoroughly enjoyed revealing the ins and outs so far as he had got wind of them or could embroider on what he had heard. He too is of course turning events into story and illustration. Cleopatra was for Antony a powerful political ally in his attempts to gain hegemony over the whole Middle East, an attempt that even before the break-up of the triumvirate had not been entirely successful. It was not only personally congenial to him but a part of Antony's political manoeuvring to 'go native', a move which though it made him popular in the East compromised his reputation in Rome and Italy. Shakespeare of course ignores such success as he had: what must have struck the playwright's imagination was the way in which the hero's luck had turned. Even the loyalty of Octavia to himself and his family became a political liability, because her dignity and forbearance could not but make excellent propaganda for the Roman side: a consequence on which her brother had no doubt calculated.

Cleopatra, for her part, had put her money on Antony as the best bet not only to retain her kingdom but to further her ambition to become mistress of the Middle East. Her decision to accompany Antony on the Actium campaign, which Shakespeare artfully transmutes into the eternally vacuous wilfulness of the eternal feminine, was in reality a pre-emptive move to ensure that her colleague did not do a deal of his own with Octavius, leaving her out. The treachery and defection of client kings which Antony's Eastern policies had already set in train, was no doubt her fault as much as his, but no more. Though his narrative purposes required him to show how Antony was ruined by Cleopatra and his love for her, Plutarch's narration also reveals them in the clearest fashion as *colleagues*. And colleagues they remained, even in their last days, which in Plutarch's account have something pretentious and repellent about them, as well as sinister, for such episodes occurred as the handing over of Seleucus' wife and children to Antony for torture and death. Seleucus was commandant of the frontier fortress of Pelusium, and Cleopatra committed this deed in order to clear herself of suspicion when the town fell easily to the forces of Octavius Caesar. Shakespeare gives the name to the comic treasurer, who gives her away when she makes a declaration of her assets to Caesar, and he smilingly reassures her: 'Nay, blush not, Cleopatra. I approve / Your wisdom in the deed.'

That seems indeed the extent of Cleopatra's 'naughtiness' in her comedy role. The change, and its significance, are clear. Cleopatra is to be as unremitting in her frivolity as Caesar in his pursuit of power. Between these two blank walls Antony's consciousness drifts to and fro. He can make nothing of them, and impose himself upon neither of them. And this pattern of course determines the general drift and image of the play. The hero is helpless in a unique sense, not like the conditions of any other tragedy.

The second clue which Shakespeare may have taken in his creative imagination of this process is Plutarch's comment on Antony's marriage in his young days, when he was a dissolute favourite of the older Caesar, to Fulvia. Plutarch remarks that in order to exercise self-control over his rackety existence Antony needed the help of a woman of character and strong personality.

> a woman not so basely minded to spend her time in spinning and housewifery, and was not contented to master her husband at home, but would also rule him in his office abroad, and command him that commanded legions and great armies; so that Cleopatra was to give Fulvia thanks that she had taught Antonius this obedience to women, that learned so well to be at their commandment.

Fulvia no doubt made a man of him in some sense, and loved him, for with the help of his brother she did her best to start a civil war in Italy to bring him home. But Cleopatra is a very different sort of woman. She may think herself powerful, and may have appealed to Antony because she seemed so, but in Shakespeare's presentation she is nothing of the sort. She demands attention; she affects authority and purpose; but really, and in her own robust way, she clings and vapours. She loves games and dreams and dressing up, and Antony's past makes him here the most congenial of playfellows. Their deep affection and love for each other here is undoubted, but she is not the woman to inspire him to action, as Fulvia was. Plutarch portrays her as a worthy successor to Fulvia, an enterprising if not altogether trustworthy colleague and comrade; but Shakespeare makes her a wholly different woman, not at all the sort that we may guess Fulvia to have been.

It is a part of Antony's helplessness that he never seems quite to find this out. She teases him, exasperates him, but fascinates him because he will go on against all the evidence in believing her to be stronger than he is. Her 'strength' is like Octavius' 'luck'—an impalpable thing whose influence is fateful to Antony because he so implicitly believes in it. If he is with her she is happy, and it matters not what is going on—peace or war. The latter seems to her a special sort of dressing up. 'I'll give thee, friend, an armour all of gold: it was a king's,' she tells Scarus, after Antony has praised his conduct in the last battle. She buckles on Antony's armour for him and he praises her: 'Thou fumblest, Eros, and my queen's a squire / More tight at this than thou.' This final desperate contest, nothing more than a forlorn gesture against an overwhelmingly strong and prudent enemy, seems in its excitement and innocence just like their Alexandrian revels, their inquisitive wanderings through the night streets together, the joke with the salt fish on the hook which Antony 'with fervency drew up.'

Shakespeare has of course introduced a degree of romantic simplification and stylisation here which is in keeping with the taste of the age. Samuel Daniel had portrayed a very similar Cleopatra in his tragedy of 1594, and Dryden in *All for Love* was to take the hint from Shakespeare and give a total passivity and helplessness to both lovers. Mars and Venus, the conventions of tapestry and emblem, are convenient to the change, and exercise a traditional influence in the scene. But behind it is our sense of the woman herself, and the presentation of her as fatal for Antony in a touching and homely sense. Shakespeare joins on romantic preconceptions of the part to his portrait of a weak woman with a strong personality. Such a woman could not be—as Plutarch's Cleopatra is—in constant communication with Caesar behind Antony's back: when Thidias (Thyreus in Plutarch) comes to treat with her, she behaves with a genuinely girlish naïvety, gratified to flirtatiousness by his courtesies, and professing respectful submission to his master. Neither means anything at all; they are merely symptoms of her instant, effortless way of dealing with every situation by being herself; the impression she gives is one of unbounded equanimity, whether she is giving audience to Caesar's representatives, mourning the fate of Antony, or ordering the asps *sotto voce* from Charmian while saying of Caesar: 'He words me, girls, he words me. . . .'

Shakespeare's sense of omission, and of timing, is perfect to this presentation of her. This Cleopatra could not be mentioned as experimenting on prisoners to see which death was the easiest, though we don't in the least mind hearing after her death that 'She hath pursued conclusions infinite / Of easy ways to die.' Nor could she have joined in the intellectuals' pact, mentioned by Plutarch as the *Synapothanumenon*—'the order and agreement of those that are to die together'—which she and Antony used to celebrate in the last days with their friends. Our Cleopatra is no bluestocking, and neither coldhearted nor methodical. Oddly enough the touch in Plutarch that Shakespeare would normally have delighted to use, and whose incongruity would not in the least have disturbed her self-possession, is that the soldier to whom she gave the golden armour, 'when he had received this rich gift, stole away by night and went to Caesar.'

The most moving thing about their relation is the sense of two people, who have, in the misfortunes they bring on each other, become inextricably close. It is a closeness easily ruptured, as so many knots of style are easily dissolved in the play, and death itself seems gentler and easier for being prolonged, the 'knot intrinsicate of life' insensibly untied. But the lovers are close rather than intimate. It is the only subtlety that can survive in their relationship, changed as it is from the sexual and professional intimacy of lovers and colleagues to Shakespeare's representation of the eternal feminine bewitching the grand captain, the greatest prince in the world. It is the only subtlety, I should say, that survives in the portrayal of the relationship, the most famous but also the most public love spectacle, not only in Shakespeare but anywhere in literature. The lovers are never alone together and there is no invitation to us to imagine them alone.

The role of Enobarbus, who hardly appears in Plutarch, is crucial here. Dramatically he is the confidant, unique in being the confidant of both lovers, as well as the candid friend and salty commentator. Typically, the role of confidant is naturalised by Shakespeare to the point where we feel that both lovers really do need him to inquire and consult with about each other. At the outset the matter is plainly put by Enobarbus, who is not, like most clever and cynical bystanders, seeing through the situation, but stating that there is no situation to see through:

> ANT.: She is cunning past man's thought.
> ENO.: Alack, sir, no. Her passions are made of nothing but the finest part of pure love. We cannot call her winds and waters sighs and tears: they are greater storms and tempests than almanacs can report. This cannot be cunning in her: if it be she makes a shower of rain as well as Jove.
> ANT.: Would I had never seen her!
> ENO.: O, sir, you had then left unseen a wonderful piece of work, which not to have been blest withal would have discredited your travel.
>
> (I. iii. 141ff.)

'Alack, sir, no. . . .' That is just the trouble. If she were cunning past man's thought, as her original may well have been, and as in a distant and unamiable fashion she appears in Plutarch's account, there would, in one sense, be no problem. Antony would still be overcome by Caesar, but he would be overcome making use of her, and being used by her. Her not being cunning makes for the innocence and openness of their love that transforms the play. The play is what it is, and not like any other, because of this.

Dramatically, a cunning Cleopatra who redeemed herself in Antony's last days, coming to love him absolutely in his defeat and their *liebestod*, would be effective but also banal. Shakespeare was in any case no doubt content to give his audience the traditional figure they expected, the love's martyr of Chaucer and Gower and Garnier's *Marc Antoine*, which Sir Philip Sidney's sister had translated. What he added was his own kind of simplicity, which echoes the simplicity—and the tradition—in the handling of the two great Caesars. The presentment of them all is absolute and on the surface: there is nothing to find behind it. But the sublime simplicity of Cleopatra has its inimitable Shakespearean quality, and as we should expect it is that of the comedy sublime. At the beginning of the Actium campaign we have the perfect example of it. Antony is discussing with his general the reports of Caesar's swift progress:

> ANT.:   Is it not strange, Canidius,
> That from Tarentum and Brundusium
> He could so quickly cut the Ionian sea
> And take in Toryne? You have heard on't sweet?
> CLEO.: Celerity is never more admired
> Than by the negligent.   (III. vii. 20–5)

The intended put-down of that reply, its silliness and its self-possession, is impenetrable. An actress like Joyce Grenfell might do it justice, but she would not be able to play a straight Cleopatra, for Cleopatra never gives the faintest hint of parodying herself. If it were so she might indeed be cunning. The scene, just before Actium, is one of the most brilliant and compact in the whole play, opening with Cleopatra and Enobarbus alone together:

CLEO.: I will be even with thee, doubt it not.
ENO.: But why, why, why?
CLEO.: Thou has forspoke my being in these wars,
And sayst it is not fit.
ENO.: Well, is it, is it?

Enobarbus' exasperation, with its despairing repetitions, is an open and comic outcry of the powerlessness that Antony feels before both Cleopatra and Caesar. Critics have suggested that Shakespeare is inconsistent through his usual rapidity (or carelessness) and concentration on the scene rather than the play. Here is the politically steely Cleopatra who does not appear elsewhere? But surely Shakespeare has deftly substituted a Cleopatra determined not to leave Antony for a Plutarchan one who couldn't afford to let him out of her sight. The idea that the queen and her maids 'manage this war' is absurd, as everybody knows it to be, including Cleopatra herself: that is the point of her observation about celerity. It shows what a card she is, a 'great fairy'—it is just the sort of remark that Cleopatra *would* make. Her presence, we might note, divests every scene she is in of military and man-like seriousness: contrast with these scenes the ones—no less supple and brilliant—where Antony is alone in Italy with Caesar, Agrippa, Lepidus and the others. There the tone is genuinely businesslike—hard, watchful, courteous, dangerous. Antony there is holding his own in a real man's world.

Such a world of power is not of course any less inherently and humanly absurd than Cleopatra's world of feminine self-satisfaction. That is wonderfully suggested in the messenger's account of Antony's words for her, and when he spoke them:

'All the east,
Say thou, shall call her mistress'. So he nodded,
And soberly did mount an arm-gaunt steed,
Which neighed so high that what I would have spoke
Was beastly dumbed by him.   (l. v. 46–50)

It has its animation, its triumphs and its poetry as well as the comedy which in Shakespeare is indivisible from these things, but it is basically as odious as the world of violence and intrigue must always be. The scene on board Pompey's galley, and the decency of its commander, does not obscure the fundamental truth of what he is tempted to do, and what his subsequent murder at the hands of the triumvirate shows he should have done.

But this realism does not extend to the later campaign scenes in which Cleopatra is present. There romance takes over, or rather the kind of feminine reality she represents, a reality none the less moving for being here shown as wholly powerless. All her influence can do is to remove any kind of represented seriousness from the concluding acts and battles. The skirmish outside Alexandria is portrayed in the play as a last chance to recoup Antony's fortunes. In fact it was nothing of the sort, a truth the play tacitly acknowledges in the dressing up for the encounter and the banquet after it, as well as in Cleopatra's womanly yearnings over Antony's challenge of Caesar to single combat (a challenge which—to further compound our issue—he may well have made in historical fact). She does not manage the wars, but her attentions have indeed effectively demoralised those who do, and it is true that both in the play and the historical events behind it her mere existence has made it impossible for Antony to come to terms with Caesar.

It is her presence which makes it possible for this play to make a virtue out of the artificiality of having battles take place just off-stage: a battle in Cleopatra's vicinity automatically becomes a make-believe, depriving of any conviction the masculine ploys which the play attempts to represent. The business of battle is put on one side in a somewhat similar, if less grand and touching, way at the end of *Julius Caesar*, where the represented events at Philippi are transformed by parting and the emotions of friendship—the farewells of Brutus and Cassius, and the Roman friendship that can still be invoked between the conspirators, their victim, and his avengers.

'Here's sport indeed—how heavy weighs my lord?' This is the reality which dominates and transforms the ending of the play, the surrender of the whole issue to helplessness and childhood. The price paid by the play is the impression that the disasters and imminent death that bring the lovers so close are not quite real anyway, no more real in terms of the play's imagination than they are in the necessary artifice of enactment. For Plutarch as for Shakespeare a legend died with Antony, the god Hercules forsaking him in music by night; and, taking the hint, Shakespeare gives the play up to something like music, and its 'strong toil of grace'. The transforming comedy truth of Cleopatra as 'no more but e'en a woman' takes over, folding in its arms both the hero and the heroine herself.

The departure of Enobarbus is significant here, for in spite of Antony's final explosion after his last ships join the enemy it brings the pair, as lovers, more helplessly together. 'Is Antony or we in fault for this?' the queen had asked him at their last meeting alone, and the query is dazed and child-like in the same way as Antony's own query to his sardonic lieutenant a little later on, when Caesar has refused the challenge to single combat. ' "He will not fight with me, Domitius?" "No." "Why should he not?" ' It is the same note as the break in Antony's voice when he addresses her after the outburst of rage over Thidias—'Cold-hearted toward me?'—to which her reply is the warmest, most enfolding she has yet given him:

> Ah, dear, if it be so,
> From my cold heart let heaven engender hail. . . .

To Antony's rhetorical indignation her reply has been 'Not know me yet?'—a question in which there is nothing wise or fathomless. Antony has never known her because he has been so insistent on his image of her as all-powerful queen of love and serpent of old Nile. But in that sense there is nothing to know. The query is the reverse of the species of telling stroke in tragedy which suddenly reveals a psychological truth. Such are Lady Macbeth's 'had he not resembled / My father as he slept. . . .' Hermione's cry to Oreste in Racine's *Andromaque*—'Qui te l'a dit?'— when he has slain on her orders the man she loved; Clytemnestra's grief when told the lie that her son, whom she knows will try to kill her, is dead. Such a stroke of truth is the reverse of anything that will happen in *Antony and Cleopatra*. What moves as its tragedy is that only in dying will the pair be close to one another, but then they will be close indeed. Their weakness blurs all distinctions and brings them, at last, into a deep intimacy with the audience. They are no longer social types, living in Plutarch's larger-than-life world of the powerful and great. Her rhetoric of death turns again to a child's game as she gives instructions to Charmian:

> when thou hast done this chare, I'll give thee leave
> To play till doomsday. Bring our crown and all.

And it is with a child's idea of comfort that she remembers Antony in death:

> As sweet as balm, as soft as air, as gentle—
> O Antony—[*To the asp*] Nay, I will take thee too:
> What should I stay—

She is asleep before she can finish the sentence. Charmian completes it for her, and straightens her up like a nurse removing a toy: 'Your crown's awry. / I'll mend it, and then play.' Fortune has followed them all, in its own way, throughout; as requested, the Soothsayer at the beginning told 'but a workday fortune'. To be sleepy is the proper end to a working-day.

Irene G. Dash

UNION OF ROLES:
ANTONY AND CLEOPATRA

Give me my robe, put on my crown,

....

... Husband, I come! (V.ii.280, 287)

In *Antony and Cleopatra,* Shakespeare suggests that a woman of power has the unusual opportunity of combining her sexual and political selves. She commands others and is sovereign over herself. Because she lives in a patriarchal society, however, she may still be limited by the stereotypes for female behavior and subject to the rules established by the dominant group. To illuminate the problems even a woman who is queen may face, the dramatist creates male characters who express the views of society: they derisively challenge her right to self-sovereignty, suggesting that she thereby dominates a man, and minimize or forget her role as a political person. "Nay, but this dotage of our general's / O'erflows the measure" (I.i.1–2), exclaims Philo, a friend of Antony's in the play's opening lines. Preceding the entrance of the two principals, Philo describes Cleopatra in terms of her impact on Antony. She is a "strumpet" and a "gipsy"; he "a strumpet's fool," "a bellows," and a "fan" "to cool a gipsy's lust" (13, 9–10). Although reference to Antony as "Mars" as well as "general" occurs, Cleopatra is seldom dignified by the title of queen.

When, however, she and Antony sweep onto the stage, the close interweaving of her roles as sexual being and political person becomes immediately apparent. "If it be love indeed, tell me how much" (I.i.14), she insists, seeming to illustrate Philo's observation. But talk of love quickly gives way to discussions of political strategy when a messenger from Rome enters with news. Compared with Antony's wish for a brief summary of the message, Cleopatra repeatedly insists "Nay, hear them, Antony" (19), "Call in the messengers" (29), and again later pleads with him to attend to them. Although she refers to those back in Rome with mockery— Antony's wife, Fulvia, and his fellow Triumvir, Caesar—Cleopatra reveals a sensitivity to the angry feelings of a neglected wife and the ambitions of a young man seeking full control of power. With remarkable insight, she anticipates the scene that will occur in Rome:

From *Wooing, Wedding, and Power: Women in Shakespeare's Plays* (New York: Columbia University Press, 1981), pp. 209–47.

> ... who knows
> If the scarce-bearded Caesar have not sent
> His pow'rful mandate to you: "Do this, or this;
> Take in that kingdom, and enfranchise that;
> Perform't, or else we damn thee."   (I.i.20–24)

Gliding quickly back and forth between pragmatic political advice and subjective personal response, Cleopatra chides, "Fulvia perchance is angry" (20). Wondering if his wife is summoning him back to Rome, the Queen teases:

> As I am Egypt's queen,
> Thou blushest, Antony, and that blood of thine
> Is Caesar's homager; else so thy cheek pays shame
> When shrill-tongu'd Fulvia scolds.   (29–32)

The speech is interesting for its contrast between Cleopatra's self-image as "Egypt's queen," and her derisive portrait of Fulvia as a "shrill-tongu'd" wife. Throughout, Cleopatra's advice that he listen to the messenger beats a refrain.

Always, in answer, Antony speaks only to her as a woman.

> Let Rome in Tiber melt, and the wide arch
> Of the rang'd empire fall! Here is my space,
> Kingdoms are clay; our dungy earth alike
> Feeds beast as man; the nobleness of life
> Is to do thus—when such a mutual pair
> And such a twain can do't.   (33–38)

One of the great speeches of the play, it nevertheless follows Cleopatra's advice that Antony listen to the messengers from Rome. This hyperbole to love seems to have been prompted by his desire to silence her request. He will counter any rational arguments with what appears primary—the love between two people. But Cleopatra is not to be deterred. Again she returns to the subject of Rome.

Does he wish to speak of a "mutual pair"? Then why not speak of his wife? Is she not the person with whom he is paired?

> Excellent falsehood!
> Why did he marry Fulvia, and not love her?   (I.i.40–41)

Cleopatra asks, rebutting his reference to a "twain," a pair of lovers. Thematically, the concept of the direct relationship between love and marriage weaves through the text, illuminating one aspect of Cleopatra's personality. Unsurprisingly, in the play's last moments when she speaks of meeting Antony in death, she does not say "Beloved, I come," but, reinforcing her earliest comment, "Husband, I come" (V.ii.287).

Although brief, that early reference to Fulvia has resonances throughout the drama as Cleopatra keeps questioning Antony's ideas about the meaning of a "mutual pair" and wondering at his perception of marriage. An artist at the height of his power, Shakespeare, one must assume, knew what he was doing when he wrote this drama with only two major characters—one of whom, Cleopatra, spans the entire work. He would not have given her lines that contradict the portrait or seem inconsistent with the whole. Addressing an audience already familiar with the story, an audience bringing its own prejudices toward the pair to the theater, an audience also familiar with the rule of a queen—Shakespeare probably sought to develop a believable, if extraordinarily complex woman.[1] Strangely, however, some critics have had difficulty accepting Cleopatra as one of Shakespeare's more finely wrought, fully realized portraits. Others have theorized that she changes at mid-point in the drama.[2] A recent article by an astute Shakespeare critic, Leeds Barroll, offers one possible explanation. Barroll writes about the danger of ascribing to the dramatist the ideas expressed by one of the characters and warns against calling a character "choric" unless designated as "chorus" by Shakespeare. And yet this has occurred in interpretations of Antony and Cleopatra. Comments Barroll:

> Approving of the statements of a specific character whom we then choose as the "choric figure," we are simply using our own approval as guide to what we "deem" the ethical orientation of the play itself.[3]

In Antony and Cleopatra, the ethical orientation coincides with the point of view of Antony's most trusted adviser, Enobarbus, frequently dubbed the "choric figure." Like Philo, he too denigrates Cleopatra, particularly as a person of power. Because he praises her "infinite variety" as a woman, we believe him an objective commentator. But Enobarbus misdirects us if we identify with his point of view rather than listen to the characters themselves. As another critic suggests in a warning against accepting Philo's words, "May not Shakespeare's play be, after all, intended to persuade Philo to revise his accepted ideas?"[4]

In Cleopatra, Shakespeare portrays a woman whose self-sovereignty saves her from self-denigration. She likes herself and moves with confidence. Although she makes mistakes, she has a clear sense of herself as a woman and a ruler—as a sexual being and person of power. In contrast with the women of the histories, she refuses to separate her political from her sexual self. She sees no need to "unsex" herself in order to prove her role as political person. But the men in the play, representing the attitudes of the patriarchal society, find it difficult to accept such a woman who is sexually alive and politically aware of her role as ruler.

Karen Horney writes of the power struggle between the sexes:

> At any given time, the more powerful side will create an ideology suitable to help maintain its position and to make this position acceptable to the weaker one. In this ideology the differentness of the weaker one will be interpreted as inferiority, and it will be proven that these differences are unchangeable, basic, or God's will. It is the function of such an ideology to deny or conceal the existence of a struggle.[5]

We may apply this theory to *Antony and Cleopatra*. The more powerful side, the male side, creates an ideology that does not permit a woman to combine the two qualities that can be observed in Cleopatra: political power and sexual independence. Although Cleopatra's "differentness" consists merely in the fact that she is a woman, she may not behave as would her male counterpart, a king, without eliciting societal condemnation. The ideology of our society mandates marriage for a woman as the stamp of approval for a sexual alliance with a man, no matter how permanent, how faithful, the union.

Unfortunately, the rules of our society also establish a hierarchy of power within marriage. Therefore a woman who wishes to live as a sexually fulfilled being must, if she is to retain the sanction of society, marry. If she is a queen with real powers, she sacrifices a great deal for societal approval. The people of Shakespeare's time had wrestled with the problem of what to do when a woman monarch chose to remain a virgin queen rather than relinquish power by marrying. Surely an artist, living under such a ruler, would have incorporated this experience into his portrait of Cleopatra.

Perhaps he speculated with an ideal, wondering what might result if the concept of marriage were not hierarchical but more equal. What if the kind of relationship envisioned meant mutual respect between two equals, people of power and self-respect, who also loved one another? As Mill suggests, we might then have a richer society because one half of it would not be limiting the role of the other half.[6]

In the play's first scene, this possible equality is still an uncertainty. While Cleopatra has the confidence and independence required of a woman monarch, Antony perceives her primarily as a sexual being. Pursuing their debate, Antony lyrically chides: "Now for the love of Love, and her soft hours, / Let's not confound the time with conference harsh" (I.i.44–45). "Hear the ambassadors" (48), she succinctly answers. If he is a strumpet's fool, a "bellows" and "a fan" to cool a gypsy's lust, this first scene fails to illustrate her strumpetlike qualities. We do not hear a lusting Cleopatra. Rather Shakespeare presents a woman with a range of interests and a man who thinks only of love-making even when in the last moments before they exit he calls her Queen. "Fie, wrangling queen!" (48), he asserts before leading her off stage and dismissing the messengers. He, not she, commands the situation, but she has the potential for equality because of her self-sovereignty.

The men standing on the sidelines see only what they wish to see. "Is Caesar with Antonius priz'd so slight?" (I.i.56), challenges Philo's companion. The narrator assures his listener that such shortcomings may be observed only when Antony is not himself. The men have failed to see Cleopatra in any role but seductress although Shakespeare has presented her as a woman with political as well as personal interests.

In the following scene, still another of Antony's men, Enobarbus, offers his perceptions of Cleopatra. A light scene at the start, it opens with Cleopatra's women entreating a soothsayer to tell them their fortunes. It closes with Antony resolved to leave Egypt and break the "Egyptian fetters" (I.ii.116) in which he believes himself enslaved. Enobarbus links the two groups, appearing first with Cleopatra's court, and later alone with Antony. The scene, frequently transposed, partially cut, or moved to another section of the play, offers a first clue to this supposedly objective "choric figure."[7] Joking with the group surrounding the soothsayer, Enobarbus suddenly warns, "Hush, here comes Antony" (I.ii.79). In quick response, Charmian, one of Cleopatra's women, corrects him, "Not he, the Queen" (79). To emphasize the irony of Enobarbus' remark, Shakespeare has Cleopatra ask the whereabouts of Antony, "Saw you my lord?" Enobarbus replies, "No, lady" (80). The stage directions in these speeches assure the reader that Antony is nowhere visible. Enobarbus' reference to Cleopatra as "Antony" therefore reflects his own critical attitude toward this woman whose strength, self-confidence, and individuality continually assault and confuse him. Frequently, those attending a production, however, never hear this exchange. Occasionally they, like the audience at the 1909 Winthrop Ames production, may even see Antony enter after Enobarbus' announcement, the irony of the comment completely lost.[8]

Not only Cleopatra, but all women are seen through this lens by Enobarbus. When Antony, hearing of Fulvia's death, suddenly reminds himself of her virtues, Enobarbus, the pragmatist, offers no conventional comfort to the widower, only congratulations for the happy accident of being able to replace an "old smock" with a "new petticoat." He assures Antony, "If there were no more women but Fulvia, then had you indeed a cut, and the case to be lamented . . . your old smock brings forth a new petticoat" (I.ii.165–69). Once again this revealing aspect of Enobarbus' character tends to disappear in the theater. The references to "smock" and "petticoat" are altered for the sake of audience sensibilities.[9]

Anticipating Cleopatra's response to the unwelcome news of Antony's departure for Rome, Enobarbus observes, "Cleopatra, catching but the least noise of this, dies instantly; I have seen her die twenty times upon far poorer moment" (140–42). Elizabethan audiences would have heard the sexual inferences in the word "die." Later audiences still recognize the hostility and condescension in Enobarbus' comment. John Stuart Mill offers the background of such an attitude:

> Think what it is to a boy, to grow up to manhood in the belief that without any merit or any exertion of his own, though he may be the most frivolous and empty or the most ignorant and stolid of mankind, by the mere fact of being born a male he is by right the superior of all and every one of an entire half of the human race: including probably some whose real superiority to himself he has daily or hourly occasion to feel.[10]

This sense of superiority to women pervades Enobarbus' speeches. He perceives Cleopatra only as a sexual being, never as a politically aware person. He speaks of her magic powers, renaming her "sighs" and "tears" as "greater storms and tempests than almanacs can report" (I.ii.148–49). He protests Antony's decision to leave Egypt. But his most telling comment follows Antony's despairing "Would I had never seen her!" (152). Swiftly Enobarbus exclaims, "you had then left unseen a wonderful piece of work" (153–54). The sexual connotations of his remark are obvious. Enobarbus presents a male attitude toward Cleopatra, perceiving her always as "Other."

In these early scenes, Antony himself appears confused as to who the Queen is and what role she plays in his life. He oscillates between extremes: dismissing the messengers in favor of nights of love, then swearing "I must be gone" (136), "She is cunning past man's thought" (145), "Would I had never seen her" (152). Although protesting her power over him, Antony dominates in the early scenes. At the close of scene two, he asserts

> I shall break
> The cause of our expedience to the Queen,
> And get her leave to part. (I.ii.177–79)

As we discover in the next scene, however, his expression, "get her leave to part," is a mere formality. Determined to go, whether she willingly consents or not, he offers her no option. In these first scenes then, not Cleopatra, but Antony wields the power. Nevertheless, Cleopatra, because of her role as Egypt's Queen and her sense of confidence in herself, retains her composure. Because of this, too, she arouses male hostility.

"What holds women back," according to the psychologist, Florence Denmark, who recently completed a study of antagonism to women in the job market, "is something not quite so amenable to change as a woman's personality: the very fact that she is female."[11] Although Denmark's findings appeared in 1979, they confirm what Shakespeare knew and illustrated in this play. The general hostility expressed by Enobarbus, Philo, and even Antony in the second scene—the perception of woman as "Other," and as seducer of men—supports Denmark's thesis. To succeed, therefore, a woman must bring all of her strengths, her knowledge, and her ability to any endeavor. For Cleopatra these strengths derive, as do Antony's, from a combination of learned patterns of behavior and native inner resources—of nurture and nature. The fact that she is sovereign over herself gives her greater leverage than most women have. Nevertheless, to present a well-rounded character, Shakespeare must exhibit her learned behavioral characteristics as well as those qualities nurtured by her unusual position as queen.

She exhibits this learned behavior in scene three. Hoping to keep Antony in Egypt and realistically aware of the power of Roman life to separate him from her, Cleopatra directs her servant:

> See where he is, who's with him, what he does.
> I did not send you. If you find him sad,
> Say I am dancing; if in mirth, report
> That I am sudden sick. Quick and return. (I.iii.2–5)

Although her woman, Charmian, considers this a poor device for retaining a man's affection, believing that a better method exists—"In each thing give him way, cross him in nothing" (9)—Cleopatra scorns such acquiescent behavior: "Thou teachest like a fool: the way to lose him" (10). Here Cleopatra applies some of the learned behavior patterns for a woman—patterns noted and decried by Wollstonecraft. Antony in Rome will also rely on learned behavior patterns.

Later in the scene when they confront one another, Cleopatra, angry at the news of his intended departure, returns to the theme introduced in the first scene:

> What, says the married woman you may go?
> Would she had never given you leave to come!   (I.iii.20–21)

Questioning the permanence of his vows, Cleopatra again refers to Fulvia. "Why should I think you can be mine, and true / ... Who have been false to Fulvia?" (27–29). Finally, when Antony announces Fulvia's death, assuring Cleopatra that she should feel safe about his leaving, the Queen poses the question: "Where be the sacred vials thou shouldst fill / With sorrowful water?" (63–64). She also proposes a parallel between herself and his late wife:

> I prithee turn aside, and weep for her,
> Then bid adieu to me, and say the tears
> Belong to Egypt.   (76–78)

Accusing him of dishonesty in his dealings with her, Cleopatra understands what Antony fails, at this early point in the play, to recognize—that their union is more than one of sexual attraction, that it represents, as Ruth Nevo, the contemporary critic, observes, the best type of love between a man and a woman, "a consonance of the imagination and the senses"; that it is a love that includes companionship.[12] Furness, writing much earlier than Nevo, considers many of the qualities she describes in the relationship between a man and a woman as characteristics of a good marriage.[13] In this the *Variorum* editor was challenging the generally prevailing critical opinion that Cleopatra was primarily a sensual, seductive woman—a point of view reinforced by stage productions. A good example is the treatment of this scene recorded in a late nineteenth-century promptbook. The lines beginning "I prithee turn aside, and weep for her"—Cleopatra's admonition to Antony that he not confuse his tears for his late wife with those for the Egyptian Queen—are accompanied by the stage direction: "Cleopatra shields her face with veil but joyfully says, 'O most false love.'"[14] The promptbook offers valuable evidence of the persistence of a point of view. Dated in the late 1880s, it reconstructs an 1874 production in which Jean Davenport Lander played Cleopatra and James H. Taylor played Antony. Undoubtedly, the promptbook was then used, or read, by those who would later produce the play. Thus this hypocritical Cleopatra was assured survival on the stage.

Along with questions about marriage and love, those first scenes also stress Cleopatra's awareness of herself as a political person, another theme that weaves throughout the play. As if to stress the naturalness of these two major interests in a ruler, Shakespeare, during the scene of Antony's leavetaking, gives him lines where they alternate. Like Cleopatra, Antony shifts back and forth between presenting himself as a sexual being and presenting himself as a political person. Explaining the reasons for his return to Rome, he begins, "Our Italy / Shines o'er with civil swords" (I.iii.44–45), then addresses the woman:

> Quarrel no more, but be prepar'd to know
> The purposes I bear; which are, or cease,
> As you shall give th' advice. By the fire
> That quickens Nilus' slime, I go from hence
> Thy soldier, servant, making peace or war
> As thou affects. (66–71)

This natural combination of political and sexual being, acceptable in a man, is unusual in a woman. Nevertheless, recognizing the inevitability of his departure, Cleopatra, too, interweaves the roles. Gallantly she acknowledges the validity of his reasons:

> Sir, you and I must part, but that's not it;
> Sir, you and I have lov'd, but there's not it.
> . . . .
> . . . Your honor calls you hence,
> Therefore be deaf to my unpitied folly,
> And all the gods go with you! (87–99)

Moments later, Shakespeare presents a scene that can only remind us of Cleopatra the political person rather than the sexual being. We are transported to Rome and listening to the "scarce-bearded Caesar" damning Antony. Caesar's words so closely approximate Cleopatra's description that Shakespeare's intention of creating a woman of political wisdom appears clear. Addressing Lepidus, the third member of the triumvirate, Caesar assures his colleague:

> It is not Caesar's natural vice to hate
> Our great competitor. (I.iv.2–3)

Nevertheless, Caesar manages to catalogue, in detail and with embellishment, Antony's faults.

> Let's grant it is not
> Amiss to tumble on the bed of Ptolomy,
> To give a kingdom for a mirth, to sit
> And keep the turn of tippling with a slave (16–19)

He mentions adultery and whoring, implying that these are pardonable if they do not interfere with responsibility to one's work. The young Roman general also accuses Antony of familiarity with bums on the street—"and stand the buffet / With knaves that smell of sweat" (20–21). Despite Lepidus' protests, "I must not think there are / Evils enow to darken all his goodness" (10–11), Caesar, the superb politician, continues until Lepidus finally admits, " 'Tis pity of him" (71). As Cleopatra had predicted, the ambitious young Caesar finds Antony "th' abstract of all faults / That all men follow" (9–10).

Promptbooks of *Antony and Cleopatra* frequently omit the beginning of this scene where Caesar emerges as a manipulative, unscrupulous partner. The strong language describing the carousing in Egypt disappears. Instead of a conniving Caesar, a politically motivated head of state is presented, someone difficult for the audience to hate since he faults Antony only for political and military irresponsibilities.

Stage productions can also affect our impression of Cleopatra waiting in Egypt for Antony's return. Shakespeare creates two separate scenes of longing and loneliness for her. Between them, he wafts his audience to Rome to observe the far less lonely Antony. When the scenes in Egypt are grouped together and their order shifted a less sympathetic Cleopatra emerges, the contrast with Antony diminished.

In her first scene alone, Act I, scene v, she reminisces about their days together and thinks only of "sleeping out" the great gap of time while he is gone. She muses on his greatness, "The demi-Atlas of this earth, the arm / And burgonet of men" (23–24). Imagining him longing for her as she does for him, she is less perceptive as a lover than as a politician. "He's speaking now, / Or murmuring 'Where's my serpent of old Nile?' " (24–25), she assures her women. In Rome, however, Antony is feeling very unattached to her as she discovers when news of his marriage interrupts her second scene, one act later.

Shakespeare contrasts her loyalty with Antony's although critics tend to accuse her of deception and attribute to Antony the desire to reestablish himself in the Roman world. Heinrich Heine, the nineteenth-century German poet and critic, for example, writes:

> Cleopatra is a woman. She loves and betrays at the same time. We err in thinking that women cease to love us when they betray us. They do but follow their nature.[15]

One might ask, "What then is the nature of men, as illustrated by Antony's actions here?" Horney's observation that the power struggle between the sexes is masked by generalizations about the basic, unchangeable difference between men and women would seem to apply here. Actually, the juxtaposition of scenes heightens the contrast between the loyalty of the lovers.

In Rome, vulnerable to attacks on his "manhood," Antony rejoins the male clique that looks on women as inferior beings. Reacting with almost knee jerk response to Caesar's insinuation that Cleopatra controls him, Antony contracts to marry Caesar's widowed sister, Octavia. Manipulating language, Caesar adroitly reprimands one of his men who suggests the marriage:

> Say not so, Agrippa;
> If Cleopatra heard you, your reproof
> Were well deserv'd of rashness.   (II.ii.120–22)

The wording of Caesar's comment reminds us of Leontes' reproach to Antigonus for permitting a woman to determine his actions. Playing the stereotypically approved male role, Antony immediately responds, "I am not married, Caesar" (122). He has grabbed the bait.

Continuing to act according to learned patterns of behavior for his sex, he next adopts the classic suitor role while Octavia, in turn, follows the correct pattern of a woman being wooed. To his apology that he may at times be absent from her, she merely says that she will pray to the gods for him when he is away. He then asks her tolerance for his past weaknesses:

> My Octavia,
> Read not my blemishes in the world's report.
> I have not kept my square, but that to come
> Shall all be done by th' rule. Good night, dear lady.   (II.iii.4–7)

Moments later, following the soothsayer's advice to return to Egypt, Antony becomes totally immersed in his role of the typical male, one that conflicts with Cleopatra's ideas on the meaning of allegiance between a man and a woman. He soliloquizes:

> ... I make this marriage for my peace,
> I' th' East my pleasure lies.   (40–41)

He has divided women into two categories—wives, and women to satisfy men's pleasures. The mutual pair joined in love that Cleopatra believed should also be joined in marriage is an ideal he rejects. Instead, he accepts the traditional male view, perceives women as lesser beings, and commits himself to an inevitably tragic path.[16] Antony has failed to understand the soothsayer's advice, translating it to its most limited meaning:

> Thy daemon, that thy spirit which keeps thee, is
> Noble, courageous, high unmatchable,
> Where Caesar's is not; but near him, thy angel
> Becomes a fear, as being o'erpow'r'd.   (20–23)

In contemporary terms, one may read this as the wisdom of the adviser who counsels departure from a life whose values conflict with one's own and espousal of the life where one's "unmatchable" spirit may flourish. In such a world, Cleopatra, far from inhibiting Antony's greatness, nourishes it.

Back in Egypt, Cleopatra, laughing with her women, remains the completely unconventional person. Happy with herself—an independent woman—she listens while Charmian recollects a trick Cleopatra played on Antony:

> 'Twas merry when
> You wager'd on your angling; when your diver
> Did hang a salt-fish on his hook, which he
> With fervency drew up.   (II.v.15–18)

But laughter quickly gives way to shock, disappointment, and the beginning of her own tragedy. Because while she can look at herself as a total person, the male world in which she moves refuses to accept her. She hears that Antony is married to Octavia. Reacting with rage and anger, Cleopatra strikes the messenger and even draws a knife on him. By the scene's close, however, she says: "Pity me, Charmian, / But do not speak to me" (118–19).

Flashing back to Rome, Shakespeare presents the prototypical, acceptable woman: Octavia. But he editorializes on the portrait. Plutarch tells us that Antony and Octavia were married for many years and that they had children. He also tells us that Antony sought to rid himself of Octavia as a wife. Finally acquiescing to Cleopatra's demand, Antony commanded Octavia to leave his home. Shakespeare omits this information, compresses time, eliminates the children, and offers little hint of any intimacy between Antony and Octavia.[17] The dramatist instead presents an Octavia whose allegiance to her brother equals her loyalty to her husband— suggesting, perhaps, an incestuous bond between brother and sister. Thus, Shakespeare minimizes audience sympathy for Octavia and implies a seemingly sexless, short-lived marriage.

Alternating scenes between her and Cleopatra, he contrasts their allegiance, self-confidence, and conformity. In Act III, Octavia's first two scenes frame Cleopatra's; her last precedes Cleopatra's affirmation of her role as political person. Obvious in the first is Octavia's divided loyalty between brother whom she loves and husband to whom convention binds her. Parting from Caesar, she hesitantly begins, "Sir, look well to my husband's house; and—" (III.ii.44). But she can speak no further. "What, / Octavia?" (45–46), asks the loving brother who has married her off for political reasons. "I'll tell you in your ear" (46), she confides. What a remarkable bit of character definition, particularly since later Cleopatra, although defeated in battle, refuses the request of Caesar's ambassador for a private audience. Insisting that "none but friends" are present, she conducts the interview publicly. Here, Octavia, amidst friends, in a social situation, chooses to whisper to her brother.

The illusion of time standing still, the almost dizzying superimposition of one picture on another, seeming to anticipate modern film technique, returns us to Egypt and the messenger threatened by Cleopatra. In an amusing interlude she quizzes him for details of Octavia's appearance. Seeking specifics of voice, height, carriage, and hair color, the Egyptian Queen finally satisfies herself that Antony will return to her, for she concludes that his wife is "dull of tongue," and "dwarfish" (III.iii.16), "she creeps" (18), and her face is "long and round" (29).

A pure invention of Shakespeare's, the scene has sometimes been cited as an example of Cleopatra's pettiness. Recent scholarship, however, has uncovered parallels with reports of Queen Elizabeth's behavior.[18] If Shakespeare's audience knew of these incidents—a possibility since, at the time of this play's production, Elizabeth was no longer alive—the scene would have strengthened the impression that the dramatist was accurately describing a real queen, a woman of power. The successful woman ruler had been a reality. She had governed for forty-six years, had survived far beyond her "salad days," had never relinquished complete control of power (although in her late years the people complained of her relying on favorites) and, in her seventieth year, still proclaimed that she was "Prince" of her kingdom.[19] Through analogy, the dramatist would have been reinforcing the known portrait of a woman monarch.

The next scene, in Athens, sharpens the contrast between wife and Queen. Octavia, troubled and uncertain, divided by news of a conflict between husband and brother, bewails her position:

> A more unhappy lady,
> If this division chance, ne'er stood between,
> Praying for both parts.
> . . . .
> Husband win, win brother,
> Prays, and destroys the prayer.   (III.iv.12–19)

Compared with Cleopatra's overwhelming loyalty to Antony, Octavia's divided loyalty reflects her uncertain sense of self. She would conform to the role of wife. Antony, too, adopts a properly conventional posture. Chiding her first, he then asks that she strive to be fair, but warns of the difficulty:

> . . . our faults
> Can never be so equal that your love
> Can equally move with them.   (34–36)

Nowhere does one sense the mutuality that Cleopatra affirmed was a vital part of marriage.

Octavia's last scene stresses the usual, familiar pattern that governs the behavior of women of power. Like the women of the early histories, the Roman matron derives her identity from her relationship with husband and brother. Returning to her brother's home and expecting to act the mediator between Caesar and Antony, she finds herself berated instead for improper behavior:

> Why have you stol'n upon us thus? You come not
> Like Caesar's sister. The wife of Antony
> Should have an army for an usher, and
> The neighs of horse to tell of her approach.   (III.vi.42–45)

She is told exactly how she should be traveling, then is given a report of Antony's return to Egypt, told of his adulterous life and his "abominations" and, lastly, offered the standard palliative for women, "Pray you / Be ever known to patience" (97–98). The portrait seems intentionally designed to enhance the individuality of Cleopatra through contrast, for Plutarch's Octavia was a woman of more initiative than Shakespeare's.

"I will be even with thee, doubt it not" (III.vii.1) explodes Cleopatra to Enobarbus a moment later, catapulting us back to Egypt. "But why, why, why?" (2), repeats Enobarbus. If time stood still between earlier scenes in Egypt and those in Rome, now it spurts ahead. The contention between Antony and Caesar that Octavia had planned to mediate has burst into war. And Cleopatra, as "president" of her kingdom, intends to be present at the battle:

> CLEOPATRA: Thou has forspoke my being in these wars,
> And say'st it is not fit.
> ENOBARBUS: Well; is it, is it?
> CLEOPATRA: If not denounc'd against us, why should not we
> Be there in person?   (III.vii.3–6)

The swift shift of scenes contrasts the two women—the uncertain, compliant sister, torn between husband and brother, and the spurned Cleopatra, now asserting her rights as head of her kingdom. Unfortunately, the Octavia scenes, whole or in part, frequently disappear from the stage either because of excision or because someone else's version of Shakespeare's play replaces the original.[20] This occurred during the Restoration and eighteenth century when Dryden's *All for Love* became the popular stage favorite and Shakespeare's work remained in the study.[21] A different Octavia emerges. The mother of Antony's children, she brings them with her to Egypt to plead with him to return home. In Shakespeare's drama, not Octavia, but Cleopatra is the mother of Antony's children. Dryden's Antony, torn between the women, chooses to sacrifice "all"—home, family, empire—for love. No such contrast exists for Shakespeare's Antony. Nor are the women equally strong. Rather, as we see here, Octavia's uncertainty dramatizes Cleopatra's sense of independence.

In the above scene with Enobarbus, she asks a logical question. Although perhaps motivated, as some critics suggest, by the fear that Antony will join with Caesar, she may also wish to exercise her role as queen. Political power means the right to function as more than decoration. It means the right to make wrong decisions and have them obeyed. It means the right to command the actions of a nation. If her decision proves wrong, not female wiles but poor judgment should be the accusation; but it is not. Antony attributes his defeat to her action—a foolish retreat that he unthinkingly follows because, he claims, of his love for her.

During these moments before the battle, Shakespeare gives Cleopatra lines that emphasize her position as monarch. Again, he may have hoped that his audience would hear echoes of the words of their late Queen. Enobarbus explains that Cleopatra should withdraw because of rumors in Rome that Photinus, "an eunuch," and her maids "Manage this war." The Queen rationally replies,

> A charge we bear i' th' war,
> And as the president of my kingdom will
> Appear there for a man.
>
> (III.vii.16–18)

The audience may well have been reminded of Elizabeth's "Golden Speech" to her parliament of 1601. There she defined her role as defender of her kingdom.

> ... from peril, dishonour, tyranny and oppression.
>   There will never Queen sit in my seat with more zeal to my country, care for my subjects, and that will sooner with willingness venture her life for your good and safety, than myself.[22]

Some scholars believe that Shakespeare may have waited to write his play until after Elizabeth's death because of such parallels.[23]

No resemblance, however, existed between the sexual lives of the two Queens. Did this mean that Elizabeth would have been less openly attacked for womanliness? Perhaps. Enobarbus, having failed to convince Cleopatra through argumentation, finally relies on a more expected answer—one still being used three hundred years later to exclude women from participation in the public activities of society:

> Well, I could reply:
> If we should serve with horse and mares together,
> The horse were merely lost; the mares would bear
> A soldier and his horse.
>
> (III.vii.6–9)

The speech reinforces the portrait of Enobarbus already begun in the first act. But it also intensifies the portrait of Cleopatra, adding fine lines of shading, particularly if one rejects the stage direction added by Samuel Johnson: an "[Aside]" preceding the speech.

Together, lines and stage direction project an attitude at once protective and disparaging of women because they assume that Cleopatra did not hear Enobarbus and would rage had she heard him. She responds with the question, "What is't you say?" Such a conclusion, however, denigrates Cleopatra's talents as a political being, one who is realistically aware of her position. She understood the limits of her power well enough to announce that without Antony's support she could not wield the same extensive control. As a woman, she understood herself well enough to exclaim, "Pity me, Charmian, / But do not speak to me" (II.v.118–19). She had accepted Antony back at her court despite her disappointment and disillusionment. Historically, she had no choice. May she not also have had little choice in the type of comments Antony's trusted companion would make to her? Her words—"What is't you say?"—would then indicate the self-possession and regal manner of a political figure who had already learned to adjust to disappointment.

Although Enobarbus' speech frequently disappears from the stage, probably because it so clearly defines his point of view toward women, the argument he presents persists into the twentieth century. Virginia Woolf quotes a 1936 "Report of the Archbishops' Commission on the Ministry of Women." Offering several reasons for excluding women from the ministry, the report notes:

> We believe . . . that it would be impossible for the male members of the average Anglican congregation to be present at a service at which a woman ministered without becoming unduly conscious of her sex.

Woolf comments:

> In the opinion of the Commissioners, therefore, Christian women are more spiritually minded than Christian men—a remarkable, but no doubt adequate, reason for excluding them from the priesthood.[24]

To adapt Woolf's observation to Cleopatra's experience, women at war are more single minded than men. Apparently Cleopatra was. Although she fled the battle, she had not expected Antony to follow her. She had acted as a political person whose poor military judgment dictated flight. He had reacted to her as a woman, not as a head of state. When she answers his query: "O, whither hast thou led me, Egypt?" (III.xi.51), she is expressing an honest response to his behavior:

> O my lord, my lord,
> Forgive my fearful sails! I little thought
> You would have followed.   (54–56)

His departure for Rome, his marriage to Octavia, his too easy separation of wife and mistress all fail to prepare her for this dramatic shift in Antony's behavior. Nor can the audience easily accept his claim:

> Egypt, thou knew'st too well
> My heart was to thy rudder tied by th' strings,
> And thou shouldst tow me after.   (56–58)

She, not he, should evoke our pity.

Despite his complaint, he has dominated her rather than she him. Until this moment in the drama, his words have determined events, whether something as slight as the dismissal of the messengers, or as important as the decision to return to Rome. Nor has the relationship of equals existed between them, despite his claim that they were a "mutual pair." In his actions he has committed himself to the idea that mutuality cannot exist between a man and a woman. By marrying Octavia, but determining to return to Egypt for his pleasure, he has opted against mutuality. In this scene, when he suddenly asserts that she is responsible for his behavior, he again rejects mutuality—a concept that means mutual respect as well as love between a man and a woman. As the scene draws to a close, Cleopatra, pitying his anguish, adopts the female role only, taking sole responsibility for the defeat by repeating, chorus-like, the word "pardon."

But Cleopatra's self image mandates that she question rationally the areas of human responsibility. A political person, she too suffers a great loss. After Antony leaves, she wonders: "Is Antony or we in fault for this?" (III.xiii.2). Enobarbus confirms her own belief. "Antony only" (3), but this friend of Antony then continues: "that would make his will / Lord of his reason" (3–4). Hoping for military or political analysis, she receives an answer based only on her sexual identification. That she is Queen, monarch of a kingdom to be captured by Caesar, does not affect Enobarbus' perception of her. Nor does she receive political advice to her earlier question, "What shall we do, Enobarbus?" He responds with a purely personal, defeatist answer, "Think, and die" (1). His answer is inadequate.

Political realities face her immediately. She must use all of her talents—learned traits and native strengths—to confuse her enemy. Ironically, Caesar, the victor, although he would take her as a political trophy, also thinks of her only as a woman—a person of lesser intelligence and greater vanity than men. He instructs his messenger, Thidias, to promise her anything, explaining:

... Women are not
In their best fortunes strong, but want will perjure
The ne'er-touch'd vestal.
(III.xii.29–31)

This expectation that women can be easily bought, this sense of the superiority of men—that Mill observes begins when men are boys—persists. Quick to discern this weakness in Thidias' opening words, Cleopatra responds with equal guile. For Thidias assures her that Caesar "knows that you embrace not Antony / As you did love, but as you fear'd him" (III.xiii.56–57). "O!" exclaims Cleopatra in astonishment. Aware that she is being wooed as a political person, she allows him to continue:

The scars upon your honor, therefore, he
Does pity, as constrained blemishes,
Not as deserved.
(58–60)

The humor of this suggestion, the implied insult to Cleopatra's intelligence and political wisdom, leads her to answer: "Mine honor was not yielded, / But conquer'd merely" (61–62). Playing with words, she would match his wit and cordiality. But neither he nor Enobarbus, who is listening, understands her.

Believing she is betraying Antony, Enobarbus in soliloquy muses:

Sir, sir thou art so leaky
That we must leave thee to thy sinking, for
Thy dearest quit thee.
(III.xiii.63–65)

Eventually he, not she, deserts. Because of his misogyny, observed in his earliest references to Cleopatra as "Antony," in his comments on her as "a wonderful piece of work," "a new petticoat," and, obliquely, as a "mare," Enobarbus has little difficulty misreading her political maneuverings. This is the man critics have mistaken for the voice of the dramatist because of his extensive description of her coming to meet Antony at Cydnus, and the famous lines, "Age cannot wither her, nor custom stale / Her infinite variety" (II.ii.234–35). Norman Holland, for example, writes that Shakespeare, the man,

> was probably . . . a sort of Enobarbus, a man's man, aggressive, competitive, at home in the world of men, the kind of man one thinks of as rather puzzled by and a little afraid of women whom he tends to see either as ideal figures (in God-home-and-mother terms) or as mere amusements put on earth for a man's convenience.[25]

I believe, however, that the confusion in values that leads Enobarbus to desert Antony and then regret his actions is part of a larger portrait, not of the dramatist, but of a male whose inability to understand women as human beings leads him to other aberrations. Enobarbus is, as Holland suggests, "a man's man," but not a self-portrait of the dramatist. Nor does this character represent attitudes that are specifically Roman. Unfortunately, they tend to be universal.

Cleopatra, contending with such attitudes, uses her intelligence and skill. Continuing her interview with Thidias, she sends conciliatory messages back to Caesar:

> I kiss his conqu'ring hand.
> . . . .
> Tell him, from his all-obeying breath I hear
> The doom of Egypt.   (III.xiii.75–78)

Aware of defeat, she acts as she does later on when, Antony dead, she bows to Caesar. Perhaps because men tend to perceive women as easily blinded by flattery, Thidias approvingly comments: "'Tis your noblest course. / Wisdom and fortune combating together" (78–79). They are engaged in a verbal game that reminds us of the first play discussed, *Love's Labour's Lost.*

Storming in on this interview at the moment when Cleopatra has extended her hand to be kissed by Thidias, Antony rages, "Moon and stars! / Whip him. . ." and then, turning to the Egyptian Queen, he speaks of her in third person, "So saucy with the hand of she here—what's her name, / Since she was Cleopatra?" (III.xiii.95–99). In a long series of expletives and descriptive phrases, he calls her whore: "You were half blasted ere I knew you" (105), "boggler" (110), "a morsel, cold upon / Dead Caesar's trencher" (116–17), "a fragment / Of Cneius Pompey's" (117–18). Again, promptbooks tend to omit these lines, erasing Antony's violent name-calling and lack of self-control toward Cleopatra.

Patiently, she waits. "Not know me yet?" (157), she asks, wondering, presumably, if he ever will. Oscillating between extremes of temperament—tenderness, warmth, and faith combating jealousy, suspicion, and accusations of betrayal—Antony has great problems "knowing" Cleopatra.[26] When, in this scene, he finally accepts her answer, he confides new plans for battle and for redeeming his reputation:

If from the field I shall return once more
To kiss these lips, I will appear in blood;
I and my sword will earn our chronicle.   (III.xiii.173–75)

Assuring him of her confidence and acting the supportive female role, she exclaims,
"That's my brave lord" (176).

Believing he wants the woman only, she becomes just that, suppressing her
political self when with him. But they are engaging in an impossible game; neither
can erase from consciousness her role as queen. The irony mounts when, buckling
on his armor, she listens to him boast:

                    O love,
That thou couldst see my wars to-day . . .
. . . thou shouldst see
A workman in't.   (IV.iv.15–18)

Would he really like her to "see" his wars? The rhetoric masks the truth. Nevertheless, Cleopatra acts Woolf's magic mirror, encouraging him and buoying his
self-confidence. Only after he departs does she reveal her deep skepticism based
on her political wisdom, confiding to Charmian:

He goes forth gallantly. That he and Caesar might
Determine this great war in single fight!
Then, Antony—but now—Well, on.   (36–38)

She knows, even as he heads for battle, that he has little chance of success. This
broken last line with its pause contrasts what might have been with what will
inevitably occur. Its hesitation reflects Cleopatra's less than confident belief that
Antony can win. But he does.

Then follows a brief interlude in which Shakespeare emphasizes Antony's
inability to accept Cleopatra as an astute political person, someone who had to
match Thidias' duplicity in the earlier scene. "Not know me yet?" she had then
asked. In this later scene, following Antony's temporary victory, he resembles the
men in the *Henry VI* plays.

Sending word to the woman—"Run one before, / And let the Queen know of
our gests" (IV.viii.1–2)—he would have her bestow the gift of a queen. The right
to kiss her hand is the reward he would offer one of his men for great feats in battle
that day. With defeat, his confusion returns. Raging against her when he discovers
that the fleet has defected, Antony again reveals extremes of temperament before
arriving at some truce, some temporary knowledge. He lacks confidence in Cleopatra's loyalty. Because she owns herself and is not dependent except when she
herself wills a dependency, Antony has great difficulty trusting her. Perhaps he
imposes his own earlier, pragmatic approach to political alliance on her actions. Or
perhaps he fails to overcome cultural biases that often lead men to view strong
women with suspicion.[27]

Once again Shakespeare relies on contrast to illuminate relationships. News of Enobarbus' desertion precedes Antony's final defeat as a result of the defection of the fleet. Blaming himself for the first, Antony exclaims, "O, my fortunes have / Corrupted honest men!" (IV.v.16–17). Enobarbus' treasures are sent after him. No such generosity extends to Cleopatra. "This foul Egyptian hath betrayed me" (IV.xii.10), Antony rages, believing her disloyal, then vows, "The witch shall die" (47). Nor can he accept responsibility for his fate: "I made these wars for Egypt, and the Queen, / Whose heart I thought I had, for she had mine" (IV.xiv.15–16), he dishonestly asserts, determined to remain the hero. In reality, he made the wars because of a political error, his marriage to Octavia, a marriage presented here as cold, passionless, and sexless. But Antony refuses to confront the question rationally. Furiously, he accuses Cleopatra of entering an alliance with Caesar and being responsible for the action of the fleet.

Exhausted by this man of extremes and frightened by his threats, Cleopatra takes Charmian's advice: "To th' monument! / There lock yourself, and send him word you are dead" (IV.xiii.3–4). Earlier, when more confident, Cleopatra had dismissed another of Charmian's suggestions with the comment: "Thou teachest like a fool" (I.iii.10). At this point in the action, however, the distraught Queen accepts her woman's advice. By transferring the major responsibility for this deception from Cleopatra to Charmian, Shakespeare retains sympathy for Cleopatra, the character who is to dominate the last act.

During the scenes following the defeat at Actium, Shakespeare also offers glimpses of the Antony Cleopatra loved. One such moment occurs shortly before Antony receives false news of Cleopatra's death. Calm, and accepting defeat, he muses on the dreams we all have, the fleeting visions that transform our everyday lives:

> Sometime we see a cloud that's dragonish,
> A vapor sometime like a bear or lion,
> A tower'd citadel, a pendant rock,
> A forked mountain, or blue promontory
> ... that nod unto the world,
> And mock our eyes with air.   (IV.xiv.2–7)

We hear in his poetry the wonderfully imaginative and creative qualities that distinguish him. The man behind the armor of convention emerges: the man the soothsayer directed to return to Egypt where his greatness might flourish. And when news of Cleopatra's death leads him to choose suicide, we also discover a fresh analogy for marriage. Earlier, shortly before preparing for the battle he expected to lose, he used the word "married" to describe the relationship between himself and his men:

> Mine honest friends,
> I turn you not away, but like a master
> Married to your good service, stay till death.

Tend me to-night two hours, I ask no more,
And the gods yield you for't!   (IV.ii.29–33)

Among the cruxes of the play, these lines have been variously read depending on
the shift of punctuation. Either reading retains the concept of a master-servant
relationship surrounding the word "married." Only at his death does Antony alter
his perception of marriage to include love. Finally, he accepts Cleopatra's ideal,
enunciated at the play's opening, of the bond between love and marriage. About
to run on his sword, Antony says:

                    . . . but I will be
          A bridegroom in my death, and run into't
          As to a lover's bed.   (IV.xiv.99–101)

Until this point in the drama, the bridegroom had not been a lover, but a cold,
calculating politician. We have already witnessed Antony as bridegroom and lis-
tened to the successive statements:

                    My Octavia,
          . . . .
          I have not kept my square, but that to come
          Shall all be done by th' rule   (II.iii.4–7)

followed by, "I make this marriage for my peace, / I' th' East my pleasure lies"
(40–41). Although after Fulvia's death Antony could speak generously of her virtues, Enobarbus assured us that little love existed between them when she was
alive. If Antony's words shortly before his death express his true feelings, then he
has finally come to some new understanding of marriage.

Again Shakespeare uses dramatic situation as well as language to convey ideas
and define character. When Antony bungles his suicide attempt, he survives long
enough to meet with Cleopatra one last time. The text tells us that she is "aloft" in
the monument, hoping to protect herself from Caesar. Rather than permitting
Antony to die on the bare stage before us, Shakespeare insists that the dying lover
be hoisted to the upper platform where Cleopatra has barricaded herself.[28] Refusing to come below, and insisting that her women help lift him, she reveals her
independence and political awareness:

          I dare not, dear—
          Dear my lord, pardon—I dare not,
          Lest I be taken.   (IV.xv.21–23)

The same conjunction of references then occurs as were mentioned at the beginning of the play: love, politics, Caesar, wife. "O sun, / Burn the great sphere thou
mov'st in!" (9–10), Cleopatra exclaims at the sight of the dying Antony. Then, aware
that she will be exhibited by Caesar, she speaks of killing herself. Next, even at this
moment of closeness, she mentions Antony's wife:

> Your wife Octavia, with her modest eyes
> And still conclusion, shall acquire no honor
> Demuring upon me.   (27–29)

Finally, she offers to lift him up to the monument: "Help me, my women—we must draw thee up" (30). If we think back to the history plays, we realize that never did a woman there function as these women do, alone but together. Nor did a queen rely on women's help as Cleopatra does here.

Once aloft, Antony, too, finally acknowledges the duality of her roles—political person and woman he loves. "One word, sweet queen: / Of Caesar seek your honor, with your safety. O!" (IV.xv.45–46). But Cleopatra answers knowledgeably, "They do not go together" (47). When Antony then tells her whom to trust, she replies, "My resolution and my hands I'll trust, / None about Caesar" (49–50).

Moments later, Antony dies. Cleopatra swoons and exclaims:

> No more but e'en a woman, and commanded
> By such poor passion as the maid that milks
> And does the meanest chares.   (IV.xv.73–75)

Identifying with other women, even the most modest, who suffer emotionally at the death of a beloved, Cleopatra then continues, linking her personal with her public self:

>   It were for me
> To throw my scepter at the injurious gods,
> To tell them that this world did equal theirs
> Till they had stol'n our jewel.   (75–78)

Some critics have suggested that the earlier lines indicate a sudden awakening of a new Cleopatra. Harold C. Goddard, for example, writes:

> It is as if she must compensate for having been queen by being not merely a woman, but the humblest of women, a menial, a servant.[29]

But the later lines remind us of her awareness of role—an awareness that will dictate many of her actions in the last act. Despite the passion of her outburst, she also reveals a sense of responsibility to Antony's men. She comforts them, promising a proper burial for their general:

>   Good sirs, take heart,
> We'll bury him; and then, what's brave, what's noble,
> Let's do't after the high Roman fashion.   (85–87)

The strength and independence that led her to challenge Enobarbus and to question Antony's honesty when speaking of Fulvia sustain Cleopatra here. Shakespeare's portrait is consistent, but the environment has shifted. Whereas earlier her self-dependence led her to disagree with allies, now it saves her from being a cripple when confronting an opponent. Fuller suggests that self-dependence must "unfold" from within, but that women frequently have rules of behavior imposed on them from without. "This is the fault of Man, who is still vain, and wishes to be more important to Woman than, by right, he should be."[30] Cleopatra is censured for her independent behavior during the early scenes, leading some critics to find two different women in her—or one who had radically changed. But skill in performing the job of monarch does not occur suddenly at the moment when necessity demands independence of action. It evolves slowly and derives from self-confidence as well as knowledge of contemporary affairs. When the character is well developed, the actions seem to grow naturally from the earlier outlines. Shakespeare's Cleopatra is well prepared when, in the last act with neither Antony nor Enobarbus any longer alive to censure, direct, inhibit, or motivate her immediate behavior, she must confront her problems alone.

   She must evaluate the honesty of each of Caesar's ambassadors as well as that of Caesar himself. She must attempt to understand each man's attitude toward women in general as well as to her as Queen. Ultimately, she must outwit the conqueror who plans to take her back to Rome as hostage. Caesar asserts to his men:

> Go and say
> We purpose her no shame. Give her what comforts
> The quality of her passion shall require.   (V.i.61–63)

Concluding, he reveals his aim, "for her life in Rome / Would be eternal in our triumph" (65–66). The political contest she must enter is immediately apparent, demanding the guile and verbal dexterity of its participants. In the first encounter, she loses, tricked by Proculeius, a man whom Antony had told her to trust. To him she reveals her true aim, to die.

> Shall they hoist me up,
> And show me to the shouting varlotry
> Of censuring Rome?   (V.ii.55–57)

she challenges, after Proculeius has thwarted her first suicide attempt. Even worse, however, is the thought of being "chastis'd with the sober eye / Of dull Octavia" (54–55), Antony's second wife. Dishonestly, Proculeius assures her that Caesar will treat her with kindness.

   When Dolabella, the next of Caesar's men, takes command, Cleopatra, with no previous instruction from Antony, must judge the messenger by his words. Unlike his predecessor who, upon entering, proclaimed:

> Caesar sends greeting to the Queen of Egypt,
> And bids thee study on what fair demands
> Thou mean'st to have him grant thee.   (V.ii.9–11)

Dolabella introduces himself tentatively with a question: "Most noble Empress, you have heard of me?" (71). Her answers, evasive, tell us little: "I cannot tell" and then "No matter, sir, what I have heard or known" (72–73). Cleopatra then paints the

portrait of the man she loved—an Antony we have hardly seen—a man recol-
lected in a dream:

> O, such another sleep, that I might see
> But such another man!
> ....
> His face was as the heav'ns, and therein stuck
> A sun and moon, which kept their course, and lighted
> The little O, th' earth.   (77–81)

As she continues to describe in hyperbole this man whose greatness was past the
size of dreaming, she reveals her own poetic imagination, the soaring images drawn
from the vast range of nature. Has she, indeed, heard of Dolabella? Or is she, in her
despair, recollecting another time—another world? Her grief, her poetry, her loss
capture her hearer's sympathy. "Think you there was ... such a man?" (93), she
asks. Her listener assuringly answers, no. Then Cleopatra, the political person, asks
a more mundane question, the same one she asked Proculeius: "Know you what
Caesar means to do with me?" (106). This time she receives a more honest answer.
She will be led in triumph in Rome.

Certain now of her fate Cleopatra, when she meets Caesar, bows low, hailing
him with the words, "Sole sir o' th' world" (V.ii.120). Listening to his false promises
of gentleness and kindness, she matches dishonesty with dishonesty. She speaks of
her wish to bring "lady trifles" to Rome as gifts for Octavia and Caesar's wife that
they might mediate on her behalf. She speaks of her womanly frailties—frailties she
knows Caesar believes belong exclusively to the weaker sex. She rages at her
treasurer when he accuses her of deceit. This permits Caesar to act the magnanimous male role. Intent on dying, she knows she must convince Caesar of her great
desire to live if he is to be open and careless about guarding her.

"He words me, girls, he words me, that I should not / Be noble to myself"
(V.ii.191–92), she confides to her women the moment they are alone. She then
describes the life they may anticipate:

>   Mechanic slaves
> With greasy aprons, rules, and hammers shall
> Uplift us to the view.   (209–11)

Some critics have objected to Cleopatra's logical wish to know her fate, believing
that she should have chosen suicide for love without thought of what would happen
in Rome. Eugene Waith offers a well-reasoned defense of her actions:

> If she pauses to find out what would happen to her in Rome, she is no more
> disloyal to Antony than he is to her when he speaks to Eros about the shame
> of a Roman triumph after he has already vowed to follow Cleopatra.[31]

During her last moments, Cleopatra knows her direction. Perceptive, uncompro-
mising, she achieves her goal. A political person as well as a woman of genius, she

has no difficulty convincing the guard to allow the Clown with the basket of figs—and the asp—to enter. She suggests the potential for women if they could have self-sovereignty and function as complete people, not in a sexless world or a world where, like Queen Elizabeth, they must choose between marriage and career, but in a world where true mutuality might exist between men and women.

The conjunction of roles that marked her from the start illuminates her poetry at her death:

> Give me my robe, put on my crown, I have
> Immortal longings in me.
>
> (V.ii.280–81)

The political person, the Queen, speaks of her office. She would join Antony, a god, and also immortal. The interweaving continues:

> Methinks I hear
> Antony call . . .
> . . . I hear him mock
> The luck of Caesar, which the gods give men
> To excuse their after wrath.
>
> (V.ii.283–87)

Echoes of the soothsayer's lines comparing Caesar and Antony take on a new cast, for now luck becomes a paltry, momentary thing. Then she thinks of her personal self, mentioning the role she has longed for, "Husband, I come! / Now to that name my courage prove my title!" (287–88).[32] Although in some of the analogues Antony and Cleopatra marry, Shakespeare retains the concept as an ideal. Perhaps he thought that the mutuality she believed must characterize marriage was unattainable. "Why did he marry Fulvia, and not love her?" Cleopatra had asked in the first scene. Now she suggests that a different kind of mutuality exists, one of courage.

Shakespeare dramatizes the question of the meaning of power in a relationship between a man and a woman by creating two rulers who love one another. He presents the conflicts between them, conflicts frequently born of the struggle for mastery of one human being over another. He stresses the concept of mutuality nourishing the complete development of each of them.

By insisting that Antony die in the fourth act and Cleopatra have the last act alone, Shakespeare forces us to observe her as the one character who spans the entire drama. Capable, politically astute, imaginative, she hardly seems to be a character who should lose her identity in a hierarchical arrangement because she is a woman. Fittingly, Shakespeare continues to intertwine her two selves—lover and political person—at her dying moment: "The stroke of death is as a lover's pinch, / Which hurts, and is desir'd" (V.ii.295–96), she declares, then, to the asp at her breast:

> O, couldst thou speak,
> That I might hear thee call great Caesar ass
> Unpolicied!
>
> (306–8)

NOTES

[1] Madeleine Doran, *Shakespeare's Dramatic Language* (Madison: University of Wisconsin Press, 1976), p. 162; see also S. L. Bethell, *Shakespeare and the Popular Dramatic Tradition* (Durham, N.C.: Duke University Press, 1944), pp. 25ff.

[2] See review article, J. C. Maxwell, "Shakespeare's Roman Plays: 1900–1956," *Shakespeare Survey* 10 (1957): 1–11; Joseph Allen Bryant, *Hippolyta's View: Some Christian Aspects of Shakespeare's Plays* (Lexington: University Press of Kentucky, 1961), pp. 183–86; Reuben A. Brower, *Hero and Saint: Shakespeare and the Graeco-Roman Heroic Tradition* (New York: Oxford University Press, 1971), p. 318; L. T. Fitz, "Egyptian Queens and Male Reviewers: Sexist Attitudes in *Antony and Cleopatra* Criticism," *Shakespeare Quarterly* 28 (1977): 297–316.

[3] J. Leeds Barroll, "Ethical Premises in Shakespearean Criticism," *Shakespearean Research Opportunities* 2 (1966): 27; see also Peter Bilton, "Shakespeare Criticism and the 'Choric Character,'" *English Studies* 50 (1969): 257.

[4] Maurice Charney, *Shakespeare's Roman Plays* (Cambridge: Harvard University Press, 1961), p. 114.

[5] Karen Horney, *Feminine Psychology* (1967; rpt. New York: W. W. Norton, 1973), p. 116.

[6] John Stuart Mill and Harriet Taylor Mill, *Essays on Sex Equality*, edited by Alice S. Rossi (Chicago: University of Chicago Press, 1970), p. 236.

[7] See the following promptbooks of *Antony and Cleopatra:* Folger Prompt Ant 3 (London: J. Tonson, 1734; marked by Edward Capell [ca. 1758]); Folger Prompt Ant 8 (title page lacking; marked by Samuel Phelps; Theatre Royal, Sadler's Wells; London, 1849); Folger Prompt Ant 9 (Israel Gollancz, ed.; London: J. M. Dent, 1896); Charles Calvert, adaptor, *Antony and Cleopatra*, arranged in four acts (Edinburgh: Schenck and M'Farlane, 186–); Herbert Beerbohm Tree, adaptor, *Antony and Cleopatra*, Mansfield Theatre, New York, November 1937 (New York Public Library *NCP + Shakespeare). See also [David Garrick and Edward Capell], *Antony and Cleopatra* fitted for stage by abridging only (London: Tonson, 1758); [David Garrick and Edward Capell], *Antony and Cleopatra* (Dublin: Peter Wilson and Wm. Smith, Jr., 1759); John Philip Kemble, *Antony and Cleopatra*, ms. in Kemble's hand, believed to be in preparation for the 1813 production (Folger Library S.a. 125); [John Philip Kemble], *Antony and Cleopatra*, with alterations and additions from Dryden, Theatre-Royal, Covent-Garden (London: J. Barker, 1813).

[8] Winthrop Ames, dir., *Antony and Cleopatra*, New Theatre, New York, 1909 (New York Public Library *NCP .51625; typescript *NCP + 51624B).

[9] Folger Prompt Ant 1 ([London:] Thomas Hailes Lacy, n.d. [Princess's Theatre, 1867]; marked by George Becks, actor [ca. 1888]; reconstructs performance of 1874).

[10] Mill, *Essays on Sex Equality*, p. 218.

[11] Virginia Adams, "Women Held Back by Their Sex, Not Personality, Study Suggests," *New York Times*, July 12, 1979.

[12] Ruth Nevo, "The Masque of Greatness," *Shakespeare Studies* 3 (1967): 126. See also her *Tragic Form in Shakespeare* (Princeton: Princeton University Press, 1972). See also Thomas McFarland, *Tragic Meaning in Shakespeare* (New York: Random House, 1968), p. 68.

[13] Furness challenges Coleridge's thesis that this is the "love of passion and appetite opposed to the love of affection and instinct" that we see in *Romeo and Juliet*. Furness notes that the activities of Antony and Cleopatra might be those of a husband and wife. "Where is there a word which, had it been addressed by a husband to a wife, we should not approve? . . . Is wandering through the streets and noting the quality of the people sensual? Is fishing sensual? Is teasing past endurance sensual? Such are the glimpses that we get into the common life of this 'sensual' pair." Horace Howard Furness, *A New Variorum Edition of Shakespeare* (Philadelphia: J. B. Lippincott, 1871–1955), 15:xiv.

[14] Folger Prompt Ant 1, interleave facing page 16. See also Charles H. Shattuck, *The Shakespeare Promptbooks* (Urbana: University of Illinois Press, 1965), pp. 35–36 and 3–5.

[15] Heinrich Heine, *Heine on Shakespeare: A Translation of His Notes on Shakespeare Heroines*, translated by Ida Benecke (Westminster: Archibald Constable, 1895), p. 63; see also G. Wilson Knight, *The Imperial Theme* (1931; rpt. London: Methuen, University Paperbacks, 1965), p. 294, who writes, "She is unfair, quite irrational, typically feminine."

[16] As Maynard Mack observes, "Antony . . . never . . . reflect[s] for our benefit on his betrayal of Cleopatra in marrying Octavia or his betrayal of Octavia and Caesar in returning to Cleopatra." "*Antony and Cleopatra:* The Stillness and the Dance," in *Shakespeare's Art*, edited by Milton Crane (Chicago: University of Chicago Press, 1973), p. 81.

[17] "Plutarch's Lives of the Noble Grecians and Romanes," in Geoffrey Bullough, ed., *Narrative and Dramatic Sources of Shakespeare* (London: Routledge and Kegan Paul, 1957–75), 5:254–321.

[18] Helen Morris, "Queen Elizabeth I 'Shadowed' in Cleopatra," *Huntington Library Quarterly* 32 (1969): 271–78.

[19] Jonathan E. Neale, *Elizabeth I and Her Parliaments 1584–1601* (London: Jonathan Cape, 1957), p. 428.

[20] Folger Prompt Ant 3, 9, and 1. The sequence of scenes is altered in the stage version of 1937, Herbert Beerbohm Tree, *Antony and Cleopatra.*

[21] John Dryden's *All for Love* was first performed in 1677. See William Van Lennep et al., eds., *The London Stage 1660–1800* (Carbondale: Southern Illinois University Press, 1960–68), for its history on the Restoration and eighteenth-century stage. See George C. D. Odell, *Shakespeare from Betterton to Irving* (1920; rpt. New York: Dover, 1966), for an account of the relationship between Dryden's and Shakespeare's works. In the advertisement for the combined version (London: J. Barker, 1813), appears the following comment. Shakespeare's play has

> ... stood the test of modern times less than many of our great Bard's revived Dramas.... Something has been wanting to render it what is termed a Stock Play:—Dryden's Play has been long upon the shelf; nor does it appear suited to the present taste, without much departure from the original; but there is much to be admired in both the Plays. Under these circumstances, an amalgamation of wonderful poetic powers has been considered the best method to be adopted; and it is hoped, that the present arrangement will be found sometimes to have softened the violations of those Unities in Shakespeare, which it cannot easily encrease.

[22] Neale, *Elizabeth I*, p. 391.

[23] Bullough, *Narrative and Dramatic Sources*, 5:216.

[24] Virginia Woolf, *Three Guineas* (New York: Harcourt, Brace & World, 1938), p. 161.

[25] Norman N. Holland, *Psychoanalysis and Shakespeare* (New York: McGraw-Hill, 1964), p. 140.

[26] For interesting analyses see: Janet Adelman, *The Common Liar: An Essay on* Antony and Cleopatra (New Haven: Yale University Press, 1973), and Earnest Schanzer, *The Problem Plays of Shakespeare* (London: Routledge and Kegan Paul, 1963).

[27] Mill, *Essays on Sex Equality*, pp. 201, 242; Virginia Woolf, *A Room of One's Own* (New York: Harcourt, Brace & World, 1929), pp. 27–37.

[28] This detail appears in Plutarch (Bullough, *Narrative and Dramatic Sources*, 5:309).

[29] Harold C. Goddard, *The Meaning of Shakespeare* (Chicago: University of Chicago Press, Phoenix Books, 1951), 2:200; see also Bryant, *Hippolyta's View*, p. 185.

[30] Margaret Fuller, *Woman in the Nineteenth Century* (1845; rpt. New York: W. W. Norton, 1971), p. 40.

[31] Eugene M. Waith, *The Herculean Hero* (New York: Columbia University Press, 1962), p. 214.

[32] For other interpretations, see J. L. Simmons, *Shakespeare's Pagan World* (Charlottesville: University Press of Virginia, 1973), p. 162; Derek Traversi, *Shakespeare: The Roman Plays* (Stanford, Ca.: Stanford University Press, 1963), p. 199; Philip J. Traci, *The Love Play of* Antony and Cleopatra (The Hague and Paris: Mouton, 1970), pp. 153–57.

Derek Hughes
ART AND LIFE
IN *ALL FOR LOVE*

In an article published some years ago, Professor J. Douglas Canfield argued that *All for Love* emerges from a large and uniform dramatic tradition, modified only by Shakespeare, in which the love of Antony and Cleopatra invariably exemplifies the triumph of transcendent constancy over sublunary change; in Canfield's view, Dryden's perpetuation of the tradition is confirmed by his use of jewel imagery, which repeatedly identifies Cleopatra as "the jewel of great price," a heroine sublimely and victoriously constant.[1] In examining the place of *All for Love* in the Antony and Cleopatra tradition, Canfield has performed two valuable services: though he exaggerates the number of plays probably known to Dryden, he rightly asks us to see him not simply as the imitator of one or two isolated predecessors but as a contributor to a large and genealogically intricate tradition; and, in discussing the jewel images, he calls attention to a centrally important aspect of the play. Regrettably, however, his account also has flaws. His discussion of Dryden's antecedents is marred by factual error;[2] he imposes a false uniformity on the Renaissance tradition; and he misunderstands the jewel imagery of *All for Love*. In this essay I shall argue that *All for Love* does not recreate an established and inviolable set pattern but is rather a wholly individual response to a complex and divided tradition; and I shall argue that the jewel imagery expresses the characters' tragically misguided attempts to establish an unblemished and unchanging ideal in a world of change and imperfection.

I

Discussion of the tradition must, of course, begin with Plutarch, not only because his account is the fullest and most influential of the ancient sources but because his unusually complex moral judgments provide an essential basis for

From *Studies in Philology* 80, No. 1 (Winter 1983): 84–107.

appreciating later and much changed assessments of Antony and Cleopatra.[3] In his account, Cleopatra unleashes the evil in a soul whose virtues are already marred by the vices of irrationality and excess. Her advent, of course, provokes a decisive subjugation of reason to passion,[4] a surrender to the lowest element in the triform Platonic soul, whose dominance confines the soul to the world of transitory reflections and forbids its ascent to a transcendent, immutable reality.[5] Plutarch cites the image of the triform soul expounded in the *Phaedrus* (of the charioteer, obedient horse, and unruly horse), suggesting that Antony yields to the unruly horse and, hence, to Plato's basest and most earth-bound category of love (36.1); indeed, Plutarch's Antony recalls Plato's "tyrannical man"—the man enslaved to his darkest and most disordered desires, whose deranged constitution corresponds to the most corrupt and chaotic of political communities (*Republic* 571a–76b). Throughout, Antony violates the ideal of *sōphrosunē* (temperance, the virtue which orders the soul):[6] he is characterized by *akolasia* (intemperance), *akrasia* (lack of self-control), and *ametria* (excess);[7] above all, he is characterized by *hubris* (wantonness, insolence) and its cognates—common and flexible terms, to be sure, but ones repeatedly used (in opposition to *sōphrosunē*) in Plato's description of the unruly horse.[8] Although Plutarch respects Cleopatra's intelligence and courage, he sees her as a pernicious deceiver, ensnaring Antony with flattery (*kolakeia*)—the deception which, according to both Plato and Plutarch, nurtures and releases the least rational part of the soul.[9] Repeatedly, Plutarch describes Cleopatra's flattering corruption of Antony's soul in images of enchantment: Antony is the victim of witchcraft (*goēteia*) and of *pharmaka* (drugs, philtres, or poisons [37.4, 60.1]) and has been subdued by Cleopatra's spells (*Comparison* 3.3). Perhaps significantly, the word that Plutarch uses here (*katathelgein*) is an uncommon form whose chief previous occurrence is in Homer's account of Circe's dehumanizing magic, and its appearance here may reveal the analogy that lurked in Plutarch's mind and shaped some of his imagery.[10] Two other debilitating mythic females are more explicitly used: Omphale, inevitably, is cited (*Comparison* 3.3), and Plutarch introduces the Cydnos voyage by reworking the line which in the *Iliad* introduces Hera's deception and seduction of Zeus,[11] itself accomplished with the aid of enchantments (*thelktēria* [XIV.215]).[12]

The transformation of Antony and Cleopatra in the sixteenth and seventeenth centuries is most neatly illustrated in some striking alterations—even inversions—of the ethical basis of Plutarch's narrative. In Giulio Landi's *La vita di Cleopatra reina d'Egitto* (Venice, 1551) the infatuation of Cleopatra's lovers is still deplored (pp. 18ᵛ, 23ʳ), but her own career is now a sustained demonstration of *magnanimità*,[13] manifested even at Actium (pp. 30ᵛ–31ʳ): the theme is no longer deformity of soul but greatness of soul.[14] Plutarch is still further inverted at the end of Girolamo Graziani's epic poem *La Cleopatra* (Venice, 1633), where the soul of Antony summons his mistress to Platonic illumination in the stars (XIII.34–48).[15] And Dryden's Cleopatra exactly reverses Plutarch's use of the *Phaedrus* by claiming the "noble madness" (II.17) of love which, in that dialogue, brings ascent to the realm of transcendent forms (244a–57b). Indeed, the ethical implications of Plutarch's narrative are nicely overturned every time Antony and Cleopatra transcend bodily death through immortal love. The Antonies and Cleopatras bequeathed by the Renaissance can sometimes seem like precisely reversed images, mirror reflections, of other classic originals.

Transcendent love certainly figures in many sixteenth- and seventeenth-century treatments of Antony and Cleopatra. The flaws of passion are always admitted (sometimes extensively) but can be outweighed by a heroic constancy that triumphs over the grace: triumphant love is portrayed in Cinthio Giraldi's *Cleopatra* (c. 1543), Guillaume de Belliard's narrative poem "Les Delitieuses Amours de Marc Antoine, & de Cleopatre" (1578), Nicolas de Montreux' *Cleopatre* (1595), and Jean de Mairet's *Le Marc-Antoine* (1637); in Sir Charles Sedley's *Antony and Cleopatra* (1677), somewhat differently, Elysium permits the realization of heroic ideals that have proved blunderingly ineffectual in a deviously pragmatic world.[16] Shakespeare's Cleopatra, of course, creates her own drama of transcendent death, but here the rites of immutability do not quite efface memories of the heroine's earlier, changeful self and earlier, Protean histrionics. In other works, however, idealization is more muted or is altogether absent. In *Los áspides de Cleopatra* (1645) Francisco de Rojas Zorilla contrasts the lovers' noble (though not transcendent) constancy with the cycles of mutability but gives at least equal emphasis to the fatal and disruptive powers of passion.[17] Graziani's *La Cleopatra* at first stresses Antony's degeneracy and Cleopatra's guileful "lusinghe" (*kolakeia*),[18] and depicts Cleopatra as trying to arouse Octavius' love after Antony's death (XIII.1–32); and, though Antony's love finally transcends the illusions of the earth, Cleopatra's final loyalty to him is not explicitly transcendent. Elsewhere, too, Cleopatra originally offends against the (non-Plutarchan) ideal of amorous constancy, usually by seeking Octavius' love; normally, however, she redeems her failings, and finally defeats mutability, by following Antony to Elysium. Atonement for inconstancy is portrayed in Samuel Daniel's *The Tragedie of Cleopatra* (1599), Thomas May's *The Tragedie of Cleopatra Queen of Ægypt* (1626), Giovanni Capponi's *Cleopatra* (1628), Isaac de Benserade's *La Cleopatre* (1636), and Daniel Casper von Lohenstein's *Cleopatra* (1661).[19] May and Lohenstein, in particular, show the last-minute redemption of an unprincipled and faithless schemer, and Lohenstein's Cleopatra (like Dio's) actually tricks Antony into suicide in the hope of gaining Octavius' love.[20] In *Cléopâtre* (1648) La Calprenède treats our Cleopatra (his heroine's mother) sympathetically, idealizing her relationship with Julius Caesar; but her years with Antony bring a moral decline, and her execution of Artabasus [Artavasdes] is a crime whose consequences dog her children.[21] In Robert Garnier's *Marc-Antoine* (1578) love is constant, but the play ends not with transcendence but with waste, loss, and lamentation (V.1793–2000). And there is no hint of transcendent love in the accounts of Hans Sachs and Georg Neumark, who are both as sternly concerned with the evils of passion as any classical author. Both respond to the pathos of the lovers' deaths, but both also allow moral condemnation the last word:[22] Sachs's Octavius briefly praises Cleopatra's "trew" (VII, p. 231), but a moralizing epilogue (pp. 232–3) renews the attack on the lovers, stigmatizing Cleopatra as "untrew" and much more. This is hardly praise of transcendent constancy.

In other works, love is not the all-important theme. Cesare de' Cesari's *Cleopatra* (Venice, 1552) is primarily the tragedy of a fallen queen, and, though Cleopatra envisages eternal reunion with Antony, the reunion is to take place in regions of Tartarean gloom.[23] Moreover, the narration of Cleopatra's death dwells not on her love for Antony but on her love for her daughters, maids, and slave (V, pp. 41^r–45^r); the choric praise of immutable love (V, p. 44^v), which Canfield applies to the love of Antony and Cleopatra (p. 41), quite explicitly refers to the loyalty of Charmion and Iras to their mistress. Étienne Jodelle's *Cléopâtre captive* (1552) is primarily concerned with the heroine's indomitable courage: the Act III chorus, for instance, contrasts the inconstancy of Fortune with the "constance" that Cleopatra displays in thrashing the treacherous Seleucus.[24] Indeed, far from celebrating transcendent love, the play opens with a sombre monologue for the damned ghost of Antony, who deplores his infatuation with Cleopatra and takes grim comfort from the certainty that she will soon be sharing his torments (I, pp. 95–7). In Celso Pistorelli's *Marc' Antonio, e Cleopatra* (Verona, 1576), finally, Cleopatra's tragedy is interlaced with, even overshadowed by, the tragedies of her children. In first electing death, the heroine does envisage Elysian reunion with Antony (IV, p. 34^v), but during her suicide she thinks only of her nurse, her children, and her sins (V, pp. 48^r–50^r).

Even were the tradition as unanimous as Canfield suggests, it would of itself prove nothing about Dryden. But, in fact, the tradition is so varied that it does not even provide us with a new presupposition about Dryden's likely approach to the subject. And the fact remains that Dryden was chiefly influenced by Shakespeare, whom even Canfield exempts from his supposed tradition. In particular, Dryden took over and transformed one important strand of Shakespeare's play: the lovers' self-exalting self-dramatization in a world increasingly alien to their aspirations. In *All for Love* the role-playing remains but the self-exaltation is largely gone, for the roles are stifling and unwanted, imposed by uncomprehending outsiders on an exhausted hero and on a bewildered heroine who secretly longs for quiet, obscure domesticity. But Dryden did also respond to a wider spectrum of the Antony and Cleopatra tradition: in portraying the often conflicting roles thrust on his hero and heroine, he exploited the very antinomies of earlier tradition, creating his own subtle mirror-relationship between the extremes of idealization and condemnation.

II

The action in *All for Love* proceeds almost wholly from the stagecraft of its characters (most overt in the laborious rehearsals and counter-rehearsals of Act

IV).[25] Throughout, they attempt to exercise a dramaturgic control over increasingly uncontrollable events, to efface a world of change and menace and give substance to the ideals of a vanishing order, with the result that the play is a sequence of scenes staged by rival dramatists: Antony's sylvan fantasy (I.231–44) and his numerous re-enactments of the past; Ventidius' and Alexas' alternating reconstructions of the hero's personality, in which his desires and words are at first shaped with an unerring, puppeteering skill; Charmion's embassy to Antony (II.47–77), where—like Alexas later (II.154–87)—she actually plays the role of Cleopatra, rehearsing all her mistress's "sighs and tears" (59); Antony's unsuccessful attempt to preordain the pattern of his first dialogue with Cleopatra by permitting her to speak only if he lies (II.251–5); the sublime pageant of Venus and Mars (III.1–28); and, in the midst of the surprises that Ventidius pulls from the wings in Act III, Antony's recreation of the great, theatrical display on the Cydnos (156–87), with Cleopatra posing as the "Sea-born *Venus*"(166). Thus, at the mid-point of the play, memories of Cleopatra's elaborate, histrionic début on the Cydnos immediately precede Octavia's no less carefully stage-managed re-entry into Antony's life. But then comes Antony's surrender to the infamous barrage of titles—"Emperour," "Friend," "Husband," "Father" (III.362–3)—and here we witness the last and (designedly) the crudest demonstration of triumphant role-making. For hereafter the manipulative scenarios go disastrously astray: Alexas and Ventidius, the chief contrivers, reveal passionate and even erotic complexities that destroy their own assumed identities and herald their failure to control the identities and passions of others (III.379–92, IV.232–47); dabbling in passions which they resentfully desire but cannot understand, they preside over the disastrous fictions of Act IV, using identical schemes to create antithetical roles for Antony and finding that he can act neither. By the end of his act theatre and life are hopelessly confounded: faced with Octavia, Antony cannot feign a Roman part by forcing "a smile at *Cleopatra's* falsehood" (IV. 438); but, faced with his friend and his mistress, he cannot distinguish the man and the woman from the actors created by Alexas and Ventidius. In Act V, Antony briefly recovers his Roman role, resolving to die in sustained mimicry of Ventidius (173–7); but news of Cleopatra's death renders him "weary of [his] part" (285), and there begins the final reassertion of love, culminating in the final piece of character-contrived dramaturgy: Cleopatra's dying re-enactment of the Cydnos pageant.

In their dramaturgic endeavors, the characters repeatedly try to shape and control the utterances of their fellows, even forcing them to silence in order to compose for them the speeches which hope or preconception dictate. For example, when Antony first gropes towards renewed Roman identity his speeches are not the outpourings of a reasserted self but *anticipations of the words he imagines to be in Ventidius' mouth*: "Thou ... speak'st not half thou think'st" (I. 284), he interposes; "I'll help thee" (291); "I know thy meaning" (292). Here, Antony is attempting to discover the speeches that Ventidius has devised for him. More frequently, however, characters flagrantly arrogate the privilege of speech-writer to themselves. When Dollabella hesitantly reproaches Antony's decline, Ventidius butts in with a polemic account of what Dollabella "would say" (III.188–98). When Octavia's cold self-righteousness repels Antony (III.255–330), Dollabella promptly gives his own version of Octavia's feelings, of the love implicit in her *"silence"* (335; italics added); and, though Octavia's *ipsissima verba* had grated upon Antony, Dollabella's suppositious account moves him to "a secret yielding" (337), so that the Octavia of Dollabella's creation proves more powerful than the Octavia of Dryden's. Scheming to maneuvre Antony into an incurably Roman view of Cleopatra, Ventidius again bolsters preconception with the speculative elucidation of silence:

> She look'd methought
> As she would say, Take your old man, *Octavia;*
> Thank you, I'm better here.   (IV.228–30)

The script-writing continues even in the last, ecstatic reassertion of love. When Cleopatra reaffirms her constancy to Antony, she speaks according to her lover's dictation: "Say but thou art not false," he urges (V.374). And the compulsive exegesis of silence persists even in the play's final speech, where Serapion confidently (but questionably) unravels the meaning couched in Cleopatra's "smile" (V. 510).[26]

Through their dramaturgic contrivances the characters attempt to give substance to the two most opposed verdicts of art and history on the events comprised in the play. The eunuch Alexas strives to sustain the vision of divine eroticism enacted on the Cydnos, briefly recaptured in the Venus and Mars pageant, and finally reasserted in Cleopatra's death and Serapion's valediction. Conversely, those who would create a Roman Antony endeavour also to create the Cleopatra of Rome and its apologists: the foe to temperance and manhood, the adept in sorceries, the flatterer, the Siren, the whore. And, unseen amidst the visions of demonic darkness or divine radiance, wanders an increasingly vulnerable woman, a "harmless" infant (III.485), a "harmless household Dove" (IV.92), whose mundane weakness is most fully exposed in the venial but tragic compromise of Act IV; for Dryden's Cleopatra is neither Circe nor Aphrodite, and she is destroyed as much by the apotheoses of her admirers as by the execrations of her antagonists.

Indeed, Dryden suggests a surprising kinship between the rival views of the heroine. Disclosing his own painful fascination with Cleopatra, Ventidius produces a tortured reworking of Antony's exultant worship. For Antony, Cleopatra had represented a timeless simultaneity of fruit and blossom, and a source of endless self-fulfillment:

> There's no satiety of Love, in thee;
> Enjoy'd, thou still art new; perpetual Spring
> Is in thy armes; the ripen'd fruit but falls,
> And blossoms rise to fill its empty place;
> And I grow rich by giving.   (III.24–8)

Ventidius, by contrast, sees natural cycles and personal identity transmuted by
malign sorcery: "Her eyes have pow'r beyond *Thessalian* Charms [*pharmaka*] / To
draw the Moon from Heav'n" (IV.233–4); her Siren "flatt'ry" permits night to steal
unnoticed upon the day (235–7); and

> The holy Priests gaze on her when she smiles;
> And with heav'd hands, forgetting gravity,
> They bless her wanton eyes.   (IV.239–41)

To claim with Canfield that Ventidius is "praising the timeless quality of Cleopatra"
(p. 54) is simply to ignore what Ventidius says. Nevertheless, there is a disturbing
symmetry between idealization and malign fascination, not least because Antony
and Ventidius echo consecutive sentences of Shakespeare's Enobarbus;[27] and the
symmetry is improved in Serapion's concluding panegyric, when a holy priest does
indeed gaze at Cleopatra's "smile" and bless it (V.510, 515). In Antony's mouth the
Shakespearean imagery is heightened, whereas in Ventidius' it merges with imagery
of flattery and evil enchantment familiar from Plutarch and Dio. But Dryden derives
the traditional terms of condemnation from a grudging yet irrepressible attraction,
so that the impulses to vilify and deify Cleopatra seem alternative but strangely
related responses to a single experience: the impact of a mesmeric and seemingly
superhuman beauty. The two responses combine in Dollabella, whose courtship of
Cleopatra is at first actuated by a malignant fascination akin to Ventidius': though he
blames "the love of ruin'd *Antony*" (IV.51), he helplessly envies his ruin, at once
overwhelmed by the goddess of the Cydnos and convinced that the goddess is a
destructive and corrupting Siren.[28] Even Octavia expresses her hatred of Cleopatra
in fascination, poring over "th' inevitable *charms,* that catch / Mankind so sure"
(III.437–8; italics added). If Antony vacillates between the roles purveyed by his rival
puppeteers, Cleopatra is imprisoned and finally destroyed by the opposed but
equally unwanted roles thrust on her by her admirers and enemies, for her true
character is persistently obscured as those who surround her transmute a good,
loyal, but mundane woman into a figure of either barbaric evil or divine radiance.
The nature and consequences of their misapprehensions remain to be examined.

III

In their dramaturgic attempts to resurrect and perpetuate a dying order, the
characters attempt to give the transient, ever-changing patterns of life the permanence of art. Nor is drama the only vehicle for their artistry, for they consistently
invest organic life with the condition of the mineral artefact, which can to some
degree be changed or fixed according to the demands of the will, giving the
transformations wrought by the human imagination a limited immunity to those
wrought by time. Characters even think of each other as statues, and regard the
transmutation of character as the melting and recasting of a moulded image: An-

tony, for example, imagines that Dollabella might "melt" Caesar from his "hard rugged Image, . . . / And mould him in what softer form he pleas'd" (III.87–8).[29] But even in these images there are often hints of a discrepancy between the nature of the material and the intentions of the artist: Ventidius, the "true-stampt Roman" (I.106), proves adamantly resistant to Alexas' attempts at transformation, and Dollabella, conversely, protests that he has been "cast . . . in so soft a mould" (IV.12) that he will not be able to receive the form that Antony wishes to give him; and, of course, he does resist his friend's shaping hand, though not in the manner anticipated.

The artefacts of Rome are of iron: Antony boasts to Ventidius that he will appear "once again in Iron" (I.426) and to Charmion later seems "Incompass'd . . . with Iron *Statues*" (II.48; italics added). In Egypt, however, iron belongs only to the dead—an "Iron Wicket" guards the Ptolemies' funeral vault (I.21)—and the artefacts of the living are rich and varied in substance: silver, gold, purple silk, and, above all, jewels. But even art is not eternal, and the images of brilliant, dead lustre are overshadowed and contradicted by other images: we are reminded that even art can be evanescent, and that life cannot in any case attain the purity and perfection of art; for life is marred by stain, taint, and poison. The play's first statue image— Serapion's "Fortune striding, like a vast *Colossus*" (I.69)—is of a statue ruined long before the events of the play, and the image of destroyed artefact becomes explicit when Alexas (employing a recurrent idea) complains that Cleopatra "winds her self" about Antony's "mighty *ruins*" (I.78; italics added).[30] But, mutable though it may be, art occupies a realm that life cannot enter, and we do not share Ventidius' fear that ancestral souls may "animate their Marbles, / To blush at their degenerate Progeny" (I.154–5). Statues are obdurately lifeless, and the blush (another recurrent idea)[31] betokens the blood of life; but the blush also acknowledges the shame and blemishes that deny life the marmoreal perfection of art.

The most complex artistic images are those which combine ideas of inorganic lustre with those of human stain, defilement, and decay. Ventidius, for example, laments that Cleopatra has *"deck'd"* Antony's

> *ruin* with her love,
> Led him in *golden* bands to *gaudy* slaughter,
> And made *perdition* pleasing. (I.170–2; italics added)

Related to the imagery of corruption and decay is that of poison. Ventidius likens Antony to a scorpion driven to sting itself (I.314–15), and images of poison first combine with those of aesthetic splendor when Ventidius reviles the jewels and silks which Alexas offers on Cleopatra's behalf:

> Touch not these poyson'd gifts,
> Infected by the sender, touch 'em not,
> Miriads of blewest Plagues lye underneath 'em,
> And more than Aconite has dipt the Silk. (II.203–6)

Ventidius' choice of poison is perhaps infelicitous, since aconite was held to cure scorpion bites,[32] but his morbid fears magnify and distort realities which Antony would merely wish away. For, haunted by the inanimate perfection of the Cydnos apparition, Antony cannot come to terms with the blemishes endemic to organic life; consequently, when the stains of life unavoidably intrude on his radiant memories, he responds with the same uncomprehending visions of poisoned splendor as does Ventidius. Antony's blind worship contains the seeds of Ventidius' blind horror: hence the suggestive parallels between Antony's adoration and Ventidius' malign attraction, and the parallels between Ventidius' attraction and Serapion's final homage, which transmits Antony's ideals to exponents in the distant future; parallels, in short, between the views recorded by ancient Rome and "late Posterity" (V.518).

The dissonant combination of splendor and corruption—unblemished art and discolored life—reappears when Antony himself joins Ventidius in denouncing Cleopatra for her conduct at Actium: "Oh stain to Honor!" (II.310), Antony exclaims, to be seconded by Ventidius:

What haste she made to hoist her purple Sails!
And, to appear magnificent in flight,
Drew half our strength away.   (II.313–15)[33]

The image of tainted honor is incongruously followed by the memory of the unchangingly beautiful sails, themselves both magnificent and corrupting, sapping away the strength of the navy. Significantly, moreover, Antony regains faith in Cleopatra only by turning his eyes from the flaws of life and transforming her once more into a (literally) immaculate figure. He reproaches her as "stain'd by *Cæsar*" (II.276) and as staining his honor (310),[34] and in reply Cleopatra pointedly avoids claiming flawlessness, craving rather to be seen as a human figure with the frailties inherent in human life: her liaison with Caesar was a pragmatic concession to power (346–59), she wrongly urged a naval engagement at Actium (374–5), and she fled from it through fear (376–7). But Antony misunderstands her explanations and impulsively renews his trust in a figure of imagined divine immaculacy, reproving Ventidius as the "Blasphemer" of "wrong'd Innocence" (436, 437).

The contrast between Antony's aesthetic and Cleopatra's organic views of life recurs at the beginning of Act III. When Cleopatra looks forward to the night of love that never comes, she imagines an Antony whom she will *"mark . . . red with many an eager kiss"* (10; italics added), whereas Antony responds by hailing her as his "Brighter *Venus!*" (11), again investing her with a perfect, superhuman, but incorporeal radiance. At the end of the act, by contrast, Cleopatra sees—and fears—*Octavia* as the embodiment of inhuman splendor, remaining aware that she herself is sullied by the stains of life; Octavia, she imagines, will be *"Bright* as a Goddess" (III.403; italics added); she herself embodies the "rubbish" remaining after her rival's creation (406). And, when Octavia's arrival has dispelled fears about her beauty, Cleopatra persists (far less affectedly) in her contrast:

You bear the specious Title of a Wife,
To *guild* your Cause, and draw the pitying World
To favour it: the World contemns poor me;
For I have lost my Honour, lost my Fame,
And *stain'd* the glory of my Royal House,
And all to bear the *branded* Name of Mistress.   (III.460–5; italics added)

Cleopatra's tragedy is that no one else views her with such sober realism.

The fullest exposition of the aesthetic view of Cleopatra is provided in Antony's recollections of the Cydnos voyage. Cleopatra comes to the Cydnos slurred with suspected complicity in the death of Dollabella's brother and determined to counter the charges against her; indeed, in a significant metaphor, she comes "To clear her self" (III.160), and does so in the most literal manner, dazzling her accusers with the flawless radiance of "Gold" (163), "Purple" (164), and "Silver" (177), and smiling with an equally lifeless radiance, so that "A darting glory seem'd to blaze abroad" (174). Here life abdicates before art, for the living figures are immobile and inert—"plac'd" (165), lying (166, 168), standing (172)—and all motion is accomplished by the artefacts: the waving streamers (163), fanning wings (172), and the oars (177), whose beating of time preserves a sense of temporal flow even in this first assertion of timeless divinity. And Antony responds with a sensory delight in external, aesthetic splendor that barely distinguishes the woman from the trappings:

> but if she smil'd,
> A darting glory seem'd to blaze abroad:
> That men's desiring eyes were never weary'd;
> But hung upon the object: to soft Flutes
> The Silver Oars kept time; and while they plaid,
> The hearing gave new pleasure to the sight;
> And both to thought.   (III.173–9)

Despite the echoes of Plato with which they claim a transfiguring and elevating love,[35] Antony and Cleopatra inhabit that world of artistic fiction which for Plato was three times removed from the reality of transcendent forms (*Republic* 596a–99a). For Antony, Cleopatra is a mimetic "object" (176) of the senses, and Cleopatra's misfortune is that her conduct at the Cydnos determines the conduct of her life, for she can only ever hold the admiration of her lover by disowning the mundane frailties of her nature and sheltering behind a blaze of perfect but lifeless brilliance. And in Act IV she is destroyed when art becomes inescapably discrepant from life and can no longer even seem to perfect it. It is ominous, indeed, that Dryden's Cleopatra should pose as "another Sea-born *Venus*" (166), mimicking the famous *Aphrodite anadyomene* of Apelles; for that work too exemplifies the tragic impermanence of art, and had decayed irreparably when Pliny came to describe Apelles' work.[36]

The fragility of art and ugliness of life are most subtly combined, early in Act
IV, in a brief exchange between Cleopatra and Dollabella:

CLEOPATRA: Your *Roman* Wits, your *Gallus* and *Tibullus,*
Have taught you this from *Citheris* and *Delia.*
DOLLABELLA: Those *Roman* Wits have never been in *Egypt.*   (IV.106–8)

Love poetry is a fit enough vehicle for flirtation, but the poetic compliments conceal
some complexities: Cleopatra's reference to Cytheris is painfully appropriate, since
she too was a former mistress of Antony; Gallus' works provide one of the saddest
testimonies to the transience of art; and Gallus was soon to remedy his inexperience of Egypt—as first Roman governor of the conquered province.

   Throughout Act IV the imagery stresses the discrepancy between the blemishes of life and the alien lustre of art. When Alexas urges Cleopatra to recover
Antony's love, his imagery suggests the sullying of a polished object: jealousy, he
argues, is like "A polisht Glass held to the lips when life's in doubt:/If there be
breath, 'twill catch the damp and show it" (IV.72–3). Like the blush, the discolor-
ation of the mirror is at once a sign of life and a symbol of imperfection. In her reply
Cleopatra maintains the imagery of corporeal defect, though she wishes that me-
dicinal art could cure sick nature: jealousy, she claims, "puts out the disease, and
makes it show,/But has no pow'r to cure" (IV.76–7). When the flirtation gets
under way, moreover, both parties instinctively and guiltily seize on images of
poison: "Love may be expell'd by other Love,/As Poysons are by Poysons" (IV.
136–7), Cleopatra reassures Dollabella; and, when Dollabella is giving his feigned
account of Antony's parting speech, he too turns to the idea of poison, representing
his friend's climactic words as "She'll poyson to the Center" (IV.167). Once the
pretence has been dropped, however, Dollabella does restore Cleopatra to the
status of art:

I find your breast fenc'd round from humane reach,
Transparent as a Rock of solid Crystal;
Seen through, but never pierc'd. My Friend, my Friend!
What endless treasure hast thou thrown away,
And scatter'd, like an Infant, in the Ocean,
Vain sums of Wealth which none can gather thence.   (IV.201–6)

As Canfield notes (p. 52), Dollabella here uses jewel imagery to praise Cleopatra's
constancy. Nevertheless, the imagery is too equivocal to constitute mere auctorial
panegyric. According to ancient theory rock crystal consists of water petrified by
extreme cold,[37] and as such it represents a stabilization of one of the play's chief
images of mutability: the element that, from Serapion's description of the Nile
onwards, has combined ideas of flood and exhaustion, life and death (for even the
Cydnos witnessed not the genesis of Antony's love but that of a rival and fatal
affection). The suspension of flux is, however, at best precarious, since rock crystal
derives its value solely from its fragility,[38] and water is released from its stasis in

Dollabella's second image, where a hostile and intractable element engulfs the alien substances which man insecurely transforms into expressions of human value. The inanimate, inorganic image of the "Sea-born *Venus*" (III.166) is here, in effect, claimed by the element over which it feigned a brief mastery.

Antony's return, however, renews the imagery of corruption and poison. Although he at first refuses to believe Cleopatra "tainted" (IV.318), he soon accepts her guilt and begins to see in Dollabella a further mocking synthesis of aesthetic beauty and human corruption: "With how secure a brow, and specious form / He *guilds* the secret Villain!" he exclaims (IV.445–6; italics added); similarly, he reverts to imagery of poison, seeing his friend and mistress as "Serpents" (IV.470) whom he has fatally warmed in his bosom. Dollabella and Cleopatra both beg Antony to forgive their stains, Dollabella pleading that repentance may *"wash away"* his crime (IV.512; italics added), Cleopatra again urging her lover to accept a life necessarily tarnished and stained: " 'Twas I blew up the fire that *scorch'd* his Soul," she confesses (IV.518; italics added). But Antony still cannot accept the blemishes attendant on life, and, though Cleopatra's flirtation with his friend presents him with clear evidence of her bewilderment and vulnerability, he cannot understand what he sees, transforming her not from goddess to woman but from goddess to infernal monster, worthy of pains exceeding all that Tartarus has hitherto inflicted (IV.475–82). And, embittered and uncomprehending, he retreats from the spectacle of human frailty to the unyielding artifice of Rome: "Oh Iron heart!" Cleopatra laments (IV.568). Antony has exchanged the illusions of the Cydnos for those of the Tiber.

By the end of Act IV the beauties of art have become quite alien to the blemishes of life, and the discrepancy between them is confirmed by the events of Act V. In his final fiction, Alexas attempts to "clear" Cleopatra once more (V.105, 117, 219); but, out of all the analogies afforded by history, he chooses to compare his mistress to the defiled *"Lucrece"* (V.227); and his fictive attempts to restore the immaculate ideal create only the messy reality of Antony's death. Cleopatra's own death, moreover, conclusively reaffirms the unbridgeable disparity between art and life. She does, as Canfield observes (p. 53), complete the pattern of jewel images by calling for her regalia; but she also completes the pattern of poison images by calling for the serpents. Bejewelled without, poisoned within, she sustains the antithesis between corporeal corruptibility and mineral splendor that has dominated the play;[39] in the end, jewelry joins iron as the artefact of the dead. Significantly, moreover, when Cleopatra receives the snakebite she *"Turns aside, and then shows her Arm bloody"* (s.d., V.489)—that is, she shows her arm *stained*. To the end, reality resists the transformations attempted by art. It is therefore perhaps appropriate that in her final histrionic recreation of the past, preparing to meet Antony as when she "saw him first, on *Cydnos* bank" (V.459), Cleopatra should act out a dramatic tradition that is at odds with the facts of this play. Cleopatra here acts out the tradition of Daniel, Shakespeare, and May;[40] but, with the authority of Appian,[41] Dryden has laboriously established that the pair met and loved long before the Cydnos incident (II.262–77, 346–59). The final pageant of transcendent love still declares the uncertainty of art and history.

The jewel imagery, then, is not simply panegyric, but serves rather to stress the inevitable disparity between the actualities of life and the creations of art; between the woman of Egypt and the divinity of the Cydnos. And in Dryden's account it is the latter image that, in various but strangely linked ways, has haunted the imaginations of antiquity and late posterity. Consider the first two jewel images in the play: Ventidius' complaint that Cleopatra "new names her Jewels" (I.363) taxes and provinces, and Alexas' production of the "Ruby bracelet, set with bleeding hearts" (II.199). Canfield (p. 52) sees in these incidents symbols of Cleopatra's transcendent constancy (though Ventidius is abusing her reckless prodigality and Alexas is being singularly devious and unsublime). But we need not distort the tone and context of these passages: in both Cleopatra is associated with jewels and in both she works on them with the transforming power of her imagination, successively treating them as symbols of empire and love. The jewels are not symbols of Cleopatra herself but manifestations of the artistic imagination that she showed most consummately on the waters of the Cydnos; for her, jewelry *per se* is something fit to be given only to Alexas (III.411–12). Antony's jewel images, however, are very different from Cleopatra's, for he simply identifies the woman with the artefact, as he has done ever since the Cydnos voyage; to the end, the illusions of art blind him to the actualities—and the needs—of life. Grieving over imagined betrayal by his dearest intimates, he delivers a coarse and revealing lament for the disintegration of the Cydnos image, likening himself to a "Merchant" watching a sinking cargo of inanimate "Wealth" (V.206, 208). Trustful once more, and overwhelmed by his mistress's reported death, he sees his former "Pow'r" and "Empire" as mere "Merchandise to buy her love" (V.271–2), and it is this mercantile metaphor that reintroduces the cult of the artefact: the world is "An Empty Circle, since the Jewel's gone," and now lacks "all the bribes of life" (V.274, 276); and, in the lovers' last encounter, Cleopatra is the "one dear Jewel" (V.367) that the traveller returns to add to his baggage. Moving as these last two tributes are, they are the tributes of an imagination at once idealizing and insensitive, unable to grasp the human reality it faces. And it is an imagination that is, once again, curiously akin to that of the opposition: in using "Empire" as "Merchandise" to gain Cleopatra's love, Antony becomes uncomfortably like the Octavius who was "fit indeed to buy, not conquer Kingdoms" (III.215), and still more like the Octavius who tempted Cleopatra with the "price" of "Kingdoms" (II.442, III.235). Yet throughout the play Cleopatra shows that Antony means everything to her and the world nothing; and, as Alexas coaches her in the unwanted role of Siren, she longs to escape from magnificent eroticism into the inglorious respectability of "a silly harmless houshold Dove" (IV.92). Antony, no less than Ventidius or Octavia, is inhibited by his Roman imagination from understanding Cleopatra's nature: throughout his career of suicidal prodigality he has sought to purchase the divine apparition on the Cydnos, wastefully courting the "Sea-born *Venus*" (III.166) and wastefully returning her to "the Ocean" (IV.205) in his incomprehension at finding her a mere woman. And so, especially during the period of fatal misunderstanding, his imagery suggests an unexpected but fitting equivalence between the destructive worship of Antony, the "Merchant," and the destructive hostility of Octavius, the tradesman *manqué*.

The reconciliation of Act V brings no new understanding, but simply resurrects the false pageantry of the past—pageantry in part expressed through the final jewel images. Intimations of Elysian love (common in the dramatic tradition)[42] abound, but they are framed and counteracted by hints of final extinction. Immediately before his suicide and reconciliation, Antony falls into Epicurean doubts about the soul's survival (V.346), believing that death may be "but to think no more" (with the result that his speedy conversion to Elysian rapture [V.394–7] seems arbitrary and capricious). And, after all the transcendent visions, the dying Cleopatra, blinded by the asp bite, loses her triumphant (and conventional) sense of reunion with Antony (494–5) and instead gropes unseeingly for his corpse (496–500)—for the lifeless remnants of an irrecoverable past. Moreover, the intervening ecstasies are solitary experiences, uncommunicated to the partner; for during Antony's raptures Cleopatra is aware only of hastening change, and when she begins her own transports Antony is "gone too far, to hear" her (V.408). Dryden thus provides not transfiguration but a final conflict between the idealizing, dramaturgic imagination and the terrors of transience. "Say but thou art not false" (V.374), Antony prompts in his last act as script-writer; and, when Cleopatra has obeyed his prompting, he believes her because death induces a wish to believe (382–4). But the affirmations of eternal love are juxtaposed—even interlinked—with a continuing awareness of fugitive time: "A moment more" (364); "Removing in a hurry" (366); "His fleeting life" (372); "my life's not long enough for more. / . . . I believe thee" (381–2). Even when Antony hymns reunion "in Groves below" (395), Cleopatra notices only the transience of his words, which are "like the Notes of dying Swans, / Too sweet to last" (398–9). And, most remarkably, Antony's final affirmation of a love surpassing the world itself serves as a paradigm of transience:

> CLEOPATRA: Were there so many hours
> For your unkindness, and not one for love?
> ANTONY: No, not a minute.——This one kiss——more worth
> Than all I leave to *Cæsar.*   *Dies.*   (V.399–402)

Cleopatra attempts to transmute and perpetuate the vanished moment in her imagination, to metamorphose the fleeting kiss into "ten thousand kisses" (404). But Antony has "gone too far, to hear" her, and his senseless "leavings of a Soul" are deaf to the transforming power of language (408, 410).

Throughout her entire, final conversation with Antony, Cleopatra is obsessed with transience, and she gains thoughts of immortality only when, deprived of her lover, she resumes the histrionic pageantry of the Cydnos. But even here discords persist, for the splendors of art are still contaminated by the stains and poisons of the world, and the beckoning of Antony's spirit at last dwindles into the touch of his corpse. Greatly though Dryden differs from Plutarch in his human judgments, he resembles him in confining the lovers' passion to the realm of death and change. Then Serapion enters and blesses Cleopatra's smile, unaware that it records not an entry into immortality but a final dalliance with the mortal world. Dead, the lovers have passed finally into the condition of art, their lifeless postures and mute expressions now the property of Serapion's vivifying imagination.[43] Like so much of the earlier verbal creation in the play, Serapion's is elaborated around silence; for the figures of the past are inexorably silent, alike to the historian and the dramatist. Throughout the play, the living Cleopatra has been engulfed by the extinct, wordless image from the Cydnos; now, still unrecognised, she enters a past and a silence that are still more final and impenetrable.

NOTES

[1] "The Jewel of Great Price: Mutability and Constancy in Dryden's *All for Love*," *ELH*, XLII (1975), 38–61. For a more reliable account of the tradition as far as Shakespeare, see Marilyn L. Williamson, *Infinite Variety: Antony and Cleopatra in Renaissance Drama and Earlier Tradition* (Mystic, Conn., 1974). Canfield's article was a reply to my own "The Significance of *All for Love*," *ELH*, XXXVII (1970), 540–63. I shall not repeat or defend my earlier arguments, though I shall incidentally offer new confirmation for some of them. I should, however, like to recant my claim that Dryden denies all objective validity to human perception and judgment. He certainly portrays characters whose constricted imaginations vitiate their understanding of their fellows, but it is unnecessary to conclude that he propounds an all-embracing scepticism.

[2] Canfield slips up particularly in his readings of three plays. The cornerstone of his interpretation of Cesare de' Cesari's *Cleopatra* (Venice, 1552) is a choric passage in praise of immutable love (V, p. 44^v), which he cites as a celebration of Antony and Cleopatra's constancy (p. 41). In fact, the chorus is quite explicitly praising the loyalty of "Eras, e Cherimonia" (Iras and Charmion) to their queen. According to Canfield, the heroine of Isaac de Benserade's *La Cleopatre* (Paris, 1636) is "From the beginning ... constant to Antony" (p. 46). In fact, she tries to gain Octavius' love (IV, pp. 37^r–40^r) and dies lamenting her *inconstancy* to Antony (V, pp. 47^v–48^r, 49^v). Moreover, Antony's "Ajouste la constance à tes autres vertus" (III, p. 24^v) is not, as Canfield claims (p. 46), a tribute to Cleopatra's fidelity; rather, Antony is telling her to dry her tears and be brave. Indeed, Canfield's persistent failure to distinguish the different senses of "constancy" (chiefly fortitude and fidelity) makes his whole argument misleadingly equivocal. In discussing Sir Charles Sedley's *Antony and Cleopatra* (1677), Canfield misrepresents the heroine's death scene by means of deceptively selective quotation: Cleopatra he claims, "kills herself to pursue a good that is 'real' and transcendent: 'Love alone can to the Dead extend,' where 'Lovers in Eternal Roses Love'" (p. 48). "Love alone can to the Dead extend" in fact expresses Cleopatra's hope that Octavius will forgive her once she is dead (V.ii.94–7, in *The Poetical and Dramatic Works of Sir Charles Sedley*, ed. V. de Sola Pinto [London, 1928], I). The Elysian "Lovers in Eternal Roses" appear seven lines later (103), after Cleopatra has mentioned such other Elysian inhabitants as heroes and poets (100–2). The sense that Canfield imposes on the passage—that love alone triumphs over the grave—simply is not there. There are also a couple of slighter errors. In claiming that Robert Garnier's Cleopatra dies "'happie' in the end" (p. 42), Canfield ignores the concluding anguished threnody that follows the heroine's brief flicker of joy (*The Tragedie of Antonie*, trans. Mary Sidney, Countess of Pembroke [1595], V.1963–2000, in *Narrative and Dramatic Sources of Shakespeare*, ed. Geoffrey Bullough [London, 1957–75], V). And Philostratus and Arius, the philosophers in Samuel Daniel's *The Tragedie of Cleopatra* (1599), are decidedly not men whom misfortune has "taught a *contemptus mundi*" (Canfield, p. 43). The pair have in fact learned quite the opposite lesson: namely, that for all their homilies on the vanity of life they are still very anxious to go on living (III.469–592, in Bullough, V).

[3] For other classical assessments of Antony and Cleopatra, all more or less hostile, see Appian, *The Civil Wars* II.33–V.145, esp. V.8–11; Cassius Dio, *Roman History* XLI–LI; Florus, *Epitome of Roman History* II.16, 19–21; Horace, *Odes* I. xxxvii, *Epodes* ix; Josephus, *Against Apion* ii.56–61, *The Jewish War* I.243,

359–63, VII.300–3, *The Jewish Antiquities* XV.88–103; Pliny, *Natural History* IX.119, XIX.22; Propertius, *Elegies* III.xi.39–72; Strabo, *Geography* XVII.i.11; Velleius Paterculus, *Roman History* II.60–1, 66, 82–6; Virgil, *Aeneid* VIII.688–713. Though Appian and Dio are for the most part very hostile, Appian concedes some good qualities to Antony (V.65, 136), and in his retrospect upon the lovers' lives Dio concedes some virtues to both (Ll.15). Josephus sees Antony as restraining Cleopatra's malice, despite his passion for her (*J. W.* VII.302, *Ant.* XV.93–4). Like Plutarch, Horace (*Od.* I.xxxvii.21–32) and Velleius Paterculus (II.87) admire Cleopatra's courageous death. For Pliny (IX.119) and Propertius (III.xi.39), however, Cleopatra is simply a whore ("meretrix"). In citing classical works I use the universally accepted subdivisions and consequently specify texts only of those works whose verbal details I discuss. In my study of later works I have been guided by Theodore Besterman, *A Bibliography of Cleopatra* (London, 1926), rpt. from *Notes and Queries*, February 6 and 13, 1926. I have, however, been unable to locate the operatic versions, A. Olearius Adonis, *Historia von der Cleopatra* (n.p., 1606), and Francesco Pona, *Cleopatra* (Venice, 1635). I am not equipped to read Guilliam van Nieuwelandt, *Ægyptica ofte Ægyptische Tragoedie van M. Anthonius, en Cleopatra* (Antwerp, 1624), and I omit consideration of Giovanni Delfino, *La Cleopatra* (acted 1660), since it was not published until 1733.
[4] *Life of Antony* 25.1, 31.2, in *Shakespeare's Lives*, trans. Bernadotte Perrin, Loeb Classical Library (London, 1914–26), IX.
[5] *Phaedrus* 246a–48e, 253d–57b; *Republic*, 436a–44e; *Timaeus* 69c–72d.
[6] For discussions of *sōphrosunē*, see, e.g., *Republic* 430d–32a; *Gorgias* 491d–e, 493a–94a, 506e–08a; Aristotle, *Nicomachean Ethics* II.7–8, III.10. In his preamble to the *Life of Demetrius*, which also serves as an introduction to the parallel *Life of Antony*, Plutarch justifies the portrayal of blameworthy lives by arguing that, as the study of disease is necessary to the art of medicine, so the study of evil is necessary to "the most consummate arts of all": *sōphrosunē*, *dikaiosunē* (justice), and *phronēsis* (wisdom) (1.2–6). Commenting on Antony's conduct after the murder of Caesar, Dio writes, *"ouket' esōphronēsen"*—"he no longer acted with moderation" (*Dio's Roman History*, trans. Earnest Cary, Loeb Classical Library [London, 1914–27], XLIV.53.2).
[7] 2.3, 21.1, 28.2, 36.1; *Comparison of Demetrius and Antony* 4.3. Antony is implicitly contrasted with the *sōphrones* in 9.5, 21.1–2. For the antithesis of *sōphrosunē* and *akolasia* see the passages from Plato and Aristotle cited in note 6.
[8] *Antony* 9.6, 16.2, 20.2, 21.2, 24.7, 53.1, 54.1; *Comparison* 3.1; *Phaedrus* 238a, 251a, 253d–e, 254c–e.
[9] 29.1, 53.4. *Cf.* 59.3. Plutarch leads up to Antony's first meeting with Cleopatra by stressing his susceptibility to flattery (24.7–8). For Plato's discussions of flattery see *Republic* 590b and, especially, *Gorgias* 463a–66a, 501a–04e. Plato opposes flattery to true rhetoric, which produces the ordered dispositions of soul represented by the virtues of *sōphrosunē* and *dikaiosunē*. In *How to Tell a Flatterer* Plutarch recalls Antony's susceptibility to flattery and goes on to suggest that flattery nurtures the irrational part of the soul (61a–f).
[10] *"tous autē katethelxen, epei kaka pharmak' edōken"* (*Odyssey*, ed. W. W. Merry [Oxford, 1870–8] X.213). The association between Circe and Cleopatra is also implicit in the *Aeneid*: both feature in a large group of sinister female figures who threaten man's civilized self (VII.10–24, VIII.688–713), and both are partly recreated in the figure of Dido. Ariosto twice associates his Circe-figure, Alcina, with Cleopatra (*Orlando Furioso* VII.20, X.56), and Tasso's Circe-figure, Armida, has a representation of Actium (closely modelled on Virgil's) engraved on one of her palace doors, the other bearing a representation of Hercules and Omphale (*Gerusalemme liberata* XVI.3–7). Cleopatra is also associated with the debasement of man's rational or spiritual potential in Spenser, *The Faerie Queene* V.viii.2, and in Pierre Le Moyne's Tassoesque epic *Saint Louys ou la sainte couronne reconquise* (Paris, 1658) XIII, p. 392.
[11] *Antony* 25.2; *Iliad* XIV.162.
[12] Dio and Josephus also portray Antony as overcome by enchantments or *pharmaka* (*Rom. Hist.* XLIX.34.1, L.5.3–4, 26.5; *Ant.* XV.93).
[13] Pages 27ᵛ, 34ᵛ, 44ʳ, 45ᵛ, 46ʳ.
[14] Other writers also stress the lovers' greatness of soul: see Celso Pistorelli, *Marc' Antonio, e Cleopatra* (Verona, 1576), V. p. 50ᵛ ("magnanima"); Ollenix du Mont-Sacré [pseudonym and near-anagram of Nicolas de Montreux], *Cleopatre* V, p. 99 ("genereux esprit"), in *Œuvre de la chasteté ... Ensemble la tragedie de Cleopatre* (Paris, 1595); Daniel V.1586 ("the minde that's great"); Shakespeare, *Antony and Cleopatra*, ed. M. R. Ridley, The Arden Shakespeare (London, 1954) IV.xv.89 ("huge spirit"); Girolamo Graziani, *La Cleopatra* (Venice, 1633) XII.12 ("Egualmente magnanima, e constante" [expressing a resolution that Cleopatra does not wholly fulfill]); Paganino Guadenzio, *Di Cleopatra, reina d'Egitto, la vita*

considerata (Pisa, 1642), p. 8 ("grandezza dell'animo"); Daniel Casper von Lohenstein, *Cleopatra* (1661), ed. Ilse-Marie Barth (Stuttgart, 1965) V.32 "gross-müttig"); Dryden, *All for Love* I.125 ("vast Soul"), in *John Dryden: Four Tragedies*, ed. L. A. Beaurline and Fredson Bowers (Chicago and London, 1967). In addition, Daniel repeatedly stresses the honor and indomitability of Cleopatra's soul, and Shakespeare repeatedly stresses the lovers' concern with their greatness of character. Plutarch sees nobility (*euge-neia*) in Cleopatra's suicide (86.4); by translating this as "lofty spirit," Perrin adds his own contribution to the magnanimity tradition. The magnanimity attributed to Antony and Cleopatra is not strictly the *megalopsuchia* of Aristotle and his Renaissance commentators, for the essence of this was perfect virtue: see *Nicomachean Ethics* IV.3 and, e.g., Alessandro Piccolomini, *De la institutione di tutta la vita de l'huomo nata nobile, e in città libera* (Florence[?], 1543), pp. 105–9; Felice Figliucci, *De la filosofia morale libri dieci* (Rome, 1551), pp. 156–65; Agostino da Sessa, *Ragionamenti ... sopra la filosofia morale d'Aristotele* (Venice, 1554), pp. 105–15. Da Sessa complains that poets and orators confuse *magna-nimità* with *fortezza* (p. 105) and cites Antony as the antithesis of the magnanimous man, referring to his "molte ... sceleratezze" (p. 114).

[15] See *Timaeus* 41e–42b.

[16] For love conquering the grave see Cinthio, *Cleopatra* (Venice, 1583) V, pp. 123–4 (where, however, the motif of love after death is not heavily stressed); Belliard, "Les Delitieuses Amours," in *Le Premier Livre des poemes* (Paris, 1578), pp. 18ʳ⁻ᵛ; Montreux III, p. 60, V, p. 108; Mairet, *Le Marc-Antoine ou la Cléopatre* (Paris, 1637) V, p. 83; Sedley, *Antony and Cleopatra* (V.ii.98–105, 130–3). For criticism of love see Cinthio I, pp. 37–40, III, pp. 84–6; Belliard, pp. 12ᵛ–13ᵛ, 24ʳ; Montreux II, pp. 47–8. Mairet stresses the lovers' original pride and folly (e.g., III, pp. 36–7, V, p. 87), seeing them as manifestations of the blindness that is the play's central metaphor; and he repeatedly dwells on the anguish of the rejected Octavia.

[17] For the lovers' constancy, see *Los áspides de Cleopatra* II, pp. 432, 434, III, p. 437, 439, 440, in Zorrilla, *Comedias escogidas*, ed. Rámon de Mesonero Romanos, Biblioteca de Autores Españoles, LIV (Madrid, 1861). For a good account of the play, emphasizing its concern with the fatality of passion, see Raymond R. MacCurdy, *Francisco de Rojas Zorilla and the Tragedy*, University of New Mexico Publications in Language and Literature, XIII (Albuquerque, 1958), pp. 98–108. Zorrilla anticipates Dryden in portraying an encounter between Octavius' sister ("Irene") and Cleopatra (III, pp. 436–7). With still greater poetic license, he represents Octavius and Antony as friends whose ideal relationship is destroyed by rivalry for Cleopatra, and portrays Cleopatra at first as a chaste queen who punishes lechery with death (I, p. 427).

[18] V.16, VII.11, 32.

[19] For Cleopatra's inconstancy see Daniel I.149–70; May, the *Tragedie of Cleopatra* (London, 1639) V, sigs. [D10ᵛ]–[D12]; Capponi, *Cleopatra* (Bologna, 1628) I, p. 18, II pp. 34–5, V, pp. 80–1; Benserade IV, pp. 37ʳ–40ʳ; Lohenstein IV.351–510. In all the plays but Daniel's Cleopatra seeks Octavius' love, as she does in Dio LI. 12. For Cleopatra's union in death with Antony's spirit see Daniel IV.1175, V.1608; May V, sigs. [D12ᵛ]–E2ᵛ (an unfortunate misprint in Canfield's article [p.45] entirely alters May's emphasis by locating Cleopatra's redemption in the *fourth* act); Capponi III, p. 48 (though, it is later suggested, Cleopatra's inconstancy may frustrate her hopes of Elysian reunion [V, pp. 80–1]); Benserade V, p. 49ᵛ; Lohenstein V.14, 33–4, 124–6.

[20] Lohenstein III.1–565; Dio LI.10.

[21] *Hymen's Præludia, or Love's Master-Piece. Being that so much admir'd Romance, entituled Cleopatra*, I [containing Books I–VI], trans. Robert Loveday et al. (London, 1665); II [containing books VII–XII], trans. J[ohn] C[oles] and J. D. (London, 1663). Cleopatra's history is briefly related in I. iii, pp. 54–63. For the consequences of Artabasus' execution see, e.g., IV.i–ii, pp. 339–87, V.ii. pp. 505–20.

[22] Sachs, *Die königin Cleopatra* (1560), in *Hans Sachs*, ed. A. v. Keller and E. Goetze (Tübingen, 1870–1908), XX; Georg Neumark, "Die verführerische Kleopatra" ["Cleopatra the seductress"; a narrative poem], in *Poetisch-historisch Lustgarten* (Frankfurt, 1666). Neumark asserts at the beginning and end of his poem (pp. 173, 228) that passion turns man into a beast ("Thier") and throughout stresses Antony's degeneracy. His account of the lovers' suicides, however, is quite moving (pp. 208–26).

[23] IV, pp. 33ʳ⁻ᵛ, 36ᵛ, 39ᵛ, V, p. 44ʳ.

[24] III, pp. 132–4, in Jodelle, *Œuvres complètes*, ed. Énea Balmas (Paris, 1965–   ), II.

[25] For discussions of role-playing in *All for Love* see Anne Davidson Ferry, *Milton and the Miltonic Dryden* (Cambridge, Mass., 1968), pp. 200–18; Hughes, "The Significance of *All for Love*," pp. 551–63; Frank J. Kearful, " 'Tis Past Recovery': Tragic Consciousness in *All for Love*," *Modern Language Quarterly*, XXXIV (1973), 227–46. Also relevant is Alan S. Fisher, "Necessity and the Winter: The Tragedy of *All*

for Love," *Philological Quarterly*, LVI (1977), 183–203. Daniel also uses theatrical imagery (I.33–42, 245–8, V.1602–7). Plutarch uses such imagery frequently in the *Life of Demetrius* but only twice in the *Life of Antony*, though he does turn from Demetrius to Antony with the words, "And now that the Macedonian play has been performed, let us introduce the Roman" (*Demetrius* 53.4): see *Demetrius* 18.3, 25.6, 28.1, 34.3, 41.3–4, 44.6, 53.1; *Antony* 29.2, 54.3.

[26] See also II.35–47, III.351–2, IV.17–52, 158–67. Such dramaturgic attempts to dictate the deeds and words of others account for the phenomenon extensively documented but, I think, imperfectly explained by Anne Davidson Ferry (pp. 178–218)—the characters' tendency to regard words as concrete objects. Seeking to override a threatening reality with their more comforting dramaturgic imaginings, to unmake the world and enthrone the will, the characters come to equate the expression with the actualization of desire, so that the words which express the will become indistinguishable from the objects that the will craves: a "word" can defeat Octavius (I.429); a jewel can be *named* into a province (I.363–5); and the language of others is so threatening that it must be silenced and replaced by words of one's own devising. The catalogue of Antony's titles (III.362–4) is the last and most blatant fusion of speech and creation. But, as the artifices of the will fail in the last two acts, language becomes impotent or positively refractory: "spare me and imagine it" (V.79); "His fury cannot be express'd by words" (V.100); "O those two words! their sound shou'd be divided" (V.238).

[27] Age cannot wither her, nor custom stale
Her infinite variety: other women cloy
The appetites they feed, but she makes hungry,
Where most she satisfies. For vilest things
Become themselves in her, that the holy priests
Bless her, when she is riggish.   (II.ii.235–40)
This proceeds from Enobarbus' recollections of the Cydnos (II.ii.190–226).

[28] For Canfield, Dollabella's perplexed and painful reaction is merely another tribute to transcendent love (p. 54).

[29] For other imagery of melting see II.214, 407, III.2.

[30] For other imagery of ruin see I.56, 164, 170, 304, II.245, 258–9, 316, 333, 361, 386, 432, III.47, 63, 343–4, 438, 452, 476, IV.51–2, 62, 572, V.22, 112. Moody E. Prior identifies "ruin" as "The most persistent single word in the play" (*The Language of Tragedy* [1947; rpt. Gloucester, Mass., 1964], p. 207). See also Canfield, p. 49.

[31] I.269, II.54, 268, 305, 345–6, III.21, 160, 292, 309, 354, 443–4, IV.287.

[32] Pliny, *Natural History* XXVII.5.

[33] Neither Plutarch nor Dio record that Cleopatra used purple sails at Actium, though this detail is mentioned in Pliny, *Natural History* XIX.22 and Florus II.21.

[34] In addition to the imagery of staining discussed in my text, see I.383, III.286.

[35] As Cleopatra echoes the *Phaedrus* in first expressing her love, so Antony echoes the *Symposium* (214a–15a) in first addressing Cleopatra. See Hughes, "The Significance of *All for Love*," p. 550, and *All for Love*, ed. N. J. Andrew (London, 1975), p. xxv.

[36] *Natural History* XXXV.91–2. Plutarch merely notes that Cleopatra was "adorned like Venus in a painting" (26.2) Daniel compares her to Venus descended "from heaven" (V.1463), and Enobarbus describes her as "O'er-picturing that Venus where we see / The fancy outwork nature" (II.ii.200–1). Graziani, however, uses the idea of *Aphrodite anadyomene* (IV.41).

[37] Pliny, *Natural History* XXXVII. 23; see also Strabo II. 3.4, Seneca, *Naturales Quaestiones* III. 25. 12.

[38] "Murrina . . . et crystallina . . . quibus pretium faceret ipsa fragilitas" (Pliny, *Natural History* XXXIII. 5). The fragility of rock crystal provides the basis for one of Lohenstein's images (*Cleopatra* II. 301–2).

[39] Is Dryden working against the old idea that certain jewels confer immunity to poisons? Diamonds, twice associated with Cleopatra (I.364, II.189), are attributed with such power by Pliny (*Natural History* XXXVII.61).

[40] Daniel V. 1460–7; Shakespeare V.ii.226–8; May V, sig. E2ʳ.

[41] Appian V.8. The debt to Appian is noted by Canfield, who oddly suggests that Dryden's aim in mentioning the early meeting "is to make Cleopatra constant to Antony from the beginning" (p. 50). But Cleopatra's liaison with Julius Caesar is more embarrassing if it follows the first meeting with Antony than if it precedes it.

[42] Pistorelli IV, p. 34ᵛ; Belliard, p. 18ᵛ; Montreux V, p. 108; Daniel V.1608; Shakespeare V.ii.279–84; May V, sigs. [D12ᵛ]–E2ʳ; Benserade V, p. 49ᵛ; Mairet V, p. 83; Lohenstein V.124; Sedley V.ii.98–105.

43 "Serapion . . . creates verbally the surviving stage-image of the corpses which we are bidden to sustain" (Kearful, p. 246), Kearful, however, sees the ending as more affirmative than I do. Since Serapion here becomes the spokesman for Antony's Egyptian self, it is interesting to recall a passage that Dio puts in the mouth of Octavius: "Therefore let no one count him a Roman, but rather an Egyptian, nor call him Antony, but rather Serapion" (L.27.1).

J. Leeds Barroll

CLEOPATRA AND THE SIZE
OF DREAMING

I

What is Cleopatra? To some she is the scheming, serpentlike embodiment of
that typological land of bondage and of the devil, ancient Egypt. To others she is
Bernard Shaw's ingénue: youthful, captivating, the lass who entices the preoccupied
Julius Caesar anxious over battles and musing on empires. To younger eyes Cleopatra is somewhat more mature—ageless enchantress, fable of Egypt come to
vibrant life, affirmation of the power of love and grace: Juliet at middle age to
Antony's virile, masterful, and aging Romeo. Remote, mysterious, cinematic gypsy,
essence of all women, spirit of deep Nile mysteries, Aphrodite and Juno, sexually
imperious and imperiously sensual, Shakespeare's Egyptian queen remains a monument to his genius and the antagonizing seductress of his critics, whose responses
to her are as disparate as her own vices and charms.

She is a study in contrasts. She loves Antony yet she sends him word that she
has killed herself. She can be teased by her servingwomen but threatens her
messenger with a knife. She grandly speaks of having Herod's head and threatens
her attendant with bloody teeth, trades bawdy jests with her eunuch and dreams
of lovers who were kings, taunts Mark Antony, flatters Caesar's servant, quarrels
with Enobarbus. In fact it is this frank soldier who, acting in his own capacity as
"critic," has left us with our cliché, a phrase for her varying forms. She is what she
is because of her "infinite variety."

But "infinite variety" does not necessarily relate in the long run to the important question of how Cleopatra, with all her élan, is to share with Hamlet—and with
Mark Antony—the role of tragic protagonist. For example, when we think of
"tragedy" we imagine certain constants. The term *anagnorisis* comes to mind,

From *Shakespearean Tragedy: Genre, Tradition, and Change in* Antony and Cleopatra (Washington,
DC: Folger Shakespeare Library, 1984), pp. 130–48, 152–87.

among other things, since something akin to "recognition" seems to lie within the dramatic experience of most of Shakespeare's tragic protagonists.[1] Othello learns it is Iago, not the dying Desdemona, who has deceived him. Or there is Antony looking at life just after the Battle of Actium—or after he learns that Cleopatra has not committed suicide. Forcing agonized speech or frenzied utterance, such moments hold an audience in that painful empathy we so associate with the tragic. Truth's brutal assault shakes the one we watch, and we too suffer—but also we are relieved. It is time that an Othello or a Macbeth finally begins to understand his own complicity in the deterioration of the events around him.

Cleopatra scarcely seems troubled by such moments. She grieves, collapses, remembers, blames the gods, broods, but it is impossible to recall in her any agonized or even disturbed sense of her own part in events. After Actium, when her own flight made Antony swerve and follow, we do not see her wrestle with awareness of her role. (When she later asks Enobarbus who was at fault, even he does not blame her.) Even Lear at one point mutters, "fool," and his word summarizes those responses found in "recognition." They show the dawn of a tragic comprehension which Cleopatra seldom or never seems to see. And while such inklings may themselves not be definitive of tragedy, they seem typical of it. Certainly their absence in Cleopatra's case can lead us to wonder—dare one say it?—whether she ought, in fact, to be taken at all seriously in just this way. If she never comes to doubt herself—as does even Coriolanus eventually—or to question her own world view, can she, in effect, be a tragic figure at all?

But the stuff of Cleopatra's tragedy may lie elsewhere: her response to Antony's death: her grief, her feeling of desolation, her intention to commit suicide. It is this event that reduces her in her own mind to "no more but e'en a woman," as she emerges from her fainting. That, and her resolution to kill herself, are perhaps her real catastrophe, a tragic process of which her spectacular death is the capstone. But yet. . . . Is this how we, or how many Shakespearean dramas themselves, view the scope and flow of the tragic vision? Do we or the plays consent to or demand such strait restriction?

This would be the story. An Egyptian queen is in love with one of the Roman rulers of the world. For various reasons he begins to lose his grip on events, meets political and personal disaster, and kills himself, much to the queen's wracking grief. And in her sorrow, which embraces no sense of any personal complicity in the great Roman's death, she finds that she can no longer exist on this earth without him. So she too ends her life.

It is, in effect, Juliet's story. Yet when *Romeo and Juliet* is described as Shakespearean tragedy, many informed students of that play join one of its choruses to speak in terms of "star"-crossed lovers, crushed not by themselves but by the ossified hates of their families. There is pity for Juliet's youth, and perhaps too for her headstrong temperament. And when Romeo dies, it is hard to see where else the helpless young woman can turn but to romantic suicide. Her case is pathetic.

But we do not view Lear, Hamlet, or Othello as "star-crossed." We expect some accounting from them. They are not fourteen years old, and we are not willing, for the most part, to shrug and ask, "What was Lear expected to do, after all?" Nor do we excuse Othello, holding him blameless because he believed some one who he thought was his friend. Yet if Cleopatra's story is to be the tale of her lover's death followed by her own sorrowful suicide, we are being asked, in effect, to deal with another Juliet, with a woman pathetically responding to the death of someone she loves. Such a case, true, is disastrous misfortune, hardly to be coveted by any one, but the distinctions I speak of are aesthetic, not moral. Disaster is not necessarily *tragic*. And while Cleopatra's grief at her bereavement is affecting as the height of pathos, the pathetic is not the tragic either; otherwise, in *Hamlet,* the greatest tragic moment might be experienced in the singing of Ophelia.

There is, perhaps, "tragic" material in the Egyptian queen's remarkable and resolute killing of herself, dressed anew in her royal garments, again for Cydnus. This response to her huge misfortune is pitiable, breathtaking, rivaling, and perhaps exceeding Juliet's pathetic surrender to the forces overwhelming her. Yet in these present times, and in Shakespeare's era too, the notion that it is simply "natural" to kill oneself because of the crushing death of a loved one is actually more romantic than real, especially when there is no question about sanity or about such psycho-physiological circumstances as prevail over Lear in his final collapse over the body of Cordelia.[2] In fact, any notion that Cleopatra, grieving over Antony's death, "naturally" committed suicide from sorrow seems melodramatically *simpliste,* a view of reality which, if it is to be attributed to the author, is uncharacteristically adolescent. Indeed, if "tragedy" is a situation in which a character contributes to her own disaster, then to accept such a melodramatic version of the queen's story as Shakespeare's is to stop seeing Cleopatra herself as a tragic figure. For little tragic choice is involved if one kills oneself simply to escape an overwhelming sorrow imposed from without. One thinks again of the "star-crossed" Juliet.

What of another version then? The Egyptian queen finds that she is going to be led in triumph by Octavius Caesar, but, too great of spirit, she eludes him and his power by contriving that death which also permits her to rejoin Antony and to claim "that kiss which is my heaven to have." Surely this triumph, this greatness of spirit must speak eloquently to Cleopatra's overwhelming claim to tragic stature. Yet what of Lear? To escape the kinds of humiliation threatened by a Caesar did not interest this old king—if only he could have his once-rejected Cordelia alive again. And he had endured some humiliations. Nor are the Roman jeers Cleopatra wants to avoid as deep as the kinds of condemnations Othello wishes visited upon himself before he kills himself as his own inflicted punishment. Is the avoidance of disgrace really the high summation of tragedy?

Indeed, the notion of an all-embracing triumph in Cleopatra's act of suicide raises questions having something to do with form: with the aesthetic nature of "tragedy." For if we derive Cleopatra's tragic stature from her triumph over Caesar and her encounter with Antony, then "tragedy" changes meaning. If Cleopatra really rises above Caesar by understanding that he is "Fortune's knave," if she really becomes worthy of calling Antony "husband," looking toward a glorious afterlife which leaves the dingy world far behind, then there is victory. It is good, Cleopatra says toward the end of her contemplations on Antony's death, to do that thing which "shackles accidents and binds up change." Her course through the drama has thus served as anticipation of this conclusion, and Cleopatra stands magnificent, triumphant. But hardly tragic.

The "tragic" in Shakespeare implies the kind of thing which we believe has happened to Lear as he looks down at his dead daughter. Or it implies Antony's new knowledge that Cleopatra is still alive, or Macbeth's melancholy wondering about why he feels nothing when news comes to him of his wife's suicide. Triumphing over Caesar and meeting one's lover in some Elysian Cydnus does not replicate such moments. Rather, we associate triumph with the comic ending of the *Odyssey* or the benign conclusions of *The Winter's Tale.* Conclusions impressive and moving, to be sure, but they are no more the aesthetic material of the thing we call "tragedy" than is the vision of triumph in Cleopatra's end. For it is a vision which, if we share it, must render the Egyptian queen not as an Othello, but as a complex and enchanting, yet comic, heroine.

This Cleopatra has been sufficiently celebrated by critics, and little can be done to add to this viewpoint except to grant the perception and sensitivity of the best of these writings.[3] Here I will argue a viewpoint opposite to these. I propose adhering as closely as possible to a fundamental concept of tragedy as a process of the kind undergone not by Viola or by Prospero, but by Brutus, by Macbeth, or by Mark Antony himself. And to do this, to look at Cleopatra's story as of a kind similar to Lear's or Coriolanus's, we cannot casually grant the Egyptian enchantress even the pagan truth in her magniloquent vision. For her concept of death as a floating to meet Mark Antony in a physical afterlife to attain marriage and "that kiss which is my heaven to have" was a vision which few if any of the intelligent thinkers of the ancient world would have granted her, especially those whom Shakespeare and his contemporaries were likely to know.[4]

All well and good, it might be answered, but Shakespeare's queen cannot be so easily judged! She may have her illusions, but we must consider the broader context of her final situation. Her lover is dead, her kingdom is gone, and in these circumstances her reactions seem rather grand and magnificent as a display of life and of defiant bravery. Certainly this is true. But grant it and we have lost our tragedy again. We may congratulate Cleopatra on magnificence under stress, celebrate her grand comedy, and go our smiling ways.

On the other hand, rather than praising her pluckiness while secretly scorning or being startled by those other responses painted so vividly by Shakespeare—her speeches, her spectacular death, her metaphors—we can do the queen the honor of taking her seriously as a tragic character fashioned by the world's greatest playwright. So if at times Cleopatra appears grandly egoistic and thus ridiculous, we need not grudgingly praise her while secretly despising her or relegating her to the comedy of triumph. We can as aptly pity her for this ridiculousness and for her fantasy against the Roman empire and try to understand how and why she evolved her visions. Little is gained by dismissing some of Cleopatra's odder moments as "typically female." To see Cleopatra as tragic, in other words, is to cease praising her and to begin considering her as seriously—may one say it with any originality at all in this day and age?—as we do the tragic figures who are men.

A typical Shakespearean technique used in *Antony and Cleopatra* is especially misleading for those who do not take Cleopatra seriously. Unlike Macbeth or Hamlet, figures such as Richard II, Lear, and Cleopatra are exempt from certain kinds of situations. They are not characters striving for goals for which they are prepared to stake and pawn all their formidable talents and even themselves. For when it comes to achieving, a Lear, a Richard II, and a Cleopatra have, as monarchs, already attained to all that is possible. They do not begin their plays, as do Macbeth and Othello, with the whole world to gain and the means to gain it. Rather, at their outsets, the Lears and Richards do not have everything to gain: they have everything to lose. They are monarchs waiting to be unseated. It is Cleopatra's situation too. Queen of Egypt, mistress of the co-ruler of the whole world, she does not begin her play with a ravenous desire to seize it all: to kill Octavius and rule Rome. Politically, she is content. Her only aesthetic course is to go down, losing all, like Lear and Richard stripped figuratively and literally to a nakedness. From her stasis, Cleopatra is pushed into loss by the playwright. With Actium she loses the stature and manhood of her lover. She loses her lover himself through his suicide, and finally she loses her kingdom and her personal freedom.

Thus, with everything not to gain but to lose, such Shakespearean figures do not yearn as do the Macbeths and the Richard III's who desire hugely, plot for and pit themselves against the world to seek vast prizes. The Lears and Richard II's (and Cleopatra) attempt smaller, even minute, things. They strive for goals and have desires which, when compared to Macbeth's, must even seem trivial. A Lear already has all that a Macbeth wants. So, as Shakespeare pictures them, such possessors of everything can only go retrograde to pursue small social or domestic victories, as the only immediate triumphs available. Lear strives for petty tyrannies over his endowed daughters and for a vacation, for authority to make Kent keep quiet, or to demand a fast dinner. Richard II loves the panoply of kingship and personal stances. Thus, though they are complicated persons, compared to the magnitude and wonder of their enveloping tragedies their immediate goals seem trivial and captious. Scenarios come to seem curiously domestic and un-Wagnerian, ambitions constricted, life almost petty.

Cleopatra misleads and causes difficulty in the same way. Her stage life yields the same residue, the same kinds of triviality. She too has nothing more to desire except a continuation of her present grand existence: the magnitude of her immediate wishing is as diminished as Lear's before his crisis. But Shakespeare, in her characterization, makes her unambitious activities even more trivial, even more inconsequential than those of Lear or of Richard II in their early scenes. She jokes with messengers, she teases Antony, she threatens her waiting women. If one were to be judgmental, one might even rate such activity below that of being bossy with one's daughters or speechifying about crowns, but, paradoxically, Cleopatra's own behavior shapes a mode of Shakespearean characterization not to be found in his other figures.

An audience takes the process of characterization as a kind of explanation. Lady Macbeth says she is reminded of her father by the sleeping Duncan; later she understandably kills herself brooding about Duncan's murder. Lear enunciates his comfortable ideas about kingship; later he is understandably unable to grasp what is happening with his newly empowered daughters. However, it is difficult at first to see "explanation" coming from much of the activity of Cleopatra. In the early parts of the play especially, we are offered such seeming trivia as to tempt critics to dismiss merely as "local color" or "comic relief" the teasings, or the boredoms, or messenger threatenings. But the fact is that these "trivial" activities indeed constitute the greater part of what Shakespeare has chosen to make available to us as data about Cleopatra. Indeed, we have been presented a dramatic proposition interestingly anticipating the manner, if not the matter, of contemporary psychological analysis, a manner we have seen anticipated too by Plutarch and Montaigne in their own ideas about how we can get to know the character of a person. Trivial incidents or responses, that is, serve as indicators of the whole personality. And even if, with Cleopatra, such material seems too inconsequential for serious art, serious tragedy, yet because most of the play offers us for a long time little else about her, we must either dismiss the queen as a significant character or accept the material we have been given for analysis. Then let us accept what we have been offered by Shakespeare and seek his Egyptian queen, his tragic protagonist, where he has told us to seek her.

II

Why does Cleopatra resist Antony's departure from Egypt? This is not at all a serious question for those who see the tragedy as a study in dualities. For them *Antony and Cleopatra* contrasts Cleopatra's mysterious Egypt with Rome and shows Antony in dilemma, caught and poised between these two worlds. Thus when the queen begins her resistance to Antony's going, she seems to sound a keynote reverberating through the drama.

> He was dispos'd to mirth, but on the sudden
> A Roman thought hath strook him.   (1.2.82–83)

But Cleopatra's resistance should be tempered, in theory, at least, by the fact of Fulvia's death, by the notion of the deterioration of Antony's own political position, and by the possibility that if Antony takes steps now, he can maintain not only his, but her position too, since this depends on his own strength. Furthermore,

Cleopatra's resistance, even though it has been with us from the very beginning of the play, and with us at some length, does nothing to change Antony. He still departs. Dramatically, then, what happens here is little beyond the prospect of Cleopatra's resistance itself. One cannot even say that her attitude has been "planted" in this scene to build for later. For after the hero's departure Cleopatra is not disconsolate, brooding, angry, revengeful—or worried. She thinks about Antony, but not anxiously, and when the messenger comes to tell her that Antony and Caesar have become "greater friends than ever" she exclaims "Make thee a fortune from me." In fact, the extent of Cleopatra's unworried security will only be emphasized by the violent emotion that then strikes her when she learns of Antony's remarriage. She is enraged by surprise.

Even then, Cleopatra's anger at the remarriage does not make her remind us that she was always opposed to Antony's leaving, nor later, when Antony returns to Egypt and to Cleopatra, does she initiate (or repudiate) a reconciliation scene to bind up their estrangement. In other words, the queen's resistance to the departure of Antony from Egypt does not begin a dramatic motif or sequence. A reconciliation, it is true, might best be left to the imagination, but the poet actually points away from shaping a dramatic sequence of departure-return-reconciliation. In 3.7, the first Egypt scene in which Antony is back, Cleopatra's only topic is her quarrel with Enobarbus about whether she should be at Actium. Thus, while Antony's departure from Egypt does indeed affect the play by isolating him from Cleopatra, her own carefully displayed resistance does not prevent the departure, nor does it operate as a basis for later activity.

It is often argued, therefore, that the early scenes of this tragedy serve simply to demonstrate the power of Cleopatra's variegated personality.[5] If so, then it is extremely interesting to note how Shakespeare, showing us the queen's variety, effected an immediate and radical contradiction of his Plutarchian source. Here is the ancient biographer's account of how his own Egyptian queen commanded the affections of Marcus Antonius:

> So sweete was her companie and conversacion, that a man could not possiblie but be taken. And besides her beawtie, the good grace she had to talke and discourse, her curteous nature that tempered her words and dedes, was a spurre that pricked to the quick.[6]

Furthermore, Cleopatra, "were it in sport, or in matters of earnest, still devised sundry new delights to have Antonius at commandment, never leaving him night nor day, nor once letting him go out of her sight." When, however, Plutarch's Cleopatra had to reckon with another woman (Octavia), then, instead of flying into a rage, she "subtly seemed to languish for the love of Antonius," and whenever Antonius came into her presence, "she cast her eyes upon him like a woman ravished for joy." Allowing herself also to be "discovered" weeping, she would seem suddenly to notice Antonius, and then "made as though she dried her eyes and turned her face away, as if she were unwilling that he should see her weep."

Most clearly this is not Shakespeare's approach! His Cleopatra's *modus op-erandi* not only differs drastically from what is in his source, but Charmian comments on the queen's method in a warning couplet. Her hint even becomes prophecy.

CHAR.: Madam, methinks if you did love him dearly,
You do not hold the method to enforce
The like from him.
CLEO.:   What should I do, I do not?
CHAR.: In each thing give him way, cross him in nothing.
CLEO.: Thou teachest like a fool: the way to lose him.
CHAR.: Tempt him not so too far. I wish, forbear.
In time we [haste] that which we often fear.[7]   (1.3.6–12)

Furthermore—very importantly for our understanding of Shakespeare's tragedy—Plutarch sketched his Cleopatran traits to describe what he saw as a *success:* Cleopatra's ability to retain her influence over Antonius. But Shakespeare, at the outset of his drama, has taken pains to describe a Cleopatran technique of "crossing" which is, ultimately, a failure.

Othello is illustrative by contrast. When he is initially presented, the Moor has already managed an elopement with Desdemona. Then, despite the efforts of her father, a powerful senator, and despite Roderigo and Iago, Othello succeeds in maintaining his reputation before the senate, as well as his freedom and his new wife. We have at once been exposed to a series of successes: the Moor's first appearances on stage have thus been a demonstration of power. Cleopatra stands in contrast. She may momentarily have diverted Antony from the messengers at the beginning of the play, but, despite greater efforts, she does not succeed in staving off the very situation she began the play trying to prevent: Antony's departure.

Indeed, throughout the drama, Cleopatra's carefully shown and enunciated technique, her mode of "crossing," never achieves its intended effect. It is not that Antony is impervious to the queen's techniques: it is simply that this specific approach to him does not profit her. In fact, results are quite contrary to Cleopatra's own desires in such instances. For not only does she fail to keep Antony in Egypt, but, later in the play, she will most disastrously fail again. What is her "piteously" worded message of her "death"—she does, as Enobarbus says, have a "celerity in dying"—but this familiar form of "crossing?" Crossing is, as Charmian says, a tempting, and Antony will indeed be tempted too far.

When we watch a character on stage praise some *modus operandi* (however trivial) that really does not work, we are very likely to wonder why on earth that person believes in the method. And Cleopatra's early display of failure has this result. Pursuing this question, Shakespeare proceeds to remove Antony from the Egyptian scenario as if isolating Cleopatra to suggest answers. We are thus presented with "Egyptian" scenes: Cleopatra with her eunuch; Cleopatra in wit-battles with her waiting women; Cleopatra with the messenger.

Such a sequence is 1.5, where we find Cleopatra greeting Alexas by speaking with an extravagance not often seen in other Shakespearean heroes or heroines of her age.

> How much unlike art thou Mark Antony!
> Yet coming from him, that great med'cine hath
> With his tinct gilded thee.[8]

(1.5.35–37)

Charmian's teasing response suggests similar Cleopatran effusions in different circumstances.

> CLEO.:   Did I, Charmian,
> Ever love Caesar so?
> CHAR.:   O that brave Caesar!
> CLEO.: Be chok'd with such another emphasis!
> Say "the brave Antony."
> CHAR.:   The valiant Caesar!
> CLEO.: By Isis, I will give thee bloody teeth,
> If thou with Caesar paragon again
> My man of men.
> CHAR.:   By your most gracious pardon,
> I sing but after you.

(1.5.66–73)

Her lover, whoever he is, must always be "a man of men." Why? Is she politically rapacious? Hardly. For where is the political sense that should go with such greed? Indeed, Cleopatra's initial resistance to Antony's departure from Egypt raised this question, and so does her response to Alexas here, as she listens to Antony's message.

> "Say the firm Roman to great Egypt sends
> This treasure of an oyster; at whose foot,
> To mend the petty present, I will piece
> Her opulent throne with kingdoms. All the East,
> Say thou, shall call her mistress." So he nodded,
> And soberly did mount an arm-gaunt steed,
> Who neigh'd so high that what I would have spoke
> Was beastly [dumb'd] by him.

(1.5.43–50)

If the Egyptian queen was to be portrayed as scheming for empires, it is here that we could know it, for at this Antonian message it would not be inappropriate to be gratified, to boast, to express Cleopatran satisfaction were world politics her sphere. But she ignores the promises and prospects, concentrating on a view.

> What, was he, sad or merry?

"He was nor sad nor merry" is the answer which prompts this response from the queen:

> Oh well-divided disposition! Note him,
> Note him, good Charmian, 'tis the man; but note him:
> He was not sad, for he would shine on those
> That make their looks by his; he was not merry,
> Which seem'd to tell them his remembrance lay
> In Egypt with his joy.

Such is her "political" sense. The play began with one of Antony's followers denouncing him for dotage. But as Cleopatra sees it here, the soldiers are radiating a kind of worship and respectful approval as now, Mark Antony sits remembering his "joy" with the brooding solemnity of a young Romeo. Antony's men render this homage, presumably, because they acquiesce in Cleopatra's vision of Antony's transcendent superiority.

Cleopatra believes that the soldiers feel this worship because her own words about the absent Antony redound with an appreciation of the "intrinsic" value of those who happen to be kings. Kings and gods bump together in her speeches.

>   Think on me,
> That am with Phoebus' amorous pinches black,[9]
> And wrinkled deep in time? Broad-fronted Caesar,
> When thou wast here above the ground, I was
> A morsel for a monarch; and great Pompey
> Would stand and make his eyes grow in my brow;
> There would he anchor his aspect, and die
> With looking on his life.   (1.5.27–34)

It has often been said that much of the language of *Antony and Cleopatra* leans toward supernatural terms, but it is not often pointed out that most of this exuberance comes from the speeches of the queen herself. Yet, for all that, her lines do not necessarily speak for the play: they describe her own nature. Apparently part of this nature is her opinion that to be loved by gods or kings is much the same thing. Without, in fact, comprehending the enormous stature Mark Antony does enjoy in the affairs of the drama's world, Cleopatra thinks of him as vaguely but hugely elevated. Thus her responses elude any ideas of Antony's real political status for perceptions she can better comprehend. These are informed, it seems, by a kind of aesthetic sense: What is he doing now? How is he? He "is" ultimately handsome, supremely "photogenic": a stasis, not an action.

> O heavenly mingle! Be'st thou sad or merry,
> The violence of either thee becomes,
> So does it no man's else.

Where do you think he is now? she asks Charmian.

> Stands he, or sits he?
> Or does he walk? Or is he on his horse?
> O happy horse, to bear the weight of Antony!
> Do bravely, horse, for wot'st thou whom thou mov'st?
> The demi-Atlas of this earth, the arm
> And burgonet of men. He's speaking now,
> Or murmuring, "Where's my serpent of old Nile?"
> (For so he calls me). Now I feel myself
> With most delicious poison.[10]
>
>   (1.5.19–27)

He does not evoke the striving of Hercules, whose carrying of the world was memorialized by Shakespeare's own Globe theater, a Hercules to whom Cleopatra likened him only in ridicule—"Look, prithee, Charmian how this Herculean Roman does become the carriage of his chafe." Rather, Antony, in her mind, stands as Hercules' antithesis, as Atlas, who bears the world not in temporary task but forever, simply standing there universally, gigantesquely.[11] It is a pose in a different mood from, but of the same order as, Antony-not-sad-not-merry-on-his-horse, in thoughtful splendor before his troops, thus heartened to see their radiant leader touched with reminiscent melancholy.

Are we perhaps too quick in our response to Cleopatra's word "brave"? We think of Antony's own pride and achievements and it is easy to assume that the queen admires him too for mastering fear, for being brave in battle. But in Shakespeare's time "brave" was also "pretty" or "handsome"—the sense of Miranda's "brave new world which has such people in it."[12] So when she greets the ill-favored Alexas, Cleopatra pays homage only to what she herself admires.

> How much unlike art thou Mark Antony!
> Yet coming from him, that great med'cine hath
> With his tinct gilded thee.
> How goes it with my brave Mark Antony?
>
>   (1.5.35–38)

It is because of these admirations, however, that we may be assured the queen indeed *is* in love. But then we learn from her that she is not simply in love. She is more in love and more impressively in love than most people have ever been. So even her deprivations are huge. The second time we see her after Antony's departure shows these magnitudes.

> CLEO.: Charmian!
> CHAR.: Madam?
> CLEO.: Ha, ha!
> Give me to drink mandragora.[13]
> CHAR.:   Why, madam?
> CLEO.: That I might sleep out this great gap of time
> My Antony is away.

CHAR.:   You think of him too much.
CLEO.: O, 'tis treason!
CHAR.:   Madam, I trust not so.   (1.5.1–7)

This idea of herself seems extremely important to Cleopatra. Enobarbus hinted as much in jest when, at the beginning of the play, Antony saw her manipulations as (of course) "cunning past man's thoughts." Enobarbus replied:

Alack, sir, no, her passions are made of nothing but the finest part of pure love. We cannot call her winds and waters sighs and tears; they are greater storms and tempests than almanacs can report. This cannot be cunning in her; if it be, she makes a show'r of rain as well as Jove.[14]   (1.2.146–51)

Whatever "love" may indeed be, Cleopatra wants to be involved with it emphatically—as if it were a state to which one aspires for its own sake. "Met'st thou my posts?" she asks Alexas.

ALEXAS: Aye, madam, twenty several messgers.
Why do you send so thick?
CLEO.:   Who's born that day
When I forget to send to Antony,
Shall die a beggar. Ink and paper, Charmian.
Welcome, my good Alexas. Did I, Charmian,
Ever love Caesar so?   (1.5.62–67)

Charmian's teasing rejoinder irritates the queen who must then explain why she was equally carried away with Julius Caesar.

                          My salad days,
When I was green in judgment, cold in blood,[15]
To say as I said then! But come, away,
Get me ink and paper.
He shall have every day a several greeting,
Or I'll unpeople Egypt.   (1.5.73–78)

Yet while it may be very important to think of love warmly and to show that one loves warmly, it is just as crucial—Cleopatra seems often characterized through apparent paradox—to think in terms of control. Certain speeches Shakespeare gives to her in these same Egyptian scenes have in fact stood as the basis for one longstanding interpretive tradition of Cleopatra as plotter for empires. But when we observe the articulation of this would-be control, her aims seem more curious and more covert.

Give me mine angle, we'll to th'river; there,
My music playing far off, I will betray
Tawny[-finn'd] fishes; my bended hook shall pierce
Their slimy jaws; and as I draw them up,

I'll think them every one an Antony,
And say, "Ah, ha! y'are caught."   (2.5.10–15)

In the first scene Cleopatra spoke of "crossing": it was a way of keeping Antony. Though it does not try to "catch" him, "crossing" is much like angling, because it is designed to control Antony as if by continually dragging a lure back and forth.

See where he is, who's with him, what he does.
I did not send you. If you find him sad,
Say I am dancing; if in mirth, report
That I am sudden sick. Quick, and return.   (1.3.2–5)

Such is the motion of her thought, the revolving of the opposites, control and worship, both in pictures, during these early scenes of the play. It is a motion which, though the suppleness and magnificence of her own rhetoric tend to conceal it from us, shows a sense of the love between her and Antony which differs from that with which Shakespeare's other lovers are endowed. For those lovers the stuff of love is not necessarily power, or its opposite, self-abasement. Yet how importantly such opposite notions of Antony's stature and of her own control of him dominate Cleopatra's thinking. His own role becomes clear, now she is deprived of him. It is Antony only who opts for the Neoplatonic—

Our separation so abides and flies,
That thou residing here goes yet with me;
And I hence fleeting, here remain with thee.   (1.3.102–5)

As long as one can go fishing. For in Cleopatran love something must constantly be enacting "love" for it to be real. One dreams of pictures wherein a Mars murmurs her name, or one goes fishing, writes letters, many letters, for many messengers are much love. A final vignette enhances Shakespeare's picture. What a theory of herself and of Antony to react as she does to her eunuch's talk!

CLEO.:   Hast thou affections?
MAR.: Yes, gracious madam.
CLEO.: Indeed?
MAR.: Not in deed, madam, for I can do nothing
But what indeed is honest to be done;
Yet have I fierce affections, and think
What Venus did with Mars.
CLEO.:   Oh, Charmian!
Where think'st thou he is now?   (1.5.12–19)

Venus and Mars: the perfect expression of what she, Antony, and their love should be. A picture, again, but a picture of deities in static embrace: it is her life-role to translate this picture (somehow) to action, action equally symbolic. To sustain illusions one cultivates trivial realities as their symbols: fishing; queening; complaining of deprivation.

III

Plutarch, Shakespeare's source, writes of Cleopatra's charms.

Now her beawtie (as it is reported) was not so passing, as unmatchable of other women, not yet suche, as upon present [immediate] viewe did enamor men with her: but so sweete was her companie and conversacion, that a man could not possiblie but be taken.[16] And besides her beawtie, the good grace she had to talke and discourse, her curteous nature that tempered her words and dedes, was a spurre that pricked to the quick. (6:26–27)

Shakespeare clearly rejected this whole line. He stresses in his Cleopatra an almost unearthly beauty. Her chief herald is Enobarbus whose description of her arrival in her barge on the Cydnus has become a part of English anthology literature.

> For her own person,
> It beggar'd all description: she did lie
> In her pavilion—cloth-of-gold of tissue—
> O'er-picturing that Venus where we see
> The fancy outwork nature.   (2.2.197–201)

It is a description which ends with a tellingly hyperbolic encomium on this beauty as Antony, himself holding court, is left alone in the marketplace by the crowd which rushes to see this fabulously shipped queen.

> Antony,
> Enthron'd i'th'market-place, did sit alone,
> Whistling to th'air: which, but for vacancy,
> Had gone to gaze on Cleopatra too,
> And made a gap in nature.   (2.2.214–18)

Cleopatra invites Antony to dinner and Plutarch tells us that "when Cleopatra found Antonius' jests and slents to be but gross and soldier-like, in plain manner, she gave it him finely, and without fear taunted him thoroughly." Shakespeare alters this in the comments of Enobarbus to maintain the emphasis on beauty. Antony is invited to a supper by the queen and there "for his ordinary, pays his heart for what his eyes eat only." "I saw her once," he continues,

> Hop forty paces through the public street;
> And having lost her breath, she spoke, and panted,
> That she did make defect perfection,
> And, breathless, pow'r breathe forth.   (2.2.229–32)

So there is a basis for Shakespeare's queen reacting to the details of Octavia's features as she does when she hears of Antony's remarriage, even though we ourselves may either be puzzled by her simplicity or become sufficiently patronizing as to regard Cleopatra's response as "typically feminine." Yet to think of the "typically Shakespearean feminine" is to think of Volumnia, Portia, Olivia, Lady Macbeth, none of whom is overmuch absorbed in hair color or skin tones, so we may well wonder at Cleopatra's own way. She requires the messenger to "report the features of Octavia: her years, her inclination." Let him not leave out, she adds, "the color of her hair." "Did you Alexas bring me word how tall she is."

CLEO.: Bear'st thou her face in mind? Is't long or round?
MESS.: Round, even to faultiness.
CLEO.: For the most part, too, they are foolish that are so.
Her hair what color?
MESS.: Brown, madam; and her forehead
As low as she would wish it.
CLEO.:   There's gold for thee.   (3.3.29)

"Is she as tall as me?" and

What majesty is in her gait? Remember,
If e'er thou look'st on majesty.

Although she is reassured on all these points so that she concludes that "all will be well enough," we ourselves may become increasingly concerned that Cleopatra here especially rates herself so small in such petty concerns as to risk comic, not tragic, stature. For the least that might be said of the Egyptian queen as a competitor to other women is that she is interesting. Enobarbus himself, though he feels that women should be esteemed as nothing to a great cause, has given us another memorable assessment.

Age cannot wither her, not custom stale
Her infinite variety. Other women cloy
The appetites they feed, but she makes hungry
Where most she satisfies.   (2.2.234–37)

It is as if the queen, in a way, shares Antony's misperception of self. Despite his own many other magnificences, he insists upon his fantasy of military masculinity even to daring the triumphant Caesar to duel "sword against sword, ourselves, alone." Cleopatra is wedded to the feminine cliché, the pageant of beauty-queens. The challenge to the Roman Octavia is not to see who can prevail, say, in wisdom, cunning, or imagination, but in prettiness—"face against face," as it were, "ourselves, alone."

One of Shakespeare's most interesting ways of characterizing his figures is having them describe their friends or enemies. They often do this by recourse to a kind of synecdoche, summing up people in terms of the "summer-up's" own predilections. A frolicsome Falstaff sums up the morally flawed Prince John simply as "sober." A sexually agonized Hamlet isolates "lecherous" to epitomize Claudius's villainies; Antony's infatuation with rugged physical maturity leads him to condemn Caesar as "boy." Macbeth judges the degree of treachery in men; Iago assesses their naïveté. Here is how Cleopatra sums up the messenger who displeases her in this particular way.

> But there's no goodness in thy face, if Antony
> Be free and healthful—so tart a favor
> To trumpet such good tidings! If not well,
> Thou shouldst come like a Fury crown'd with snakes,
> Not like a formal man.   (2.5.37–41)

Or again:

>   Go get thee hence!
> Hadst thou Narcissus in thy face, to me
> Thou wouldst appear most ugly.   (2.5.95–97)

And when she is displeased with Antony:

> Let him forever go—let him not, Charmian—
> Though he be painted one way like a Gorgon,
> The other way's a Mars.[17]   (2.5.115–17)

In the writings of the times, Narcissus represented physical beauty; Gorgons, on the other hand, were synonymous with purely physical ugliness.[18] Ugliness and beauty, of course, are both rather subjective polarities, but they stand there in Cleopatra's universe, persisting in her response to Charmian's helpfulness, after the messenger has finally succeeded in pleasing her.

> CHAR.:   A proper man.[19]
> CLEO.: Indeed he is so; I repent me much
> That so I harried him. Why, methinks, by him,
> This creature's no such thing.   (3.3.38–41)

The messenger passes from ugly to handsome, sharing this attainment with Alexas whose ill-favored appearance, Cleopatra once said, seemed gilded when he was returning from Antony.[20]

Let us think further about epithets. If King Lear calls Kent "recreant," or if Hamlet calls Claudius "lecherous," both name-callers use epithets denoting inclinations of the human will: treachery, lechery. And even when such name calling modulates to metaphor—as when Lear describes his two older daughters as "she-wolves"—the will or inclination is still the point of reference. Lear is obviously saying something about his daughter's wills, about the quality of their desires. If their natures were to be made visible, his daughters would appear as wolves because wolfishness, Lear believes, represents the quality of their wishing, their wills. The case is the same when Hamlet calls Claudius a "satyr." But those whom Cleopatra dislikes—and in certain instances this obviously includes Antony—she epitomizes as . . . "ugly." So when she expresses this quality in metaphor she does not speak of "she-wolves" but of Furies crowned with snakes, and of Gorgons. For Lear's "To be vicious is to be like a she-wolf," Cleopatra offers: "To be vicious is to be like . . . something ugly." Ugliness (and beauty too) rather than being understood as subjective judgment thus assume the quality of reality usually accorded to shapes and to visible behavior—"she-wolves."

For subjective estimates such as beauty and ugliness to hold the status of fact, not of opinion, was not without precedent in the writing of Shakespeare's time. Contemporary versions of Neoplatonic thought, we recall, held that abstract Beauty, like Truth, was a form of God. Thus, went the intellectual sequence, physical beauty in a human being could suggest that beautiful person's potential closeness to God. Of course, in a Christian Neoplatonic universe, the human possession of mortal, physical beauty could hardly assure anything about the nature of the physically beautiful person, for "the body where the beauty shineth, is not the fountain from whence beauty springeth."[21] Therefore, though Cleopatra's thinking about beauty skirts Neoplatonism, it is, as always with Cleopatra, the difference that is interesting. In her own universe of cognition, Beauty serves a far different master. Messengers attain beauty simply by pleasing the queen. But if messengers do not please her, then,

> Had'st thou Narcissus in thy face, to me
> Thou would'st appear most ugly.

Beauty and ugliness are *facts* to Cleopatra because she believes that visible shapes define intangible qualities in a one-for-one relationship. Again, her description of Antony's new wife.

> CLEO.: Bear'st thou her face in mind? Is't long or round?
> MESS.: Round, even to faultiness.
> CLEO.: For the most part, too, they are foolish that are so.

Such physiognomical lore may indeed have been popular at certain levels of society in the early seventeenth century, but this general naïveté can hardly be imputed to a Shakespeare or to other sophisticated persons living in his time. It is Cleopatra, not the poet, who sees, like Duncan, the mind's construction in the face—and with rather interesting implications for her thinking. For the queen is suggesting that even if Octavia were to stand as still as a stone she could be detected as foolish since her face is round. Just as nonpoisonous snakes are nevertheless to be considered dangerous because they have "snakey" looks.

⟨. . .⟩ Cleopatra really is not Aphrodite or Venus at all, even though, in the words of Enobarbus, she can be seen as "o'erpicturing that Venus where we see the fancy outwork Nature." Rather, the Egyptian queen is an extremely beautiful woman who oddly tries to enact mythological "enslavement" to feed her sense of validity.

But they should never, these fancies, be taken seriously. There is no room for god-
and goddess-worship in that world of power politics inhabited by such figures as
Enobarbus, Menas the pirate, Ventidius the general, Maecenas and Agrippa, cynical
molders of public opinion whenever Antony puts an Egyptian foot wrong. There is
no room here for ideas which forlornly try to sustain such attitudes as this:

> ALEXAS: Good Majesty!
> Herod of Jewry dare not look upon you
> But when you are well pleas'd.
> CLEO.:   That Herod's head
> I'll have; but how, when Antony is gone,
> Through whom I might command it?   (3.3.2–6)

Or again (to her messenger):

> There is gold, and here
> My bluest veins to kiss—a hand that kings
> Have lipp'd, and trembled kissing.   (2.5.28–30)

Or again:

> Broad-fronted Caesar,
> When thou wast here above the ground, I was
> A morsel for a monarch; and great Pompey
> Would stand and make his eyes grow in my brow;
> There would he anchor his aspect, and die
> With looking on his life.   (1.5.29–34)

Cleopatra as the planetary vamp who enslaves the kings of the earth is a colorful
and poetic notion. But gorgeous, Egyptian, mysterious, and Eastern as she may be,
king-enslavement is an idea which in this tragedy is real to no one but herself. It is
perhaps "real," for very different reasons, to Antony who sees things in a more
quasi-Platonic way than Cleopatra—his heart is tied to her rudder, he says. But a
Julius Caesar and a Cnaeus Pompey, both of whom the Egyptian queen mentions,
we know left her for their greater mistress, Rome, and the play begins with Antony
leaving too, but against her wishes. And even Enobarbus, Cleopatra's most sympathetic admirer outside of Antony, observes at the beginning of the tragedy that
"compared to a great cause" such women should be esteemed nothing.

        Thus, because what she pursues is, in the end, only a metaphor, Cleopatra's
goal in the grand articulation of her "self" can never be attained, except in metaphor
too. Owning a "triple pillar" of the world who seems to transcend mere politics,
owning too her messengers who must be able to "create" the very news they bring,
Cleopatra must continue to enact some sort of control that can never be achieved
except figuratively. Therefore her way of passing time in Antony's absence. She
luxuriates in the imaginings of being Circe or Acrasia, playing against the background
of her music, which she has called the "moody food of us that trade in love."

Give me mine angle, we'll to th'river; there,
My music playing far off, I will betray
Tawny[-finn'd] fishes; my bended hook shall pierce
Their slimy jaws; and as I draw them up,
I'll think them every one an Antony,
And say, "Ah, ha! y'are caught."

(2.5.10–15)

If Cleopatra would "possess" Antony, she can only do so through some metaphor of possession. Plutarch said Cleopatra especially intrigued Antonius by participating in such male activities as dice and heavy drinking. In the play, however, this revelry becomes something that helps Cleopatra realize "possession."

O times!
I laugh'd him out of patience; and that night
I laugh'd him into patience; and next morn,
Ere the ninth hour, I drunk him to his bed;
Then put my tires and mantles on him, whilst
I wore his sword Philippan.

(2.5.18–23)

To have and to hold Antony, that colorful king of panoramas, as if he were an idea, like soldiership or virtue, can also be achieved, Cleopatra thinks, by loving. For Antony "the business that we love" is soldiering and it is his commitment to his version of warriorship that makes him feel worthy of being a "soldier." Cannot Cleopatra then think that "loving" this giant figure who towers over half the world will make her worthy of participating in that greatness which she sees in him? As the faithful Christian hopes to love God and thus be close to Him, Cleopatra can hope to love Antony so that she can be part of the great hero.

But how can she make sure she loves (at least in her terms)? She can send a message to Antony every day while he is away from Egypt. This sending of letters will show, presumably, how much she loves him. In her own mind, indeed, Cleopatra will have less trouble than Cordelia dealing with some one such as Lear. Show me how much you love me, Lear would demand—and Cleopatra, who thinks she knows how to quantify love, would easily obey. For she is unconcerned with criteria established by Western traditions. Cordelia may have to return to Lear from France to show the audience her love for her father, since traditional discussions insisted that this unseeable entity called "love" did not exist unless confirmed by appropriate deeds. But why must Cleopatra attend to all this? Why must feelings of "love," to be considered "love," be complemented by any deeds at all? Why cannot love be "real" when it is merely "felt"? As she says to Mardian, the eunuch, who consents to play (billiards) with her as well as he can:

And when good will is show'd, though't come too short,
The actor may plead pardon.

(2.5.8–9)

These words of Cleopatra, though they are partly a joke about Mardian's eunuchry, do represent the queen's general views about intent, act, and what they show about emotion. They guide us, these words, to later events:

> O my lord, my lord,
> Forgive my fearful sails! I little thought
> You would have followed.   (3.11.54–56)

There is also Diomed's message to Antony from the queen.

> when she saw
> (Which never shall be found) you did suspect
> She had dispos'd with Caesar, and that your rage
> Would not be purg'd, she sent you word she was dead;
> But fearing since how it might work, hath sent
> Me to proclaim the truth.   (4.14.121–26)

There is little question of scheming or malice in these situations. Cleopatra does to others what she wants done unto her. We know that she does not insist on deeds of huge fidelity or devotion as proof that others worship her. She herself merely requires that "good will" be "shown," as in the obeisance of the chastened messenger with his purged news, or in her dreams of Julius Caesar kissing her hand or Pompey gazing at her face. Of course, to insist on the expression of, rather than the deeds of, love is to see love as ballet or even mime, "love" as merely body movement or facial expression, gesture, and, in life, the mere words. Thus this way of looking at things can complicate one's own emotional self-knowledge. To decide that one is in love because one *should* be, and then to strive to convince oneself of the existence of this love by doing the things you fancy one might do if one *were* in love—this is to risk confusions. How are you to know when you are really in love? By the things that you do? Cleopatra is prone to such confusion.

> Who's born that day
> When I forget to send to Antony,
> Shall die a beggar. Ink and paper, Charmian.
> Welcome, my good Alexas. Did I, Charmian,
> Ever love Caesar so?   (1.5.63–67)

In the long run, these confusions are what an actor or actress might face living a life of constantly impersonating both people and emotion. His life in the playhouse may have led Shakespeare to imagine both Cleopatra and Hamlet from the perspective of these confusions. For in both characters we see the problem of distinguishing between one's own emotions and those which one pretends or feels one ought to have. What is the true emotion, such persons seem to ask: the physical manifestation or the "feeling"?—"I suppose I am happy; but then why am I crying?"[22]

Is Cleopatra glad to be bored in Antony's absence? Does this tell her that she loves him? Possibly she might even wish boredom in order to prove her love!

CLEO.: Charmian!
CHAR.: Madam?
CLEO.: Ha, ha!
Give me to drink mandragora.
CHAR.:   Why, madam?
CLEO.: That I might sleep out this great gap of time
My Antony is away.
CHAR.:   You think of him too much.
CLEO.: O, 'tis treason!   (1.5.1–7)

Cleopatra frequently has to scan her own pretenses to know how she feels. When she hears that Antony is going to leave Egypt, she tries to prevent him with:

Cut my lace, Charmian, come
But let it be; I am quickly ill, and well,
So Antony loves.   (1.3.71–73)

Through this metaphor she attributes vacillation to Antony, imaging it either in earnest or in jest. Yet when she hears of Antony's marriage, when there seems no reason for pretense, her very first reaction is

I am pale, Charmian

as if the pallor were the feeling itself. Later, in a further reaction to the marriage, still in Antony's absence, she says to Charmian:

                    lead me from hence.
I faint, oh Iras, Charmian! 'Tis no matter.

Does she feel faint because she is so used to pretending, or because she thinks she ought to feel faint? The effect of her fainting upon her waiting women will hardly be the same as that of a faint before Antony!

Cleopatra's difficulty with the reality of emotion is one of the most important elements in her characterization. This characterization, to recall where we have been, presents Cleopatra as a beautiful woman who has fallen into the trap of believing in the existential validity of herself not as a human but as a superhuman entity known as a "beautiful woman"—indeed, as the most beautiful woman on earth. This is very like thinking of a man as "essentially royal," for it is as if—as we might say today—some people had been produced through royal or beautiful genes and chromosomes. In Shakespeare's day one might have said that someone such as Cleopatra thought in terms of "royal" or "beautiful" souls.

The attitude is racist, but even more exclusive than racism because Cleopatra's "race" may contain only two or three persons. And just as the "inferior" race may be identifiable by color, which becomes part of the "inherent" inferiority, so the "superhuman" race is to be discovered by visible attributes too. Beauty, or kingliness becomes as "real" as skin color.

A writer such as Augustine or Montaigne might say that humans are always worshipers, always idolatrous of themselves or others. But because they remain humans, people have emotions. And no matter what the misperceiving inner orientation makes a person think about her emotions, they still exist, uncontrollable, pushing us in their reality. There are no such things as "queenly" emotions. There are only human emotions.

Thus Cleopatra, however she puts it to herself, may want the power represented by Antony the Triumvir. She may also want to call that desire "love" because she needs to see herself as the greatest of "lovers." She may think that a woman with genes that make her the most beautiful queen in the world naturally has the best kind of love too, for the best kind of man. But when Cleopatra's normal human emotion and desirings impel that structure of self-styled superhumanity against the rock-face of events, her tragedy will begin.

IV

The Battle of Actium is the turning point upon which Shakespeare pivots our view of Cleopatra, and we may understand his approach by the poet's divergence again from Plutarch. Plutarch's queen made it a point, for political reasons, to keep Antonius under her constant surveillance and immediate influence; and this policy had to be maintained by her presence even at Actium lest he be allowed to swerve toward Rome again. But Shakespeare introduces Actium by bringing Cleopatra on stage quarreling with Enobarbus.

> CLEO.: If not denounc'd against us, why should not we
> Be there in person?
> ENO.:   Well, I could reply:
> If we should serve with horse and mares together,
> The horse were merely lost; the mares would bear
> A soldier and his horse.   (3.7.5–9)

He goes on to observe that Antony is already being traduced in Rome for levity. This triggers her angry reply.

>   Sink Rome, and their tongues rot
> That speak against us! A charge we bear i'th'war,
> And as the president of my kingdom will
> Appear there for a man. Speak not against it,
> I will not stay behind.   (3.7.15–19)

To Cleopatra "war" is not a physical struggle in which bravery, with disciplined and intelligent use of force, can carry the day. Her "war" is the grand gesture, as we might expect. It is an event which needs her presence as inevitably as would a painting of the Battle of Actium. There, as Leader of Egypt and in brilliant colors, she would be holding the silent and decorous foreground position, an appropriate expression of this huge world-conflict. When Antony comes in, she embellishes this decorum, enacting the role of Warrior in military conference with the Hero. Fellow strategist, nautical expert, military maximist, she supports Antony's own poor judgment with enthusiasms more ignorant. Antony is exclaiming about Caesar's unbelievable speed in taking Toryne: "You have heard on't, sweet?"

> CLEO.: Celerity is never more admir'd
> Than by the negligent.
> ANT.:   A good rebuke,
> Which might have well becom'd the best of men,
> To taunt at slackness, Canidius, we
> Will fight with him by sea.
> CLEO.:   By sea? What else?
> . . . .
> I have sixty sails, Caesar none better.   (3.7.24–49)

Despite this new "becoming," Cleopatra proves no Amazon, no Zenobia. Indeed, when the naval battle is at its crucially balanced stage—"when vantage like a pair of twins appear'd, / Both as the same, or rather ours the elder"—she bolts in the panic of inexperience. She has no deep, vile plots to betray Antony. Nor can she be blamed for any great tactical errors in the disposition of her forces. The whole play so far has emphasized the vagueness of the queen's concepts of political and military cause and effect and, indeed, her message to Caesar after the disaster emphasizes her removal from the reality of the war.

> Next, Cleopatra does confess thy greatness,
> Submits her to thy might, and of thee craves
> The circle of the Ptolomies for her heirs,
> Now hazarded to thy grace.   (3.12.16–19)

It is as if the defeat had been purely theoretical—a game in which, no matter the outcome, she retains her world. Otherwise, could she really believe that Caesar would give her country to her son—simply because Cleopatra thinks that, in some puzzlingly intrinsic way, she remains "queen" of Egypt? Yet, after the disaster, far from putting heads together with Antony to assess the extent of ruin she only wants to clarify her own status and relationship with him. Cleopatra cannot see catastrophe because she cannot imagine what there is to lose.

> EROS: Nay, gentle madam, to him, comfort him.
> IRAS: Do, most dear Queen.
> CHAR.: Do? Why, what else?
> CLEO.: Let me sit down. O Juno!
> ANT.: No, no, no, no, no.
> EROS: See you here, sir?

ANT.: O fie, fie, fie!
CHAR.: Madam!
IRAS: Madam, O good Empress!
EROS: Sir, sir!
ANT.: Yes, my lord, yes; he at Philippi kept
His sword e'en like a dancer, while I strook
The lean and wrinkled Cassius; and 'twas I
That the mad Brutus ended. He alone
Dealt on lieutenantry, and no practice had
In the brave squares of war; yet now—No matter.
CLEO.: Ah, stand by.
EROS: The Queen, my lord, the Queen.
IRAS: Go to him, madam, speak to him,
He's unqualitied with very shame.
CLEO.: Well then, sustain me. O!
EROS: Most noble sir, arise, the Queen approaches.
Her head's declin'd, and death will seize her, but
Your comfort makes the rescue.   (3.11.25–48)

The queen's confusion may be worse than Antony's, for she too had a sword.
Her sword is Antony, and for her there is little refuge in continuing to indulge
herself in the weapon which, in some mysterious way, seems to be coming apart
in her hands. Antony tries to explain.

CLEO.: Oh my lord, my lord,
Forgive my fearful sails! I little thought
You would have followed.
ANT.:   Egypt, thou knew'st too well
My heart was to thy rudder tied by th'strings,
And thou shouldst [tow] me after. O'er my spirit
[Thy] full supremacy thou knew'st, and that
Thy beck might from the bidding of the gods
Command me.
CLEO.: Oh, my pardon!   (3.11.54–61)

Did Antony reach her? Who knows? But Cleopatra opens the next Egyptian
scene (3.13), for the first time, with questions.

CLEO.: What shall we do, Enobarbus?
ENO.:   Think, and die.

She ignores this:

Is Antony or we in fault for this?

She has violated the decorum of a particular pose, empress of the sea, and in a distressingly visible way. But if one evasion was to throw the blame on Antony, his rejoinder made for dilemma. Here is her choice. Either she is dominant and therefore responsible for what Antony has done, or she is not responsible. And therefore not dominant? The dilemma is scarcely resolved here by Enobarbus's approach to her question. Who is at fault?

> ENO.: Antony only, that would make his will
> Lord of his reason. What though you fled
> From that great face of war, whose several ranges
> Frighted each other? Why should he follow?
> The itch of his affection should not then
> Have nick'd his captainship, at such a point,
> When half to half the world oppos'd, he being
> The mered question. 'Twas a shame no less
> Than was his loss, to course your flying flags,
> And leave his navy gazing.
> CLEO.:   Prithee, peace.   (3.13.1–12)

This is worse. To Enobarbus Cleopatra is not culpable at all, because she is as irrelevant to the issue as a dancing-girl watching the fight from the porch of a whore house. Fortunately the entrance of Antony breaks off this chat, but it introduces other problems for the queen. Antony is fretting over Caesar's message and he says to her:

> ANT.: To the boy Caesar send this grizzled head,
> And he will fill thy wishes to the brim
> With principalities.
> CLEO.:   That head, my lord?
> ANT.: To him again, Tell him, etc.   (3.13.17–19)

It is this section of the play which has fueled critical argument about Cleopatra's fidelity to Antony. Indeed, if Shakespeare wished us to imagine his Cleopatra as steadfast and faithful, he has scarcely assured us of these traits by depicting her doubts and unanswered questions. But, in the long run, the issue of Cleopatra's loyalty is a red herring. For despite Antony's accusations and doubts, we have seen that it will be his own soldiers, not Cleopatra's Egyptians, who gladly surrender to Caesar's fleet at the last. And if in this present scene Antony sees fit to raise with Cleopatra the issue of "principalities" versus his decapitation, matters can hardly seem so clear-cut to Cleopatra. Her interest in (or understanding of) political power has always been slight. If decisions there then must be, they have to be in her own mode. She cannot betray Antony in terms she does not understand.

Thus her equivocal reactions to Antony's words do not suggest problems in fidelity so much as they do shapes of cognition. Her vacillations are not as important in determining political events as they are in delineating her outlook. For the questions she debates now are new ones: ethics, cause and effect, relative values. Who is to blame for this highly undesirable post-Actium situation? She is surrounded by matters different from those she has ever encountered before. Hence Shakespeare's brilliance in introducing Thidias to exacerbate this conceptual confusion.

> CLEO.:   Caesar's will?
> THID.: Hear it apart.
> CLEO.:   None but friends: say boldly.
> THID.: So haply are they friends to Antony.
> ENO.: He needs as many, sir, as Caesar has,
> Or needs not us. If Caesar please, our master
> Will leap to be his friend; for us, you know
> Whose he is we are, and that is Caesar's.
> THID.:   So.   (3.13.46–52)

It was Cleopatra's response, innocent to the point of political naïveté, which forced Thidias's bluntness. But here Enobarbus shields the queen from immediate reaction, just as Antony's new challenge of a duel with Caesar had forestalled her answer to the question about the "grizzled head." Yet Thidias ignores Enobarbus and continues.

> THID.: Thus then, thou most renown'd: Caesar entreats
> Not to consider in what case thou stand'st
> Further than he is [Caesar].
> CLEO.:   Go on: right royal.
> THID.: He knows that you embrace not Antony
> As you did love, but as you fear'd him.
> CLEO.:   O!
> THID.: The scars upon your honor, therefore, he
> Does pity, as constrained blemishes,
> Not as deserv'd.
> CLEO.:   He is a god and knows
> What is most right. Mine honor was not yielded,
> But conquer'd merely.   (3.13.53–62)

Conversation is beginning to touch upon the subject Cleopatra was debating with Enobarbus: her responsibility. And the temptation is extreme: Thidias offers a way out. Nothing was Cleopatra's fault. So her own approach to the matter was perhaps right after all! And when Thidias presses further, showing, in effect, how Caesar supports her notions of her own distance from the pettiness of causation, it is interesting that Octavius, who began the play as (in her words) "scarce-bearded Caesar," begins to rise in her esteem. It would warm Caesar's spirits, we gather, to hear that Cleopatra had left Antony and put herself under Caesar's "shroud."

> Shall I say to Caesar
> What you require of him? for he partly begs
> To be desir'd to give.

So perhaps here is another king who understands how the universe is orga-nized, that Cleopatra's only duty is to assure the proper majesty for herself. Thus, though evasive, the queen's response here to Thidias is familiar as she now looks more closely at the one who has brought the news.

> CLEO.:   What's your name?
> THID.: My name is Thidias.
> CLEO.:   Most kind messenger,
> Say to great Caesar this in [deputation]:
> I kiss his conqu'ring hand. Tell him, I am prompt
> To lay my crown at's feet, and there to kneel.
> Tell him, from his all-obeying breath I hear
> The doom of Egypt.   (3.13.72–78)

Regressing to the tones of the first two acts, reinforced in the idea of herself as cynosure, how can she then be averse to offering that reward for good news granted a previous messenger?

> THID.:   Give me grace to lay
> My duty on your hand.
> CLEO.:   Your Caesar's father oft
> (When he hath mus'd of taking kingdoms in)
> Bestow'd his lips on that unworthy place,
> As it rain'd kisses.

What is the reality behind this decorous painting of herself as refurbished goddess? Would she have yielded to Caesar? We can only speculate, wondering how a submissive Cleopatra would have responded then to, say, another bland request for Antony's head. But Shakespeare again shields the queen from us. Antony's raging entry breaks in upon her musing about Caesar musing, and the violent disposal of Thidias brings one train of possibilities to an abrupt end.

We must, I think, believe that Cleopatra never would have knowingly be-trayed Antony—what does she know of the idea of the quid pro quo where she herself is concerned? But how could she resist thinking about being a goddess again, her own natural "greatness" having won over Caesar?

In her limited self-knowledge, she can hardly explain herself succinctly and swiftly to an Antony now shouting over issues of virility and warriorship. But he, in his despair, unknowingly flings the challenge that tells.

CLEO.: Have you done yet?
ANT.:   Alack, our terrene moon
Is now eclips'd, and it portends alone
The fall of Antony!
CLEO.:   I must stay this time.
ANT.: To flatter Caesar, would you mingle eyes
With one that ties his points?
CLEO.:   Not know me yet?
ANT.: Cold-hearted toward me?   (3.13.153–58)

Now Cleopatra does not at all like to see herself as "cold." "Cold" means unloving, and in her world "love" has the status of a moral virtue. One therefore responds to the accusation of "coldness" as would the erring Christian who has been told he hates God—with protestations that one is indeed good, or, in Cleopatra's case, that one is indeed "warm." So Cleopatra's involved figure insists that she is not green in judgment, cold in blood (as in her salad days).

                 Ah, dear, if I be so,
From my cold heart let heaven engender hail,
And poison it in the source, and the first stone
Drop in my neck; as it determines, so
Dissolve my life! The next Caesarion [smite],
Till by degrees the memory of my womb,
Together with my brave Egyptians all,
By the [discandying] of this pelleted storm,
Lie graveless, till the flies and gnats of Nile
Have buried them for prey!   (3.13.158–67)

The challenge, then, and the "change" in Antony, have their effect on her. She needs to see herself as warm and loving. Antony tells her of his own change as he exclaims:

ANT.: Where hast thou been, my heart? Dost thou hear, lady?
If from the field I shall return once more
To kiss these lips, I will appear in blood;
I and my sword will earn our chronicle.
There's hope in't yet.
CLEO.:   That's my brave lord!

Brave. She has certainly nothing to gain by egging him on in this mood, which Enobarbus sees as disaster. Yet these words reassert the Antony which the queen always envisioned: the spectacular, rhetorical, colorful man of men, lord over all: a "brave" lord indeed. Perhaps it is not all collapsing around her. Antony is acting like a "king" again in his pleasures and his rages. And if this vision of Antony no longer wavers, then Cleopatra as an idea is still real too!

ANT.:   Call to me
All my sad captains, fill our bowls once more;
Let's mock the midnight bell.
CLEO.:   It is my birthday,
I had thought t'have held it poor; but since my lord
Is Antony again, I will be Cleopatra.   (3.13.182–86)

So, until Antony threatens her with death, Cleopatra changes with him. Accused of coldness, she acts submissive, even though her ongoing dilemma is dramatized by her continuing silence, one which yields only two comments in forty-five lines. And these are comments which only stress her distance. They come during the party, during Antony's half-melodramatic, half-intuitive farewell to the men who have served him. And then she is almost naïve.

ANT.:   Give me thy hand,
Thou hast been rightly honest—so hast thou—
Thou—and thou—and thou. You have serv'd me well,
And kings have been your fellows.
CLEO.: [*Aside to Enobarbus.*] What means this?
. . . .
ANT.: Well, my good fellows, wait on me to-night.
Scant not my cups, and make as much of me
As when mine empire was your fellow too,
And suffer'd my command.
CLEO.: [*Aside to Enobarbus.*] What does he mean?   (4.2.10–24)

Enobarbus weeps too, with the other hard officers in this moment together, leader and captains at the end of the long, daring road they have all traveled together since Philippi to seize an empire. But outside this grieving circle the queen is removed, uncomprehending, silent: this is alien stuff. A king is beyond the faith of mere followers. So why all this? Kings don't depend on anybody. They are just there. Why all this? The chasm between her and the mood of the others urges, more sharply than any other moment we see, Cleopatra's vast incomprehension about what the game has been.

But the next day, before the fight, the queen is everywhere.

ANT.: Eros, mine armor, Eros!
CLEO.:   Sleep a little.
ANT.: No, my chuck. Eros, come, mine armor, Eros!
                    Enter Eros [*with armor*].
Come, good fellow, put thine iron on.
If Fortune be not ours to-day, it is
Because we brave her. Come.
CLEO.:   Nay, I'll help too.
What's this for?

ANT.:   Ah, let be, let be! Thou art
The armorer of my heart. False, false; this, this.
CLEO.: Sooth law, I'll help. Thus it must be.
ANT.:   Well, well,
We shall thrive now. Seest thou, my good fellow?
Go, put on thy defences.
EROS: Briefly, sir.
CLEO.: Is not this buckled well?
ANT.:   Rarely, rarely

Serving him now, playing the ingénue, the charming servant, she acts, in her eyes, the truer lover. She will do anything not to be "cold," to stay "loving." But, significantly, after Antony has departed, she is no longer the child. She is, after all, a tragic protagonist. The lull of her silence—she did not return Antony's melodramatic farewell—may be what prompts Charmian's suggestion.

ANT.: Follow me close; I'll bring you to't. Adieu.
          Exeunt [Antony, Eros, Captains, and Soldiers].
CHAR.: Please you retire to your chamber?
CLEO.:   Lead me.
He goes forth gallantly. That he and Caesar might
Determine this great war in single fight!
Then, Antony—but now—well, on!   *Exeunt.*   (4.2.34–38)

How can he look so grand and not be king of the world? Always, it is the theoretical, picturesque Antony, devoid of human reality, that captivates her. And here, in its fitful half-life, the image is still potent enough to help her resist a growing awareness.

He returns from this battle and she greets him astoundingly.

                    Lord of lords!
O infinite virtue, com'st thou smiling from
The world's great snare uncaught?[23]   (4.8.16–18)

That "world" before which she had wanted to appear at Actium, as president of her kingdom, has now become a different thing. It is a "snare," but not because she lately has been reading the Bible. Cleopatra tends to deprecate what she cannot have—we recall how she spoke of Antony when he remarried. And so Antony's power (the seventeenth-century meaning of "virtue"), which she saw as limited by the refusal of the world's affairs to be settled by a duel, must be translated. It becomes "infinite" in a new transcendental conception within which all mere sublunary matters begin to show as the hindrance and snare to new nobility, new greatness.

It is a conception which never leaves her, but it is momentarily and violently arrested after the last battle when Antony has seen his fleet evaporate. As Cleopatra wanders in his path:

> ANT.:   Ah, thou spell! Avaunt!
> CLEO.: Why is my lord enrag'd against his love?

Antony threatens her with death, raises before her too the prospect of being led in triumph by Caesar, and this tumbles her back into a pre-Thidias mode.

> Help me, my women! O, he is more mad
> Than Telamon for his shield. The boar of Thessaly
> Was never so emboss'd.[24]

Cleopatra's speech is puzzlingly coarse, but its very insensitivity does reiterate, and at a crucial juncture, one of the strongest emphases in this tragedy. If she is not overly empathic with the complications of Antony's emotional experience in witnessing the desertion of his soldiers in the fleet, we need not be astonished. We saw her at Antony's "last supper." And here, from her viewpoint it is Antony the *Übermensch* who rages. A Superman cannot lose power: but he can get angry and harm a person.

Her reaction to his rage is no decision. It is a response. At the threat of hard reality in the form either of Antony's sword or of a march through a jeering Roman crowd—he reminded her of this danger when he threatened her—she can only flee. Charmian structures the response, it is true, but once the familiar form has been suggested, Cleopatra immediately knows where she is. She can, in this remarkable sequence, elaborate on that "crossing" which we witnessed in the first act and which here has not a comic but a dangerous effect.

> CHAR.:   To th'monument!
> There lock yourself, and send him word you are dead.
> The soul and body rive not more in parting
> Than greatness going off.
> CLEO.:   To th'monument!
> Mardian, go tell him I have slain myself;
> Say that the last I spoke was "Antony,"
> And word it, prithee, piteously. Hence, Mardian,
> And bring me how he takes my death. To th'monument!   (4.13.3–10)

Perhaps she has forgotten what she said to him early in the play.

> my becomings kill me when they do not
> Eye well to you.   (1.3.96–97)

When Mardian enters to the dying Antony, we know the queen's man is supposed to lie. So when he describes Cleopatra killing herself in a way that differs radically from her actual suicide later, we are importantly instructed by the contrast.

```
ANT.:                             O, thy vile lady!
She has robb'd me of my sword.
MAR.:                             No, Antony.
My mistress lov'd thee, and her fortunes mingled
With thine entirely.
ANT.:                        Hence, saucy eunuch, peace!
She hath betrayed me, and shall die the death.
MAR.: Death of one person can be paid but once,
And that she has discharg'd. What thou wouldst do
Is done unto thy hand; the last she spake
Was "Antony, most noble Antony!"
Then in the midst a tearing groan did break
The name of Antony; it was divided
Between her heart and lips. She rend'red life,
Thy name so buried in her.
ANT.:                        Dead, then?
MAR.:                             Dead.               (4.13.22–34)
```

Antony comments on this death-scene, imagining the whole idea. "I," he says

```
                    condemn myself to lack
The courage of a woman—less noble mind
Than she which by her death our Caesar tells,
"I am conqueror of myself."                           (4.14.59–62)
```

Waiving the grim humor of Antony's aspiration to become his "self" again through the heroic emulation of that mere fiction of a self which Cleopatra presented, we can see that the exaggerated sentimentality of the eunuch's story is ultimately a Sophonisban alternative to the plot of the play itself. For Cleopatra to die in this fashion would indeed be the sentimental solution. Yet the very grossness of the cliché, the movie-ending as Cleopatra plays an Egyptian Juliet, is enough to warn us that if she does ever kill herself, the queen will take that step consistently with her own outlook—with that cognitive kaleidoscope which Shakespeare has assembled for us as Cleopatra, his tragic protagonist.

V

Before we follow Cleopatra to her conclusion and tragedy, we must think again of symbols, of what they are and are not. They are not, for instance, logically inevitable: it takes agreement to establish what something will stand for. This is one way of differentiating symbols from signs. A sign points out: it indicates the larger whole of which it is a part. The paw-prints of the jackal in the sand cannot help but point the jackal's presence. But we have to *agree* that, say, a sounded horn may symbolize an approaching danger. Thus symbols and signs in most cases are fairly simple concepts.

But then comes something, such as "Decorum" which, in these contexts will seem queer. For this fascinating medieval and Renaissance idea which informed the criticism of poetry, and painting, as well as some ways of thinking about theological and political matters, strongly opposes, in its own emphasis on symbols, the principle underlying symbols themselves. Decorum does this by introducing the idea of the "appropriate," even by admitting the concept of the "appropriate" symbol.

To seek the "appropriate" symbol, however, is to require a symbol to participate in something like the "quality" of what it must represent. It would, for instance, be grossly "indecorous" to symbolize a monarch by the picture of a mad dog. The mad-dog symbol would be unsatisfactory because it would presumably suggest undesirable qualities in the monarch so symbolized. But, in theory, all objects may be used to symbolize anything as long as all agree about what the symbol is to be. Black sails have no inherent meaning beyond what Theseus and his father might establish. There is nothing necessarily black about death. So if a Renaissance sense of "decorum" rejects the picture of a mad dog as the symbol of a monarch, then that picture is not being treated as a symbol at all: it is being treated as a sign. If a sign is the part of a whole, then one can say that a rabid animal has little to do with a human king. What "decorum" does, therefore, is require symbols to be moral signs conveying the moral quality of an object rather than, say, its height.

In *The Merchant of Venice,* Bassanio's task of choosing the casket that will win him Portia aptly epitomizes the general complexity of "decorum." The "correct" casket to symbolize Portia and the attaining of her is not the silver or the gold one, but the leaden vessel, even though the unsuccessful choosers are somewhat justified in thinking that a privileged sixteenth-century lady might "appropriately" be symbolized by precious metals. Yet when the Christian tradition is present to invoke such virtues as lowliness, humility, or risk-taking as the way to "treasure" in a homiletic sense, then a different "decorum" may rule what is to symbolize the attaining of Portia.

Shakespeare's Cleopatra frequently insists on a decorum too. This is understandable, since in her world all things must have visible, capable-of-being-photographed existences to be "real." Her situation is thus rather like that which prevails when one scrutinizes a dollar bill to make sure it is not counterfeit. For financial reasons, this dollar bill must be the "real" manifestation of a hundred cents—even identical. But why cannot a counterfeit dollar symbolize a hundred cents? Because the counterfeit dollar is not the "correct" (decorous?) symbol of a hundred cents! The dollar, to be "genuine," must "contain" its own worth. The dollar does not function merely as some symbol, but as the "right" symbol: as, in fact, the "sign" of a hundred cents. These matters are important in Shakespeare's characterization of Cleopatra because of the abstractions with which she must deal.

One such abstraction is her own self-awareness. Renaissance thinking did not regard human "being," as an autonomous state (the Satanic fallacy). Human "existence" depended on God for its objective "reality." But fallen yearnings or "affections," postlapsarianly directed away from God and the Good, sought earthly and thus transitory, "unreal" joys and satisfactions. These, to fallen imaginings, could, of course, seem more "real" than the ultimate Reality of Heaven—and so forth. The text was familiar to all of Shakespeare's contemporaries, but perhaps not to his Cleopatra for whom the "affections" or emotions seem the products of her reason.

And as reason can make us decide to take a journey or to stay home, so can it make us decide to feel an emotion, or not to feel it. One can manipulate emotion precisely because one can imitate it. One can imitate it because, like all things in her world, emotion is somehow visible, tangible, quite literally. And because one can imitate emotion, it must "look like" something. And because it looks like something, it becomes "real." In brief, an emotion, like all other things in Cleopatra's world, is not intangible, abstract. It can always be seen, observed in others (as Lear would have love observable), and it certainly can be noted in the self. What these emotions look like, how one can "tell if they really exist," however, is up to Cleopatra who, like Lear, will decide what something as complex as love must "look like" too.

There must be standards. All things must look "like themselves." They must appear "correctly." One cannot have such things as anger, kingship, love, greatness, beauty, wisdom, and the like constantly changing their looks; otherwise one will never know where one is. What then establishes what these things will look like? Decorum. But this will be a "decorum" shaped by the vagaries of Cleopatra's assumptions, desires, knowledges, and ignorances. It is a sense of such decorum, in fact, which informs those scenes just before and after Antony's death, bringing the play to a close. Indeed, Cleopatra's insistence on a kind of order largely contributes to the quality of her own tragedy, beginning to consummate itself now quickly.

> CLEO.: O Charmian, I will never go from hence.
> CHAR.: Be comforted, dear madam.
> CLEO.:   No, I will not.
> All strange and terrible events are welcome,
> But comforts we despise; our size of sorrow,
> Proportion'd to our cause, must be as great
> As that which makes it.   (4.15.1–6)

To live statically in a huge tomb is the mighty, the queenly, way to grieve, but this operatic decorum will not be allowed her for long. Antony will not die so refined a death for her. She is to see him again, but this time bleeding, and heavy with physical helplessness.

>   O sun,
> Burn the great sphere thou mov'st in! darkling stand
> The varying shore o'th'world! O Antony,
> Antony, Antony! Help, Charmian, help, Iras, help;
> Help, friends below; let's draw him hither.   (4.15.9–13)

But even this drawing must be made decorous to the magnitude of the occasion.

CLEO.:   Had I great Juno's power,
The strong-wing'd Mercury should fetch thee up,
And set thee by Jove's side. Yet come a little—
Wishers were ever fools—O, come, come, come.

They heave Antony aloft to Cleopatra.

And welcome, welcome! Die when thou hast liv'd,
Quicken with kissing. Had my lips that power,
Thus would I wear them out.
ALL: A heavy sight!
ANT.: I am dying, Egypt, dying.
Give me some wine, and let me speak a little.
CLEO.: No, let me speak, and let me rail so high,
That the false huswife Fortune break her wheel,
Provok'd by my offense.   (4.15.34–45)

In these wishful metaphors, she not only lingers on as a goddess and agent of resurrection, but Antony is placed with Pompey who would "die with looking on his life." She must even complete the picture that so moves those below: repeated kisses that show love as did the daily letters. The railing against Fortune; the lack of interest in what Antony might say. But then he begins to fade into death and her static hero, demi-Atlas, still holder of the throne of Jove, at last yields to reality.

CLEO.:   Noblest of men, woo't die?
Hast thou no care of me? Shall I abide
In this dull world, which in thy absence is
No better than a sty? O, see, my women,
                              [*Antony dies.*]
The crown o'th'earth doth melt. My lord!
O, wither'd is the garland of the war,
The soldier's pole is fall'n! Young boys and girls
Are level now with men; the odds is gone,
And there is nothing left remarkable
Beneath the visiting moon.
CHAR.:   O, quietness, lady!
IRAS: She's dead too, our sovereign.   (4.15.59–69)

We must fully comprehend her shock, not only in terms of those obvious, human reasons to which Shakespeare always attends, but in terms of the poet's complexity as artist. Antony was, after all, the *Übermensch*, the "remarkable" in Cleopatra's wishfully hierarchical thinking. He *cannot* die. It is one thing sentimentally to half-experience a picturesque and heroic expiring of one's great lover in one's lap, but what has actual death to do with all that? She speaks to Antony but he does not answer. He is dead—"dead as earth" in the words of Lear about

Cordelia—and death, when by Antony's very dumb immobility it begins to be comprehended, evokes not the would-be faint which we have come to know in Cleopatra so well, but a fall into that deep unconsciousness which is scarcely a "becoming" any more than is Othello's trance at the feet of Iago or Lear's unconsciousness in Cordelia's camp. The event in Cleopatra's lap has fantastically deranged the degreed cadences of that strange world which is her order.

We must look ahead for a moment to that time when the queen and Dolabella will be talking as she tries to comprehend what has happened, for then we may see just how much of an "order" this idea of Antony actually was to her. For with Dolabella she will be asking herself whether, after all, this superman was no superman at all. How can this be? She says to Dolabella:

> CLEO.: You laugh when boys or women tell their dreams;
> Is't not your trick?
> DOL.:   I understand not, madam.
> CLEO.: I dreamt there was an Emperor Antony.
> O, such another sleep, that I might see
> But such another man!
> DOL.:   If it might please ye—
> CLEO.: His face was as the heav'ns, and therein stuck
> A sun and moon, which kept their course and lighted
> The little O, th'earth.
> DOL.:   Most sovereign creature—
> CLEO.: His legs bestrid the ocean, his rear'd arm
> Crested the world. His voice was propertied
> As all the tuned spheres, and that to friends;
> But when he meant to quail and shake the orb,
> He was as rattling thunder. For his bounty,
> There was no winter in't; an autumn it was
> That grew the more by reaping. His delights
> Were dolphin-like, they show'd his back above
> The element they liv'd in.[25] In his livery
> Walk'd crowns and crownets; realms and islands were
> As plates dropp'd from his pocket.   (5.2.74–92)

In the beauty of her vision—and visions are supposed to be beautiful—one might recall Hamlet's words about his father. But in Cleopatra's world where qualities must "appear," Antony's superhumanity is best expressed not by a recounting of his moral qualities, but by a description of his gigantism. For his essence must ultimately be a visual thing. To churchmen, the ultimate may be ineffable; for Cleopatra, since the ineffable cannot be seen, the ultimate has to be . . . enormous.

> Think you there was or might be such a man
> As this I dreamt of?

This is not simply rhetorical. It recalls the astonishing simplicity of those questions put to Enobarbus about Actium and blame, and the questions Cleopatra asked during Antony's final banquet. But Dolabella answers her. He tells her a truth, and she tells him one back.

DOL.:   Gentle madam, no.
CLEO.: You lie up to the hearing of the gods!
But if there be or ever were one such,
It's past the size of dreaming. Nature wants stuff
To vie strange forms with fancy; yet t'imagine
An Antony were nature's piece 'gainst fancy,
Condemning shadows quite.   (5.2.94–100)

Though the world of the real cannot compete with Fancy most of the time, it can when an Antony is created. Yet it is her metaphor that tells the tale. With the Renaissance sense of "shadows" as "pictures" or "images," Antony stands as a work created by the artist Nature to compete with all those "shadows" created by the artist Fancy. And in this vying, Antony triumphs: he is the ultimate . . . painting.[26]

This, I think, will be the most vivid projection of the way in which Cleopatra ultimately thinks of Antony, of what he means to her. His qualities she imagines not in any abstraction: she sees him as a sight. Not great but gigantic; not compelling but picturesque; not powerful but loud: visible, decorous giant of the world. Not the striving god Hercules, but the static god Atlas, colossal in his changeless holding of the heavens. But there is more too, for in this speech to Dolabella, Antony is something else than giant. He has a quality which Cleopatra visually translated as proportion, decorum.

Be'st thou sad or merry,
The violence of either thee becomes,
So does it no man's else.   (1.5.59–61)

So when Cleopatra finally revives from the dead faint into which Antony's lifelessness threw her, we can understand that more than one thing has begun to crumble. There is, of course, her sense of her self. In her world, emotion was exactly what one wished it to be: proportional, decorous, appropriately expressive of high, queenly thinkings. One does not lose control: one may feel faint, but this has nothing to do with actually falling unconscious. One does not lose consciousness: one throws scepters. Her reviving words talk of this, but they also show how the loss of Antony has caused disorder.

CHAR.:   O, quietness, lady!
IRAS: She's dead too, our sovereign.
CHAR.:   Lady!
IRAS: Madam!
CHAR.: O madam, madam, madam!

IRAS: Royal Egypt!
Empress!
CHAR.: Peace, peace, Iras!
CLEO.: No more but [e'en] a woman, and commanded
By such poor passion as the maid that milks
And does the meanest chares. It were for me
To throw my sceptre at the injurious gods,
To tell them that this world did equal theirs
Till they had stol'n our jewel.   (4.15.69–78)

But with Antony dead, the principle of decorum is gone anyway. Nothing becomes anything: no reaction is appropriate. Appropriateness is dead.

All's but naught:
Patience is sottish, and impatience does
Become a dog that's mad. Then is it sin
To rush into the secret house of death
Ere death dare come to us?[27]   (4.15.78–82)

The suicidal impulse, but also this enormous strength and stature as a tragic figure. The effort at recovery, the will to retain fragments. Now, when Antony has dwindled to nothingness, she must seek other analogies. Once we heard of her trading clothes with him; we saw her trying to be his kind of soldier at Actium; now she tries to be another part of him: magnanimous Antony who, even when dying, could speak in this way to his men:

Nay, good my fellows, do not please sharp fate
To grace it with your sorrows.

We knew this Antony well, and so does Cleopatra as she herself becomes like him.

Ere death dare come to us? How do you, women?
What, what, good cheer! Why, how now, Charmian?
My noble girls! Ah women, women! Look
Our lamp is spent, it's out. Good sirs, take heart.
We'll bury him;   (4.15.82–86)

She is no longer the messenger-beater. She is the magnanimous holder of those "Roman" thoughts which have heretofore been so antipathetic to her.

And then, what's brave, what's noble,
Let's do it after the high Roman fashion,
And make death proud to take us. Come, away,
This case of that huge spirit now is cold.
Ah, women, women! Come, we have no friend
But resolution and the briefest end. *Exeunt.* (4.15.86–91)

VI

But ideally, Romans did not use anesthetic asps. They grimly disemboweled themselves like Cato in the Elizabethan play *Caesar's Revenge*. There, although interrupted and disarmed by his son, Cato found another sword with which to reopen his stomach, into which his intestines had already been shoved back by a doctor. And there was Cato's daughter, Portia, Brutus's wife, who had the incredible fortitude to swallow hot coals. So we must contrast what Cleopatra calls her "resolution"—that Renaissance Stoic term—with that moment when she will abandon this neo-Stoic parlance for her own way of death. And though that moment is not now, her clinging to life need not merely bespeak the political opportunist. She is no more this than Lear. Her dilemma, like Lear's, is a conceptual one. No baldly stated choice between being faithful to Antony's memory and forming a new liaison with Octavius, her problem is most importantly a matter of visualization.

Can Greatness, Absoluteness, the Transcendent, be grasped through some sense of an Antony now visible only in her imaginings as giant, or is this ineluctable sense of hugeness to be attained through Caesar? Is it he who can fulfill all those infinite notions of "Kingship," which she supposed was the property of Mark Antony alone? As Cleopatra appears in 5.2, for the first time since her rhetoric about suicide, her opening words bespeak her dilemma. "What should one be to be great?"

> My desolation does begin to make
> A better life. 'Tis paltry to be Caesar;
> Not being Fortune, he's but Fortune's knave,
> A minister of her will: and it is great
> To do that thing that ends all other deeds,
> Which shackles accidents, and bolts up change;
> Which sleeps, and never palates more the dung,
> The beggar's nurse and Caesar's.[28]
>
> (5.2.1–8)

This quasi-Boethian disparagement of Fortune may indicate, as critics have argued, some beginning of wisdom, but her approach is hardly the homiletic way. Boethius, we recall, saw Fortune as the myth produced by man's ignorance of the intricate workings of Divine Providence, and this view was, too, the general understanding among Shakespeare's contemporaries. But the queen always finds it difficult to think of anything transcending her. If there are higher Powers, she has confined them within competitively anthropomorphic, ultimately Cleopatran, terms. Her infrequent "religious" thoughts, in fact, imply a pantheon paralleling, illustrating, and thus justifying her own activities. "What Venus did with Mars" once struck her as a decorous metaphor of her own affair with Antony, and she excused her almost comic irritation at her blameless messenger with the assertion that

> Some innocents 'scape not the thunderbolt.
>
> (2.5.77)

That wielder of lightning is much like the other "gods"—like Lady Fortune, who strikes at the nearest object in anger, and like those gods too who "did steal our jewel" because Cleopatra's world, she says, "did equal theirs." And if, at the end, she imagines Antony to mock

> The luck of Caesar, which the gods give men
> To excuse their after wrath,   (5.2.286–87)

the gods are thus always mirrors of herself. They lure, like her, but with gifts of "luck" to the end that mankind, seduced by the remembrance and hope of good fortune, will obey and understand a "wrath" which seems to be the gods' only form of meaningful assertion. It is as if the Immortals exercise their godhood merely to derive gratification from the submission of humans. And were they indeed all like Cleopatra, that would be perfectly true. Thus if, in her pseudo–*contemptus mundi* the world can indeed become "dung," Caesar "paltry," we may, in contrast, recall a very different point of view.

> Here is my space,
> Kingdoms are clay; our dungy earth alike
> Feeds beast as man; the nobleness of life
> Is to do thus.   (1.1.34–37)

It is merely a question of taste. For Antony, kingdoms are so much dross compared to the Cleopatran experience. For the queen kingdoms are so much dross compared to being a goddess.

So in comes Proculeius whom Antony told her to trust. She had replied:

> My resolution and my hands I'll trust,
> None about Caesar.   (4.15.49–50)

To be sure, Cleopatra was right and Antony was wrong, but she could not have known this in advance. For her the world is always a snare. She says as much here to Proculeius.

>   Antony
> Did tell me of you, bade me trust you, but
> I do not greatly care to be deceiv'd,
> That have no use for trusting.   (5.2.12–15)

Proud of distrust, she fought Antony's return to Rome: for the wrong reasons. Thus she was surprised by his remarriage. She outfoxed his attempt to murder her—she thought—but she did not anticipate his suicide. So if there are traps and snares, Cleopatra sees only those visible to her in the first place. Otherwise, her prideful perspicacity generally precedes a fall, as now. She is lulled by the kind of language which she does not realize she can be lured with.

PRO.:   This I'll report, dear lady.
Have comfort, for I know your plight is pitied
Of him that caus'd it.
                    [Enter Roman Soldiers *behind Cleopatra*]
You see how easily she may be surpris'd.
Guard her till Caesar come.   (5.2.32–36)

Has Cleopatra already planned suicide—even before Proculeius captured her? Some critics think so and point to Dolabella's conversation with the queen just before Caesar enters.

CLEO.: Know you what Caesar means to do with me?
DOL. I am loath to tell you what I would you knew.
CLEO.: Nay, I pray you, sir.
DOL.   Though he be honorable—
CLEO.: He'll lead me then in triumph?
DOL. Madam, he will. I know't. *Flourish.*   (5.2.106–10)

When she now speaks submissively to the Roman leader, her words are thus to be construed as a way of deceiving him so that she may find the opportunity of killing herself. After showing Caesar the list of her treasures, her rage at her treasurer who betrays her becomes, by this token, one more element in her successful deception. And so it goes in Plutarch to whom critics refer for this interpretation, especially since the marginal gloss in North's translation describes the queen's rage: "Cleopatra finely deceiveth Octavius Caesar, as though she desired to live." But if we compare Shakespeare's approach with Plutarch's, we find that the poet did not abandon the carefully wrought consistency of his characterization at all.

In Plutarch, Dolabella speaks to Cleopatra *after* the interview with Caesar, and it is then that Dolabella tells her that she will be sent to Rome within three days.

When this was tolde to Cleopatra, she requested Caesar that it would please him to suffer her to offer the last oblations of the dead unto the soule of Antonius. This being graunted her, she was caried to the place where his tombe was, and there falling downe on her knees, imbracing the tombe with her women, the teares running down her cheekes, she began to speake in this sorte.... Then having ended these dolefull plaints, and crowned the tombe with garlands and sundry nosegayes, and marvelous lovingly imbraced the same: she commaunded they should prepare her bath, and when she had bathed and washed her selfe, she fell to her meate and was sumptuously served. Now whilest she was at dinner, there came a countrieman, and brought her a basket. The souldiers that warded at the gates, asked him straight what he had in his basket. He opened the basket, and tooke out the leaves that covered the figges, and shewed them that they were figges he brought. They all of them marvelled to see so goodly figs. The countrieman laughed to heare them, and bad them take some if they would. They beleved he told them truely, and so bad him carrie them in. After Cleopatra had dined, she sent a certaine table written and sealed unto Caesar and commaunded them all to go out of the tombes where she was, but the two women. Then she shut the doors to her. . . . Some report that this Aspicke was brought unto her in the basket with figs, and that she commaunded them to hide it under the figge leaves, that when she should think to take out the figges, the Aspicke shoulde bite her before she should see her: howbeit, that when she would have taken away the leaves for the figges, she perceived it, and said, Art thou here then? And so, her arme being naked, she put it to the Aspicke to be bitten.   (6:161)

Clearly this is a version emphasizing a suspense. So close is the supervision that the countryman with the figs must make his way artfully past the guards at the tomb. But Shakespeare's Cleopatra never leaves the place where she was captured, summoning there the snakes with ludicrous ease. The guards' dealing with the countryman is, in fact, limited to this.

GUARD: Here is a rural fellow
That will not be denied your Highness' presence.
He brings you figs.
CLEO.: Let him come in.   (5.2.233–36)

Comme ça.
So Shakespeare has let her and us know through Dolabella of Caesar's plan in advance and furnished the means of suicide with casual speed, leaving no suspense at all except in one case: Cleopatra's own intentions. And it is in this context that we must observe Caesar's visit to her. After Dolabella has said "It is the emperor, madam," the stage direction reads: *"Cleopatra kneels."* Caesar would have her rise, but she:

                    Sir, the gods
Will have it thus, my master and my lord
I must obey.   (5.2.115–17)

With what we know of her opinion about the gods, the colossal humility may be amusing and more so as she persists to paint the portrait of a frail woman who does not have the gift of eloquence.

                    Sole sir o'th'world,
I cannot project mine own cause so well
To make it clear, but do confess I have
Been laden with like frailties which before
Have often sham'd our sex.

Caesar tut-tuts and takes his leave, or is about to, when the queen adds something else.

CAES.: I'll take my leave.
CLEO.: And may, through all the world; 'tis yours, and we,
Your scutcheons and your signs of conquest, shall
Hang in what place you please. Here, my good lord.
CAES.: You shall advise me in all for Cleopatra.
CLEO.: [*Giving a scroll.*] This is the brief: of money, plate, and jewels
I am possess'd of; 'tis exactly valued,
Not petty things admitted. Where's Seleucus? (5.2.133–40)

Do we catch here a glimpse of some ludicrous future in which such a daily treasure-list becomes a form of her showing love to this new kind of earthly god?—"Did I ever love Antony so?"

Only when she is bewildered, or when she is pretending, does Cleopatra adopt humility, and then its purpose is to regain domination. "My good lord," in fact, the phrase so often upon her lips now, were words always used to placate Antony. So her rage at Seleucus is not unpredictable and restores the balance—for us, at least, if not for Caesar. Rage is one emotion she never pretends, and whereas Plutarch's Egyptian queen is merely angry to be betrayed by her own servants, Shakespeare's Cleopatra exclaims:

See, Caesar! O, behold,
How pomp is followed! Mine will now be yours,
And should we shift estates, yours would be mine.
The ingratitude of this Seleucus does
Even make me wild. O slave, of no more trust
Than love that's hir'd! What, goest thou back? Thou shalt
Go back, I warrant thee; but I'll catch thine eyes
Though they had wings. Slave, soulless villain, dog!
O rarely base! (5.2.150–58)

Always, in her eyes, she is intrinsically deserving of loyalty and love, so she must soothe this betrayal with clichés about the mutability of high estate, showing what she never learned, especially when she compared the enraged Antony to the wild Caledonian boar. Neither Antony nor Cleopatra ever understands what loyalty is—that lords are followed not because they are gods but because there is reciprocity. The Charmians, Irases, and Eroses are few and far between. But Cleopatra tells Seleucus to leave "or I shall show the cinders of my spirits through th'ashes of my chance." "Chance" and "change," the world's mutability, have caused all this, not she. So Seleucus becomes unnatural even for not steadfastly seeing her intrinsic worth, her intrinsic Aphroditean quality.

Wert thou a man
Thou would'st have mercy on me.

"Be it known," she continues with Caesar,

> that we, the greatest, are misthought
For things that others do; and when we fall,
We answer others' merits in our name,
Are therefore to be pitied.   (5.2.176–79)

When one would be a goddess, it is difficult to know just what to do.

Plutarch's Seleucus betrayed Cleopatra merely by noting items absent from her list of treasure. Shakespeare's official tells us something else. Cleopatra withheld "enough to purchase what you have made known." Why not? Her dilemma is understandable enough. She has not yet resolved herself of her best way. But Caesar makes his mistake. He does not grasp what Thidias and Proculeius intuited so well. Instead of praise, of worship, of feverishly sought-after hand-kissing, only a series of good, solid bargains whose greatest flattery amounts to:

> CAES.:   Feed, and sleep.
Our care and pity is so much upon you,
That we remain your friend; and so adieu.
CLEO.: My master and my lord!

She has been flattered by experts, and now she is being asked to believe that a regal "we" sounds the signal to romance! The contrast with what the queen is used to in these respects is pointed right after Caesar leaves. Dolabella speaks to Cleopatra of obeying "your command which my love makes religion to obey." But Caesar was talking "nonsense" as it were—to the effect of

>   if you seek
To lay on me a cruelty, by taking
Antony's course, you shall bereave yourself
Of my good purposes, and put your children
To that destruction which I'll guard them from
If thereon you rely.   (5.2.128–33)

And so, for the wrong reasons, Cleopatra does prove right. As she sees it, because Caesar shows her none of the homage that is her due, he therefore cannot mean her well. According to *her* lights, then, he is all talk and no truth, and it is thus that she has verified for herself Dolabella's previous warning.

> He words me, girls, he words me, that I should not
Be noble to myself.

And thus have the possibilities been stripped from her life. But because her urge for power lingers, to kill herself is not escape: it is response.

> Now Charmian!
Show me, my women, like a queen, go fetch
My best attires. I am again for Cydnus
To meet Mark Antony. Sirrah Iras, go.

Now, noble Charmian, we'll dispatch indeed,
And when thou hast done this chare, I'll give thee leave
To play till doomsday. [*To Iras.*]—Bring our crown and all.   (5.2.226–32)

There is this, and there is also:

My resolution's plac'd, and I have nothing
Of woman in me; now from head to foot
I am marble-constant; now the fleeting moon
No planet is of mine.[29]   (5.2.237–40)

The difficulty of Cleopatra's death is its very spectacle: donning regalia to commit suicide is the very soul of what theater is about. And if that were not enough, there are the wriggling asps which Cleopatra does not chastely place to her arms, as so many medieval accounts and even Plutarch would have it. Shakespeare's queen, played by a boy, puts the asps to her breast, and with this she enacts her last audacious metaphor. Through it she joins Othello, for the two stand apart from those who merely kill themselves. Othello stabbed his traitor "self" with the violence with which he says he knifed the Turk traducing the state; the queen, not for warriorship but for control, shapes Death too. It is a fussy infant. One assuages it by giving suck, in turn oneself being lulled.

CLEO.: Come, thou mortal wretch,
With thy sharp teeth this knot intrinsicate
Of life at once untie. Poor venomous fool,[30]
Be angry, and dispatch. O, couldst thou speak,
That I might hear thee call great Caesar ass
Unpolicied!
CHAR.:   O eastern star!
CLEO.:   Peace, peace!
Dost thou not see my baby at my breast,
That sucks the nurse asleep?   (5.2.303–10)

Some see fantastic suggestings in all this. A Satanic Virgin Mary, perhaps, suckling a viper at her breast, that age-old image, in the Renaissance, of sin and repentance. But such furious imagings seem scarcely vital to Shakespeare's intent. For no matter when her end might come, quiet things would be beyond the pale of all we know about the queen for whom life is enactment and enactment is life. Thus it is Shakespeare's, not Cleopatra's which is the more audacious conception.

A tragic figure whom the poet has driven, perhaps further than he drove Lear, to a delirium of desperation, she has been stripped, as Lear, of grandiose conception after grandiose conception—in the melting of the godhood of Antony and his empire, the lapse of her own greatness, the death of her lover, Caesar's utter indifference—and still she concedes nothing. For just as Antony would insist, however strangely, to the end, on his quintessential, unshaken, steadfast Romanness, so

Cleopatra insists on her sense of her own, towering self. She will not yield. If she is not the cynosure of earthly gods, empress of beauty, controller of reality, then so much the worse for reality. It is no longer real.

There is another country "far beyond the stars," but not Henry Vaughan's. There Antony waits, if Iras does not get him first. Of what Antony may be king now, however, Cleopatra does not stop to reason. But if, in the afterlife she, for him, will be Dido to his Aeneas in the Elysian Fields trooping with their retainers where the nobleness of death is to do thus, he, for her, will be something different, somewhere. For she is going where gorgeous, curled giants over reality reign ripe for the seducing and where, thus, she will shackle all accidents.

If the existential nature of death's aftermath may be taken by her for granted, then the whole idea of dying itself is nothing but in the pain. And because this pain can be eliminated, it is nothing either. Thus the passage to death is nothing, and the asp becomes another messenger to be confused with his message. Because there is no pain in the asp, there is no hurt in death.

But those that Shakespeare creates into tragedy, despite their proud natures, he does not see as gods. And even though Cleopatra's violent intellectuality insists on constant and consistent dominations, the title she gives Antony is not "king," but "husband." Whether the Renaissance Shakespeare assumed such feeling would suggest a woman's proper sense of fulfillment, or whether he meant us to know the depth of her human love for Antony, however confused, it is difficult to tell. Perhaps she imagines herself the Roman matron, Lucrecian or Portian, another becoming.

> Husband, I come!
> Now to that name my courage prove my title!

She has her dreamy asps, not a sword, yet she speaks Antony's name at the last and we know her Antonian hope, confused as it is with delusions of greatness. She dies as does Lear, forever in the grip of those urgent visions so seductive and destructive of oneself and of those one may love. Such spirits are left with nothing but the hope they see in the death they move to so grandly and, as do all of us, alone.

NOTES

[1] J. C. Maxwell's fine essay, "Shakespeare's Roman Plays: 1900–1956" in *Shakespeare Survey 10* (Cambridge: Cambridge University Press, 1957), pp. 1–11, is helpful here, as is A. P. Riemer's incisive and reasonable view of studies about *Antony and Cleopatra* up to 1968: see *A Reading of Shakespeare's* Antony and Cleopatra (Sydney: Sydney University Press, 1968), chap. 3.

[2] Castiglione is to the point. Caesar and Gaspar converse about the ancient and modern stories of women who would rather commit suicide "than to lose their honesty" and Gaspar rejoins: "These, my Lord Caesar, be not, I believe, in the world nowadays." Caesar responds: "And I will not alledge unto you them of old time." See Baldassare Castiglione, *The Courtier*, trans. Sir Thomas Hoby (London, 1577), pp. 258–61.

[3] Most lately Reuben Brower in his essay on the play—chap. 8 of *Hero and Saint* (Oxford: Clarendon Press, 1971), esp. pp. 351–53.

[4] Illustrative is Montaigne speaking of the heaven of the Moslems: see M. de Montaigne, *Essays,* trans. John Florio and ed. George Saintsbury (London: David Nubb, 1892): Bk. 2.12.

[5] A good statement about the power of this variety is Rosalie Colie's interesting essay on the play in *Shakespeare's Living Art* (Princeton, N.J.: Princeton University Press, 1974), pp. 188ff.

[6] Plutarch, *The Lives of the Noble Grecians and Romans,* translated by Sir Thomas North and edited by George Wyndham (London: David Nutt, 1895), 6:26–27.

[7] The First Folio reads "hate" instead of "haste." This makes superficial sense: one hates things that one fears. But the intent is to warn Cleopatra not to bring about what she is actually trying to prevent. For such a use of "haste" with a direct object, see *Romeo and Juliet* (2.1.11): "hastes our marriage." Cf. *1 Henry IV* (3.1.43) "haste the writer."

[8] Antony is the Philosopher's Stone which with its power has "gilded" Alexas. See *All's Well That Ends Well* (5.3.101ff.): "Plutus himself that knows the tinct and multiplying medicine, hath not in Nature's mystery more science than I have in this ring."

[9] This reference to "black" has caused discussion about Cleopatra's appearance—and, indeed, "black" is used variously in the writings available in Shakespeare's time. Vergil, *Eclogues,* trans. J. Brinsley (London, 1620), has a gloss for ll. 15–18 of the second Eclogue ("Nonne Menalcan / Quamvis ille *niger* quamvis tu candidus esses? / O formosa puer nimium ne crede colori / Alba ligustra cadunt baccinia *nigra* leguntur."). He translates the second line: "Although he [be] black, and albeit thou wert passing fair." Then he glosses "black": *"Foul, or at least not so fair, or of a swart color."* Again: *"White [viz. beautiful]"* (sig. D2). This follows earlier commentary: see Vergil, *Bucolica* (London, 1514)—STC 24814—sigs. A6–A6ᵛ. Eclogue 10.38 also alludes to blackness in this manner. Thus the traditional glossing of the *Bucolics* may have established "black" as meaning "not beautiful." Various comments on the Song of Songs make the same point as the Church, in the allegorical interpretations of this biblical poem, speaks apologetically about her "blackness." One commentator observes: "And so indeed the Church is made black and duskish, that is to say, deformed and unhandsome, by the adversities of her oppressions." See Antonio Brucioli, *A Commentary upon the Canticle of Canticles,* trans. Thomas James (London, 1598), sig. B3. Other approaches to the *Song of Songs* have "black" as sunburnt. Joseph Hall, *Solomon's Divine Arts* (London, 1609), sigs. N5ᵛ–N6 was one such commentator, as was George Gifford, *Fifteen Sermons upon the Song of Solomon* (London, 1598), sig. C3. He interprets: "I know that I am black: but yet withal I am comely, I am well-favored.... I am black indeed, as the men in the tents of Kedar which are sunburnt." (Cf. Henoch Clapham, *Three Parts of Solomon his Song of Songs* (London, 1603), sigs. D2ᵛ–D3. Many other constructions in the period use "black" as a contrast-word to "beautiful" or as a synonym. G. de la Perrière, *Theatre of Fine Devices* (London, 1614), Emblem 37: "If she find / That she is fair ... / If she be black...." Valentine in *Two Gentlemen of Verona* (3.1.102–3) says of women: "Flatter, and praise, commend, extoll their graces: / Though ne'er so black, say they have angels' faces." In Cleopatra's case, furthermore, some punning is involved. Since a sunburned face was not fashionable in Shakespeare's England, Cleopatra is "unhandsome" because "black" with Phoebus's amorous pinches: the pun on both senses of "black" makes her "sunburnt" and thus "unattractive". But, of course, as Enobarbus says, she also "o'erpictures" Venus, so the "blackness" is relative. She is equally elusive in being "wrinkled deep in time." *OED* offers usages wherein a "wrinkle" is a blemish and Gifford (sig. C3ᵛ above) suggests a collocation: "what shall her beauty be, when all her blackness shall be taken away, and Christ shall wash her and make her a glorious Church not having spot or wrinkle?" Cleopatra sees herself, I think, as sunburnt and therefore conventionally flawed. Janet Adelman has carefully surveyed Elizabethan associations of blackness with Africa. See her Appendix C: "Cleopatra's Blackness," in *The Common Liar* (New Haven: Yale University Press, 1973).

[10] The idea of the poison here is somewhat more complicated than the *Variorum* (p. 73n) suggests: "It is poison because the reminiscence 'works like madness in her veins.'" Actually we are dealing with the notion that whatever a serpent eats turns to poison. See La Primaudaye, sign. 2X3: "as venomous serpents turn all they eat, how good soever it be, into venom...." Thus our serpent of old Nile feeds herself with thoughts, but because she is a serpent, the thoughts she "eats," although naturally poison now, are paradoxically delicious.

[11] Cf. *3 Henry VI* (5.1.36): "Thou art no Atlas for so great a weight."

[12] See Shakespeare's Sonnet 15, where "brave" is contrasted to "bare," and see Alexander Schmidt, *Shakespeare-Lexikon* (Berlin: G. Reimer, 1902), *brave* adj. 3.

[13] Mandragora is indeed referred to as a soporific by Iago, but a 1633 usage is at least suggestive. "Rachel indeed was gracious and extreme fair, but barren, that with all her mandragoras was hardly able to bring her Jacob a Joseph, and the little Benjamin cost her her life." See H. A., *Parthenia Sacra* (London, 1633), ed. Iain Fletcher (Aldington: Hand and Flower Press, 1950), p. 129.

[14] Enobarbus plays on "cunning" (see Schmidt, *cunning* 1, 2). Since Cleopatra exaggerates her tears and sighs, they have to be taken as real storms. As such, they are a natural manifestation. Indeed, to ascribe such meteorological phenomena to her skill as artificer (to think she is fooling) is to give her the supernatural power of Jove.

[15] Salads were thought of not only as green but as cold. Cf. Barnabe Barnes, *Devil's Charter* (London, 1607), sig. L[v]: "Will you eat any salad, my Lord? Faith here are excellent herbs if you love them. / *Caesar.* They be, my Lord, too cold for my stomach."

[16] "Conversation" means "deportment." Cf. Thomas Wright, *The Passions of the Mind* (London, 1601), sig. K6 and *Antony and Cleopatra* (2.5.131–32); Octavia is of a "holy, cold, and still conversation."

[17] Variorum and New Arden comment on how Cleopatra here alludes to the "perspective," or double picture, but the point has perhaps been missed. No one refers to *Richard II* (2.2.16ff) where "perspective" pictures are defined. "For sorrow's eye, glazed with blinding tears / Divides one thing entire to many objects, / Like perspectives, which rightly gazed upon, / Show nothing but confusion—ey'd awry / Distinguish form. So your sweet majesty, / Looking awry upon your lord's departure, / Finds shapes of grief more than himself to wail, / Which look'd on as it is, is naught but shadows / Of what is not." Cf. *All's Well That End's Well* (5.3.48). However (after all this) Variorum is more to the point when it speaks of "double or turning pictures," "cousoning picture," or "turning pictures." Here contrast is the principle: a fair maid, an ape, an owl; a crow vs. a swan; "a lion on the one side, a lamb on the other." Cf. Thomas Adams, *The Devil's Banquet* (London, 1614), sig. B2. "As I have observed in some beguiling pictures: look on it one way, and it presents to you a beautiful damsel; go on the adverse side, and behold, it is a devil, or some misshapen stigmatik. Sin shows you a fair picture," etc. Cleopatra is making a sharp contrast between Antony's ways.

[18] For Narcissus as beautiful, see *The Rape of Lucrece*, ll. 264ff. One also assumes Shakespeare's familiarity with Golding's Ovid and with such conventional Narcissus emblems as found in Alciati's *Emblemata* (1608), Emblem 69, or G. Whitney's, *A Choice of Emblems* (Leyden, 1586), sig. T3. For Gorgons as signifying ugliness as an idea, see John Grange's *Golden Aphroditis* (London, 1577), sig. N[v]: "ugly Medusa," and Sir Thomas Elyot, *The Governor* (London, 1580) on anger [sig. N4], and *OED*. On the other hand, Fritz Saxl, *Lectures,* 2 vols. (London: Warburg Institute, University of London, 1957), 1:75 alludes to Arabian drawings of the constellation of Perseus (who killed Medusa) which show Perseus holding the head of a bearded *man.* These drawings were faithfully copied by Western draughtsmen. Antony could thus be referred to as a supremely ugly bearded man. (However, in Christine du Castel's *Histories of Troy*, trans. R. Wyer [London, 1540], sig. M[v], the woodcut depicts "the serpent Gorgon" as a dragon.)

[19] For "proper" as handsome, see *Nobody and Somebody* (London, 1606), sig. A4[v], and also *As You Like It* (3.5.51): "You are a thousand times a properer man / Than she a woman. . . . And out of you she sees herself more proper / Than any of her lineaments can show her."

[20] In this sense beauty is, for Cleopatra the efficient, not the material, cause of love, instead of the reverse as we have it from Pico della Mirandola, *A Platonic Discourse upon Love*, trans. Thomas Stanley and ed. E. G. Gardner (London: G. Richards, 1914), p. 29.

[21] See, for example, La Primaudaye, sig. 2S6 and Pierre Charron, *Of Wisdom* (London, 1612: SR July 17, 1606), sig. C2[v].

[22] Charron, sigs. I[y] and I2, are relevant. "To play the mourner, the afflicted person, to weep for the death or unhappy accident of another, to think that not to be moved at all, or very little, is for want of love and affection—there is also vanity in this."

[23] Based upon Ps. 17:6, this concept of the world's snare was common as a religious motif. See Francis Quarles, *Emblems* (London, 1639), Bk. 3, Emblem 9; Joseph Hall, *Works*, sig. D[v]; P. I. Iurisc, *Pieux Désirs Imités des Latins du R. P. Herman Hugo* (Paris, 1627), Emblem 9.

[24] Cleopatra is disparaging here, even if she does not grasp the point of Antony's anger. Telamon's suicidal fury was the subject of one of Seneca's tragedies, and the queen means that Antony's rage is misdirected: see *2 Henry VI* (6.1.26–27): "Like Ajax Telamonius, / On sheep or oxen could I spend my fury." The Calydonian boar of Thessaly was a figure of anger and manslaying, *The Tragedy of Meleager* being one work concerned with this. But boars were symbols of lechery too. See Thomas Nashe, "Christ's Tears over Jerusalem," in *Works,* ed. R. B. McKerrow and rev. F. P. Wilson (Oxford: Basil

Blackwell, 1958), 2:112–113: "luxury, riot, and sensuality [we borrow] from the hog, and therefore we call a lecherous person a boarish companion." Cf. *Cymbeline* 2.5.15–17.

[25] Henry Peacham's *Minerva Britanna* (London, 1612), sig. N3, clarifies the queen's metaphor. "The friendly dolphin, while within the main, / At liberty delights to sport and play, / Himself is fresh, and doth no wit retain / The brinish saltness of the boundless sea / Wherein he lives. Such is the secret skill / Of Nature working all things at her will. / So you, great lady, who your time have spent / Within that place where dangers oft abound, / Remain untainted of your element, / And, to your praise, yet keep your honor sound, / Diana-like, whose brightness did excell, / When many stars within your climate fell."

[26] For "shadows" as "pictures" or "paintings," see Shakespeare's *Sonnet* 53; *The Merchant of Venice* 3.2.126–30; *Julius Caesar* 1.2.55–58; *Two Gentlemen of Verona* 4.4.190ff.

[27] For an extended description of the "House of Death" or "Thanatus" (*sic*), see John Davies, *Humor's Heaven on Earth* (London, 1605), stanzas 127–55.

[28] As Simmons aptly observes, this is the voice of a Senecan heroine. But Cleopatra, he continues, is going to discover more than is dreamt of in this philosophy. See J. L. Simmons, *Shakespeare's Pagan World* (Charlottesville: University Press of Virginia, 1973), p. 158.

[29] It is often pointed out here that the moon is a symbol of inconstancy, but Cleopatra invokes a more general cliché indicated by Peacham in *Minerva Britanna,* sig. X3ᵛ, where the symbol of inconstancy is a *woman*—with the moon in her hands. By this token, Cleopatra would be disavowing not her personality traits, but, like Lady Macbeth, her femininity as viewed in the early seventeenth century.

[30] For "fool" as infant, see the various commentaries on Polonius warning Ophelia to stay away from *Hamlet* lest she "tender" him a "fool." For "wretch" as having the same meaning, see *The Winter's Tale* 3.3.49; *Romeo and Juliet* 1.3.44.

Alexander Leggatt
ANTONY AND CLEOPATRA

In *Julius Caesar* the title character casts a giant shadow. There is the Caesar the actor is given to play, and there is the Caesar other characters talk about; the play is in the end more concerned with the latter. Shakespeare's interest in this doubleness of character, shadow and substance, can be traced back to Talbot's encounter with the Countess of Auvergne; it finds its most elaborate development in *Antony and Cleopatra*. The Soothsayer who warns Antony that in any contest with Octavius Caesar he is bound to lose puts it in this way:

> Thy demon, that thy spirit which keeps thee, is
> Noble, courageous, high, unmatchable,
> Where Caesar's is not. But near him, thy angel
> Becomes afeard; as being o'erpower'd.   (II. iii. 18–21)

The attendant spirits are in fact projections of the men themselves; behind the political drama, with its closely observed personalities, is a shadow-play of demigods. At that level, as the Soothsayer insists and Antony confirms, Caesar wins because he is lucky:

> The very dice obey him,
> And in our sports my better cunning faints
> Under his chance: if we draw lots, he speeds.   (II. iii. 32–4)

In her death scene Cleopatra mocks 'The luck of Caesar' (V. ii. 285). But in the historical action the play shows luck has nothing to do with it. Caesar is crafty and skilful; Antony is inept. At the start of the war, Antony's astonishment at the speed with which Caesar has captured Toryne shows he is simply outgeneralled (III. vii. 20–57). As a negotiator Antony is equally out of his depth. Through his ambassador he 'Requires to live in Egypt, which not granted, / He lessens his requests' (III. xii. 12–13). This is not the way to open a bargaining session with a tough opponent.

From *Shakespeare's Political Drama: The History Plays and the Roman Plays* (London: Routledge, 1988), pp. 161–88.

The play's action offers what looks like a full explanation of the course of the war in the relative skill of the antagonists. The Soothsayer's insistence that Caesar is simply lucky seems to refer to another action on another plane of reality, one in which men's fates are made not by themselves but by Fortune. In that respect it is like the apocalyptic speeches of Margaret in *Richard III*, which give the political action a dimension of myth it could not attain on its own.

Characters are likewise idealized in defiance of what the play actually shows. Cleopatra's dream of the Emperor Antony, 'His legs bestrid the ocean, his rear'd arm / Crested the world' (V. ii. 82–3), is not the Antony we have seen, any more than the giant Henry V we hear of in the opening of *I Henry VI*, whose 'arms spread wider than a dragon's wings' (I. i. 11), is the skilled role-player and leader of men Shakespeare will later put on the stage. Cleopatra knows this as well as we do. Her dream is presented in a defiant, even quarrelsome spirit, introduced by one of those passages of sharp comic observation so characteristic of this play. Dolabella tries to impress her:

> DOL.: Most noble empress, you have heard of me?
> CLEO.: I cannot tell.
> DOL.:   Assuredly you know me.
> CLEO.: No matter, sir, what I have heard or known:
> You laugh when boys or women tell their dreams,
> Is't not your trick?
> DOL.:   I understand not, madam.
> CLEO.: I dreamt there was an Emperor Antony.
> O such another sleep, that I might see
> But such another man!
> DOL.:   If it might please ye,—
> CLEO.: His face was as the heavens, and therein stuck
> A sun and moon, which kept their course, and lighted
> This little O, the earth.
>   (V. ii. 71–81)

Cleopatra's first reaction to this self-important fool is icy; then she decides that he will do to stand for the prosaic, diminished world against which she sets her dream. She casts him in the role of sceptic, overrides his interruptions, and then, when she has quite finished, dares him to contradict her:

> CLEO.: Think you there was, or might be such a man
> As this I dreamt of?
> DOL.:   Gentle madam, no.
> CLEO.: You lie up to the hearing of the gods.
> But if there be, or ever were one such,
> It's past the size of dreaming: nature wants stuff
> To vie strange forms with fancy, yet to imagine
> An Antony were nature's piece, 'gainst fancy,
> Condemning shadows quite.
>   (V. ii. 93–100)

At the most literal level, the play supports Dolabella's 'Gentle madam, no.' His reply is given extra force by its attractive balance of courtesy and firmness, so unlike the silliness of his first address to Cleopatra; unexpectedly, she is bringing out the best in him. At first she simply gives him the lie; then her language suddenly becomes difficult as she admits he could be right ('if' and 'were' make the dream conditional, not absolute) and goes on to argue her case by changing the meanings of words. Shadow and substance, as normally conceived, are reversed: the imagined Antony is the work of nature; it is prosaic reality that is a fantasy-world of shadows.

Cleopatra's dream is not an isolated aria but arises from a dramatic situation, and is one side of a real debate. Dolabella's 'no' is a simple way of stating the case for prose, for history, for fact. Caesar makes the same point—again, with unexpected courtesy—when he hears of Antony's death:

> The breaking of so great a thing should make
> A greater crack. The round world
> Should have shook lions into civil streets,
> And citizens to their dens.   (V. i. 14–17)

He misses the portents that really did surround the death of Julius Caesar;[1] there is a distinct note of regret as he registers the fact that the world he now lives in does not recognize the greatness of men in this way. There are no miracles; man is on his own. The play's one supernatural moment is offstage music signalling the departure of a god. If there is to be a supernatural dimension in life, men and women are responsible for creating it themselves, in their own minds and imaginations. And they must do it not by imagining gods but by seeing what is godlike in each other. Caesar and Dolabella cannot or will not make the effort: Cleopatra can, and does.

She presents her Antony as a dream; that is one way of challenging the facts of nature. Another is through the creations of art. Earlier in the play Cleopatra has been exalted as she exalts Antony here: this is done not by Antony but by Enobarbus, in a speech that, having nothing literally supernatural about it, none the less challenges reality in its own way:

> The barge she sat in, like a burnish'd throne
> Burn'd on the water: the poop was beaten gold;
> Purple the sails, and so perfumed that
> The winds were love-sick with them; the oars were silver,
> Which to the tune of flutes kept stroke, and made
> The water which they beat to follow faster,
> As amorous of their strokes . . .
>   At the helm
> A seeming mermaid steers: the silken tackle
> Swell with the touches of those flower-soft hands,
> That yarely frame the office. From the barge
> A strange invisible perfume hits the sense
> Of the adjacent wharfs.   (II. ii. 191–7, 208–13)

A barge is a throne, fire burns on water, perfume hits with the impact of something *felt*. Where a sensible shipbuilder would use wood and rope we have silver and silk. Instead of real sailors there are women with 'flower-soft hands', and they in turn impersonate sea-nymphs and mermaids. The impersonation extends to 'pretty dimpled boys, like smiling Cupids' (202) and Cleopatra herself, 'O'er-picturing that Venus where we see / The fancy outwork nature' (200–1). The speech is not overtly about Cleopatra, yet in a deeper sense she is its centre and subject. Though she is hidden beyond description, glimpsed only in the role of Venus, the sensual artifice of the whole scene radiates outward from her, expressing her power to delight and fascinate through deception. And Enobarbus, the realist, is clear that all this *is* a deception. From the opening line he deals in similes, not metaphors. He himself is impressed and delighted but never fooled; he knows the barge is steered by a 'seeming' mermaid. He admits that fancy can outwork nature, but they do not change places for him as they do for Cleopatra. As we listen to the speech, the categories of reality seem to dissolve and the senses melt into each other; but Enobarbus' phrasing makes it clear that all this is the product of human art. It is also, like Cleopatra's debate with Dolabella, offered as a challenge and defiance to his listeners. Maecenas has taken a vulgar tourist's view of Egypt: 'Eight wild-boars roasted whole at a breakfast, and but twelve persons there, is this true?' (II. ii. 179–80). He is fascinated by quantity; he imagines the delights not of the epicure but of the glutton. The words that begin Enobarbus' speech, 'I will tell you' (II. ii. 190), give it the quality of a set piece designed to impress. He is out to dazzle his listeners, and in the process to expose the feebleness of their own attempts to imagine Egypt.

The speech also has the effect of bringing Cleopatra and Egypt to the mind's eye during a long Roman sequence. For all the vast distances its action covers, this is a play in which one land impinges on another quickly and easily. Geographically much smaller, the England of *Henry IV* was a fragmented place where the flow of information was blocked and twisted by rumour. *Antony and Cleopatra* is full of messengers, who always tell the truth. The flow of information is clear and constant, and annihilates distance. But the crucial factor is the mind itself, which can call up instantly an absent character or an absent world. Cleopatra complains of Antony, 'He was dispos'd to mirth; but on the sudden / A Roman thought hath struck him' (I. ii. 79–80). As in *Julius Caesar* characters found their identities in the eyes of others, so in *Antony and Cleopatra* characters seem most vivid and powerful when they are absent, living in the imaginations of those who remember them. We see the greatness of Antony through Cleopatra, the glamour of Cleopatra through Enobarbus. In the first three scenes, when Antony and Cleopatra are together onstage, she plays manipulative games in which he can do nothing right; once he is safely in Rome, he can do nothing wrong:

> CLEO.: What, was he sad, or merry?
> ALEX.: Like to the time o' the year between the extremes
> Of hot and cold, he was nor sad nor merry.
> CLEO.: O well-divided disposition! (I. v. 50–3)

Even their sexual relationship thrives on absence; Cleopatra's strongest erotic feelings for Antony come when all she can do is daydream.[2] At this level even the eunuch Mardian can have a rich sex life: 'Yet have I fierce affections, and think / What Venus did with Mars' (I. v. 17–18).

Idealizing others, the characters reveal their own natures. Everything we hear about Antony's wife Fulvia indicates that the world is a simpler and pleasanter place without her. But as soon as she is dead Antony takes a generous view—'There's a great spirit gone!'—and adds, revealingly, 'she's good, being gone.' (I. ii. 119, 123). Enobarbus may be right when he insists, 'the tears live in an onion, that should water this sorrow' (I. ii. 167–8), but Antony's reaction, whatever it tells us about Fulvia, is a clear sign of his own chivalry and courtesy. When Caesar idealizes Antony for his heroic endurance, he inadvertently tells us something about himself:

> When thou once
> Wast beaten from Modena, where thou slew'st
> Hirtius and Pansa, consuls, at thy heel
> Did famine follow, which thou fought'st against,
> Though daintily brought up, with patience more
> Than savages could suffer. Thou didst drink
> The stale of horses, and the gilded puddle
> Which beasts would cough at.   (I. iv. 56–63)

His admiration of Antony is genuine; but, where Cleopatra's dream-Antony overflows with power and generosity, Caesar's is grotesquely degraded. He pictures Antony in defeat, and his own imagination lingers over foul images, taking the speech in a direction very different from his overt intention. If we are inclined to think of Caesar as simply cool and rational, we have to think again.

The recurring device of celebrating an absent character in a set speech takes an ugly turn here; and it is subject to direct parody when Cleopatra and the messenger between them reconstruct the absent Octavia:

> CLEO.: Is she as tall as me?
> MESS.:   She is not, madam.
> CLEO.: Didst hear her speak? is she shrill-tongu'd or low?
> MESS.: Madam, I heard her speak; she is low-voic'd.
> CLEO.: That's not so good: he cannot like her long.
> CHAR.: Like her? O Isis! 'tis impossible.
> CLEO.: I think so, Charmian: dull of tongue, and dwarfish!
> What majesty is in her gait? Remember,
> If e'er thou look'st on majesty.
> MESS.:   She creeps:
> Her motion and her station are as one:
> She shows a body, rather than a life,
> A statue, than a breather.   (III. iii. 11–21)

Lear's reference to Cordelia's low voice as 'an excellent thing in woman' shows what the conventional attitude was. But Cleopatra takes Octavia's virtues as well as her neutral qualities, and turns them to malicious caricature. The messenger quickly sees the game she is playing and joins in. This is Cleopatra at her most petty and vindictive; and yet the sheer brazenness of it is irresistible. The very next scene shows us the 'real' Octavia, a woman of feeling with a deep sense of responsibility, concerned as no one else in the play is for the suffering the war will cause, and offering to act as peacemaker. In *Henry IV* the full reality of the characters over-shadowed the caricatures they made of each other; but that is not what happens here. Such is the unfairness of Shakespeare's art at this point that we find it hard to concentrate on Octavia's virtues. A nice girl, of course, but terribly dull; our minds, like Antony's, turn back to Cleopatra, and the caricatured Octavia overrides the 'real' one.

Elsewhere in Shakespeare, the idealizing set pieces are about the state: Gaunt's England, Canterbury's commonwealth of bees, Menenius' body politic, Cranmer's vision of Elizabeth. Here they are about people. Apart from Cleopatra's parody of Octavia, they celebrate the greatness of the great. The common people, who make vivid contributions of their own elsewhere, have all but vanished. (There is, as we shall see, one important exception.) Octavia's concern for the casualties of war, 'As if the world should cleave, and that slain men / Should solder up the rift' (III. iv. 31–2), finds no echo. While Enobarbus shows a similar awareness of the scale of the conflict, he views it with equanimity:

> Then, world, thou hast a pair of chaps, no more,
> And throw between them all the food thou hast,
> They'll grind the one the other.   (III. v. 13–15)

There is no hint there of the pain and outrage of the Towton allegory. When the great make war, they consume their subjects; the process is as natural as eating. It is the same when they make love: Cleopatra talks of consuming her whole nation to create a messenger service: 'He shall have every day a several greeting, / Or I'll unpeople Egypt' (I. v. 77–8). The focus on the great individual rather than the general community has another effect. Speeches like Gaunt's and Canterbury's arise from particular dramatic situations, and support particular interests; but as they express an ideal of the state they have, or claim, qualities of timelessness and impersonality we do not find in the idealizing speeches of *Antony and Cleopatra*. Here the needs of the characters and the demands of the moment are more in the foreground, and the speeches have an impulsive, improvised quality. There is no sense of permanent reality, larger than any of the characters, to which a final appeal can be made. The characters' own tendency to live intensely for the moment—'There's not a minute of our lives should stretch / Without some pleasure now' (I. i. 46–7)—is reflected in the dramaturgy of the play, as several critics have pointed out. For Julian Markels each action of Antony's 'seems uncaused, self-generated, a new creation whose spontaneity disarms our challenge'.[3] For Maynard

Mack, this leads to difficulties of interpretation, since we are unsure 'how to reconcile one action with the next'.[4] As in *Henry V*, the problem of knowing how to
make connections is compounded by the lack of knowledge of the characters' inner
states of mind.[5] What is Cleopatra really up to with Thidias, with Seleucus, even
with Antony? Does Antony seriously want to make his marriage with Octavia
work? Does Caesar really hope that it will? Do the characters themselves know
what they want? As knowledge of them eludes us, so self-knowledge seems to
elude them. They respond to the needs and desires of the moment, not to some
consistent inner reality.

There is no sense of a fixed political state; no sense, either, of a fixed private
self. Nor is there a fixed perspective from which to judge the action. As Margery
M. Morgan has argued, Cleopatra's line about Antony, 'Though he be painted one
way like a Gorgon, / The other way's a Mars' (II. v. 117–18), suggests a perspective-
trick painting, 'contrary distortions imposed one upon another'.[6] We recall the
perspective tricks of *Richard II*. Which is the real Antony, Cleopatra's or Dolabella's?
Which is the real Caesar, the skilled general and politician or the minion of Fortune?
And how do we grasp the quicksilver that is Cleopatra? The play's first two words
suggest an ongoing debate: 'Nay, but' (I. i. 1). Philo and Demetrius are arguing about
Antony even as they come onstage. The first words belong to Philo, who tells us
to use our eyes:

> Look, where they come:
> Take but good note, and you shall see in him
> The triple pillar of the world transform'd
> Into a strumpet's fool: behold and see.   (I. i. 10–13)

His perspective is firm, and he appeals to the stage picture we see before us. He
sees what Bernard Shaw was to see: 'a faithful picture of the soldier broken down
by debauchery, and the typical wanton in whose arms such men perish'.[7] But later,
if we take Lear's advice and look with our ears, we see Cleopatra's barge burning
on the water and Antony bestriding the ocean. Nor is this a simple conflict between
picture and word. Within the dialogue itself the debate goes on. We hear it in the
first words of the lovers. Having been told to look, we listen:

> CLEO.: If it be love indeed, tell me how much.
> ANT.: There's beggary in the love that can be reckon'd.
> CLEO.: I'll set a bourn how far to be belov'd.
> ANT.: Then must thou needs find out new heaven, new earth.   (I. i. 14–17)

Playing the realist, Cleopatra challenges Antony to express his love within the limits
of language. He declares language inadequate to express that love and the present
world too small to contain it; but of course he uses words to say this. The
characters' imaginations are constantly trying to create new heaven, new earth, in
which Caesar and Antony are at war in the realm of the spirit and Antony and
Cleopatra are avatars of Mars and Venus. But the dream of 'What Venus did with

Mars' is also the prurient fantasy of a eunuch, and the characters have to live, act—and dream—in a world of hard reality in which the voices of Philo and Dolabella can be argued against, but not silenced. This does not mean, however, that Philo has the last word; he only has the first. And Shakespeare is no more content here than he was in *Richard II* to play perspective games and leave it at that. Having looked at the play's idealizing visions, we should now consider more closely the 'reality' out of which they arise.

The play's political scenes have a remarkable quality of sharp, close observation. We see not demigods but men between five and six feet tall (closer to five, as a rule) with recognizable faces. The relations of Caesar and Lepidus are caught in a matter of seconds:

LEP.: Farewell, my lord; what you shall know meantime
Of stirs abroad, I shall beseech you, sir,
To let me be partaker.
CAES.:   Doubt not, sir,
I know it for my bond.   (I. iv. 81–4)

Legally they are equal partners in the triumvirate; but their relative strength and authority as men have created a very different relationship. Against Caesar's curt acknowledgement of legal obligation we can set the kindness of Antony:

ANT.:   Let us, Lepidus,
Not lack your company.
LEP.:   Noble Antony,
Not sickness should detain me.   (II. ii. 168–70)

A small matter, perhaps, but, as Granville-Barker observes, 'The little man is grateful.'[8] If Lepidus is a nonentity, Pompey seems at first a man seduced by his own rhetoric. He begins his first scene full of self-confidence, celebrating his own achievements and pouring scorn on his opponents. His reaction to bad news is 'Where have you this? 'tis false' (II. i. 18). But he betrays his real view of his own enterprise when he learns of Antony's return to Rome:

I did not think
This amorous surfeiter would have donn'd his helm
For such a petty war.   (II. i. 32–4)

There is nothing petty about taking on the rulers of the known world. Pompey shows here the small-scale thinking that leads him to make peace on very modest terms and to refuse Menas' offer to make him lord of all the world.

The real contest is between Caesar and Antony; the smaller figures are there to help establish the scale. For these natural enemies, nothing is too small to cause a power struggle:

CAES.: Welcome to Rome.
ANT.:   Thank you.
CAES.:   Sit.
ANT.:   Sit, sir.
CAES.:   Nay, then.   (II. ii. 28)

Caesar lets Antony win this round; and in the ensuing confrontation he seems at first on the defensive, offering complaints Antony can easily deny. But he soon has Antony driven into a corner, admitting he has 'Neglected' (89) the commitments that go with his oath. When the marriage with Octavia is proposed, he forces Antony's hand, refusing to speak 'till he hears how Antony is touch'd' (II. ii. 140). Caesar is guarded and calculating. When he feasts his army, it is only after checking the budget: 'we have store to do't, / And they have earn'd the waste' (IV. i. 15–16). Antony's style in such matters is rather different. We have seen their differing treatments of Lepidus; and Antony will defy Pompey only after thanking him for past courtesies (II. ii. 154–8). His attention to such niceties is of a piece with the old-fashioned chivalry that looks so pathetic in the war sequence, as he challenges Caesar to single combat and his followers shake their heads in disbelief. Hal, though a pragmatist, was prepared to meet Hotspur on his own terms, hero against hero, letting the whole enterprise depend on him. Caesar does not work in that way. In a small touch—'I do not know, / Maecenas; ask Agrippa' (II. ii. 16–17)—we hear the voice of an administrator who is quite comfortable about delegating responsibility. There is no discernible affection between him and his associates, but they work together easily. Antony does inspire affection, and it causes practical problems: the messenger who brings him bad news at the start of the play can hardly bear to speak, and Antony has not only to wring the message from him but to complete it himself (I. ii. 91–102). It is easier doing business with Caesar; his messengers report bad news briskly and frankly, and he accepts it in the same spirit (I. iv. 34–40). Working for the most part in small details, Shakespeare builds a decisive picture of the two men, pointing to Caesar's ultimate victory.

As in *Julius Caesar,* and in the England of the Bolingbrokes, appearance and reputation count. The final breaking of the triumvirate is preceded by a propaganda war in which accusations are hurled back and forth (III. vi) and Caesar, in order to make Antony look bad, pretends that Octavia has 'come / A market-maid to Rome' (III. vi. 50–1), though she has entered *'with her Train'* (38SD) and 'To come thus was I not constrain'd, but did it / On my free will' (56–7). Octavius, I think, genuinely loves his sister. But the needs of propaganda come first. Finally, Caesar consolidates his victory by offering evidence of

How hardly I was drawn into this war,
How calm and gentle I proceeded still
In all my writings.   (V. i. 74–6)

In fact the great men spend a remarkable amount of their time and effort on propaganda, while much of the real work is done by underlings. Ventidius, having just won a victory on Antony's behalf, declares, 'Caesar and Antony have ever won / More in their officer than person' (III. i. 16–17). He goes on to point out that if the underlings do too much their superiors become jealous and turn on them; hence his own refusal to exploit his present victory. This not only exposes the inner workings of war but casts an ironic light on the great men themselves. Subordinates like Ventidius have to make a conscious effort not to outdo them.

What begins as realistic observation of the political world becomes increasingly critical and deflating. The famous names of Pompey and Caesar establish the current crop of politicians as second-generation and second-rate. Menas' complaint, 'Thy father, Pompey, would ne'er have made this treaty' (II. vi. 82–3), identifies this character as Pompey the Less. Julius Caesar was known for his generosity to old enemies, and we saw a touch of this in the earlier play in his gracious words to Ligarius (II. ii. 111–13). The new Caesar is different:

> Plant those that have revolted in the vant,
> That Antony may seem to spend his fury
> Upon himself.
>
> (IV. vi. 9–11)

Antony himself is a link with a more glorious past,[9] but this only sharpens the contrast between his former achievement and his present failure. He accuses Caesar of 'harping on what I am / Not what he knew I was' (III. xiii. 142–3) and thus admits his own decline. As in the second tetralogy, we are acutely aware of the ruinous effects of time, against which no achievement can stand. With his usual frankness Caesar tells Pompey, 'Since I saw you last, / There is a change upon you' (II. vi. 52–3). Even this younger Pompey is starting to look old. Caesar's own victory was one of the great achievements of history; but Maecenas says, of his reaction to Antony's death, 'When such a spacious mirror's set before him, / He needs must see himself' (V. i. 34–5). As in *Julius Caesar,* men see themselves through each other; Caesar, Maecenas speculates, sees in Antony his own mortality.

Reputation, on which so much depends in politics, is constantly related to the uncertain favour of

> Our slippery people,
> Whose love is never link'd to the deserver
> Till his deserts are past.
>
> (I. ii. 183–5)

Even success has a way of turning sour. Enobarbus, a realistic observer of love and politics alike, makes a pragmatic decision to follow Caesar, and finds, when he sees how Caesar treats turncoats, that he is worse off than before. He dies of a broken heart, but what could have been a sentimental effect has a sardonic edge: Enobarbus has betrayed his better self *and* made a practical blunder. The shadowy, unreal nature of worldly achievement is most fully dramatized for us in the party on Pompey's galley. In the phrasing of Menas' offer to Pompey, what could have been momentous becomes farcical:

MEN.: Wilt thou be lord of all the world?
POMP.:   What say'st thou?
MEN.: Wilt thou be lord of the whole world? That's twice.   (II. vii. 60–1)

Pompey's refusal, 'In me 'tis villainy, / In thee't had been good service' (II. vii. 73–4), not only reveals scrambled values but confirms the effect created by Menas' comic exasperation. A world that can be tossed so easily from hand to hand cannot be taken seriously. The servant who carries off the drunken Lepidus is called a strong fellow because 'A bears the third part of the world' (II. vii. 89), and later in the scene we see the whole world drunk as the great men dance hand in hand, presumably in a circle, singing 'Cup us till the world go round' (II. vii. 116).[10] Later, when we are told that Antony used to have 'superfluous kings for messengers' (III. xii. 5) and that 'realms and islands were / As plates dropp'd from his pocket' (V. ii. 91–2), the power of the world is made to look trivial. Antony, on the point of losing that world, orders:

Fall not a tear, I say, one of them rates
All that is won and lost: give me a kiss,
Even this repays me.   (III. xi. 69–71)

We might see this as lover's hyperbole; but the play has already shown dramatically how trivial the world is. The economy of the theatre, which brings great men on to the stage as life-sized figures exposed in ordinary daylight, has let us see them 'as it were, down the wrong end of the telescope'.[11] The closer we look at them, the smaller they become.

The lovers too are closely and realistically observed. As in *Julius Caesar,* love has its own politics, in which appearances count. When Cleopatra accuses Antony of betraying her, she claims she can see it in his face: 'Thou blushest, Antony, and that blood of thine / Is Caesar's homager' (I. i. 30–1). Her manipulation of him is based on countering his appearance with hers:

If you find him sad,
Say I am dancing; if in mirth, report
That I am sudden sick.   (I. iii. 3–5)

That is an obvious trick, to be played when she is working through underlings. Moments later he enters, evidently Roman and serious, and she makes a snap decision: 'I am sick, and sullen' (I. iii. 13). It is hard to cope with a player who keeps changing the rules like this. And it is hard for Antony, that most artless of men, to deal with a great actress who keeps insisting that *he* is giving a performance:

CLEO.:   Good now, play one scene
Of excellent dissembling, and let it look
Like perfect honour.
ANT.:   You'll heat my blood: no more.
CLEO.: You can do better yet; but this is meetly.   (I. iii. 78–81)

There is, however, a crucial difference between the politics of love and the politics of the world. The Romans are constantly explaining, defending, and excusing themselves. The conference on Antony's return to Rome, and the mutual accusations that precede the outbreak of war, are prolonged exercises in self-justification on both sides. Antony and Cleopatra, on the other hand, do not deal in explanations or excuses, however much they wrong each other. Cleopatra does not demand, nor does Antony offer, the reasons for his marriage to Octavia. He simply returns to her, and she simply takes him back. (There is a gap in the action here, but we are not encouraged to fill it in; for the purposes of the play, anything we do not see or hear about does not happen.) Through the war sequence Antony has every reason to accuse Cleopatra of betraying and destroying him; but, when the accusations come, Cleopatra does not counter them with arguments but simply waits till Antony's passion blows over, as she knows it will: 'I must stay his time' (III. xiii. 155). When she goes on to protest her loyalty, it is because she senses that Antony will now be receptive. Antony accuses her of betraying him in the last battle, and will not hear her speak; but when told she is dead he declares, 'I will o'ertake thee, Cleopatra, and/Weep for my pardon' (IV. xiv. 44–5). He says nothing of pardoning her. When, having wounded himself fatally, he learns that she is alive after all—learns, in fact, that her last trick has caused his death—there is no resentment or recrimination, merely a businesslike order: 'call my guard, I prithee.... Bear me, good friends, where Cleopatra bides' (IV. xiv. 128, 131). Behind the repeated accusations, even the real betrayals, the fundamental principle of their love is an unconditional acceptance of each other. To this they always return in the end, quickly and simply, with no need for the lengthy negotiations that precede reconciliation in the political world. By contrast, the politicians are bound together only by temporary expediency, however they may protest (and even want to believe) otherwise. If the final principle of love is unconditional acceptance of the other person, the final principle of politics, as this play shows it, is kill or be killed. The game is over when only Caesar is left standing.

Unconditional acceptance is not a practical or sensible attitude. It avoids analysis, judgement, and justification. But it is the attitude of a poet, and we have encountered it before in Shakespeare: 'Man is but an ass, if he go about to expound this dream.' It is a pervasive attitude in Egypt, and Antony and Cleopatra apply it to more than each other. When Caesar speaks of the people it is to analyse and judge their fickleness (I. iv. 41–7). Antony and Cleopatra just watch them: 'To-night we'll wander through the streets, and note/The qualities of people' (I. i. 53–4). At Pompey's party there is a particularly revealing discussion of things Egyptian. Antony enters, evidently in conversation with Caesar, who has apparently been asking practical questions about the economic significance of the Nile:

Thus do they, sir: they take the flow o' the Nile
By certain scales i' the pyramid; they know,
By the height, the lowness, or the mean, if dearth
Or foison follow.   (II. vii. 17–20)

The great, mysterious river is here analysed for its usefulness. If Caesar has indeed started this conversation, he is getting information helpful to someone who will one day administer Egypt. The practical attitude is linked with the desire for control. But this sensible conversation is interrupted by Lepidus, drunk and as belligerent as he is capable of being, insisting that 'the Ptolemies' pyramises are very goodly things' (II. vii. 33–4)—not useful or significant, just goodly. He is silenced by Antony's description of the crocodile: 'It is shap'd, sir, like itself, and it is as broad as it hath breadth: it is just so high as it is, and moves with its own organs. It lives by that which nourisheth it, and the elements once out of it, it transmigrates' (II. vii. 41–4). A crocodile is a crocodile is a crocodile. It was so commonly an emblem of deceit that the audience must have noticed a deliberate suppression when Antony says not 'the tears of it are treacherous' but simply 'the tears of it are wet' (II. vii. 48). Divided as he is, Antony can have a practical Roman conversation with Caesar, analysing the significance of the river; and an Egyptian conversation with Lepidus, simply accepting the crocodile for what it is. This is also a key to the differing views of sex in Rome and Egypt. Agrippa's reference to Julius Caesar's affair with Cleopatra, 'He plough'd her, and she cropp'd' (II. ii. 228), describes the movement of the sexual act as seen by an observer, and judges its significance by results. Cleopatra's line, 'O, my oblivion is a very Antony, / And I am all forgotten' (I. iii. 90–1), is not overtly sexual at all; but in its sudden surrender to annihilation it evokes and savours the feeling of an orgasm.

This enjoyment of the thing itself is the key to the way in which Shakespeare dramatizes Egypt. The local colour his audience would have expected is all there: the wealth and feasting, for which Egypt was famous; the pyramids, the serpents, the insects; and above all the mysterious, fertile river, breeding monsters generated by the sun.[12] Iras' palm presages chastity 'as the o'erflowing Nilus presageth famine' (I. ii. 47). Antony swears 'By the fire / That quickens Nilus' slime' (I. iii. 68–9). His return to Cleopatra is predicted in Enobarbus' 'he will to his Egyptian dish again' (II. vi. 123), and his sharpest attack on her is 'I found you as a morsel, cold upon / Dead Caesar's trencher' (III. xiii. 116–17). In Egypt, as in Shallow's Gloucestershire, the routines of life go on: music, billiards, drinking, fishing, and making love. The Roman scenes are full of information and business, but in Egypt there is a more palpable texture, a stronger sense of felt life. The politicians talk of ruling the world, but a few place-names and a couple of disparaging references to the fickle people do not add up to a world that one can see, much less a world that sounds worth ruling. Rome itself, a palpable city in *Julius Caesar* and *Coriolanus,* complete with streets, shops, public places, houses, famous hills, and a great river, is here as neutral and unatmospheric as a committee room. Its entire political structure seems to consist of Caesar and his entourage. If we recall the formula *Senatus Populusque Romanus,* we notice that the people are a distant rumour and the Senate has vanished completely.[13] There are three images in the play of a land sinking into a river, and they are worth comparing. In Antony's 'Let Rome in Tiber melt, and the wide arch / Of the rang'd empire fall!' (I. i. 33–4) Rome simply disappears, and the Tiber, characterless in itself, is merely the thing into which it vanishes. In Cleopatra's 'Melt Egypt into Nile! and kindly creatures / Turn all to serpents!' (II. v. 78–9) the life of Egypt does not disappear but returns transformed from the river, low and ugly but still alive. And there *is* life in Egypt; Rome is just empty scenery, if that. Later in the same scene Cleopatra wishes the messenger were lying about Antony's marriage 'So half my Egypt were submerg'd and made / A cistern for scal'd snakes!' (II. v. 94–5). Here the kingdom sinks only halfway, and the serpents, whose hissing can be heard in the sound of the line, are more alive than ever. In history, Rome absorbed the kingdom of the Ptolemies and the empire Caesar built lasted for centuries. In the play, the empire is spun into the drunken round dance on Pompey's galley, and for theatrical purposes disappears, while Egypt is alive and vivid to the end. Antony's crocodile, we remember, does not die; it 'transmigrates'. The economy of the theatre has made its own judgement: compressed and foreshortened, the business of history begins to look trivial, while the frivolities of Egypt, dramatized in a relaxed and detailed way, look solid and real. And it seems to be Egypt, not Rome, that has found a way to resist the ruin of time.

The play, having brought us to this point, is only half over. Shakespeare still has to relate his contrasted visions of Rome and Egypt to the contrast between the heroic and realistic visions we noted earlier. The relation is not a simple one, and demands a look at the mixture of triumph and defeat in the fates of the two lovers. Antony, a practical failure for most of the play, wins the second battle; for once his greatness can be celebrated as something seen and proven, not just talked about. His victory is preceded by the desertion of Hercules; this warns us that his success will be temporary,[14] but also establishes that, if he is a failure, he is a failure on a very high level; a man favoured by a god, and deserted by a god. The scene also lifts the action as a whole to a mysterious, supernatural plane: how, for example, does the soldier *know* that the music is Hercules (IV. iii. 15–16)? This prepares us for the arming of Antony. In *Henry IV*, Part 2, comedy, realism, and allegory were deliberately kept apart: there was a sharp difference between Henry's exemplary encounter with the Lord Chief Justice and the aimless ramblings of Justice Shallow; and there could be no final meeting between Eastcheap and Westminster. In the arming of Antony comedy, realism, and allegory are fused in a seamless whole:[15]

CLEO.:   Nay, I'll help too.
What's this for?
ANT.:   Ah, let be, let be! thou art
The armourer of my heart: false, false; this, this.
CLEO.: Sooth, la, I'll help: thus it must be.
ANT.:   Well, well,
We shall thrive now. Seest thou, my good fellow?
Go, put on thy defences.

EROS: Briefly, sir.
CLEO.: Is not this buckled well?
ANT.:   Rarely, rarely:
He that unbuckles this, till we do please
To dafft for our repose, shall hear a storm.
Thou fumblest, Eros, and my queen's a squire
More tight at this than thou: despatch. O love,
That thou couldst see my wars to-day, and knew'st
The royal occupation, thou shouldst see
A workman in't.   (IV. iv. 5–18)

With obvious allegory, Antony is armed as the warrior of love, flanked by Cleopatra and Eros. But the scene is ballasted by realism and comedy: in Cleopatra's
fumbling, her childish pride, Antony's amused, affectionate condescension, and Eros'
(we may imagine) discreet silence. The scene is not just airy and fantastic; practical
business is going on all through it, and Cleopatra's hands are on Antony's body.
Antony is not just a hero but a 'workman', 'master of his craft'.[16] Even the fact that
he has an attendant called Eros is not a detail Shakespeare made up but one he
found in Plutarch.

    We need this practical ballast, for the scene in other respects moves out of
history. Before this battle Antony speaks not of fighting Caesar but of fighting death
and fortune (III. xiii. 192–4, IV. iv. 4–5). By association with the spirit of the morning,
Antony seems younger: 'This morning, like the spirit of a youth / That means to be
of note, begins betimes' (IV. iv. 26–7). Time seems not just halted but reversed.
Wounds do not hurt: Scarus notes with interest, 'I had a wound here that was like
a T, / But now 'tis made an H', and adds, 'I have yet / Room for six scotches more'
(IV. vii. 7–8, 9–10). But the real magic is in Antony himself. For most of the play he
has followed initiatives taken by Caesar or Cleopatra. In the war, his followers
complain, 'our leader's led, / And we are women's men' (III. vii. 69–70). He loses the
first day's battle by following her retreat. Now at last he leads: 'You that will
fight, / Follow me close, I'll bring you to't' (IV. iv. 33–4). In the process, as realism and
allegory are fused, so Antony's different roles are fused. From Philo's opening
speech onwards, we are told that Antony's love has destroyed his generalship.
Now the warrior and the lover are one, and he celebrates his victory in powerfully
erotic language:

                    O thou day o' the world,
        Chain mine arm'd neck, leap thou, attire and all,
        Through proof of harness to my heart, and there
        Ride on the pants triumphing!   (IV. viii. 13–16)

In Cleopatra's 'O happy horse to bear the weight of Antony!' (I. v. 21) Antony as
horseman, traditionally an image of military victory and the control of the lower
passions, is transformed into Antony as lover. It is a quick summary of how

Cleopatra has changed him. Now he imagines her riding him; in a further act of poetic fusion, triumph and submission become one.

Caesar too is lifted to a new level, but only briefly. He begins the battle by announcing,

> The time of universal peace is near:
> Prove this a prosperous day, the three-nook'd world
> Shall bear the olive freely.
>
> (IV. vi. 5–7)

For a moment the future opens out, and we see the real scale of his achievement. But at once we descend to examine the means he uses, in his ugly trick of putting Antony's ex-followers in the forefront of the battle (IV. vi. 8–11). The bringer of universal peace looks small and shabby. More remarkably, he has no reaction to his day's defeat. We may take this on a realistic level and say that Caesar is the sort of politician who never acknowledges failure; or we may conclude that Antony's battle, and his victory, do not take place in the world of history Caesar inhabits. Antony's enemies are time, death, and fortune. We do not see Caesar's defeat because at his plane of reality it never happens. That is a harder reading; but it fits with the most disturbing fact about the victory, the absence of Enobarbus. The sequence is framed by his desertion and death, so that we cannot help noting that the familiar figure is missing from Antony's side. This means that, for all its air of realism, Antony's victory cannot carry full conviction, for it has not been tested against the commentary of Enobarbus, who may not stand for the whole truth but whose viewpoint, with its nice balance of sympathy, irony, and pragmatism, is an indispensable part of the truth. His absence alerts us to something shadowy in Antony's achievement: it is too close to being a matter of talk alone, and it is not quite of this world. As Antony opens the third day's battle, we know instantly that the trick cannot be played twice:

> I would they'ld fight i' the fire, or i' the air,
> We'ld fight there too. But this it is; our own foot
> Upon the hills adjoining to the city
> Shall stay with us (order for sea is given...).
>
> (IV. x. 3–6)

The cosmic poetry is suddenly empty; we are back in history. The heroic and practical visions had seemed for a while to come together; now they fall apart.

Antony loses, as we have always known he would. What he fears through the play is not just the loss of kingdoms but the loss of self: 'These strong Egyptian fetters I must break, / Or lose myself in dotage' (I. ii. 113–14). At the realistic level this means a loss of his Roman identity, even his sexual identity. Octavius declares he

> is not more manlike
> Than Cleopatra; nor the queen of Ptolemy
> More womanly than he.
>
> (I. iv. 5–7)

Cleopatra reports that they have played transvestite games (II. v. 22–3), and, when Antony celebrates his victory by imagining himself as the passive sexual partner, the misgivings of conventional Romans would be confirmed. His ultimate fear, however, is not the loss of an old or conventional identity, but the loss of any identity: 'Haply you shall not see me more, or if, / A mangled shadow' (IV. ii. 26–7). This is the fear that comes to a head in the aftermath of the final battle, when Antony imagines himself dissolving like the clouds of sunset:

ANT.: That which is now a horse, even with a thought
The rack dislimns, and makes it indistinct
As water is in water.
EROS: It does, my lord.
ANT.: My good knave Eros, now thy captain is
Even such a body: here I am Antony,
Yet cannot hold this visible shape, my knave.   (IV. xiv. 9–14)

The eerie calm of the whole passage suggests that Antony has reached 'the very heart of loss' (IV. xii. 29), where there is nothing left but the final peace of annihilation. But the scene begins with Antony's question, 'Eros, thou yet behold'st me?' (IV. xiv. 1), and even after announcing his dissolution he can still say, 'here I am Antony'. Antony's dissolving into nothing is something that can be talked of, but not seen; at the simplest level, the actor's body gives his words the lie. His loss of self, like his victory the previous day, is not quite real; Antony is still before us, as real as he ever was.

It is worth noting that if he has been submissive in Egypt—

I go from hence
Thy soldier, servant, making peace or war,
As thou affects.   (I. iii. 69–71)

—he has been equally submissive in Rome, making under pressure a marriage that puts him in a false position in which he behaves with less than his usual chivalry. Cleopatra taunts him with being at Caesar's beck and call—

'Do this, or this;
Take in this kingdom, and enfranchise that;
Perform't, or else we damn thee.'   (I. i. 22–4)

—and, more humiliating, at Fulvia's (I. iii. 20–1). This is a caricature, but based on truth: in the political scenes Antony is generally passive, following initiatives taken by others. Caesar insists that a showdown between them was inevitable—'we could not stall together, / In the whole world' (V. i. 39–40)—and the Soothsayer predicts that Antony is bound to lose. He has, in other words, the choice of being destroyed in Egypt or destroyed in Rome. It may be worth pausing at this point over the fate of Alexas. Charmian utters a comic curse on him, praying he will be cuckolded fiftyfold by a succession of bad wives; what actually happens is that he betrays

Antony for the sake of Caesar, and Caesar hangs him (IV. vi. 11–16). The political humiliation is worse than the sexual one.

Nor is Antony's choice simply two methods of destruction. It is in Rome that things disappear, including Rome itself; in Egypt they are transformed. This is what happens to Antony. After one of the most lyrical death scenes in English drama— 'Unarm, Eros, the long day's task is done, / And we must sleep' (IV. xiv. 35–6)—he fails to kill himself. The workman has bungled: 'I have done my work ill, friends' (IV. xiv. 105). And we know even as we watch his attempted suicide that he is acting on a false report of Cleopatra's death. He has to die not as a Stoic Roman in the manner of Brutus and Cassius, but as Cleopatra's lover, held for the last time in her arms. And there has to be more than lyricism in his last moments, or they will not be a full summary of him. The aftermath of his bungled stroke is cruel and embarrassing: he writhes on the stage, no one will finish him off, and Dercetas steals his sword to give it to Caesar. The business of raising him to the monument exalts him, together with Cleopatra, above the ordinary Romans on the main stage; but it is also physically difficult, even grotesque and ludicrous. In the revised version of Samuel Daniel's *Cleopatra,* there is a detail that, according to Margaret Lamb, may reflect business in the King's Men's production: Antony gets stuck halfway up and dangles in mid-air, dripping blood on the spectators below.[17] Even without this detail, there is in the stage picture a recollection of Cleopatra's earlier joke about herself as a fisher of men: 'I'll think them every one an Antony, / And say "Ah, ha! y'are caught" ' (II. v. 14–15). Anyone who has seen a Crucifixion play knows that the sheer physical difficulty of getting Christ raised on the cross has powerful dramatic impact. Shakespeare aims for a similar impact here, as Antony is drawn up to the monument, but he leavens it with comedy, some of which is sexual: 'Here's sport indeed! How heavy weighs my lord!' (IV. xv. 32). Antony, now physically passive as never before, is restored in the language to his dominant role as lover. In the sequence as a whole he is at once exalted and humiliated, and the tone of the scene veers between the grand—

> O sun,
> Burn the great sphere thou mov'st in, darkling stand
> The varying shore o' the world.
> (IV. xv. 9–11)

—and the pragmatic: 'None about Caesar trust but Proculeius' (IV. xv. 48). The scene summarizes the full range of Antony, in a way in which the second day's victory and the dissolving clouds did not. But the remarkable thing is that we never see him die. Editors usually place a stage direction for his death around Cleopatra's 'O, see, my women: / The crown o' the earth doth melt' (IV. xv. 62–3), but there is no stage direction in the Folio. The effect Shakespeare wants, I think, is that at some point, as Cleopatra talks, he fades out, so quietly that we do not see it happen. To steal another actor's death scene is, we might say, a feat that only Cleopatra could manage. But she does it for a reason. As the physical Antony fades, he is replaced by the heroic Antony for whom Cleopatra is the spokesman, the

Antony we hear of in her speech to Dolabella. For Antony, loss is a final step to transformation.

The realistic and heroic Antony are finally separate: one is seen, the other talked of. The heroic Antony, like the heroic Julius Caesar in the earlier play, is securely in place only after the other Antony is dead. Cleopatra goes one stage further. She has defined the heroic Antony for us; she must create for her own death a convincing heroic image of herself, something not just talked of but shown. She does this not by selection, as Hal defines his kingship by cutting out his former life, but by a fusion of everything she has been, high and low, grand and comic. She centres it on a political point: it matters now, as never before, that she is Queen of Egypt. Earlier, whatever political significance her affair with Antony may have had was blurred by a concentration on the affair itself. When she and Antony adopted royal images, we saw this only through Caesar's unsympathetic eyes, as a vulgar display in the market-place (III. vi. 2–12). They were surrounded by 'all the unlawful issue that their lust / Since then hath made between them' (III. vi. 7–8), suggesting not the fertility of a true royal line but the casual, prolific breeding of animals. In later negotiations with Caesar, when Cleopatra requests 'The circle of the Ptolemies for her heirs' (III. xii. 18), the idea of preserving a royal line becomes more serious. After Antony's death she demands 'conquer'd Egypt for my son' (V. ii. 19). In the end, however, Cleopatra's royalty matters more as a means of self-assertion, institutionalizing her grandeur and surrounding it with imagery that is not a matter of words alone. When she orders, 'Show me, my women, like a queen' (V. ii. 226), she emphasizes the importance of the stage picture. Characteristically, Caesar appreciates not the symbolism but the triumph of the will, saying that Cleopatra 'being royal / Took her own way' (V. ii. 334–5). But at least he recognizes that Cleopatra's nature in this respect is a function of her office. Charmian makes another political point: 'It is well done, and fitting for a princess / Descended of so many royal kings' (V. ii. 325–6). Against this regal past, Caesar is a mere republican upstart, as diminished as Napoleon among the pyramids. However we judge his victory, we know that like the Bolingbrokes he had to work for it; Cleopatra simply *is* a queen, as a crocodile simply *is* a crocodile. Thidias calls Caesar 'The universal landlord' (III. xiii. 72), and we may recall John of Gaunt's rebuke to his nephew: 'Landlord of England art thou now, not king' (*Richard II*, II. i. 113). We have seen in *Julius Caesar* how uneasily regal imagery sits in Rome, and this Caesar never attempts to use it.

If that were all that could be said, we would conclude that Cleopatra and Caesar have won separate victories on different terms. But Cleopatra has also beaten Caesar on his own terms, something Antony never managed to do. When Antony advises her, 'None about Caesar trust but Proculeius', she replies, 'My resolution, and my hands, I'll trust, / None about Caesar' (IV. xv. 48–50). Events prove her right and Antony wrong. Proculeius betrays her; Cleopatra does better on her own—enlisting, of all people, Dolabella. Given that politics deals in appearances, Caesar wants to bolster his appearance by adding Cleopatra to his train of captives: 'her life in Rome / Would be eternal in our triumph' (V. i. 65–6). This is not, as we shall see, the sort of eternity Cleopatra wants. Proculeius asks her to co-operate:

> let the world see
> His nobleness well acted, which your death
> Will never let come forth. (V. ii. 44–6)

At the same time Caesar tries to cut down her appearance of grandeur; he insults her, as the Countess's messenger insulted Talbot, by claiming not to recognize her: 'Which is the Queen of Egypt?' (V. ii. 112). But he has met his match. Grovelling before him, she puts him off his guard, and buys the time she needs to cheat him of his triumph. She imagines the asp calling 'great Caesar ass, / Unpolicied!' (V. ii. 306–7), and once again we hear the hissing of the snakes of Egypt, those symbols of indestructible life. One of the guards sums up the last phase of the political action in two words: 'Caesar's beguil'd' (V. ii. 322).

Nor is Cleopatra content with a royal Egyptian triumph over republican Rome. She takes over Rome itself, as she has taken over Antony, using her gift for transformation to embody in herself what was best in the Rome of legend: 'Let's do it after the high Roman fashion' (IV. xv. 87). The low Roman fashion of the present is indicated when Caesar talks blandly of corrupting a Vestal Virgin for money (III. xii. 29–31). Cleopatra, I think, savours the irony of being in the end the noblest Roman of them all. In the process she dismisses finally the conventional Roman view of herself and Antony, Philo's view. If she is taken to Rome in triumph, then

> saucy lictors
> Will catch at us like strumpets, and scald rhymers
> Ballad us out o' tune. The quick comedians
> Extemporally will stage us, and present
> Our Alexandrian revels: Antony
> Shall be brought drunken forth, and I shall see
> Some squeaking Cleopatra boy my greatness
> I' the posture of a whore. (V. ii. 213–20)

The Romans become dirty old men, their view of Antony and Cleopatra a vulgar play of a drunk and a whore. Shakespeare, through Cleopatra, invites us to compare that play with his, and its third-rate boy actor with the brilliant lad he trusted with this part (and with this line). The theatre that degrades, this time at least, is not Shakespeare's theatre, which has presented Cleopatra, as it presented Henry V and Julius Caesar, in a form that, though not uncritical, is full and rich and refuses the easy route of caricature.

As true theatre defies time—'we'll strive to please you every day'—so does kingship. Cleopatra's order, 'Give me my robe, put on my crown, I have / Immortal

longings in me' (V. ii. 279–80), implicitly connects kingship with immortality (and
with theatre, for she is dressing the part, though in her case this is no impersonation). The Queen is dead, long live the Queen. However, she does not aim at the
immortality that is mere survival through time. Henry V, not anticipating some
recent developments in Shakespeare criticism, could be confident about how England would remember St Crispin's Day. But, as history is written by the victors,
Antony and Cleopatra will survive through history as part of Caesar's story. Caesar
himself says as much in the speech that ends the play:

> No grave upon the earth shall clip in it
> A pair so famous: high events as these
> Strike those that make them: and their story is
> No less in pity than his glory which
> Brought them to be lamented. Our army shall
> In solemn show attend this funeral,
> And then to Rome.   (V. ii. 357–63)

Having paid his tribute, he pulls the focus to himself, and, leaving the lovers in their
graves, turns to the next stage in the story of Rome. This would not do for
Cleopatra. Enobarbus' way of surviving is even worse. Having promised himself 'a
place i' the story' (III. xiii. 46) for his loyalty to Antony, he predicts a future of infamy
for his betrayal: 'let the world rank me in register / A master-leaver, and a fugitive'
(IV. ix. 21–2). After death, survival in this world is a chancy business, dependent on
the interpretation of posterity. Antony thinks of going to another world:

> Where souls do couch on flowers, we'll hand in hand,
> And with our sprightly port make the ghosts gaze:
> Dido, and her Aeneas, shall want troops,
> And all the haunt be ours.   (IV. xiv. 51–4)

In some ways this is a legitimate reflection of their life together, especially the idea
of playing out their love in public, before an audience.[18] Antony and Cleopatra, in
striking contrast to Romeo and Juliet, are never alone. But couching on flowers
does not seem quite the style of the love we have seen, nor does strolling hand in
hand sound as though it will satisfy the Cleopatra who cried, 'O happy horse to
bear the weight of Antony!' This is to say nothing of Antony's sentimental view of
Dido and Aeneas, and his revision of their last painful encounter in the underworld,
a story Shakespeare's audience would have known from Virgil.

We have, then, no satisfying image of a life beyond death, in this world or the
next. Cleopatra's solution is simple, or at least simply phrased: 'I am again for
Cydnus, / To meet Mark Antony' (V. ii. 227–8). She imagines herself not beginning
a new life but starting the old one again; she takes time and twists it in a circle, like
an asp coiled in a basket.[19] It is repetition like that of the theatre, where the players
time and again can go back to the same starting point. If Antony's dream of
immortality is a wistful fantasy, Cleopatra's, being rooted in the repeatability of the

theatrical occasion itself, has greater substance. This is in line with the conscious dressing-up and role-playing of her last moments, and her scorn for the Roman theatre's shabby imitation of her. As her first appearance to Antony in the pageant of the barge was the product of art, so her last appearance in the play is consciously artistic, consciously theatrical. In her words, 'I am again for Cydnus', the one occasion circles back into the other, and we see before us the splendour we only heard of. Shadow and substance are joined. Cleopatra's immortality is not a dream of the future but something acted out before us, concretely, now; and something that can be acted over and over whenever the play is presented. At the end of *Henry V* the circling of time suggested the futility of history; in *Julius Caesar,* the characters' attempts to find significant form in their lives. For Cleopatra, the circle means a chance to have the same life over again, cheating time not by getting out of it but by going through it, finding transcendence as she always has, in the here and now, not shaped or analysed but felt intensely: 'Eternity was in our lips, and eyes' (I. iii. 35). We have been fairly prepared for this. Egypt has already disrupted our normal sense of time: in the long sequence from II. v to III. iii it seems that weeks pass in Rome while minutes pass in Egypt.[20] We have seen Antony briefly restored to youth on the morning of his one victory; and the Antony Cleopatra imagines in defiance of Dolabella expresses the fertility of nature in a way that ordinary time would make impossible:

> For his bounty,
> There was no winter in 't; an autumn[21] 'twas
> That grew the more by reaping. (V. ii. 86–8)

Antony has imagined banks of unchanging flowers; Cleopatra imagines a harvest that happens over and over.

At the start of her last scene, Cleopatra seems to be trying to stop the world of time, change, and fortune, the world of Caesar:

> it is great
> To do that thing that ends all other deeds,
> Which shackles accidents, and bolts up change;
> Which sleeps, and never palates more the dung,
> The beggar's nurse, and Caesar's. (V. ii. 4–8)

She sees her own nature as transformed: 'now from head to foot / I am marble-constant' (V. ii. 238–9). But marble is not her true medium: she has always appealed by change, variety, and action, not by any fixed achievement. As Susan Snyder puts it, to hop forty paces through the public street (II. ii. 229) 'is surely no way to *arrive* anywhere'.[22] Enobarbus, early in the play, gives us a clue as to how her death scene will really work: 'Cleopatra catching but the least noise of this, dies instantly. I have seen her die twenty times upon far poorer moment: I do think there is mettle in death, which commits some loving act upon her, she hath such a celerity in dying' (I. ii. 137–42). Enobarbus' jokes connect her play-acting with her capacity for multiple orgasms; the cumulative effect is to make death, like sex, a game that can be played over and over, taking away its sting by taking away its finality. By the end of the play Enobarbus is gone. But if we take his view of Cleopatra into the final scene we will find it does not destroy that scene but helps us see it more clearly. The Clown who brings the asp gives us a comic view of death. His warning, 'there is no goodness in the worm' (V. ii. 265–6), is offset by his jokes: 'his biting is immortal: those that do die of it, do seldom or never recover' (V. ii. 245–7). A recent victim 'makes a very good report o' the worm' (V. ii. 254), though the Clown suspects that her report of her death may be a little exaggerated. Death as described here hardly sounds final, and immortality is a matter of easy chat among neighbours. The Clown is the play's only commoner; his effect is not just to take the sting out of death[23] but to bring immortality down to earth.

He also combines two of Egypt's principal activities, sex and feasting, when he says, 'I know, that a woman is a dish for the gods, if the devil dress her not' (V. ii. 272–4). The asp and the figs are sexual symbols. Antony has already declared,

> I will be
> A bridegroom in my death, and run into't
> As to a lover's bed.   (IV. xiv. 99–101)

Cleopatra makes the same connection, but in a more intimate and physical way: 'The stroke of death is as a lover's pinch, / Which hurts, and is desir'd' (V. ii. 294–5). She encourages the asp as she might a clumsy lover: 'poor venomous fool, / Be angry, and despatch' (V. ii. 304–5). Though she is robed and crowned, she dies not on a throne but on a bed (V. ii. 354); her last moments are full of touching, kissing, and handling. Her action in applying the asp to her breast makes us conscious of her body as an ordinary stabbing or poisoning would not. That body is anything but marble: 'Dost thou not see my baby at my breast, / That sucks the nurse asleep?' (V. ii. 308–9). Nor is her nature really altered. She is, as before, putting on a performance for Antony as audience: 'I see him rouse himself / To praise my noble act' (V. ii. 283–4). And she is already getting ready for the next quarrel, saying of Iras, who is dead before her,

> If she first meet the curled Antony,
> He'll make demand of her, and spend that kiss
> Which is my heaven to have.   (V. ii. 300–2)[24]

As she talks through Antony's death she talks through her own: 'O Antony! Nay, I will take thee too. / What should I stay—' (V. ii. 311–12). Death interrupts her, but we may imagine she goes on talking on the other side. Nor is there a stillness on stage when she dies: Charmian's 'your crown's awry, / I'll mend it, and then play' (V. ii. 317–18) suggests that Shakespeare wants the small fussy movements, the touching and handling, to continue.

This is an intensely physical scene, alive with the full language of the theatre. It uses royal symbols as 'visual verification of the claims of the poetry',[25] allowing us to see what Enobarbus in his description of the barge only talked about. The royal Cleopatra, the crafty politician who outwits Caesar, and the sensual woman come together. As its suggestions of marriage and fertility link it with the traditional ending of comedy,[26] so the style moves easily between grandeur and laughter. The tone of the scene is caught in Cleopatra's words to Charmian, 'when thou has done this chare, I'll give thee leave / To play till doomsday' (V. ii. 230–1). *Antony and Cleopatra* is like *Richard III* in giving a mythical dimension to the world of history. The difference is that while in *Richard III* myth took over history, fixing it in simple shapes that no historian would see as true, *Antony and Cleopatra* allows us glimpses of human grandeur working through the vicissitudes of time and through closely observed reality. Its method is not selection but fusion. *Henry IV* ended with a great king publicly dismissing a representative of the sensual life, history overriding comedy. *Antony and Cleopatra* ends with a great queen, robed, crowned, and triumphant, joking with her attendants and handling her own body as she waits in bed for her lover.

NOTES

[1] See T. J. B. Spencer, *Shakespeare: The Roman Plays* (London: Longmans, Green, 1963), p. 36.
[2] See Robert Ornstein, 'The Ethic of the Imagination: Love and Art in *Antony and Cleopatra*', in John Russell Brown and Bernard Harris (eds.), *Later Shakespeare* (London: Arnold, 1966), p. 35.
[3] Julian Markels, *The Pillar of the World*: Antony and Cleopatra *in Shakespeare's Development* (Columbus: Ohio State University Press, 1968), p. 21.
[4] Maynard Mack, '*Antony and Cleopatra*: The Stillness and the Dance', in Milton Crane (ed.), *Shakespeare's Art: Seven Essays* (Chicago: University of Chicago Press for George Washington University, 1973), p. 81.
[5] See Janet Adelman, *The Common Liar: An Essay on* Antony and Cleopatra (New Haven, Conn.: Yale University Press, 1973), p. 14; David Kaula, 'The Time Sense of *Antony and Cleopatra*', *Shakespeare Quarterly*, 15 (1964), 215.
[6] Margery M. Morgan, 'Your Crown's Awry: *Antony and Cleopatra* in the Comic Tradition', *Komos*, 1 (1968), 131.
[7] George Bernard Shaw, *Three Plays for Puritans* (repr. Harmondsworth: Penguin, 1946), p. xxx.
[8] Harley Granville-Barker, *Prefaces to Shakespeare*, vol. 1 (Princeton, N.J.: Princeton University Press, 1946, repr. 1952), p. 454. Antony's courtesy to Lepidus is one sign that, while Octavius seems a logical extension of the Octavius we saw in *Julius Caesar*, Antony is essentially a new character.
[9] See Adelman, op. cit., p. 137.
[10] In Peter Brook's 1978 Royal Shakespeare Company production, the scene was played on a carpet, which during the dance was hooked on to ropes and drawn up to the flies. The great men tumbled over each other like toys tipped out of a box.
[11] H. A. Mason, *Shakespeare's Tragedies of Love* (London: Chatto & Windus, 1970), p. 242.
[12] See Maurice Charney, *Shakespeare's Roman Plays* (Cambridge, Mass.: Harvard University Press, 1961), pp. 96–107.
[13] See Paul A. Cantor, *Shakespeare's Rome: Republic and Empire* (Ithaca, N.Y.: Cornell University Press, 1976), pp. 136–7.
[14] See William Blissett, 'Dramatic Irony in *Antony and Cleopatra*', *Shakespeare Quarterly*, 18 (1967), 158.
[15] Here it may be worth recalling a general remark of Clifford Leech: 'The Elizabethan way of writing is to put things together, the Jacobean way is to fuse': *The Dramatist's Experience* (New York: Barnes & Noble, 1970), p. 159.
[16] Derick R. C. Marsh, *Passion Lends Them Power: A Study of Shakespeare's Love Tragedies* (Sydney: Sydney University Press, 1976), p. 182.

[17] See Margaret Lamb, Antony and Cleopatra *on the English Stage* (London and Toronto: Associated University Presses, 1980), pp. 180–5.

[18] See Michael Goldman, *Acting and Action in Shakespearean Tragedy* (Princeton, N.J.: Princeton University Press, 1985), p. 113.

[19] Janet Adelman reminds us, 'Popular tradition associated the serpent with his tail in his mouth with the cosmos and with eternity' (op. cit., p. 62).

[20] See ibid., pp. 153–4.

[21] I have accepted the traditional emendation here; the Folio reads 'Antony', as do some editors.

[22] Susan Snyder, 'Patterns of Motion in *Antony and Cleopatra*', *Shakespeare Survey*, 33 (1980), 117.

[23] Richard Griffiths, who played the Clown in Peter Brook's production, displayed an exaggerated fear of the worm, putting slippers on his hands before opening the basket. But the basket was seen to be empty, and the Clown then produced asps from all over his body.

[24] In Michael Langham's 1967 production at Stratford, Ontario, Zoe Caldwell gave a jealous pounce on the word 'my' and snatched another asp from the basket.

[25] Duncan S. Harris, '"Again for Cydnus": The Dramaturgical Resolution of *Antony and Cleopatra*', *Studies in English Literature*, 17 (1977), 227.

[26] See Martha Tuck Rozett, 'The Comic Structure of Tragic Endings: The Suicide Scenes in *Romeo and Juliet* and *Antony and Cleopatra*', *Shakespeare Quarterly*, 36 (1985), 162.

CHRONOLOGY

30 B.C.E.	Publication of Horace's *Odes*, Books 1–3 (including the "Cleopatra ode," 1.37)
c. 24–16 B.C.E.	Publication of Propertius' *Elegies*, Books 3 and 4 (including odes on Cleopatra, 3.11 and 4.6)
c. 110–115	Publication of Plutarch's *Life of Marc Antony*
1552	Etienne Jodelle, *Cléopâtre captive*
1578	Robert Garnier, *Marc-Antoine*
1592	Translation of Garnier's *Marc-Antoine* by the Countess of Pembroke
1594	Samuel Daniel, *Cleopatra*
c. 1607	Production of William Shakespeare's *Antony and Cleopatra*
c. 1620	*The False One* by John Fletcher and Philip Massinger
1626	Thomas May, *The Tragedy of Cleopatra Queene of Aegypt*
1642–43	Pierre Corneille, *La Mort de Pompée*
1677	Production of John Dryden's *All for Love* (published 1678)
1835	Alexander Pushkin, "Egyptian Nights"
1838	Théophile Gautier, "Une Nuit de Cléopâtre"
1898	George Bernard Shaw, *Caesar and Cleopatra*
1948	Thornton Wilder, *The Ides of March*

CONTRIBUTORS

HAROLD BLOOM is Sterling Professor of the Humanities at Yale University and Henry W. and Albert A. Berg Professor of English at the New York University Graduate School. He is a 1985 MacArthur Foundation Award recipient, served as the Charles Eliot Norton Professor of Poetry at Harvard University (1987–88), and is the author of eighteen books, the most recent being *Poetics of Influence: New and Selected Criticism* (1988). Currently he is editing the Chelsea House series Modern Critical Views and The Critical Cosmos, and other Chelsea House series in literary criticism.

HAROLD C. GODDARD was head of the English department at Swarthmore College from 1909 to 1946. In addition to *The Meaning of Shakespeare* (1951), he published *Studies in New England Transcendentalism* (1906), and in 1926 edited the essays of Ralph Waldo Emerson.

FRANKLIN M. DICKEY was Professor of English at the University of New Mexico. He wrote *Not Wisely but Too Well: Shakespeare's Love Tragedies* (1957) and, with Walter F. Station, Jr., edited and translated *Amyntas and The Lamentations of Amyntas* (1968).

STEELE COMMAGER was, until his death in 1984, Professor of Classics at Columbia University. He is the author of *The Odes of Horace: A Critical Study* (1962), *A Prologomenon to Propertius* (1974), and many articles on classical literature.

L. J. MILLS taught at Indiana University and wrote *One Soul in Bodies Twain: Friendship in Tudor Literature and Stuart Drama* (1937) and *The Tragedies of Shakespeare's* Antony and Cleopatra (1964), and edited works by Peter Hausted.

MARILYN L. WILLIAMSON is Professor of English at Wayne State University and author of *Infinite Variety: Antony and Cleopatra in Renaissance Drama and Earlier Tradition* (1974) and *The Patriarchy of Shakespeare's Comedies* (1986). She has edited Frederic Rowton's *The Female Poets of Great Britain* (1981).

GORDON W. COUCHMAN formerly taught at Elmhurst College and is the author of *This Our Caesar: A Study of Bernard Shaw's* Caesar and Cleopatra (1973).

JOHN BAYLEY, Warton Professor of English at St. Catherine's College, Oxford, is one of England's most distinguished critics. Author of works on Tolstoy (1966), Pushkin (1971), and Hardy (1978), he has also written *The Romantic Survival* (1957), *The Uses of Division* (1976), and *Shakespeare and Tragedy* (1981). His *Selected Essays* appeared in 1984, and his latest work is *The Short Story: Henry James to Elizabeth Bowen* (1988).

IRENE G. DASH is a former instructor at Hunter College. She has written *Wooing, Wedding, and Power: Women in Shakespeare's Plays* (1981) and articles on Shakespeare and feminism.

DEREK HUGHES is Professor of English at the University of Warwick in Coventry, England, and author of *Dryden's Heroic Plays* (1981) and articles on Dryden and Restoration tragedy.

J. LEEDS BARROLL, formerly Andrew W. Mellon Visiting Professor of English Literature at the University of Pittsburgh, now teaches at the University of Maryland Baltimore County. He has edited Shakespeare's *Hamlet* (1970) and *Othello* (1971) and has written *Artificial Persons: The Formation of Character in the Tragedies of Shakespeare* (1974) and *Shakespearean Tragedy: Genre, Tradition, and Change* in Antony and Cleopatra (1983). He has been the editor of *Shakespeare Studies* since its foundation in 1965.

ALEXANDER LEGGATT is Professor of English at the University of Toronto. He has written *Citizen Comedy in the Age of Shakespeare* (1973), *Shakespeare's Comedy of Love* (1974), *Ben Jonson: His Vision and Art* (1981), and *English Drama: Shakespeare to the Restoration 1590–1660* (1988).

BIBLIOGRAPHY

Adelman, Janet. *The Common Liar: An Essay on* Antony and Cleopatra. New Haven: Yale University Press, 1973.

Adler, Doris. "The Unlacing of Cleopatra." *Theatre Journal* 34 (1982): 451–66.

Bamber, Linda. *"Antony and Cleopatra."* In *Comic Women, Tragic Men: A Study of Gender and Genre in Shakespeare.* Stanford: Stanford University Press, 1982, pp. 45–70.

Bowers, John M. " 'I am Marble-Constant': Cleopatra's Monumental End." *Huntington Library Quarterly* 46 (1983): 283–97.

Burke, Kenneth. "Shakespearean Persuasion: *Antony and Cleopatra."* In *Language as Symbolic Action.* Berkeley: University of California Press, 1966, pp. 101–14.

Canfield, J. Douglas. "The Jewel of Great Price: Mutability and Constancy in Dryden's *All for Love."* *ELH* 42 (1975): 38–61.

Cantor, Paul A. *Shakespeare's Rome: Republic and Empire.* Ithaca: Cornell University Press, 1976.

Chester, Allan Griffith. *Thomas May: Man of Letters 1595–1650.* Philadelphia, 1932.

Ellis, Oliver C. de C. *Cleopatra in the Tide of Time.* London: Williams & Norgate, 1947.

Estrin, Barbara L. "The Dream of a Better Life in *As You Like It* and *Antony and Cleopatra."* In *The Raven and the Lark: Lost Children in Literature of the English Renaissance.* Lewisburg, PA: Bucknell University Press, 1985, pp. 143–57.

Everett, William. "Six Cleopatras." *Atlantic Monthly* 95 (1905): 252–63.

Fitz, L. T. "Egyptian Queens and Male Reviewers: Sexist Attitudes in *Antony and Cleopatra* Criticism." *Shakespeare Quarterly* 28 (1977): 297–316.

Frye, Northrop. *"Antony and Cleopatra."* In *Northrop Frye on Shakespeare.* Edited by Robert Sandler. New Haven: Yale University Press, 1986, pp. 122–39.

Granville-Barker, Harley. "Cleopatra." In *Prefaces to Shakespeare: Second Series.* London: Sidgwick & Jackson, 1930, pp. 203–20.

Hamilton, Donna B. *"Antony and Cleopatra* and the Tradition of Noble Lovers." *Shakespeare Quarterly* 24 (1973): 245–51.

Hughes, Derek W. "The Significance of *All for Love."* *ELH* 37 (1970): 540–63.

Kirschbaum, Leo. *Character and Characterization in Shakespeare.* Detroit: Wayne State University Press, 1962.

Knights, L. C. "On *The Tragedy of Antony and Cleopatra."* *Scrutiny* 16 (1949): 318–23.

Leavenworth, Russell E. *Daniel's* Cleopatra: *A Critical Study.* Salzburg: Institut für Englische Sprache und Literatur, Universität Salzburg, 1974.

Lloyd, Michael. "Cleopatra as Isis." *Shakespeare Survey* 12 (1959): 88–94.

Longo, Joseph A. "Cleopatra and Octavia: Archetypal Imagery in *Antony and Cleopatra."* *University of Dayton Review* 10, No. 3 (Summer 1974): 29–37.

Luce, J. V. "Cleopatra as *Fatale Monstrum* (Horace, *Carm.* 1.37.21)." *Classical Quarterly* 13 (1963): 251–57.

MacCallum, M. W. *Shakespeare's Roman Plays and Their Background.* London: Macmillan, 1910.

Markels, Julian. *The Pillar of the World:* Antony and Cleopatra *in Shakespeare's Development.* Columbus: Ohio State University Press, 1968.

Mason, Michael. *"Caesar and Cleopatra:* A Shavian Exercise in Both Hero-Worship and Belittlement." *Humanities Association Review* 25 (1974): 1–10.

Matthews, Honor. *Character and Symbol in Shakespeare's Plays*. Cambridge: Cambridge University Press, 1962.

Milhous, Judith L., and Robert D. Hume. *"All for Love."* In *Producible Interpretation: Eight English Plays 1675–1707*. Carbondale: Southern Illinois University Press, 1985, pp. 107–40.

Muir, Kenneth. "Elizabeth I, Jodelle, and Cleopatra." *Renaissance Drama* 2 (1969): 197–206.

Murry, John Middleton. *"Antony and Cleopatra."* In *Shakespeare*. London: Jonathan Cape, 1936, pp. 352–79.

Neely, Carol Thomas. "Gender and Genre in *Antony and Cleopatra*." In *Broken Nuptials in Shakespeare's Plays*. New Haven: Yale University Press, 1985, pp. 136–55.

Nethercut, William R. "Propertius 3.11." *Transactions and Proceedings of the American Philological Association* 102 (1971): 411–43.

Pelling, C. B. R. "Introduction" to *Life of Antony* by Plutarch. Cambridge: Cambridge University Press, 1988, pp. 1–47.

Rees, Joan. "Samuel Daniel's *Cleopatra* and Two French Plays." *Modern Language Review* 47 (1952): 1–10.

Reiss, Timothy J. "Jodell's *Cléopâtre* and the Enchanted Circle." In *Tragedy and Truth*. New Haven: Yale University Press, 1980, pp. 78–102.

Ribner, Irving. "The Final Paradox: *Antony and Cleopatra* and *Coriolanus*." In *Patterns in Shakespearean Tragedy*. London: Methuen, 1960, pp. 168–202.

Rosen, William. *"Antony and Cleopatra."* In *Shakespeare and the Craft of Tragedy*. Cambridge, MA: Harvard University Press, 1964, pp. 104–60.

Rothschild, Herbert B., Jr. "The Oblique Encounter: Shakespeare's Confrontation of Plutarch with Special Reference to *Antony and Cleopatra*." *English Literary Renaissance* 6 (1976): 404–29.

Schücking, Levin L. *Character Problems in Shakespeare's Plays*. London: George Harrap & Co., 1922.

Scott, Michael. Antony and Cleopatra: *Text and Performance*. London: Macmillan, 1983.

Sewell, Arthur. *Character and Society in Shakespeare*. Oxford: Clarendon Press, 1951.

Shapiro, Michael. "Boying Her Greatness: Shakespeare's Use of Coterie Drama in *Antony and Cleopatra*." *Modern Language Review* 77 (1982): 1–15.

Simmons, J. L. *"Antony and Cleopatra:* New Heaven, New Earth." In *Shakespeare's Pagan World: The Roman Tragedies*. Charlottesville: University Press of Virginia, 1973, pp. 109–63.

Stahl, Hans-Peter. "Aggressive Self-Preservation: From Cynthia to Cleopatra." In *Propertius: "Love" and "War."* Berkeley: University of California Press, 1985, pp. 234–47.

Stoll, Elmer Edgar. "Cleopatra." In *Poets and Playwrights*. Minneapolis: University of Minnesota Press, 1930, pp. 1–30.

Traci, Philip J. *The Love Play of* Antony and Cleopatra. The Hague: Mouton, 1970.

Ure, Peter. "Master and Pupil in Bernard Shaw." *Essays in Criticism* 19 (1969): 118–31.

Williamson, Marilyn L. *Infinite Variety: Antony and Cleopatra in Renaissance Drama and Earlier Tradition*. Mystic, CT: Lawrence Verry, 1974.

ACKNOWLEDGMENTS

"The Diadem of Love: An Essay on *Antony and Cleopatra*" by G. Wilson Knight from *The Imperial Theme* by G. Wilson Knight, © 1931, 1951 by G. Wilson Knight. Reprinted by permission of Methuen & Co.

"Dryden and the Analysis of Shakespeare's Techniques" by Ruth Wallerstein from *Review of English Studies* 19, No. 2 (April 1943), © 1943 by Oxford University Press. Reprinted by permission.

"Antony and Cleopatra" by G. S. Griffiths from *Essays and Studies* 31 (1945), © 1945 by Oxford University Press. Reprinted by permission.

"Antony and Cleopatra" by Willard Farnham from *Shakespeare's Tragic Frontier: The World of His Final Tragedies* by Willard Farnham, © 1950 by the Regents of the University of California. Reprinted by permission.

The Pattern of Tragicomedy in Beaumont and Fletcher by Eugene M. Waith, © 1952 by Yale University. Reprinted by permission of Yale University Press.

"Dryden in Egypt: Reflexions on *All for Love*" by Norman Suckling from *Durham University Journal* 45, No. 1 (December 1952), © 1952 by *Durham University Journal*. Reprinted by permission.

"Horace and Cleopatra: Thoughts on the Entanglements of Art and History" by Donald Pearce from *Yale Review* 51, No. 2 (Winter 1962), © 1961 by Yale University Press. Reprinted by permission.

"Dryden" by Eugene M. Waith from *The Herculean Hero in Marlowe, Chapman, Shakespeare and Dryden* by Eugene M. Waith, © 1962 by Eugene M. Waith. Reprinted by permission of Columbia University Press and Chatto & Windus.

"Literary Introduction" by Denzell S. Smith from *The Tragoedy of Cleopatra Queene of Aegypt* by Thomas May, edited by Denzell S. Smith, © 1979 by Denzell S. Smith. Reprinted by permission of the author.

"Caesar and Cleopatra" by Louis Crompton from *Shaw the Dramatist* by Louis Crompton, © 1969 by the University of Nebraska Press. Reprinted by permission.

Shakespeare's Living Art by Rosalie L. Colie, © 1974 by Princeton University Press. Reprinted by permission.

Théophile Gautier by Richard B. Grant, © 1975 by G. K. Hall & Co. Reprinted by permission.

The Evolution of the Cornelian Heroine by Mary Jo Muratore, © 1982 by Mary Jo Muratore. Reprinted by permission of José Porrua Turanzas, S.A.

Pushkin's "Egyptian Nights": The Biography of a Work by Leslie O'Bell, © 1984 by Ardis Publishers. Reprinted by permission.

"Antony and Cleopatra" by Harold C. Goddard from *The Meaning of Shakespeare* by Harold C. Goddard, © 1951 by The University of Chicago. Reprinted by permission of The University of Chicago Press.

"The Tragedy of *Antony and Cleopatra"* by Franklin M. Dickey from *Not Wisely but Too Well: Shakespeare's Love Tragedies* by Franklin M. Dickey, © 1957 by the Henry E. Huntington Library & Art Gallery. Reprinted by permission.

"Horace, *Carmina* 1.37" by Steele Commager from *Phoenix* 12, No. 2 (Summer 1958), © 1958 by The Classical Association of Canada. Reprinted by permission.

"Cleopatra's Tragedy" by L. J. Mills from *Shakespeare Quarterly* 11, No. 2 (Spring 1960), © 1960 by the Shakespeare Association of America, Inc. Reprinted by permission of *Shakespeare Quarterly.*

"Patterns of Development in *Antony and Cleopatra"* by Marilyn L. Williamson from *Tennessee Studies in Literature* 14 (1969), © 1969 by The University of Tennessee Press. Reprinted by permission.

" 'The Most Dangerous of Caesar's Conquests' " by Gordon W. Couchman from *This Our Caesar: A Study of Bernard Shaw's* Caesar and Cleopatra, © 1973 by Mouton & Co., N.V., Publishers, The Hague. Reprinted by permission of Mouton de Gruyter, a division of Walter de Gruyter & Co.

"Determined Things: The Case of the Caesars" by John Bayley from *Shakespeare and Tragedy* by John Bayley, © 1981 by John Bayley. Reprinted by permission of Routledge & Kegan Paul Ltd.

"Union of Roles: *Antony and Cleopatra"* by Irene G. Dash from *Wooing, Wedding, and Power: Women in Shakespeare's Plays* by Irene G. Dash, © 1981 by Columbia University Press. Reprinted by permission.

"Art and Life in *All for Love"* by Derek Hughes from *Studies in Philology* 80, No. 1 (Winter 1983), © 1983 by The University of North Carolina Press. Reprinted by permission.

"Cleopatra and the Size of Dreaming" by J. Leeds Barroll from *Shakespearean Tragedy: Genre, Tradition, and Change in* Antony and Cleopatra by J. Leeds Barroll, © 1984 by Associated University Presses, Inc. Reprinted by permission.

"Antony and Cleopatra" by Alexander Leggatt from *Shakespeare's Political Drama: The History Plays and the Roman Plays* by Alexander Leggatt, © 1988 by Alexander Leggatt. Reprinted by permission of Routledge.

INDEX